Contents

INTERNATIONAL
CUISINE

South-East Asia

Carl Withey

Hodder & Stoughton
A MEMBER OF THE HODDER HEADLINE GROUP

Dedicated to

Ivy Spratt
1920–2003

Orders: please contact Bookpoint Ltd, 130 Milton Park, Abingdon, Oxon OX14 4SB. Telephone: (44) 01235 827720. Fax: (44) 01235 400454. Lines are open from 9.00–6.00, Monday to Saturday, with a 24-hour message answering service. You can also order through our website www.hodderheadline.co.uk.

British Library Cataloguing in Publication Data
A catalogue record for this title is available from the British Library

ISBN 0 340 85788 9

First published 2004

Impression number   10 9 8 7 6 5 4 3 2 1

Year   2007 2006 2005 2004

Cover photo from Simon Woodgate
Typeset by Pantek Arts Ltd

Printed and bound in Dubai for Hodder & Stoughton Educational, a division of Hodder Headline Plc, 338 Euston Road, London NW1 3BH

INTRODUCTION

In today's multicultural society, there is more variety and choice in the cuisines and dishes that are on offer to the public than there was twenty years ago. Colleges now have to adapt their programmes to provide the wide range of skills and knowledge that a student chef requires on leaving college for industry. When I first qualified in 1984–85, all the programmes were geared around European cookery, mainly French classical cuisine, which was required by industry at the time, but now there are all sorts of opportunities for young chefs other than those in hotels, for example: contract catering, offshore catering, in-flight catering, hospital catering, ethnic restaurants, educational catering, fast food, pub food, coffee shops, brasserie restaurants, vegetarian restaurants – the list goes on.

I have been actively involved with the development of short courses for the business and community unit at the Birmingham College of Food, all of which are designed either around NVQ level 1/2 or the EMFEC awards. I have also designed menus and recipes for the Realistic Working Environment (RWE) kitchens and restaurants. All these cuisines are incorporated into this book, which gives the students a chance to use and learn new ideas and cookery techniques while studying their NVQ level 1 and 2 programmes.

I have also been involved with the development of an international cookery course for large contract catering companies. This involved designing courses for their head chefs and chef managers, from small units to offshore catering.

I have travelled widely – living, visiting, demonstrating and teaching in Malaysia, Thailand, Borneo, Singapore, Vietnam, Cambodia, Canada and France. I have also visited the USA, Belgium, Spain, Luxembourg, Holland, Greece and the Emirates.

I believe this cookery book will benefit both students and caterers alike as it not only provides recipes but also explains what the commodities are. In addition the book provides interesting facts, for example, how the geography, climate, religious and cultural beliefs of a region can effect and change it's cuisine. It will appeal to the general reader, and will be equally useful for a student assignment, or for the caterer who requires authentic recipes or menus for a theme day. As a chef I used to dread the manager deciding that it would be a good idea to run a theme day or week and being asked to cater for this. I did not understand the recipes, let alone know how to cook a dish from a country I knew little about.

This book will benefit students on BA, HND, PCA, CAM and NVQ programmes, who are required to conduct research, assignments and complete themed functions. The PCA, HND and CAM programmes are becoming increasingly popular courses, as they are both academic and practical, and are highly regarded qualifications within the catering industry.

I hope that this book will give you, the reader, the opportunity to be able to understand the culture and history of a country and to explain what food and dishes you can produce for your customer, by means of easy-to-follow and traditional recipes. I hope that it will be a little different, enlightening and enthusing you along the way to a whole new repertoire of cuisines and dishes.

Enjoy,

Carl B. Withey

Author's Notes

The first impression of Asian food for the uninitiated is that it is complicated, which is not really so. Although there can be a large number of ingredients, on the whole it is very simple and enjoyable. The major work is in the preparation of the pastes and base gravies and sauces. The cooking is usually very quick and simple. For me the hardest part of this book was putting together the recipes while trying to keep them as authentic as possible.

Unlike European chefs, Asian chefs, especially the traders on hawker stalls, never use written or weighed ingredients, and that is especially true where spices are concerned. So imagine the hours I have agonised and spent watching and trying to communicate in 'pigeon' Thai or Malay, etc., asking the chefs or traders what they have put into their creations, or pondering over what the chef has just thrown in the wok and how much, which has often resulted in bemused looks or laughter.

I have tried to estimate and work out the recipes through trial and error to give an accurate and authentic taste.

It is imperative to remember when trying these recipes that whether there is too much chilli or not is down to individual taste, because the same dish can be different from one stall or chef to the stall next door. What is true, however, is that Asian food requires a balance of flavours from the spices, herbs, vegetables and leaves that are used. A natural aroma and taste with colours and textures are married together.

When substituting ingredients, I have given a suitable alternative, but in some cases there is just no substitute. Please note that all the recipes in this book serve 4 people, unless specified otherwise.

Some advice when trying to order food in any part of Asia! Just point if they don't speak any English; never ask what it is, just eat it; never try to change your order – you will just confuse them; don't try to order dishes in any set order as the food will come when it is ready, so just accept it; always smile; and never try to ask for separate bills. Then you should enjoy a trouble-free meal.

ACKNOWLEDGEMENTS

Writing a book of this magnitude, with all the technical and historical data that is needed to make it as accurate as possible, would not have been achieved without help from people who I could call upon to make a valuable contribution, whether it was in the shape of recipes, advice or taking me to places that tourists would not generally see and experience.

I have been blessed with the friendship of wonderful people in the countries that I visit, whom I may not see from one year to the next. They are such utterly nice people that it always feels as if it were only yesterday that I last saw them. I always look forward to seeing them and I only wish it could be more often and for longer.

So thank you to Michael Chew and Dorothy, from Hilli City College, for their friendship and help over the years, especially with the Singapore and Malaysia chapters. A big thank you to Gurdeep Raj Chabra and Michael Liew, my translators, also from Hilli City, for their help with researching the recipes and text.

Thanks to David Chewa from Kinabalu College Sabah, Malaya, Borneo, for making me feel so welcome.

A special thanks to Miss Lee and my gratitude especially to Tan Pit Yen, from the Flamingo Institute, KL, Malaysia, who took me for some of the best meals around KL, and whose knowledge of Malay cuisine is superb. A very big thank you to my life-long friend Timo Reuss, Executive Chef at the Sun Way Lagoon Resort Hotel in KL, Malaysia, who is one of the best and most knowledgeable chefs I have had the pleasure of working with. Thanks for your friendship, advice and help with Thailand, Singapore and Malaysia.

I would like to say a big thank you to Busara Boonmakham at the Sompet cookery school, whose knowledge and help in translating, helped greatly. If anyone is planning to go to Chiang Mai, you must visit her at her cookery school. If you have time to take one or more classes, ask her to show you some of the local unknown dishes she used to cook with her mother and grandmother, as opposed to the run-of-the-mill Thai favourites.

A very big thank you to Shelia Connelly and Paul Hay, Cathy Foscatti, Arnfinn Oines and Phung, in Cambodia. Thanks for your care and support, especially after my accident, and keep up the great work you are doing.

Thanks to all my colleagues at the Birmingham College of Food, Tourism and Creative Studies who have helped, especially Rod Burton, whose advice and expertise even at the most ridiculous times of the night and day have been indispensable. Thanks also to Bill Farnsworth for his continued and enthusiastic support.

Special thanks goes to one of my NVQ students, Ngoc Tran, and his family, who helped with the Vietnamese chapter and checked my spelling and recipes.

To my editor Richard Brighton, thank you for your valued opinion, advice and enthusiasm, and also for all the hard work you have put in, night after night. Thanks mate!

Carl Withey

The author and publishers wish to thank the photographer, Simon Woodgate, and the following for their valuable assistance on the photoshoot for this book:

Sam Reader, Michael Phillips, Jason Holloway, Neil Martin, Steven Mildenhall, Adam Newman, Vicky Mabbott, John Harris, Laura Saxby, Jemma Styles, Irean Serunkuma, Rod Burton, David Hanlon, Mauro Sannio.

Also thanks to John Artis Limited and Villeroy & Boch for supplying plates for the photoshoot.

EQUIPMENT

Asian cookery is very easy and simple. There is no great need for any specialist equipment in order to recreate these dishes. In reality any pots or pans that you have will suffice. However, I would like to introduce you to some pieces of equipment that will help and that are commonly used in the countries that I have covered in this book.

To make the pastes I refer to in many of the recipes, it would help to have a pestle and mortar, which are normally made from heavy granite. Most domestic or industrial kitchens have one or more of these to grind the spices. The wooden pestles and mortars are normally used for making salads, for example papaya salad. If you are short of time you could use either a food processor or a coffee grinder instead.

The chopping boards are all wooden and there is one chopping knife that is used for every job, big or small. A small curved knife is used for carving vegetables as decoration.

The major piece of cooking equipment is the wok. This can be made from iron, brass or aluminium. It is the single most useful cooking pan there is; whether you stir-fry, deep-fry, steam, poach, or boil, the wok is the tool. The wok's shape distributes the heat effectively and it is relatively easy to handle. It is worth investing in a good one as they are quite cheap. You can use a frying pan, but you may find that pieces of food go everywhere. With a new wok you will first have to heat it up so that it is red hot, then coat the inside several times with an oil-soaked cloth and burn the oil on! This will help to season the wok and prevent food from sticking to it. Never clean the pan with a scourer, just wash it out with a cloth and very hot soapy water. If you purchase a non-stick wok then you can use it straight away.

You will find in any far eastern kitchen a double boiler and a bamboo or aluminium steamer that is used for sticky rice, fish and vegetables. The bottom of the double boiler is brought to the boil and the steamer trays are placed on top, as opposed to the bamboo steamer where the wok is filled with water and used as a base, and the bamboo steamer is placed on top. Sometimes the bamboo steamer is presented to the customer with the cooked food still in the steamer tray for the customer to remove when they are ready.

Clay pots are used for curries and soups. It is very important to ensure that you soak them overnight in water before their first use; otherwise you will find that they will crack. Small clay pots often have a small stand. This is so a flame can be placed underneath to keep the food warm.

Ladles, spoons and forks are made from coconut shells, but it is acceptable to use the modern metal versions we have in our kitchens today. Skimmers and spiders are normally made from wire and have a wooden handle.

Malaysia 1

Clockwise from bottom left: Rojak, Fish curry, Fried long beans.

MALAYSIA

Malaysia was the home of fusion cookery hundreds of years before it came to the West in the late 1990s in a blaze of glory.

Malaysia is one of the most advanced countries in Asia and is made up of 13 states, with nine of the states having sultans as governors. Every five years elections are held to choose the next king of Malaysia from these nine sultans.

It has a multiracial population in excess of 23 million. Almost 80 per cent occupy the peninsula; much of its land (approximately 75 per cent) is still primarily undeveloped jungle, famed for its indigenous Malay tigers and endangered orang-utans.

Three main races live in the country. The Malays, who are Muslim, make up approximately 54 per cent. The Chinese, whose religion is Buddhist, makes up 35 per cent, and the Indian community, whose religion is Hindu, makes up 10 per cent. Other groups such as Eurasians, Dayaks, Muruts, Ibans and Bidayuhs make up the other 1 per cent, establishing Malaysia as a pot-pourri of Asian cultures.

The official religion of the country is Islam, but other races are free to practise any religion they wish. The national currency is the ringgit (MYR). The national language is Bahasa Malaysia (Malay), although English is also widely spoken, together with other languages such as Chinese and Tamil.

There are five international airports and 14 domestic airports in Malaysia, with the main international airport in the capital city, Kuala Lumpur.

Malaysia covers some 330,000 square kilometres and is a galaxy of cultures all living in harmony and respect for each other, who welcome you with warmth. It has the natural beauty of the rain forests, wetlands, unspoilt islands with some of the world's finest coral reefs and beaches, rich flora and fauna that are home to countless rare species of insects, birds and animals, and that's not even mentioning the gastronomic heritage, which goes back many, many centuries.

Malaysia was called the Malay peninsula and is thought to be the home of the early *Homo sapiens* some 40,000 years ago. Evidence of this can be seen in the giant Niah Caves of Sarawak and other caves on the Malay peninsula and Borneo.

Because of Malaysia's geographical location, with Thailand, Burma, China, Vietnam and Laos to the north, the Philippines to the east, Singapore, Borneo, Indonesia and Sumatra to the south, and India to the west (with the Bay of Bengal, the Straits of Malacca, and the South China Sea all around), the Malay archipelago was a magnificent place of trade. Gifts from a Chinese emperor that included silk, ivory and even a princess to the Sultan of Malay, all came to the shores in great Chinese boats called

'junks'. Opium, ebony, perfumes and porcelain came from India, Arabia and China. Trade was conducted all along the coast of Malaysia.

Favourable trade winds from India to Malaysia along the Bay of Bengal had a great effect on each country's cuisine, with a constant flow of trade between the two in the northern province of Malaysia called Kedah, exchanging ideas, food and commodities around the fourth century.

The city of Malacca soon became the biggest trading port in the world for wholesale merchants, and is the oldest city in Malaysia.

Then came the Portuguese, Dutch and the British, who at various times occupied Malaysia. Their ships came in search of spices such as nutmeg and pepper, and silks. Many of the Portuguese traders settled down and married into the local population taking Malay wives. This community still exists today over 500 years later, in a small settlement on the coast of Malacca. These people are called the Bumi putra, which translated means 'people of the land'.

The Portuguese Eurasian influences on this community can be seen in their cookery with its unmistakable emphasis on fish. However, they still hold on to their Catholic faith, which permits eating pork and drinking alcohol. The main traditional regional dish is Devilled eggs, curried devil or curry Debal. With a mix of East meets West, these thick sauces are heavy with the flavour of chilli.

In 1403 the Sultan of Malay, Sultan Mansor Shah, married a Chinese princess. From this followed the intermarriage between the two cultures, which gave birth to Nyonya cuisine and culture.

The Chinese have always been great travellers. Many centuries before Marco Polo had even made his famous journey the Chinese traders, scholars and monks had already voyaged as far west as Afghanistan and as far south as Sumatra. When Melaka was established as the greatest trading centre in the world in the fifteenth century, even more Chinese rushed to work in its tin mines in the hope of a new life and riches. The provinces from which they came were in southern China, bringing a diversity of cultures, cuisines, languages and eating habits.

Most of the immigrants were Hokkien Chinese from Amoy and then Cantonese and Teochews from Kwangtung, and other smaller groups like Hakkas, Hokchian and Hailanese. Almost all were men and ended up taking Malay wives.

The word Nyonya actually refers to the female offspring of the early migrants and traders with Malay wives. The descendants of these Sino–Malay marriages became known as Straits Chinese or Peranakan. Their way of life, language, food, customs and dressing have become an amalgamation of Chinese and Malay, developing a style uniquely their own.

Nyonya cuisine was cooked mainly by the women, who combined rustic spices of Malay cookery and then mixed it with the delicate and uninspiring flavour of the Chinese cookery of that time. The basic essentials in Nyonya cooking are lemongrass, galangal, coconut milk,

3

chillies and limes as well as palm sugar, glutinous rice flour and screw pine leaves. The intermingling of soya bean, anchovies, fresh and dried mushrooms and tamarind give the cuisine its distinctive aromas and taste. Pork, which is strictly forbidden by Malay Muslims, is used in Nyonya cookery as is the odd ingredient like Worcester sauce.

The Nyonya wife would rarely leave the house due to the labour-intensive pounding of the spices in the pestle and mortar to make the all-important pastes.

In traditional match-making, the intended bride was expected to be a competent cook and would often receive an unexpected visit from her intended groom during the pounding and making of the spices and pastes. The pounding and beat of the pestle into the mortar would indicate her competency. There could be nothing worse for the bride-to-be than have her intended eat a meal she had prepared only to be told that it was coarse and lacked flavour. This was as good as being told that the wedding was off.

After the Second World War, things changed dramatically when the Nyonya wives started to work, resulting in a decline in Nyonya cuisine. However, since the mid-1980s a resurgence of interest has been seen in the cuisine. With the use of modern tools such as coffee grinders, blenders and liquidisers, gone are the long hours of pounding spices.

Nyonya restaurants can be found easily in Penang, Melaka and Kuala Lumpur.

There are three variations of Nyonya cooking – Pulau Pinang (Penang), Melaka and Singapore. The Penang style of Nyonya cooking has been influenced in part by Thailand because of its proximity to the country while the Melaka and Singapore styles are more Indonesian in influence.

Malaysia is often described as having two climates, hot and even hotter. It has a tropical climate, which is warm and humid throughout the whole year with typical temperatures ranging from 21–34°C. The monsoon rains begin in September through to February. This unique climate and geography is ideal for crops of rubber, sugar and tea.

During the period 1907 to 1928 yet another flood of immigrants was imported to work on the rubber, coffee, tea and sugar plantations. The fine-boned and slender Tamils from Madras and the long-limbed Maslayales from Kerala were ideal workers as rubber tappers. The new immigrants were Tamil Indians and Hokkien-speaking Chinese, again bringing a new diversity of art, culture, cuisine and traditions to Malaysia. There are still large communities in Penang, Ipoh and Kuala Lumpur.

The fusion of the cuisines can be seen with the inclusion of lemongrass, galangal and jackfruit in the curries, and pandan leaves (screw pine), coconut cream and star anise in a number of biryani dishes.

For anyone remotely interested in food, a trip to Malaysia is a must, and for the chef it is essential. The smells, flavours, colours, diversity and simplicity of the dishes is simply amazing. They are also very cheap and incredible value for money. The fragrances of the lemongrass, fennel, cumin, kaffir lime and galangal all give the food a distinct flavour. In hawkers' stalls, restaurants, cafés and food courts you can order as many different dishes as you can think of – delicacies from countless countries, districts and regions all under one roof.

There are many regional differences in Malayan food. For example, the northern states of Kelantan, Kedah and Perlis are influenced by the proximity of Thailand, with its heavy use of commodities such as tamarind, fish sauce and lime. In the southern state of Johur you can find influences of the Javanese. If hot curry is your delicacy then the state of Negeri Sembilan, influenced by the migration of the Minangkabaus of Sumatra, is notorious for its very hot curries.

The main meats are chicken, lamb, duck and beef. Fresh and saltwater fish, prawns and squid are also very popular. The best place to buy the raw food that has been grown or reared locally is in the local markets and night markets. You can haggle over the price and quantity, but the food here is usually of the highest quality.

Some of the best food can be seen and indulged in if you are invited to eat with a Malay family. Meals are not prepared or presented in the same way as in the West. The number of guests is not taken into account. There will be numerous dishes prepared that day and kept under fine mesh nets. The guest will be the first to help themselves. Malays usually eat with their fingers, but often cutlery is on the table. Although there are numerous dishes upon the table, you would take a helping of rice and then place a few other dishes on your plate. It is considered an insult to your host if you mix all the food on the plate together. It is also considered polite to let the older guests or family eat first.

Muslims do not consume alcohol, so it is also considered impolite to drink it while dining with them. There are a number of drinks that (considering the climate) are very refreshing, such as sugar cane juice, coconut milk, speciality teas like chrysanthemum and Jasmine tea, all of which are consumed cold. These can also be purchased freshly made, while you wait, served in plastic bags with straws to take away, at the roadside or in the markets.

National dish

Rendang is the national dish, and can be made from beef or chicken. It varies a little from one region to another, for example in the north the dish will have more sauce than in the south, where it will be much drier.

It is known as a traveller's or festival dish, which is served at the Muslim New Year and is called Hari raya. Their homes are open to all comers, regardless of faith, to sample this dish.

Festivals

Because of the rich and diverse cultural tapestry in Malaysia there are many festivals up and down the country. They include the Hari Raya Aidil Adha – for Muslims it is the end of Ramadan – and exotic festivals like the Chinese moon festival, the festival of the hungry ghost, the Buddhist Wesak day (marking the birth, enlightenment and death of Buddha), and many more.

Food plays a big part in festivals, from offerings to the monks and shrines to the consumption of it.

PERAK

Perak covers an area of some 21,000 square kilometres and has a population of over two million. According to legend the Prince of Merong Mahapudisa founded Perak, with the first governments being formed in the fifteenth century in Bruas, and Manjung was established in 1528.

Throughout the sixteenth and eighteenth centuries Perak was continually attacked by the Achinese, Dutch, Bugis and the Thais for its rich source of tin. The 1870s saw the area experience a succession of disputes in which the British were able to intercede and appoint James W.W. Birch as the first British Resident in 1874, but he was assassinated the following year. There is a memorial clock tower erected in memory of him. The tower also has a bust of Birch.

For centuries Perak relied on its world famous tin mining from the valley of Kinta, but during the collapse of world tin and the mining industry in the 1980s, Perak had to restructure its whole economy around construction, manufacturing, trade and commerce. Its fishing, forestry and tourism industries have also grown quite significantly. Twenty minutes off the coast of Lumut in the Straits of Melaka is the island of Pulau Pangkor, one of nine islands of Perak. For centuries it has been an island of refuge for seamen, pirates, adventurers, merchants and soldiers of fortune who have travelled the Straits of Melaka. The island has a fort, built in 1690 by the Dutch, as a stronghold against the attacks of pirates. At one time the island was even ruled by European conquerors, and faired little better. Now they have some of the best seafood in Malaysia. The local speciality is Satay fish and the island boasts some of the best dried seafood.

Ipoh is the capital of Perak and is the second city of Malaysia, situated on the River Kinta. Ipoh takes its name from the poisonous Ipoh tree, sought out by the natives for its poisonous sap for their blow darts, which were used to hunt wild animals. The tree was once in abundance, but can only be found in certain parts of the city today.

Ipoh is famous for its cave temples, the most famous of which is the Temple of the Thousand Buddhas, Sam Poh Tong Temple off Jalan Gopeng. Just outside the village of Tambun lies the Tambun caves, which are home to Neolithic wall paintings that are reputed to be over 2,000 years old.

The people of Ipoh take their food very seriously and Ipoh is a gourmet's paradise. The city is famous for many dishes, such as Char kuey tweow and Sar hor fun (flat rice noodles). Hawker food can be found in fan-ventilated food courts in the old town, Jalan Leech, Jalan Clark, gourmet square at Ipoh garden, and places like the railway station (called the Ipoh Taj Mahal by locals) and the Medan Selera Stadium where the stalls will sell a variety of local delights such as Ipoh bean sprouts, chicken satay, Laksa, Nasi lemak, Rojak and Kuih nyonya, just to name a few. There are many street hawkers selling their specialities all around the city from morning to night. Ipoh's other famous edible products are Menglembu ground nuts, Chart tai bean curd sticks and Kampar chicken biscuits.

Perak boasts some of the most delicious durians (dubbed King of Fruits) in Malaysia. The locals in Ipoh are proud of their local fruit, pomeloes, which are a kind of citrus fruit that grow to the size of a football, and are found only in Ipoh.

Rendang Dinding

Method

1. Soak the chillies in a little warm water. Then separately soak the tamarind with the water.

2. Cut the beef into small dice. Peel and slice the onions and 3 garlic cloves. Peel and finely slice the ginger.

3. Grind or pound the dried (soaked) chillies and peel 5 garlic cloves.

4. Heat 50ml oil in a wok or thick-bottomed pan and fry off the onions, sliced garlic and ginger for 4–5 minutes. Do not burn.

5. Drain off any excess oil and blend, but leave coarse.

6. Heat 50ml oil and fry off the ground chillies and remaining garlic until the oil begins to separate, then add the onion mixture and the beef. Fry for 5 minutes then add the soy sauce and fry for a further 10 minutes.

7. Add the brown sugar, salt and tamarind water.

Measurements	Ingredients
40	Dried chillies
30g	Tamarind paste
750ml	Water
1kg	Beef
800g	Onions
8 cloves	Garlic
6cm	Ginger
100ml	Palm oil
20–30ml	Dark thick soy sauce
20g	Brown sugar
10g	Coriander (chopped)
	Salt

continued over →

8. Stir and continue to cook over a low heat for 1 hour. The gravy must be thick.

9. Garnish with chopped coriander and serve with boiled rice.

Chef's Notes

- This recipe from the silver state of Perak is rich and dark in colour but has great flavour. Rendang is the national dish and is often eaten for breakfast by Malays.

Palm oil

The first commercial plantation of palms was planted by the British in 1917. In the 1950s the Malay government took the decision to diversify from rubber as a major revenue of the country. The country is now reaping the rewards as Malaysia is the largest provider of palm oil, and it is a major part of the economy along with petrol and timber. It is still growing in popularity, due in part to its healthy image in helping to reduce cholesterol, and studies have suggested it may help reduce some cancers. Palm oil is extensively used in Malay cooking. It was recorded being used 5,000 years ago by the Egyptians, but is believed to have come to Malaysia from Africa via Bogar in Indonesia 150 years ago.

Nasi Himpit

Rice and Pandanus

Method

1. Wash the leaves, then wash the rice and drain the water.

2. Bring the rice to the boil and add the salt and leaves.

3. When cooked, remove the leaves and start to mash the rice while it is still hot.

Measurements	Ingredients
3–4	Screw pine leaves (pandan)
400g	Jasmine rice
900ml	Water
	Salt

4. Transfer the rice to a smaller container or dish and press down hard. Cover with silicon paper, then place a heavy object on top to press well.

5. Leave overnight in the fridge, then cut into 2–3cm cubes and serve with satay or Rendang.

Chef's Notes

- Malays believe that if you add dried red chilli stalks to sacks or bins of rice you will prevent weevils.

- Pandan leaves (or screw pine leaves as they are also called) are used extensively in the making of Malay and Nyonya cakes. Malays do not normally serve desserts or puddings at the end of a meal.

Ipoh Sar Ho Fun
Flat Rice Noodles

Measurements	Ingredients
400g	Chicken leg meat
10g	Salt
2.5g	Black pepper
5ml	Sesame oil
20g	Garlic purée
45ml	Vegetable oil
400g	Freshwater prawns (shell on)
2lt	Fish or chicken stock
100g	Bok choi
450g	Flat rice noodles
20ml	Palm oil
4	Spring onions (sliced)
	Salt and pepper

Method

1. Remove the skin from the chicken and rub in the salt, pepper and sesame oil. Leave for 20 minutes and wipe off, then steam for 20 minutes. Allow to cool, then slice into 1–2cm strips.

2. Fry off the garlic purée in vegetable oil in a wok or thick-bottomed pan until just starting to colour, then add the prawns and the stock. Remove the prawns when just cooked.

3. Remove the heads from the prawns; then remove the shells and slice lengthways and reserve.

4. Chop up the shells roughly and return to the stock. Reheat the stock and remove any debris from the surface. Boil for 20 minutes and then strain through a fine muslin cloth.

5. Blanch the bok choi in boiling salted water and refresh in ice-cold water, then cut into 4–5cm strips.

6. Cut the rice noodles into 5–6cm lengths and cook in boiling water with the palm oil for 2 minutes. Divide into portions with the prawns, bok choi and chicken, and pour the stock over each portion.

7. Serve with sliced spring onion and seasoning.

Chef's Notes

- Ipoh is also famous for its flat rice noodles (sar ho fun), which are very smooth and soft textured. This has been attributed to Ipoh's hard water and the high quality of its rice flour.

- Substitute the freshwater prawns with ordinary shell-on prawns if necessary.

JOHOR

Johor (the official name is Johor Darul Takzim) occupies the southern end of the Malaysian peninsula. A few miles off the coast in the coral-rich sea stand some 60 islands, around 50 of which are uninhabited. The economy is a mix of agriculture, manufacturing, tourism and commerce. Johor boasts rich plantations of pineapples, bananas, rubber and palm oil. The population is estimated at 2.2 million, in an area of 18,986 square kilometres.

It is believed that Johor was founded in the sixteenth century by the son of the last Sultan of Melaka, Sultan Mahmud Shah, when his capital was taken by the Portuguese invaders. In 1819, Stamford Raffles acquired Singapore for the British during the rivalry and infighting in Johor. This resulted in the Johor-Riau Empire being broken up. In 1957, Johor became part of the Federation of Malaya. Singapore is now joined with Johor by a 1,038-metre causeway.

Johor Bahru is the modern-day capital of Johor, but if we go back in time to 1536 the capital was at Johor Lama on the banks of the Johor River, where a little village still remains.

Johor is strongly rooted in the Malay culture, but its cuisine has been strongly influenced by Chinese and Indian foods. Local diversifications evolved from the traditional methods of the Javanese, and ideas, tastes and flavours established by the locally-born Nyonya Chinese fused together. The Chinese population is mainly Teochew. Teochew cookery is influenced by constant use of five-spice and braised meats in dark soy sauce. The five-spice meat roll recipe typifies this influence.

There are two excellent roadside areas in Johor where large collections of hawker stalls can be found. One is known as the Tepian Tebrau stalls and is situated in Jalan Skudia, along the sea front, and the other is next to the Central Market.

Machap, a village north-west of Johor, is renowned for its pottery and ceramics, whereas the beautiful coastal town of Muar is famous for its music and inexpensive seafood. Then you can travel to the small fishing village of Kukup, west of Johor, which has numerous seafood restaurants selling locally caught fish and delicacies such as cincaluk, keropok and belacan.

The capital itself is noted for its many excellent fresh seafood dishes, notably fried cuttlefish, as well as chilli crab, steamed crab, prawns, sea cucumber and oysters. Other specialities are Laksa Johor, which is a rice noodle dish, and the rice cubes called 'Lontong'. Both of these are normally served in a spicy coconut milk sauce that is a famous speciality in Johor.

Teochew

Steamed Fish

Method

1. Gut and clean the fish (remove scales and fins) and rub salt and pepper into the fish.

2. Place the fish into a dish suitable to fit into a steamer and cover with the cabbage, pork, chillies, ginger and mushrooms. Pour the sesame oil over and leave for 15–20 minutes.

3. Cover with chopped up and freshly squeezed plums, then add to the fish.

4. Place the dish into the steamer and steam the fish for 15–20 minutes (depending on size), then remove and keep hot.

5. Fry the shallots off in hot palm oil until golden brown, then pour the oil and shallots over the fish, garnishing with the coriander and spring onions.

Measurements	Ingredients
4 × 180–200g	Pomfret
10g	Pepper
15g	Salt
150g	Tientsin cabbage (washed and sliced)
100g	Pork (cut into thin strips)
2 small	Red chillies (cut into julienne)
5cm	Fresh ginger (peeled and finely cut into strips)
6	Fresh Chinese mushrooms (cut into julienne)
15ml	Sesame oil
2–3	Pickled sour plums
4 large	Shallots (peeled and finely sliced)

continued over →

Chef's Notes

- You could use bok choi or Chinese cabbage if Tientsin cabbage is not available.
- You can also replace pomfret with threadfin fish if you wish, but pomfret is widely available from most fishmongers and Asian supermarkets.

...continued

100ml	Palm oil
120ml	Water
4 sprigs	Coriander leaves (cut into strips)
4	Spring onions (cut into large diamonds)

Teochew Five-Spice Meat Roll

Method

1. Mix the minced chicken, bacon, prawns, crab meat, carrot, Chinese mushrooms and spring onions together well with 1 egg and all of the flour, then add the spices, MSG and soy sauce. Rest for 40–45 minutes in a fridge.

2. Add the sesame oil to the mixture then divide up and place into the centre of each soy wrapper, brush the edges with egg and seal. Roll up into 4cm (diameter) rolls.

3. Place the rolls into a bamboo steamer and steam for up to 15 minutes. Remove from the steamer and cut into $2\frac{1}{2}$–3cm pieces.

Measurements	Ingredients
500g	Minced chicken
50g	Streaky bacon (minced)
250g	Prawns
250g	Crab meat (white and dark meat)
100g	Carrot (very finely diced)
8	Fresh Chinese mushrooms (very finely diced)
4	Spring onions (very finely diced)

12

continued over →

4. Place the pieces into the hot oil and fry until golden brown.

5. Drain on kitchen paper to remove any excess oil and serve hot, garnished with tomato and cucumber slices.

Chef's Notes

- The use of monosodium glutamate is optional.

- You can also seal the edges with a little flour and water mixed together instead of egg.

- The garnish of cucumber and tomato is a simple one as served in Johor, but you can garnish with lettuce and julienne of carrot.

...continued

2	Eggs (whipped separately)
30g	Plain flour
2.5g	Five-spice, salt and pepper
2.5g	Monosodium glutamate (MSG) (optional)
15ml	Light soy sauce
10ml	Sesame oil
20–30	Soybean wrappers (12cm sq, 5–6 per portion)
2lt	Palm or vegetable oil
100g	Cucumber (peeled, core removed and sliced)
100g	Tomato (washed and sliced)

Kurma Ayam

Malaysian Chicken Korma

Measurements	Ingredients
150g	Korma curry paste
450g	Potatoes (peeled)
2	Onions
15g	Poppy seeds
130g	Shallots (peeled and diced)
5 cloves	Garlic
5cm	Ginger (peeled)
4 large pieces	Chicken
5g	Salt
150ml	Palm oil
70ml	Evaporated milk
10g	Fresh coriander (chopped)
20g	Peas

Method

1. Mix the curry paste with a little water to make a paste. Peel and cut the potatoes and onions into quarters.

continued over →

13

2. Place the poppy seeds, shallots, garlic and ginger into a pestle and mortar or processor and finely grind them.

3. Clean the chicken, rub the salt into it, and keep to one side.

4. Fry off the curry paste and ground ingredients in hot palm oil until the oil separates from the paste, then add the chicken and seal it on all sides. Add the onions and cook with a lid on for 20 minutes.

5. Add 650ml water and the evaporated milk together with the potatoes and bring back to the boil for another 15 minutes until the sauce has reduced to a nice thick consistency. Adjust the seasoning.

6. Add the coriander, peas and tomatoes. Cook for 1–2 minutes and serve with chillies as garnish.

...continued

6	Tomatoes (cut into quarters)
2	Red chillies
	Salt

Chef's Notes

- You may wish to skim some of the oil and debris from the surface, but it is normally served with the excess oil.

- Serve with plain rice.

 KEDAH

The history of Kedah goes back as far as the fourth century when Indian traders stopped at Kuala Muda, using Gunung Jerai as a point of navigation, thus beginning its fame as a trading port. It became a melting pot for exchanges of ideas in cuisine. The state has since had many other influences with Hindus and Buddhists making their mark.

Around the eighth century Kedah became part of the Sumatran Kingdom, then part of Thailand, and then the Sultan of Melaka took over in the fifteenth century. The seventeenth century saw attacks on Kedah by the Chinese and the Portuguese. The eighteenth century saw Penang (at that time part of Kedah) briefly under British rule, but Kedah still fell to Thailand in 1821. Then in the nineteenth century large numbers of Tamils came from Southern India to work on the sugar, coffee and rubber plantations. In 1909, Thailand handed Kedah back to the British. Kedah was then invaded by the Japanese, and after they left, Kedah joined the Federation of Malaysia in 1948.

Kedah along with Perlis has been called the 'Rice Bowl' of Malaysia, with great green paddy fields stretching as far as you can see. Kedah has long had an economy based on agriculture, but is developing its industry and manufacturing as well. Tourism is also a source of income from its cluster of 99 islands, the largest of these being Langkawi.

Kedah has a population of 1,210,000 in an area of some 9,316 square kilometres. The capital is Alor Setar, which is on the main road to the Thai border and the turning point to Langkawi Island and to the state of Perlis.

Alor Setar has some good restaurants with a good hawker centre called the Restoran Empire, which has an assortment of stalls and delicacies. A famous bazaar called the Wednesday market (Pekan Rabu), which strangely opens every day from morning to night, sells the local delicacies called dodol durian, which are sweet cakes made from durian fruit.

The island of Langkawi has a population of 54,000 and lies in the Straits of Melaka. It is believed in times past that the island was made because of a fight that broke out between Mat Cincang and Mat Raya, two giants who lived on the island. The fight started during the engagement of the son of Mat Cincang to the daughter of Mat Raya. The huge engagement ring was thrown into the sea to become the cap of rings (Tanjung Chincin), a broken cooking pot became the village of Belanga Pecah, the gravy from the cooking pot spilled at Kuah (gravy) and seeped into the ground in Keep (seep) and the pot of boiling water landed at Air Hangat (hot water). The powers above turned the two warring giants into mountains, called Mat Cincang and Mat Raya, to stop the fight.

The staple diet of Kedahans is rice, but there are local favourite dishes that will whet the appetite of any visitor, such as jackfruit curry (Gulai nanka). Nasi ulam is another favourite dish with rice, vegetables and spices. Nasi ulam is on many menus in Kedah, especially in the month of Ramadan. Pulut (glutinous rice) is a favourite of many northern Malaysians. It is often mixed with mangoes, durians and sometimes bananas to make a fine dessert. It is said that no visit to Kedah is complete without trying Laksa, a dish of rice noodles with a thick fish sauce and cucumbers, onions and bamboo shoots.

Masak Arab Daging

Beef with Coconut and Tomatoes

Method

1. Remove any trace of fat or sinew from the meat and cut into 5cm slices.

2. Purée the tomatoes and then take 150g of the shallots, the turmeric, sesame seeds, pepper, cumin, ginger and fennel and grind to a fine paste. Then mix well into the meat and leave in the fridge for 2–3 hours.

3. Heat the oil in a suitable pan or wok and fry the remaining shallots and garlic until golden brown. Remove with a slotted spoon and then seal off the meat.

Measurements	Ingredients
500g	Beef (sirloin)
200g	Tomatoes
200g	Shallots
2cm	Turmeric root *or* 10g powder
40g	Sesame seeds
2.5g	Pepper
2.5g	Cumin

continued over →

4. Add the coconut milk to the meat and then add the browned shallots and garlic. Stir the milk until it boils then reduce the heat to a simmer until it becomes thick (approx. 15–20 minutes).

5. Add the tomato purée mixture and cook for a further 5–10 minutes, stirring to prevent burning on the bottom. Season and serve with a garnish of chilli and coriander.

Chef's Notes

• This recipe highlights the influence of the traders from Arabia with ingredients like turmeric and fennel, but it works well with ginger, tomatoes and sesame seeds.

...continued

1cm	Ginger (peeled)
2.5g	Fennel
60ml	Palm oil
4 cloves	Garlic (thinly sliced)
400ml	Coconut milk
4	Red chillies
4 sprigs	Coriander

Laksa Kedah

Measurements	Ingredients
20	Dried red chillies
15	Shallots
2cm	Belacan (dried shrimp paste)
1½ lt	Light fish stock
200g	Rice vermicelli (thick)
1 (500–600g)	Mackerel
20g	Tamarind paste
1	Wild ginger flower
2–3 sprigs	Mint
200g small	Shelled prawns
2	Red chillies
4	Eggs (hard-boiled)
1 head	Washed lettuce
1	Banana shallot
$\frac{1}{4}$	Cucumber (grated)
	Salt and pepper

Method

1. Grind the dried chillies, shallots and belacan to a fine paste. Bring half the stock to the boil and cook the vermicelli for 4 minutes then drain. Reserve the liquor.

2. Either steam the fish or lightly poach in the reserved stock. When it is cooked, remove the flesh from the bones, flake, and place into a suitable pot.

3. Add the remaining fish stock to the cooking pot together with the ground paste and the tamarind paste, wild ginger flower and mint. Cook for 15 minutes at a simmer.

4. Add the vermicelli and prawns and cook for a further 5 minutes, then season to taste.

5. Place into bowls and garnish with julienne of red chilli, egg cut into quarters, lettuce, sliced shallot and cucumber.

Chef's Notes

● Laksa is different wherever you go throughout Malaya, and can vary from one region to another.

● If you cannot obtain the wild ginger flowers, just add the juice from 1cm grated ginger.

Kanji Kedah

Kedah Porridge

Method

1. Cut the chicken breast into thin strips, lightly crush the lemongrass and deep-fry the shallot rings until crisp. Place on dish paper and reserve.

2. Bring the rice and stock to the boil until nice and thick. Then add the chicken, lemongrass, ginger, fenugreek and the coconut milk.

3. You may at this point add a little salt for taste. Add the prawns.

4. Serve hot with a garnish of shallots, spring onions and shredded lettuce.

Chef's Notes

● Beef is also often used in this dish with prawns instead of chicken.

● In this recipe you can see the influence of Indian cuisine in the fenugreek.

Measurements	Ingredients
250g	Chicken breast
1 stalk	Lemongrass
2	Banana shallots (sliced into rings)
200g	Long grain rice
2lt	Light stock (chicken, fish or vegetable)
3–4cm	Ginger (grated)
5g	Fenugreek
150ml	Coconut milk
200g small	Shelled prawns
6	Spring onions (cut into diamonds)
$\frac{1}{2}$ head	Lettuce (shredded)

KELANTAN

Called the land of lightning due to the spectacular lightning the region attracts during monsoon, Kelantan is on the north-eastern side of the Malaysian peninsula and is separated from the western side by a mountain range. It is also called the Cultural Capital of Malaysia because of its cottage industries, which are an important part of the state's tourism industry. Kelantan is the centre of some of the traditional craft industries and traditions, including the making of kaftans, pareos and also sarongs. A beautiful cloth named Songket (the cloth of gold), which has intricate weaving of gold and silver threads, is also made in Kelantan. It was once used by Kelantan royalty and has since been used for wedding ceremonies and ceremonial occasions.

Kelantan covers an area of 14,920 square kilometres, and has a population of 1.3 million.

A large part of Kelantan's economy is agriculture with rice, tobacco and rubber crops being produced on its fertile plains. Kelantan is noted for its virgin rain forests and natural waterfalls.

Other traditional areas of commerce such as fishing, managed forestry and logging play a part, along with tourism.

Kelantan's history is mainly documented with the Chinese Imperial court, with the present royal family descending from Long Yunus, a warrior ruler in the eighteenth century. After the British rule and Japanese occupation, Kelantan became part of the Federation of Malaysia in 1957. There are many influences from Thailand because of its close proximity to Thailand with many Buddhist temples.

The capital of Kelantan is called Kota Bahru, which is towards the east coast and is known as the cultural city. It has many traditional activities, such as kite flying, silat (a martial art of Malaysia), gasing (top spinning), and kertok (percussion), which take place from March until October in the Gelanggang Seni (cultural centre). A shadow puppet show (wayang kulit) is performed in the evening.

The cultural aspects also extend to food. Kelantanese food is an aromatic feast in its own right. The food is stimulated with chillies and shallots, hence the Thai influence, also gently spiced and a little sweet which shows the Chinese connection. The authentic culinary delights such as Nasi kerabu, Nasi dagang, Kuzi ayam, Ayam percik and Daging kerutuk can all be experienced in the capital's night food market in Jalan Padang Garong and on many stalls throughout the eastern coast of Kelantan. The night food market is very cheap and you will find that many locals eat there.

It is best remembered that the Malay people eat with their fingers (of the right hand), so it is best to take a fork if you are unable to cope with this.

Just outside Kota Bahru, some 15 kilometres away, are the traditional fishing villages of Kampung Sabak and Kuala Besar with their carved boats full of traditional designs and colours. You can see the daily haggling of prices for the fish from the local traders, when the fishermen land their catch, at mid-afternoon.

Daging Masak Merah

Beef in Red Sauce

Method

1. Deep-fry the sliced shallots until golden brown, then fry the sultanas for 1–2 minutes and remove.

2. Grind the ginger, chillies (no seeds), lemongrass and turmeric root to a paste. Cut the spring onions into diamonds and chop the coriander.

3. Toast the grated coconut under the grill until golden brown.

4. Boil the thin coconut milk in a pot.

5. Add the ginger paste to the beef and then put the beef into the boiled coconut milk.

6. Add the thick coconut milk and gently simmer the beef for 1 hour, then add the cashew nuts, shallots and sultanas and mix with the beef.

7. Add sugar, toasted coconut and salt, stirring cautiously to prevent sticking to the pan.

8. Add half the spring onions and coriander and stir in. Cook for a further 5 minutes.

9. Serve when the sauce is thick and garnish with the remaining spring onions and coriander.

Measurements	Ingredients
200g	Shallots (peeled and sliced)
30g	Sultanas
2cm	Ginger (peeled)
20	Dried red chillies
2 stalks	Lemongrass
2cm	Turmeric root (peeled)
4	Spring onions
10g	Coriander (chopped)
$\frac{1}{4}$	Coconut flesh (grated)
250ml	Thin coconut milk
600g	Beef (diced)
130ml	Thick coconut milk
50g	Cashew nuts (toasted)
10g	Caster sugar
	Salt

Chef's Notes

• Serve with Nasi lemak or plain rice.

• You may wish to add two jackfruit leaves when cooking the meat as this can act as a tenderiser. Remove them after 1 hour.

Ayam Percik

Grilled Chicken with Gravy

Method

1. Clean the chicken and then grind the garlic, 4 shallots, 2–3cm ginger and salt to a fine paste. Cover the chicken in the paste and leave in the fridge for 1 hour.

2. Grind the remaining ginger and shallots, dried chillies and belacan to a fine paste. Squeeze the coconut flesh to remove the milk, then soak the flesh in a little water and squeeze again. Mix the tamarind paste, sugar and a little salt into the milk and then strain, discard the pulp, then add the paste to the milk.

3. Slowly bring the milk to a simmer then squeeze the lime juice into the milk, and cook until it begins to thicken.

4. Dip the chicken into the milk and place onto a hot charcoal grill. It is important to continue to baste the chicken on both sides while cooking, until it is cooked (approx 15–20 minutes).

Measurements	Ingredients
1½kg	Chicken (cut into 4)
4 cloves	Garlic
14	Shallots (peeled and diced)
3–4cm	Ginger (peeled and diced)
2.5g	Salt
4	Dried chillies
10g	Belacan (shrimp paste)
2	Coconuts (grated and squeezed for 500–600ml milk)
20g	Tamarind paste
5g	Sugar
1	Lime (juice only)
	Salt

Chef's Notes

- The chicken can either be cut into four large portions or into pieces for sauté.

- It is said that if a coconut palm is planted outside or beside a house, the head of the house will have a very hard life.

Kuzi Ayam

Chicken

Measurements	Ingredients
500g	Shallots (peeled)
1g	Saffron powder
1 × 1½ kg	Chicken (cut for sauté)
30ml	Water
150ml	Palm or vegetable oil
50g	Sultanas
10 cloves	Garlic
6	Shallots (peeled)
30g	Coriander
20g	Fennel
20g	Peppercorns
10g	Ground turmeric
20g	Ground cumin
2cm	Galangal (peeled)
4	Green cardamom pods
3cm	Ginger
1 stick	Cinnamon
400ml	Evaporated milk
40ml	Fresh lime juice
1lt	Light chicken stock
60g	Tomato ketchup
15g	Flaked almonds (toasted)
10g	Granulated sugar

Method

1. Cut the shallots into slices and deep-fry until golden brown. Mix the saffron powder with the water and rub into the chicken.

2. Pour the oil into a suitable pan or wok and seal the chicken until golden brown, then add the sultanas and fry for a further 2 minutes. Remove the chicken and sultanas and drain on kitchen paper.

3. Slice 4 cloves of garlic and 6 shallots and fry them in the oil until golden brown and keep to one side for garnish.

4. Finely grind the coriander, fennel, peppercorns, turmeric, cumin, galangal, cardamom pods, ginger, cinnamon and remaining garlic to a fine paste. Then add the evaporated milk, lime juice, deep-fried shallots and approximately 20ml stock. Now add the fried shallots, garlic and tomato ketchup to the wok and bring to the boil.

5. Add the chicken and sultanas, bring to the boil and cook for a further 10 minutes.

6. Now add half the almonds and all the sugar and stir. Place into an earthenware dish and put in a preheated oven (170°C, 325°F, gas mark 3) until the sauce is thick – about 1 hour.

7. Remove from the oven and serve with a sprinkling of toasted almonds and the deep-fried garlic and shallots.

Chef's Notes

- Best served with simple boiled rice or rice lightly scented with coconut, and peeled, sliced cucumbers as a side dish.

- This is a classic Kelantan dish, showing the light spices and the sweetness of the region.

- You could use turmeric instead of saffron powder, but it does change the flavour of the dish slightly.

MELAKA (MALACCA)

Melaka is one of the most historically rich cities in Malaysia with a glorious and colourful past. It was founded by an exiled Sumatran Prince, Parameswara in 1400. Due to the city's location it thrived as a trading port, with merchants from China, Arabia, India and the South Americas trading in gold, silks, ivory and spices. The story goes that the Prince, after an unsuccessful battle in Sumatra against the Javanese, fled to Singapore, then called Temasik, but was ousted by the Siamese. He travelled with his warriors along the western coast of Malaysia looking for refuge. They stopped at the mouth of the Bertam River. While there, the Prince's hunting dogs were attacked by a white deer, which clearly kicked one. The Prince was so impressed by the courage of the deer that he built a settlement on the spot and called it Melaka, after the tree (a rattan) that he rested under.

In 1405, the Chinese Emperor Ming sent his Admiral Cheng Ho with gifts and the promise of protection to Melaka from the rival Siamese (Thailand). Over time Melaka grew into a powerful state and repelled many attacks by the Siamese. The Sultan's ambassador was appointed to visit China and returned with the Emperor's daughter, who married the Sultan. She brought with her over 500 handmaidens. Their residence was called China Hill, and these early settlers from China became known as Babas, or 'Straits Chinese'.

Melaka fell into the hands of the Portuguese in 1511, causing the Sultan to flee to Johor and re-establish his kingdom. The Portuguese married local women and this had a large effect on the cuisine, bringing an influence of sour and spicy combinations with dishes like Feng pada, devil kari, which is a spicy chicken dish. Another local dish is called Satay celup, a skewer of diced pork, seafood and vegetables cooked in boiling satay sauce.

Descendants of the Portuguese still live in and around the Portuguese square. In 1641, the Dutch attacked the city of Melaka and lay siege for

eight months, occupying Melaka for 150 years. It was then given to the British in 1795, to try to prevent it falling into the hands of the French when Holland was invaded by the French during the Revolution.

Melaka was returned to the Dutch in 1818 under the Treaty of Vienna, but was then exchanged for the Sumatran port of Bencoolen, now called Bengkulu, in 1826 and was run by the East India Company in Calcutta, along with the ports of Singapore and Penang.

After the Second World War the proclamation of independence was called by His Highness Tunku Abdul Rahman Putra Al-Haj, the first prime minister of Malaysia, on the warriors' field at Padang Pahlwan in Malacca on 20 February 1956.

The state's economy is mainly tourism and light industry and there is a population of 600,000.

A rich heritage of cuisine can be found in Melaka, with Nyonya, Portuguese, Dutch and Chinese influences over the centuries. Its best eating areas are along the waterfront and the Portuguese square.

Laksa Lemak Melaka

Rice Noodles with Coconut Gravy

Method

1. Place the noodles in boiling water for 3–4 minutes, then refresh under cold water.

2. Pound the shallots, turmeric root, chillies, lemongrass, candle nuts, belacan, dried prawns, galangal, coriander seeds and water in a pestle and mortar, food processor or coffee grinder and grind them to a fine paste.

3. Peel and finely shred the cucumber, wash and blanch the bean sprouts, slice the fish cake and wash and pick off the mint leaves and keep them all for garnish.

4. Heat the oil in a suitable pan and fry the paste ingredients until the paste releases oil. At this point add the prawns and cook for 3–4 minutes, then remove them and keep them warm.

5. Add the stock and bring to the boil for 5–8 minutes.

6. Add the coconut milk and keep to a gentle heat, otherwise the coconut milk could curdle.

Measurements	Ingredients
600–800g	Mifen (thick rice noodles)
100g	Shallots
4cm	Turmeric root or 15–20g powder
15	Dried red chillies
2	Red chilli
2 stalks	Lemongrass
5	Candle nuts
15g	Belacan (shrimp paste)
20g	Dried prawns (soaked)
2cm	Galangal
10g	Ground coriander seeds
60ml	Water
150g	Cucumber

continued over →

...continued

100g	Bean sprouts
1 × 30–40g	Fish cake
	Mint
50ml	Vegetable oil
240g	Jumbo prawns (3–4 per portion)
1lt	Prawn or chicken stock
250ml	Thick coconut milk
5g	Salt
2.5g	Monosodium glutamate (MSG)

7. Add the fish slices, leave for 2–3 minutes, then add the prawns and season.

8. To serve, place a helping of noodles into a bowl, followed by the bean sprouts, cucumber, fish cake slices, prawns, sauce and mint leaves.

Chef's Notes

- I have collected a number of Laksa recipes from Melaka, so this is an amalgamation of several recipes. Some recipes say remove the shells and the central vein of the prawns, others say leave the shell on.

- Cashew nuts can be substituted for candle nuts. Seasoning is up to you, you can use MSG or just salt.

- The fish cake can be either slices from a steamed puréed mixture of white fish, or a spicy Thai-style fish cake sliced, available precooked and chilled or frozen from most Asian supermarkets, or you could just add slices of steamed white fish.

Debal Chicken

Measurements	Ingredients
800kg	Chicken (diced)
5g	Salt
10	Dried chillies
15g	Mustard seeds
2	Red chillies
2–3cm	Fresh ginger
200g	Shallots
4	Candle nuts
20g	Ground coriander
5g	Ground turmeric
120g	Shallots
4 cloves	Garlic

continued over →

Method

1. Place the diced chicken into a bowl, rub the salt into the meat and leave for 30–40 minutes.

2. Soak the dried chillies in warm water until soft. Lightly toast the mustard seeds then crush them.

3. Pound 2 red chillies, dried chillies, garlic cloves, ginger, 200g shallots, candle nuts, ground coriander, ground turmeric and mustard seeds in a pestle and mortar, food processor or coffee grinder and grind them to a fine paste.

4. Peel and thinly slice 120g shallots, 2 garlic cloves, 2 red chillies and the galangal. Heat the vegetable oil in a suitable pan and fry these ingredients to a light brown colour.

5. When the sliced ingredients are brown, add the paste and fry until it smells fragrant, at which point you may add the chicken and seal it. Add the water and simmer for 20 minutes with a lid on.

6. Combine the mustard, rice vinegar, dark soy sauce and salt, stir into the chicken and cook for a further 2–3 minutes. Adjust the seasoning and then remove any excess oil. Serve and garnish with coriander and chilli.

...continued

1–2	Red chillies
1–2cm	Galangal
50ml	Vegetable oil
200ml	Water
10g	Dijon mustard
10–20ml	Rice vinegar
15ml	Dark soy sauce
10g	Fresh coriander (chopped)
1	Red chilli (cut into fine strips)
	Salt (to taste)

Chef's Notes

- This dish is meant to be hot, but adjust the ingredients to your own taste.

- The Nyonya version uses potatoes, cabbage, lemongrass and shrimp paste.

Ayam Pong Tay

Stewed Chicken

Method

1. Place the diced chicken into a bowl, rub the salt into the meat and leave for 30–40 minutes. Soak the mushrooms in water. Wash and clean the potatoes and cut into quarters.

2. Pound the shallots and garlic cloves in a pestle and mortar, food processor or coffee grinder and grind to a fine paste.

3. Place the oil into a suitable pan and fry for 3–4 minutes at which point you may add the soy beans, frying slowly until fragrant.

4. Add the chicken and seal it, then add the mushrooms. Stir for 2–3 minutes.

5. Add the water and soy sauce, and bring to the boil for 10 minutes. Add the potatoes and simmer with a lid and cook out for 15–20 minutes.

6. Adjust the seasoning and serve.

Measurements	Ingredients
800g	Chicken (diced)
5g	Salt
3–4	Dried Chinese mushrooms
200g	New or mid potatoes
100g	Shallots
1–2 cloves	Garlic
50ml	Vegetable oil
20g	Preserved soy beans
300ml	Water
5–10ml	Dark soy sauce
	Salt

Chef's Notes

- This dish is just as popular using pork (Babi Pong Tay). Simply replace the chicken with pork.

- The sauce should be thick and the meat should be nice and tender. The potatoes should be just cooked whole, and not broken up.

NEGERI SEMBILAN

Negeri Sembilan is called the 'land of Minangkabau tradition'. The earliest people to settle in the state were Sumatrans in the fifteenth century. They had a tradition of 'Adat Peratih', or a matrilineal system, which means that the wife heads the household and the inheritance passes from mother to daughter. The Minangkabau is divided into 12 clans or groups and it is forbidden for people from the same clan to marry. Today, the Minangkabau influence is seen mainly in its architecture, with many buildings showing buffalo-horn-shaped roof peaks found in traditional houses and even more modern buildings.

Negeri Sembilan is a federation of nine states. The population is 710,000 and the capital Seremban is an old town with many back alleys and narrow streets. Around 30 kilometres away is Port Dickson, which is more of a seaside town these days, with some great seafood dishes from the usual food stalls. The port also has some wonderful varieties of noodles, like Sang meen and Lor mee.

In Fort Kempas, which is approximately 23 kilometres from Port Dickson, lies the grave of a local hero who rebelled against the Sultan of Melaka. Beside the grave there are three mysterious megalithic stones, named 'The Rudder', 'The Sword' and 'The Spoon', named after their shapes. There is a fourth stone known as 'The Stone of Ordeal', which has a hole through it. According to local legend, if a person puts their hand into the hole and tells lies, the stone will tighten around it.

The local economy is mainly agricultural; as the state is a mountainous region the land is very fertile and paddy fields and rubber plantations are the main sources of income.

The cuisine of Negeri Sembilan is very hot and spicy and the dishes are usually done in the style of the Minangkabau tradition. This normally means that there will be plenty of 'cili padi', a generous portion of small hot chillies (bird's eye), which are the hottest. Some of the favourite dishes are Masak lemak cili api, which is made with coconut milk, ground chilli and turmeric, then added to meat or fish. A dish made with glutinous rice cooked in coconut and bamboo sticks is another favourite. It is called Lemang, and is normally served with a traditional (spicy) rendang dish. Both of these dishes can also be found on many roadside stalls.

Lemang

Glutinous Rice with Bamboo   *4–6 covers*

Method

1. Open the coconuts (keeping the milk) and grate the flesh. Cut the bamboo sticks down three-quarters of the length. Wash the banana leaves and cut 4–5cm longer than the bamboo sticks. Roll up the leaves individually with the outside of the leaf facing outwards, then place each leaf into a bamboo stick and tap on the ground to ensure they have reached the bottom.

Measurements	Ingredients
1–2	Coconuts
6	Bamboo sticks
6	Banana leaves
1kg	Glutinous rice
20g	Sea salt

2. Wash the rice well and then leave to soak for 1–2 hours.

3. Drain the rice and then soak in the grated coconut and milk and add salt to taste. The milk must just cover the rice.

4. Spoon the rice into the bamboo sticks, tapping gently to ensure they are filled, but leave around 20 per cent of the stick empty to allow the rice to expand when cooking. Fold the ends of the leaf over and tuck them in.

5. Traditionally the rice is cooked on an open fire, but you can either cook it on a barbeque or in the oven for 3–4 hours on a low gentle heat, turning regularly.

6. When cooked, split the stick and cut across the banana leaf approximately 3–4cm down. Serve the rice still wrapped in the cooked banana leaf.

Chef's Notes

- If you cannot obtain the bamboo sticks, wrap the rice in banana leaves and then wrap tightly in tin foil, twisting the ends to allow expansion.

- An old wives' tale relating to the banana leaf is that if a woman passes the leaf over a fire to make it more pliable, her child will be born with spots, just like those on the banana leaf.

Ikan Masak Lemak Cili Padi

Fish in Hot Coconut Gravy

Method

1. Cut the fish into 5cm pieces on the bone. Rub salt onto the fish and leave for 30 minutes to 1 hour then wipe off.

2. Pound the chillies, turmeric, tamarind pulp, ginger, shallots and garlic in a pestle and mortar or food processor.

Measurements	Ingredients
500g	Catfish or mackerel
	Salt
10	Bird's eye chillies
1–2cm	Turmeric

continued over →

Add water and bring to the boil.

3. Add all of the thin coconut milk and one turmeric leaf (torn in two) and bring to the boil for 15 minutes, then add the thick coconut milk and again bring to the boil. Add the fish and cook for 10–15 minutes, skimming any debris from the surface.

4. Season to taste.

5. Serve hot with plain boiled white rice and garnish the top with shredded turmeric leaf.

...continued

1–2cm	Tamarind pulp
1–2cm	Ginger
50g	Shallots (sliced)
1 clove	Garlic
200ml	Water
250ml	Thin coconut milk
2	Turmeric leaves
500ml	Thick coconut milk

Chef's Notes

- This dish is normally made with freshwater catfish, usually taken from a tank or bucket in the restaurant or kitchen. If your fishmonger cannot get catfish, use mackerel.

- You can add more chillies if you wish, as the recipe I was given had twice as many as I have included here.

Dodol

Glutinous Rice Cake

Method

1. Dissolve the palm sugar, white sugar, water and screw pine leaves in a suitable pan.

2. Place the flour into a bowl and mix in the coconut milk until a smooth texture is achieved.

3. Pour into a thick-bottomed non-stick pan and stir with a non-metal spatula on a low heat.

4. As the mixture begins to thicken pour the sugar syrup over the rice flour and stir in. Continue to cook for around 2 hours. It will become a dark brown-colour dough. You must continue to stir the mixture. Do not allow it to catch on the bottom of the pan and burn.

5. When the mixture stops sticking to your fingers it should be cooked.

6. Place into a screw pine basket or a suitable dish to allow to cool. Smooth the top over and let it cool overnight, then divide up evenly.

Measurements	Ingredients
400g	Palm sugar
200g	White sugar
250ml	Water
3–4	Screw pine leaves (pandan)
500g	Glutinous rice flour
875ml	Coconut milk

Chef's Notes

- This is a very sweet dessert. If you cannot get the screw pine leaves use pandan essence, which you can buy from any good supermarket or Chinese store.

PAHANG

Pahang is the largest state in Malaysia, occupying some 35,960 square kilometres, with a population of some 1.2 million.

The east coast of Pahang has some of the best beaches. The capital city of the state is called Kuantan and ten kilometres north you can still see villagers transferring their goods from the paddy fields, and the fresh fish caught that day, by way of carts pulled by buffalo. In some areas and at certain times of the year you can see green turtles, and occasionally huge leatherback turtles, which can be seen laying their eggs on the beaches.

The mainstay of the state's economy are palm oil, rubber, fruits and cocoa. Tourism and manufacturing are also increasing steadily.

The first mention of the state can be found around the seventh century in ancient Chinese records when Pahang was part of the Sumatra-based Sri Vijaya Empire. Around the thirteenth century Pahang was under Melaka Empire control, then ruled by the Johor–Riau Empire from the fifteenth to the nineteenth centuries. That rule ended when Bendahara Wan Ahmad of Pahang declared himself the Sultan in 1882. His reign was short lived, however, since the British took control in 1888. The Japanese invaded during the Second World War, and afterwards Pahang became part of the Malay Federation.

Pahang is famous for its hill resorts. The main three are Genting Highlands, Cameron Highlands, which can be reached only from Perak, and Fraser's Hill. Genting Highlands is famous for its sky lift, the highest and longest in Asia, rising to 2,000 metres at the summit. At the top there is a 24-hour casino, as well as restaurants, golf courses and numerous hotels. Fraser's Hill is approximately 40–50 kilometres north of Genting Highlands.

Many inhabitants of the capital Kuala Lumpur use Genting Highlands as a weekend and bank holiday retreat, being around 40 minutes away by car. Just before the station for the sky lift there are a number of small villages that offer some superb food, from fresh frogs' legs with rice wine to wild boar curry and Ikan jelawat, a freshwater fish that is found only in a few local rivers around Genting. Other specialities that Pahang offers are salted fish and prawn crackers (Keropok). Weaving and handicrafts support the economy.

The Cameron Highlands have some of the most excellent scenery with its landscape of tea plantations, vegetable plantations, wild flowers, rose gardens and the smell of strawberry farms. You can still see the tea plantation workers harvesting the tea leaves. Then there are the Neo Tudor-style cottages and the old colonial bungalows dotted around the hills. Around 1,820 metres above sea level the Cameron Highlands have three townships – Brinchang, Ringlet and Tanah Rata. It is quite a common sight to see many Malaysians walking around the Highlands wearing coats, due to the cold at high altitude.

Tea has been fought over, traded, and craved by Emperors. It even led the way to American Independence. It has been brewed for some 4,500 years. The first cup of tea is reputed to have been made when Emperor of China, Shen Nung's water cup had tea leaves fall into it as long ago as 2737 BC. The Chinese guarded tea as its greatest treasure until around 1721, when the Europeans stole it and transferred it to India, breaking the Chinese monopoly.

The English began to drink their tea with the addition of sugar and either cream or milk, much to the Chinese tea drinkers' disapproval as they considered this to be blasphemous. Yet the Tibetans drink it with yaks' butter and salt, and the Russians with a dash of vodka and lemon. Today with every second that passes, over 2 million cups of tea are consumed all over the world.

The tea bush is not really a bush but a wild tree, and is either green or black. All tea comes from the original wild plant called *camellia sinensis*.

In 1929, A. J. Russell travelled up 5,000 feet to the Cameron Highlands and set up a garden carved out of the hillside. He created the tea brand called Boh, taking the word from the original tea hills of China, where it also means 'precious'. The tea produced is black tea, and you can still see the original machinery being used to produce some of the tea in this area.

The following two recipes, wild boar curry and steamed frog's legs, are from the little restaurants at the foot of the Genting Highlands. The third is a typical recipe reflecting the mild spices and fragrant roots of the region.

Buas Babi Jantan Kari

Wild Boar Curry

Method

1. Pound the candle nuts, lemongrass, turmeric, galangal, garlic and shallots into a paste with a pestle and mortar, or in a food processor, until they form a smooth paste.

2. Pour the oil into a hot wok or suitable pan and add the paste. Sweat the paste until it becomes fragrant, keep stirring and do not allow it to burn.

3. Next add the chilli and curry powder to the paste and stir in and cook it out for a further 3–4 minutes.

4. Add the meat to the paste and cook for approximately 15–20 minutes on a lower heat.

Measurements	Ingredients
30g	Candle nuts
1 stalk	Lemongrass
10g	Turmeric
5cm	Galangal
2 cloves	Garlic
4 large	Shallots
60–80ml	Vegetable oil
100–150g	Meat curry powder
10g	Chilli powder

continued over →

5. Add the coconut milk and continue to cook for a further 15 minutes until it is really thick. Check the seasoning and serve with plain boiled or steamed rice, garnished with coriander.

...continued

800g	Wild boar meat (diced)
100ml	Coconut milk
10g	Coriander (chopped)

Chef's Notes

- Malaysians use two types of curry powder, one for meat and one for fish.

- The meat variety is as follows: 10–15g chilli powder, 10–15g ground coriander, 10g ground cumin, 5g ground fennel, 10g ground turmeric, 10g garam dhal, 10 curry leaves, 10g rice flour, 10–15g curry powder and 5–10g ground black pepper. For chicken or mutton increase curry powder by 15g for each 500g meat.

- If you cannot obtain wild boar meat, then use baby pork ribs.

Mengukus Katak Kaki Dan Padi Wain

Steamed Frog's Legs with Rice Wine

Method

1. Peel and finely slice the garlic and spring onions. Peel and cut the ginger into very fine strips.

2. Roughly chop the coriander leaves and then the stalks separately.

Measurements	Ingredients
2 cloves	Garlic
8	Spring onions
5cm	Ginger (peeled)
10g	Coriander

continued over →

3. Bring the rice wine to the boil and add the garlic, ginger, spring onion and the coriander stalks. Add the water.

4. Once the liquid is at boiling point, put the frog's legs in a steamer and place over the boiling liquid for 10–12 minutes. When cooked, arrange on a plate and pour the liquid over the legs and serve.

5. Garnish with chopped coriander leaves.

...continued

150ml	Chinese yellow rice wine
50ml	Water
12	Frog's legs
	Salt and pepper

Chef's Notes

- You can normally buy frozen frog's legs from most frozen food suppliers, or from Chinese supermarkets or Asian stores.

- If you do not wish to use frog's legs, use baby chicken legs instead.

Ayam Kicap Buah Asam

Spiced Fried Chicken and Plum Sauce

Method

1. Remove the chicken legs and cut each into two at the joint. Remove the wish bone and then remove the winglets and trim. Remove the wings carefully, leaving two equal portions on the breast. Remove the breast and cut into two. Discard the carcass. There should be 8 portions of chicken – 2 drumsticks, 2 thighs and 4 portions of white breast meat.

2. Dust the chicken in cornflour and deep-fry until golden brown. Remove the stalks from the chillies and cut in half lengthways and remove the seeds. Thinly slice the chillies.

3. Peel and very thinly slice the garlic. Separately in a wok, fry off the garlic until golden brown, then add the chicken, chillies and curry leaves. Fry for 3–4 minutes.

4. Add the stock and reduce by one-third on a low heat. Add the plum sauce and reduce until the sauce is thick. Serve hot.

Measurements	Ingredients
1 whole	Chicken
40g	Cornflour
2	Red chillies
2	Green chillies
4 cloves	Garlic
50ml	Coconut oil
5g	Curry leaves
100ml	Light chicken stock
120ml	Yellow plum sauce
	Vegetable oil for frying

Chef's Notes

- Serve with plain boiled rice.

PENANG

The pearl of the orient, the state of Penang is the oldest British settlement in Malaysia, founded by Captain Francis Light in 1786. He acquired it from a Kedah Sultan on behalf of the East India Company, and also acquired the land between the Kerian and Muda rivers. Legend has it that Captain Light once loaded his cannons from his ship with silver dollars and fired them into the jungle to encourage his labourers to cut back the jungle and the undergrowth.

The British named the island between the river the 'Prince of Wales Island' in honour of the heir to the throne (with the strip of land being renamed after the Marquis of Wellesley, calling it Province Wellesley). The spice trade, in particular, pepper, cloves and nutmeg, grew rapidly during the 1800s. The original population of 50 residents in Penang grew quickly with immigrant Chinese, Indian and Arab traders and merchants. Penang and Province Wellesley became part of the Federation of Malaysia in 1948.

The state is officially called Pulau Pinang, and covers an area of 1,031 square kilometres, with a population of 1.07 million. The capital of the state is the Island of George Town, named after King George III who reigned at the time. There are many historical buildings dating back to the time of British colonialism, one of which Cornwallis built in 1786 on the site of Light's first landing. The older part of George Town is like stepping back in time 50–100 years, with colourful buildings, colonial architecture and rickshaw bicycles littering the streets. Parts of it have a real 'Chinatown' feeling. It is reputed that the leader of the Chinese Revolution, Dr Sun Yat Sen, had his base at 120 Lebuh Armenian, within George Town. This uprising led to the overthrow of the Manchus in 1911.

The economy is diverse, and tourism is flourishing due to the superb beaches, food and history. The state only has around 55,000 hectares of agricultural land, producing palm oil, rice, rubber and fruits as the main crops. The deep-water port brings valuable links and custom, via routes to Thailand and Indonesia. The port also has the longest bridge in Asia, the Penang Bridge, which stretches some 3 kilometres and links George Town to Butterworth on the mainland. There is a 24-hour ferry crossing just a little south of the bridge. The biggest growth for the state in recent years has been the development of international electronic companies, leading to the state being called the 'Silicon Valley of the East'.

Penang is not only renowned for its architecture and history, but also for its superb cuisine, and not just in Malaysia but throughout Asia, with dishes such as Laksa, and then the Chinese influenced dishes Hokkien mee and Char koay teow, or the oyster omelettes called Ore chie.

There is also the highly popular Nyonya food with the slightly sour flavour provided by the tamarind paste and perfumed by lemongrass, ginger and galangal. Other dishes include Penang acar and Otak otak, but one dish that stands out is the Indian influenced Curry kapitan. It gets its name from a story that a Dutch sea captain one evening asked his Indonesian cabin boy what was on the menu that night. He replied, 'Curry kapitan' and it has retained that name ever since. There is a little Indian area where there are stalls serving Muslim and southern Indian food on Jalan Pasar and Market Street.

Penang is famous throughout Malaysia for its hawker foods, from the traditional street stalls on Gurney Drive and Ayer Itam market to those of the air-conditioned courts in Komtar and island plaza.

There are a number of markets and night markets that sell fruit, cakes, laksa and many other items through to teas that claim to cure everything.

Otak Otak

Method

1. Pound or blend the chillies, galangal, lemongrass, turmeric, candle nuts, garlic, shallots and belacan into a smooth paste.

2. Blanch the banana leaves lightly, to make them pliable. Check the fish for any bones.

3. Pour the oil into a hot wok and fry off the paste until it becomes fragrant, then remove and cool in a suitable mixing bowl.

4. Add to the paste the eggs, mackerel, limau leaves, coconut milk and then season with sugar, salt and pepper. Stir the mixture constantly.

5. Spread 20g mixture onto one of the banana leaves, then place a quarter of the threadfin fish on top of the mixture, then add another 20g of mixture, spreading it evenly over the fish.

6. Fold both ends of the leaf together and then fold the sides together, secure with a cocktail stick, and place in a steamer for 10–15 minutes over a high heat.

7. When cooked remove the stick and serve in the banana leaf with a side dish of diced cucumber.

Measurements	Ingredients
3–4	Fresh red chillies (seeds and stalks removed)
2cm	Fresh galangal (peeled)
2 stalks	Lemongrass
2cm	Fresh turmeric (peeled)
5	Candle nuts
4–5 cloves	Garlic
150–200g	Fresh shallots (peeled)
10g	Belacan (shrimp paste)
4	Banana leaves (24cm × 16cm)
300g	Mackerel (flaked or mashed)
200g	Threadfin (grouper) (flaked or mashed)
50ml	Vegetable oil
3 medium	Eggs (beaten)
2–4	Limau purut leaves (citrus leaves)

continued over →

Chef's Notes

...continued

170ml	Thick coconut milk
5–10g	Sugar
150g	Cucumber (washed and diced into 2cm sq)
	Salt and pepper

- If you have difficulty in obtaining Limau purut leaves (citrus leaves), then squeeze a little lemon into the mixture. This is not the same as using the leaves but it will help. You could also use lemon balm leaves as an alternative.

- Again there are variations on this dish, but this is an authentic version.

Nyonya Mee

Nyonya Noodles

Method

Measurements	Ingredients
30g	Shallots
4 clove	Garlic
240g	Mustard greens
180g	Bean sprouts
60ml	Vegetable oil
20g	Soya bean purée (cooked)
320g	Prawns (shelled)
800g	Yellow noodles (cooked)
250ml	Chicken or pork stock
	Salt

1. Peel and thinly slice the shallots, peel and chop the garlic, and cut the mustard greens into 6–7cm lengths. Wash and clean the bean sprouts.

2. Pour the vegetable oil into a hot wok and cook the shallots until golden brown, then lift onto kitchen paper and reserve.

3. Lower the heat and add the puréed soya beans and garlic to the oil, and cook until it becomes fragrant.

4. Add the mustard greens and bean sprouts, cook out for 2 minutes, then add the prawns, but do not allow the garlic to burn.

5. When the prawns are almost cooked, add the noodles and stock and stir in well. Bring to the boil and cook out for 2–3 minutes.

6. Add half the shallots, season and divide evenly into four portions. Garnish with the remaining shallots.

Chef's Notes

- There are many variations on this dish. If you cannot obtain mustard greens then use choy sam or bok choi.

- This is traditionally served with Sambal belacan and lime.

Sambal Belacan

Method

1. Dry roast the belacan in a pan over a medium heat until it becomes fragrant.

2. Pound the chillies in a pestle and mortar or a food processor until relatively smooth, then add the belacan to make a smooth paste. Season with the juice of 1 lime.

Measurements	Ingredients
20g	Belacan (shrimp paste)
30	Fresh red chillies (medium)
2	Limes

3. This should keep for up to 3–4 weeks if kept in the fridge in a container with a tight-fitting lid. Serve with slices of lime.

Chef's Notes

- Please note that the shrimp paste is not the same as the sandwich spread used in Europe. (See Glossary.)

Curry Kapitan

Measurements	Ingredients
12 medium to large	Fresh chillies (remove the seeds and stalks)
150g	Shallots (peeled)
5 stalks	Lemongrass
12	Candle nuts
30g	Belacan (shrimp paste)
5 cloves	Garlic
2cm	Turmeric (peeled and sliced)
2	Limes (juice only)
160g	Onions
60ml	Vegetable oil
750g	Fresh chicken (diced)
500ml	Thin coconut milk
500ml	Thick coconut milk
600g	Jasmine rice (cooked)

Method

1. Pound the chillies, shallots, lemongrass, candle nuts, belacan, garlic, turmeric and lime juice in a pestle and mortar or food processor until a smooth paste is achieved.

continued over →

2. Peel and dice the onions and then fry them in the oil in a hot wok until nicely brown. Add the paste and continually stir to prevent the paste burning, until it becomes fragrant.

...continued

Salt
Ground (fresh) black pepper

3. Stir in the chicken and cook for 10 minutes, then add the thin coconut milk and bring to the boil, then add the thick coconut milk and continue to cook for a further 10–15 minutes, being careful not to burn the curry.

4. Add the seasoning, and when the curry is nice and thick, serve with the cooked rice.

Chef's Notes

- If you like curries a little more fiery you may adjust the amount of chillies, but this is a perfect example of a Nyonya curry.

Coconuts

The Malaysia archipelago is thought to be where the magnificent coconut originated. It is also thought that the coconut palm is older than the south-east Asian civilisation.

Coconuts are graded according to age and variety. There are many varieties of coconut and in the tropics they are still used for vessels, rope, clothing, tools, fuel and then there is the culinary value of the milk, cream and the oil. Coconuts can be purchased fresh from the local coconut man or in local stores in tetra paks, tins or bottles. In Java the coconut was worshipped as a symbol of knowledge and in Bali it was believed that if a young woman touched a coconut tree it would drain it of its fruit-bearing properties.

It is believed that coconuts travelled on the ocean currents over thousands of years, landing on sandy beaches where the nuts then grew and travelled on to other islands and countries.

PERLIS

Perlis is the smallest state in the Federation, with a population of 181,000, and is the closest to the Thai border. The capital of the state is Kangar, which is surrounded by limestone hills. The main source of economy is agriculture, with seas of green paddy fields throughout the state covering some 35 per cent of the land. Other crops are grown, such

as sugar cane, rubber, maize, vegetables and fruits. Tourism is on the increase and as you travel through the state there are numerous local fishing villages, but the catches are only for local demand. One such village is Kuala Perlis and it is the departure point by sea for the biggest and most famous island of Malaysia, called Langkawi.

Perlis was part of Kedah until 1821, when the Thais captured Kedah. Then Perlis was separated and given to Syed Hussein as Raja of the principality. In 1957, under the Bangkok Treaty, Perlis was given to the British and was then joined to the federation.

The cuisine of this state mainly uses local ingredients such as coconuts and consists of spicy curries that are easy to make, like Kurma daging. The cuisine is influenced a little by the proximity of Perlis to India as well as Thailand, with its use of cinnamon, star anise, curry leaves and fenugreek in a number of recipes such as Kari Kepala Jenahak, Kurma daging and Gulai ayam.

Kurma Daging

Kurma Beef Curry

Method

1. Place 100g shallots, 3cm galangal, ginger, curry leaves, turmeric, 6 garlic cloves, lemongrass, 60–80ml thick coconut milk, peppercorns and the coconut flesh in a pestle and mortar or a food processor and pound or blend until a smooth paste is formed. Soak the tamarind paste in 200ml water for 10 minutes, then strain the liquid off and throw away the pulp.

2. Slice the beef into thin slices and marinate in the curry powder and the paste for up to 30 minutes. Take 60g shallots, 3cm galangal and 1 garlic clove and slice very thinly. Peel and thickly slice the onions.

3. Heat a suitable wok and add the coconut oil and fry off the thinly sliced shallots, galangal, garlic and spices until they become fragrant, then add the sliced beef, fry for 2–3 minutes, then add the thin coconut milk and onions. Cook for 10–15 minutes.

4. Add 350ml thick coconut milk, tamarind water and 5g freshly chopped coriander. Cook for a further 8–10 minutes.

Measurements	Ingredients
160g	Shallots
6cm	Galangal (peeled)
2cm	Ginger (peeled)
6	Curry leaves
2cm	Turmeric (peeled)
7 cloves	Garlic
3–4 stalks	Lemongrass
460-80ml	Thick coconut milk
5g	Black peppercorns (crushed)
40g	Fresh coconut flesh (flaked)
30g	Tamarind paste
200ml	Water
750g	Beef (sirloin or rump)
40–50g	Curry powder (kurma)
150g	Onions

continued over →

5. Serve in a suitable dish garnished with 50ml thick coconut milk and the remaining chopped coriander on top, and boiled or steamed rice.

Chef's Notes

- I have seen this dish with large diced beef and also served with diced cucumber as a side dish.

...continued	
60ml	Coconut oil
1–2cm	Cinnamon stick
2	Star anise
1–2	Cloves
400ml	Thin coconut milk
10g	Fresh coriander (chopped)
	Salt

Gulai Ayam

Chicken in Gravy

Method

1. Clean the chicken and ensure that there are no bone splinters, then rub with a little salt and leave to marinate for 10 minutes. Take 100g shallots, the ginger and garlic, thinly slice them and fry them with the star anise in a hot wok with the oil until fragrant.

2. Thinly shred the kaffir lime and turmeric leaves.

3. Pound the chillies, turmeric, coriander leaves, 50g shallots, fennel and cumin in a pestle and mortar or a food processor until a smooth paste is formed. Add to the wok and fry over a medium heat, quickly and gently until the oil separates from the paste. Do not allow the paste to burn or stick to the wok.

4. Once the oil has separated from the paste add the chicken and allow to cook out for 5 minutes, then add the thin coconut milk and cook for a further 5 minutes on a higher heat.

5. Add 200ml thick coconut milk and half the lime and turmeric leaves and cook out for a further 10 minutes.

6. Check the seasoning and serve garnished with the remaining thick coconut milk, shredded lime and turmeric leaves.

Measurements	Ingredients
650g	Diced chicken on the bone
	Salt
150g	Shallots (peeled)
3cm	Ginger (peeled)
2 cloves	Garlic
1	Star anise
60ml	Vegetable oil
4	Kaffir lime leaves
2–3	Turmeric leaves
10	Red chillies
4	Bird's eye chillies
3cm	Turmeric (peeled)
5g	Coriander leaves
5g	Fennel
2.5g	Cumin
350ml	Thin coconut milk
250ml	Thick coconut milk

Chef's Notes

- There are variations on this dish with the addition of tomato, lemongrass etc.

- This dish is served with plain boiled or steamed rice.

Kari Kepala Ikan Jenahak

Fish Head Curry

Method

Measurements	Ingredients
160g	Shallots (peeled)
9 cloves	Garlic (peeled)
25	Dried chillies
2 medium	Aubergines
1kg	Fish head (red snapper)
	Salt
150ml	Water
20–30g	Tamarind paste
10g	Black peppercorns
5g	Ground coriander
20g	Ground cumin
10g	Ground turmeric
60ml	Coconut oil
5g	Fennel seeds
5g	Fenugreek
4 sprigs	Curry leaves
5g	Mustard seeds
400ml	Thin coconut milk
250ml	Thick coconut milk
10g	Coriander

1. Peel and slice 4 garlic cloves and 60g shallots. Soak the dried chillies in a little water for 20–30 minutes. Cut the aubergines into thick slices.

2. Either cut the fish head into four or leave whole, but clean it under cold running water then rub the head with salt and leave for 20 minutes.

3. Add the water to the tamarind paste and leave for 10 minutes. Strain and keep the liquid, discard the pulp.

4. Take the chillies, peppercorns, coriander, cumin, 100g shallots, turmeric and 5 garlic cloves and pound them in a pestle and mortar or a food processor until a smooth paste is formed. You may need to add a dash of water.

5. Heat the oil in a suitable wok and fry off the remaining spices, shallots, curry leaves and garlic until they become fragrant.

6. Add the paste and fry and stir until the oil separates from the paste, but do not allow it to stick to the pan or burn.

7. Pour the tamarind juice into the paste, then the thin coconut milk, and leave for 10 minutes. Cook out on a medium heat for 2–3 minutes. Add the aubergines and fish head, allow to cook for a further 10 minutes.

8. Add 200ml thick coconut milk and cook for a further 10 minutes on a low heat. Check seasoning.

9. Serve garnished with the remaining thick coconut milk, freshly chopped coriander and plain boiled rice.

Chef's Notes

- If you do not like the idea of a fish head you can supplement this with diced red snapper or even large prawns.

- Again you can increase or decrease the amount of chillies in this recipe.

TERENGGANU

This state is on the east coast of Malaysia and has a seemingly endless coastline of sandy beaches, stretching from Kuala Besut in the north to Kemaman in the south, along the South China Sea. The state covers a territory of over 12,955 square kilometres, with a population of 1 million.

Historical records show that Terengganu was an Islamic state 100 years before Melaka was founded, although it later became a vassal of Melaka and then Johor. In the 1700s it became a Sultanate, and in the 1800s paid tribute to Thailand. Under the Anglo–Thai Treaty in 1909 it became a British protectorate until 1941 when Japan took control. After the Second World War the state became part of the Federation of Malaya.

Terengganu has numerous magnificent islands off its coastline and Pulau Redang is no exception with crystal waters, spectacular marine life and possibly the world's most mature coral gardens. Visitors to the island have to abide by the Malaysian Fisheries Act, which states that no fishing is allowed within 3.2 kilometres of the island and bans the collecting of coral or aquatic life.

The state is famed for its boat-building skills, which have been passed down from generation to generation. The builders on Pulau Duyung take tremendous pride in their work, building boats without plans or blueprints. Building entirely from memory, the boats are dovetailed and pegged instead of nails and screws being used. You can stroll past the workshops and watch the craftsmen at work. The state's economy is primarily based on offshore oil and gas, as well as fishing, which is a major asset. Pulau Duyung is also famed for its dried, salted fish and the fish crackers industry.

There are numerous little fishing ports like Kijal, a quiet fishing village where you can see the local fishermen return with their catch. At other times you may see them cleaning their boats and mending their nets. Along the beaches at Rantau Abang, 60 kilometres south of the capital city, Kuala Terengganu, you can see (between May and September) the giant leatherback turtles crawling ashore to bury their eggs. These turtles can weigh up to 375 kilograms and this is one of only six places left in the world where they come ashore.

Kuala Terengganu is the pioneer of Malaysia's silk weaving industry with centres and shops displaying batik and songket designs, kaftans, scarves, etc.

At the central market, or Pasar Payand as it is called locally, on the Terengganu River is Chinatown, where you can get all kinds of batik, songket, brassware, wood carvings, and mat weaving together with fresh fruits and vegetables. There is also the wet fish market selling its local delicacy made with a mixture of fresh fish and sago, called Leropok lekor. You can also see a huge array of salted and dried seafood products.

The cuisine of Terengganu is memorable for its fresh ingredients, use of spices and its Thai influences and flavors, such as Ayam percik, Nasi danang (glutinous rice and coconut milk), Rendang and Daging kerutut kering.

Nasi Ulam

Rice and Vegetables   *8 covers*

Method

Measurements	Ingredients
2.5g	Cumin seeds
5g	Fennel
5g	Coriander seeds
	Salt
10g	Tamarind paste
50ml	Water
750g	Jasmine rice (washed and drained)
300g	Glutinous rice (soaked for 8–10 hours, best overnight)
800ml	Thick coconut milk
10	Red chillies (no seeds)
2–3g	Belacan (shrimp paste)
1	Fresh lime juice
4	Tomatoes
3	Egg omelette
120g	Dried anchovies
100g	Tempeh (see Glossary)
200g	Beef or salt fish
120g	Dried prawns
5 stalks	Lemongrass

1. Place the cumin seeds, fennel, coriander seeds and salt into a dry pan and pan roast for 1–2 minutes then place in a pestle and mortar or a food processor and pound or blend until nicely ground. Soak the tamarind paste in water for 10 minutes then strain the liquid off and throw away the pulp.

2. After draining both types of rice, mix them together and place in a steamer and allow to cook for 10 minutes until half cooked.

3. Mix the coconut milk with the ground spices and then add to the rice and continue to steam until cooked and all the coconut milk has been absorbed. Then place the rice into a suitable mould and press down firmly to compress the rice. Turn out onto a large sized plate, keep the rice warm until required, then remove the mould.

4. To make the sambal pound the chillies, shrimp paste, lime, tomatoes and tamarind water in a pestle and mortar or a food processor to make a smooth paste. Serve in a small dish as an accompaniment to the main dish.

5. Take the cooked omelette and roll it up, slice it and place it around one-third of the plate edge. Then deep-fry the anchovies until golden brown, drain on dish paper and place around one-third of the plate edge. Then take the tempeh, slice it and place it around the final third of the plate edge.

6. Take the meat or fish, cut into small slices and shallow fry until cooked. Place around one side of the plate. Take the prawns and chop them into small pieces and soak and drain them, then deep-fry until golden brown. Drain on dish paper and place around one edge of the plate.

7. Finally top and tail the lemongrass, remove the root, finely slice them up and pan fry in a little oil for 2–3 minutes, then drain on dish paper and place around one edge of the plate.

Chef's Notes

- Deep-fried anchovies are a great delicacy and must be tried. They taste nothing like the tinned anchovies we have in the West and can be an excellent garnish on salads.

43

Kurma Ayam (2)

Chicken Curry

Method

1. Take the nuts, garlic, ginger, peppercorns, coriander, fennel, cumin and poppy seeds and pound in a pestle and mortar or a food processor until a smooth paste is achieved

2. Mix the evaporated milk with the paste and marinate the chicken in it for 1 hour.

3. Peel and slice the onions, chillies and garlic. Take the remaining shallots and slice finely and then deep-fry until golden brown. Drain on dish paper and keep warm.

4. Pour the oil into a hot pan and fry off the spices, onions, chillies, garlic and tomatoes until the spices smell fragrant. Then add the screw pine leaves, half of the deep-fried shallots, the chicken and marinade and bring to the boil.

5. Lower the heat to a simmer for 20–30 minutes, skimming any debris from the surface. Check the seasoning.

6. Garnish with the remaining deep-fried shallots.

7. Serve in a suitable dish with plain or coconut scented rice.

Chef's Notes

- Remember to remove the screw pine leaves and cinnamon stick before serving the dish.

Measurements	Ingredients
125g	Cashew nuts or almonds
4 cloves	Garlic
2cm	Ginger
1 × 5ml teaspoon	White peppercorns
10g	Coriander
10g	Fennel
5g	Cumin
5g	Poppy seeds
410ml	Evaporated milk
1kg	Chicken (cut on the bone into pieces)
70g	Onions
12	Shallots
2	Green chillies (no seeds)
80ml	Vegetable oil
2cm	Cinnamon stick
4–6	Green cardamoms
4	Cloves
200g	Tomatoes (cut into quarters)
2	Screw pine leaves (or 3–4 drops of pandan essence)
	Salt

Screw pine leaves

Often called pandan leaves, they give a subtle fragrance when cooking, and are bright green, long and stiff. Used in Nyonya cakes the leaves are puréed and the juice extracted for the flavour and the colour. The leaves are often used in Malay and Thai cookery to wrap round rice, meat and fish when cooking to add flavour but mainly to prevent it burning or colouring. If all the recipe calls for is to wrap an ingredient you could use old leek or banana leaves, but if it is the flavour that is required, there is no real substitute. You can buy pandan essence from most Thai or Chinese stores.

Ayam Percik (2)

Spicy Barbecued Chicken

Method

1. Soak the dried chillies in warm water. Place 2–3 incisions into the chicken legs.

2. Mix the turmeric, chilli powder, 10g sugar and salt and marinate the chicken legs in the spices for 1 to 2 hours.

3. Mix the tamarind pulp with the water, strain off the water and keep. Throw away the leftover pulp. Cut off the bottom of the lemongrass and then cut 8cm from the bottom off the stalk. Cut in half, removing the root, and discard. Finely chop the remaining lemongrass.

4. Pound all the chillies, the garlic, shallots, candle nuts and ginger in a pestle and mortar or a food processor until a smooth paste is achieved.

5. Mix the paste in a bowl with the tamarind water and lemongrass.

6. Pour the oil into a hot wok and fry off the paste for 5 minutes then pour in the coconut milk and sugar and stir for 5 minutes at a simmer. Keep one quarter of the sauce separate to baste the chicken with during grilling.

Measurements	Ingredients
8	Dried chillies
4	Fresh chicken legs
5g	Turmeric
5g	Chilli powder
25g	Sugar
2.5g	Salt
20g	Tamarind pulp
200ml	Water
4 stalks	Lemongrass
3	Red chillies
5 cloves	Garlic
100g	Shallots
4	Candle nuts
2cm	Ginger
60ml	Vegetable oil
250ml	Thick coconut milk
500g	Rice (cooked)
	Salt

7. Grill or barbecue the chicken legs over hot charcoal and baste the chicken in the sauce, turning constantly to avoid burning. Continue until the chicken is completely cooked.

8. When cooked, serve in a suitable dish with the gravy, plain or coconut-scented steamed or boiled rice, and a cucumber salad.

Chef's Notes

- Candle nuts are a cream colour nut with a waxy texture. If you cannot obtain them then substitute them with either macadamia nuts or cashew nuts.

SELANGOR

The history of Selangor is one of many struggles. The original settlers were believed to be the Minangkabaus from Sumatra, followed by the Bugis in the seventeenth century. A Sultanate was installed in the eighteenth century and later there was constant fighting with the Dutch. The Chinese then came because of the huge boom in tin mining, on which the prosperity of early Selangor was made. This caused constant feuds between the three factions: the Malay chiefs Tengku Kudin and Raja Mahdi, the Chinese miners, and the Bugis in the 1860s.

This situation was exploited by the British to appoint a British resident-in-state. The increasing prosperity made the British include the state in the Federated States of Malaya in 1896. Then, in 1948, Selangor gained independence by joining the Federation of Malaya in 1957.

Although tin ore played a huge role in the early part of Selangor's history and development, it is now almost non-existent, and the biggest tin mine in the world has been transformed into a huge resort called 'The Mines Resort City'.

The state capital is Shah Alam and has a population of 2.7 million. The state has many attractions including parks, temples, mosques, museums and natural attractions such as the Batu caves and Sungai Batangsi waterfalls.

The capital, Kuala Lumpur (called KL by the locals), was made the capital of the federal states in 1886, and in 1972 was given city status. In 1974 it was made a Federal Territory by the Sultan of Selangor. KL is a compelling and exotic blend of Moorish and colonial architecture now overshadowed by sky scrapers. The city draws on its Malay, Indian, Chinese, European and British influences, giving it an exciting and diverse feel. Kuala Lumpur actually means 'muddy river junction' and its first settlers were the Chinese tin miners who settled at Ampang. Secret societies formed as the population grew and the most powerful were the Ghee Hins and Hai Sans. The Malay Chiefs dealt with the headman of the miners or Kapitan Cina, Yap Ah Loy, who was Kapitan Cina from 1868–85 and was very much responsible for the prosperity and development of KL.

KL now has a population in excess of 1.3 million in an area of 243 square kilometres. The two most famous buildings are the two most modern ones – the Petronas Twin towers, the tallest building in the world at a height of 452 metres, and the 421-metre Menara Kuala Lumpur, which functions as a telecommunications tower, tourist attraction and viewing gallery, housing a revolving restaurant at the round top.

KL is the political centre of the nation. It has the largest centre of financial institutions and the second largest number of buildings and construction establishments in the country. In the centre of KL, leading up to Kuala Lumpur International Airport in Sepang, is an area known as the 'multi-media super corridor' which is fast becoming a big area for information-related business growth.

One of the great things about KL is the diversity of the markets and cuisines that are on offer. If you travel down to Chinatown between Jalan Benteng and Jalan Sultan you can see all sorts of goods from tee-shirts to dried and salted fish. It is best to visit around 7–8 pm when the markets are in full flow, although there are many stalls open all day. Another area worth a visit during the day is Petaling Street, where you can obtain anything from clothing through to fresh rambutans. Some of the best food can be found around these markets at a very reasonable price, from the classical Rendang, Laska and Nasi goring to Hokien mee.

The best and largest wet market (a market selling fruit, vegetables, and fish) is Chow Kit Market. This really does not get going until around 9–10 pm. Here you will see all sorts of herbs, berries, tree barks, branches and spices you may not ever have seen before, as well as a variety of pills and potions. As you walk around there are stalls selling their livestock of chickens and ducks as well fresh seafood, such as crabs, prawns, and fruit and goods – all of an outstanding quality. You can also eat from the numerous hawker stalls, selling Nasi campur and Rendang, etc.

There is also a small area called Little India along Jalan Masjid India where you can purchase and experience Indian culture such as elegant sarees, flower garlands and jewellery. It is the best place to taste the many excellent Indian snacks and dishes in the many courts and stalls in this area. The culinary influence from the Indian migrants over the centuries can be seen in the many Malay dishes like Fish head curry, Curry seku and Spicy mutton soup. However, the biggest influence here is from the Chinese with numerous provinces represented like Hokkien (Fujian), Teochew (Chaozhou), Szechuan (Sichuan) and Cantonese (Guangdong) to name but a few. There are many fine restaurants in KL that offer excellent meals in addition to the food from food courts and stalls.

Outside KL the town of Kajang is famous for the culinary delights of its satay. Skewers are packed with tender pieces of chicken or beef and then barbequed over hot charcoal to give its very distinctive flavour. The town has now built a satay centre, called the Satay Complex, located in the heart of the town.

Haka Rumput Ikan

Haka Grass Carp

Method

1. Remove the scales and head and gut the fish. Purée the ginger and spring onions and rub into and spread over the fish.

2. Steam the fish for 10–15 minutes at a high steam.

3. Serve garnished with picked leaves of coriander, fine julienne of ginger, spring onions and chillies.

Measurements	Ingredients
1–1.5kg	Whole grass carp
200g	Young ginger (peeled)
200g	Spring onion
5 sprigs	Coriander
2cm	Young ginger
3–4	Spring onions
1–2	Red chillies

Chef's Notes

- Often young ginger is referred to as green ginger.

- This dish is a simple traditional Chinese 'Haka' dish. If you cannot obtain grass carp or carp then use a large silver pomfret or threadfin.

- Young ginger can also be puréed and squeezed to make a refreshing ginger juice drink; you may wish to add a little sugar and dash of lime.

Pedas Daging Kambing Sup

Spicy Mutton Soup

Method

1. Roughly dice the shallots and put in a suitable pot with the stock and mutton, bring to the boil and remove any debris from the surface.

2. Wrap the spices and coriander stalks in a muslin cloth and tie securely. Place in the pot with the meat and simmer for 90 minutes, skimming any debris from the surface.

3. Remove the spice bag and skim any debris from the surface.

4. To make the garnish, slice and deep-fry the garlic and shallots.

5. Ladle the soup evenly into four suitable dishes and then garnish with the deep-fried garlic and shallots, with a sprinkling of spring onions cut into diamonds and chopped coriander leaves.

Measurements	Ingredients
40g	Shallots (peeled)
1lt	Light stock (chicken or lamb)
400g	Diced mutton (no fat)
3cm	Cinnamon stick
1–2	Star anise
4–5	Cloves
6	Black peppercorns
2.5g	Cumin seeds
2.5g	Fennel seeds
8 crushed	Coriander stalks (use leaves as garnish)
2 cloves	Garlic (peeled)
40g	Shallots (peeled)
4	Spring onions (cut into diamonds)
	Salt

Chef's Notes

- This is a very simple soup with a number of variations. You could use lamb, but it will not give the same flavour. You may require a much stronger stock if you do use lamb.

- Cloves are the dried flowerbuds of a native tropical evergreen tree that is found in south-eastern Asia, which is used in Malay and Indian cookery, and was a very valuable cargo in the eighteenth and nineteenth centuries.

Satay Kajang

Chicken Satay Kajang Style

Method

1. Place the peanuts, turmeric, coriander and cumin seeds, sugar, salt and cinnamon in a pestle and mortar or a food processor and pound or blend until it becomes a smooth paste. Mix this with 50ml oil and marinate the diced chicken for 1–2 hours in a refrigerator.

Measurements	Ingredients
30g	Roasted peanuts
2cm	Turmeric (peeled)
2.5g	Coriander seeds
2.5g	Cumin seeds

continued over →

2. Purée the lemongrass and mix with the remaining oil.

3. Divide the meat between the skewers (5–6 cubes per portion), then grill over hot charcoals, brushing with the lemongrass oil constantly to add flavour.

4. Turn over after 4–5 minutes and continue to cook. Brush and turn until the chicken is cooked. Serve with peanut sauce.

...continued

2.5g	Sugar
2cm	Cinnamon stick
100ml	Vegetable oil
1kg	Chicken (diced small)
1–2 stalks	Lemongrass
12–15	Wooden skewers
	Salt

Peanut Sauce

Method

1. Peel and finely dice the onion and seal off in a little oil.

2. Pound the ginger, chillies, shallots, galangal, peanuts and lemongrass in a pestle and mortar or a food processor until a smooth paste has been achieved. Add to the onions and fry until it becomes fragrant, then add the tamarind water. Cook for 2–3 minutes.

3. Add the sugar and a pinch of salt. Cook out for another 4–5 minutes, stirring constantly to prevent sticking. When a thick consistency is achieved check seasoning and serve hot or cold.

Measurements	Ingredients
70g	Onion
30ml	Oil
2cm	Ginger (peeled)
30g	Chillies (seeds removed)
30g	Shallots (peeled)
2cm	Galangal (peeled)
250g	Roasted peanuts
1–2 stalks	Lemongrass
100ml	Tamarind water
20g	White sugar

Chef's Notes

- Soak the skewers in oil or water for 30 minutes before you use them and this will help the diced meat slide onto them.

- The peanut sauce has many variations from stall to stall, state to state and even country to country. This particular one is from a stall in Kajang.

Tauhu Sumbat

Stuffed Bean Curd

Method

1. Put the soy sauce, fish sauce and sugar into a pan and bring to the boil. Add the vegetable stock and season. Thicken by adding a little cold water to 5–10g cornflour and add to the sauce to thicken it a little at a time. Skim any debris from the surface.

2. Peel and finely dice the shallots. Peel and finely dice the white of the spring onions and cut the green stems into 3cm lengths.

3. Finely chop the prawns and mix them with the beef, shallots, and white of the spring onion, season with a little salt and pepper.

4. Drain the tofu and cut into wedges. Make a cut on one side and take out a spoonful of the tofu from the centre. Sprinkle a little cornflour in the cavity and fill with the meat and prawn stuffing and then press the side closed as best you can.

Measurements	Ingredients
40ml	Soy sauce
10ml	Fish sauce
5g	Sugar
300ml	Vegetable stock
25–40g	Cornflour
30g	Shallots
4	Spring onions
30g	Dried prawns (soaked)
180g	Minced beef
200g	Tofu (bean curd)
1lt	Vegetable oil
	Salt and ground white pepper

5. Stir-fry the green spring onion lengths in a little oil.

6. Dust the tofu in cornflour and then deep-fry until golden brown. Remove and drain on kitchen paper.

7. Pour the sauce onto plates and then add the tofu. Garnish the top with the remaining spring onions.

Chef's Notes

- This dish is originally from KL and the Hakka Chinese.

- You must fry the tofu until it is really crispy. The dusting of cornflour will help with this and it will be an excellent dish. You must serve it immediately.

- Only use fresh bean curd (tofu) and not the spongy vac-packed tofu.

SABAH (MALAYA BORNEO)

Borneo is the third largest island in the world, surrounded by the Sulu Sea, the Celebes Sea and the Straits of Makassar to the east. To the south is the Java Sea and to the west and north is the South China Sea.

Borneo has been occupied for at least 5,000 years. In the ninth century AD, what is now known as Sabah was under the rule of a number of different chieftains, who traded with China and India. Later, around the fifteenth century, the Spanish and Portuguese traded with Sabah, which was then under the rule of the Sultanate of Brunei. In the seventeenth century the Dutch and British began to trade there until the Sultan of Brunei handed the land over to the Sultan of Sulu.

In the 1880s, an American called Charles Lee Moses obtained the lease for Sabah, which was then given to an Englishman called Alfred Dent. He signed a treaty with the Brunei and Sulu Sultans, converting the lease into a succession and there was born 'British North Borneo' and the North Borneo Chartered Company. After the Second World War Borneo became a British Crown Colony, and then, in 1963, it was granted independence and joined the federation of Malaysia. Politically, Borneo is divided into Sarawak and Sabah (two Malaysian states), as well as Brunei, (an independent Sultanate) and Kalimantan, which is part of Indonesia.

Borneo has a tropical climate with average temperatures of 25–26°C. It has some of the world's oldest and largest tropical rain forest and jungles and is renowned as one of the great treasure houses of wildlife, flora and fauna. Sabah also has the highest mountain in south-east Asia, Mount Kinabalu, and a huge network of rivers. The wet season runs from November to February. The economy is supported by forestry and tourism. Exports of rubber, palm oil, cocoa beans, wood, crude oil and pearls are sold, primarily to Japan.

Sabah has been called 'the land below the wind' and is home to some 30 different indigenous races having 80 different dialects. The largest of these is the Kadazan-Dusuns who live on the interior plains where they farm the paddy fields and make up one-third of the total population. Then there are the Muruts who live in the interior close to the borders of Sarawak and Kalimantan. They are hunters and agriculturists and were once the feared headhunters of Borneo. They still use their spears and deadly blow pipes to hunt. On the west coast you have the 'Cowboys of the East', the Bajaus who are farmers and are famed for their horsemanship. To the east on the coast you have the Bajaus, often called the 'sea gypsies', who are sea nomads, fishing for their living and only coming ashore to bury their dead.

The capital is Kota Kinabalu and the state has a population of 900,000 and covers some 74,500 square kilometres.

When the word Sabah is uttered one automatically thinks of 'seafood', and the mention of seafood brings to mind the capital Kota Kinabalu, or

KK, as the locals call it. Hawkers sell food on the streets from their gleaming pedal cycles, set up to cook normally very simple food, such as Sotong-kangkung (cuttlefish and vegetables) that are on the whole grilled and have been a part of the staple diet in Sabah for centuries. There are dozens of other stalls selling local specialities like Foh sang prawn mee, Sinsuran grilled fish and Sinsuran tom-yam.

Around KK you are spoilt for choice between the huge red or green lobsters and groupers of all shapes, sizes and colours to crabs, mussels, cockles, prawns, eels, sea cucumbers, squids and some of the most exotic fish you can see anywhere.

Some of the best food can be found at Jalan Haji Sam, opposite the old customs wharf, close to Merlin Point where the local fish market is located. It is a sea lover's paradise with some incredible fresh seafood straight from the sea.

The seafood in KK and Sabah is so good because it is so fresh, whether it is shipped in from the coastlines of the state, from the fish market in KK or in the restaurants. Many, like the Portview Restaurant in KK, hold the fish in tanks, not only for the customer to choose their fish but also to keep them in the very best condition possible.

There are various stalls throughout KK that take great pride in selling dried seafood such as cuttlefish and all kinds of round and flat fish, whether it is salt or freshwater fish. You can walk in and around the market in KK and see the fish and seafood on tables or in baskets drying in the midday sun.

Although Sabah is famed for its seafood, you can just as easily have some excellent duck and chicken dishes. Sabah also has a vegetable called sayur manis or 'little tree vegetable', which is grown only around Sabah. I have included a recipe for this as well as some dishes from KK.

When Borneo is mentioned in culinary terms it conjures up exotic foods like turtles and bird's nest soup. The legend as to how the bird's nest soup first came about began in China, where an Emperor's royal chef was charged with giving the Emperor something new and different every day. The first record of the edible nests is around the time of the Tang dynasty (AD 626–706), but was a prized dish for more than a thousand years. Knowing how the Emperor liked exotic dishes, the chef went to the harbour to try to find inspiration for a new dish, knowing that if he failed he would lose his position and his head!

A trader from Borneo sold him a bird's nest and the chef asked, 'How do I cook it?' The trader replied, 'I sell it, I don't cook it, but I know it has longevity properties.'

The chef made a soup from the nest and presented it to the Emperor with a phoenix on one side and a dragon on the other side. The Emperor asked, 'What dish have you made for me today?' and the chef thought and said, 'Longevity Soup, Highness.' The Emperor looked at the soup and then smelt its aromatic scent. Then he tasted it and said to the chef,

'Its flavour is bland and I can get this anywhere.' The chef then replied, 'Please take another taste, Your Majesty.' The Emperor duly took another spoonful and said, 'It is still bland.' The chef, then fearing for his life, said, 'But in Borneo the people there eat this for longevity, Your Majesty.' The Emperor's eyes lit up because to him, Borneo was exotic (the wooden pillars to the forbidden city came from Borneo). The Emperor then decreed, 'This "exotic dish" is fit for an Emperor and should be served to him regularly and not the general public.'

To prevent the Emperor and any other chef from finding out it was made from bird's nests from Borneo, the chef sent new sailors and traders to collect fresh supplies each time and had them killed, and true to the legend the Emperor lived a long life.

In the late sixteenth century the swiftlet's bird's nest aroused the interest of European traders and became part of Chinese medicine. Swallows make their nests from mud and grass whereas the swiftlets make their nest with their saliva which dries. This saliva contains 60 per cent soluble proteins; moisture is 10 per cent with traces of carbohydrates, potassium, sodium and fat, although the benefits are not scientifically proven.

The dish is very expensive to eat in restaurants, but it is easily obtainable in the more upmarket restaurants in Sabah and Sarawak.

Tujuh Bintang Kerapu

Seven Star Grouper

Measurements	Ingredients
700g	Grouper fillet (skin on)
150g	Spring onions
100g	Onion
5–10g	Garlic purée
60ml	Palm oil
5g	Cornflour
150ml	Fish stock
	Salt

Method

1. Cut the fillet into large dice (3cm sq). Peel and cut the spring onions into 5cm lengths, then peel and finely slice the onions.

2. Place the fish into a steamer and steam for 3–4 minutes.

3. Sweat off the onions and garlic purée in the palm oil, but do not get the oil so hot that it burns the garlic.

4. Add the spring onions and fry for 2 minutes then pour off the oil and sprinkle with cornflour.

5. Add the stock and stir and continue to cook for a further 2–3 minutes.

6. Carefully add the fish to the stock, check seasoning and then place into a suitable dish.

7. Serve with coconut scented rice.

Chef's Notes

- If you cannot obtain the grouper you can use red snapper.

- This dish is called seven star grouper because of the seven stars it has on its back.

- In ancient times the Kadazan of Sabah believed that man had to eat wild flowers, berries, fruit and animals. At that time rice was a wild grass with empty hulls. One day the Goddess of Mercy, Bambarazon, came and saw how her people were living and decided to help the hunter-gatherers. It is said that one evening she went into the fields and pressed her breast with one hand until her milk flowed onto the empty rice hulls, but it was not enough and she pressed with all her might until milk mixed with blood came out. It was from that moment that man had rice to eat and was able to choose between the white grains from Bambarazon milk and the red ones from the mixture of milk and blood.

- The Kadazan celebrate the 'Modsurung' or the harvest festival to the Goddess of Mercy.

Sayur Manis

Little Tree Vegetable

Method

1. Peel and very finely dice the garlic and cut the vegetables into 5–6cm lengths.

2. Mix the belacan with a small amount of water into a smooth paste.

3. Heat the oil in a suitable wok and fry off the garlic and the vegetables for 2 minutes then add the chilli and cook for another 2 minutes then add the shrimp paste. Fry off then serve in a suitable dish.

Measurements	Ingredients
2 cloves	Garlic
250g	Sayur manis
10g	Belacan (shrimp paste)
50ml	Palm oil
4–5	Green bird's eye chillies

Chef's Notes

- It is almost impossible to find Sayur Manis, but you could use mustard greens, Chinese chives or even samphire as a replacement.

Burung Sarang Hitam Sticky Padi Manis Sup

Bird's Nest, Black Sticky Rice Soup

Method

1. Soak the bird's nest overnight in fresh water. Using a fine mesh strainer, drain and rinse the nest.

2. Soak the rice for 3–4 hours in cold water. Remove the white pith from the orange peel and then divide into two. Cut half into a very fine zest, leave the other half whole.

3. Place the whole orange peel into the water and bring to the boil. Add the rice and reduce to a simmer for 15 minutes. Remove the orange peel and add the zest (keep a little for garnish).

Measurements	Ingredients
170g	Bird's nest
150g	Black sticky rice
1	Orange peel (blanched)
1,800ml	Water
113g	Palm sugar
200ml	Coconut milk

4. Add the palm sugar and bird's nest and stir in until the sugar has all dissolved. Then add the coconut milk.

5. Serve in suitable bowls and garnish with the remaining zest.

Chef's Notes

- This can be served hot or cold, but it is better hot.

- You can purchase bird's nest in tins or frozen from good Chinese supermarkets.

Burung Sarang Dan Ayam Sup

Bird's Nest and Chicken Soup

Method

1. Wash and chop the parsley, then mix the arrow root with a little water to make a smooth paste.

2. Bring the stock to the boil and stir in the chicken. Reduce to a simmer, remove debris from the surface then add the bird's nest pieces.

Measurements	Ingredients
10g	Flat parsley
10g	Arrow root
800ml	Chicken stock
150g	Chicken breast (minced)

continued over →

3. Add the water chestnut purée and pour in the arrow root paste. Stir constantly to try to avoid any lumps forming.

4. Cook out and simmer for a further 4–5 minutes. Add half the parsley.

5. Adjust the seasoning and serve in suitable bowls.

6. Serve the soup garnished with the remaining parsley.

...continued

100g	Bird's nest pieces (soaked)
20g	Water chestnut purée
	Salt and white pepper

Chef's Notes

• Each May in the state of Sabah Borneo, there is a festival called 'Sabah Fest'. Residents celebrate with traditional music, culture and food and bird's nest soup can be found on many menus.

• You can purchase bird's nest in tins or frozen from good Chinese supermarkets.

Jeruk Undang Cili Padi

Pickled Prawns and Chilli

Measurements	Ingredients
4	Onions
4	Spring onions
6	Fresh chillies
4	Red chillies
10–12	Fresh lime juice and zest
500g medium	Fresh prawns (shell on)
10g	Salt
100g	Fresh lettuce leaves

Method

1. Cut the onions and spring onions into slices. Remove the stalks and the seeds from the chillies and finely slice. Remove the skin from 4 of the limes and cut into a fine zest, then cut all the limes in half and extract the juice (200ml).

57

2. Remove the shells from the prawns and remove the black central vein.

3. Place all the prawns into a suitable bowl and season heavily with the salt. Add the other ingredients except the lettuce. Leave for a few minutes for the prawns to marinate. Serve garnished with fresh lettuce leaves.

Chef's Notes

- This is a very strong and sharp dish from Sabah and is considered a Kadazandusun delicacy in Borneo.

- Try to obtain the *limau kesturi* variety of lime, as it is smaller and has a milder flavour than the ordinary larger round and sour lime found in the UK.

SARAWAK

In the ninth century the kingdom called Po-Ni (known as Brunei) was trading with Chinese merchants, and ruled and controlled most of Borneo, but around the sixteenth to nineteenth centuries their control begin to wane.

In 1839 the English adventurer James Brooke arrived in the area called Kuching, which is now the capital of Sarawak. At the time of his arrival the locals were in revolt against the Bruneian Governor. Brooke quashed the rebellion and was duly appointed the Rajah of Sarawak in 1841. In 1888 Sarawak and Brunei became a British protectorate. Brooke and his nephew asserted independence and expanded Sarawak's borders. Brooke was succeeded by his nephew, Charles Brooke, as Rajah and he built a fabulous palace for his bride on the riverbank. The state then passed to his son, Charles Vyner Brooke, in 1917. After the Second World War he handed the state to the British and it became a British Crown Colony. There was huge opposition to this and the Governor, Duncan Stewart, was assassinated in 1949. Then, in 1963, both Sarawak and Sabah joined the Malaysian Federation. Brunei kept its independence and Sultanate, but Indonesia disagreed with the two states joining Malaysia and supported a guerrilla war which was referred to as the confrontation. This ended in 1965 when the Indonesian leader was removed from power.

Sarawak is truly multiracial with over 23 ethnic groups, for example Chinese, Ibans, Dayaks and Malays. Each group has their own customs, traditions and culture. There are many tribes still living in areas of untouched jungle up river, while Sarawak's lush interior is home to hundreds of longhouses inhabited by tattooed descendents of tribal headhunters and where whole communities live under one roof. The interior houses some very rare animals, flora and fauna; visas are required to enter this protected area.

For fascination value, you cannot beat the Niah caves in Mulu Park, where people lived some 40,000 years ago. Cave drawings can be seen in parts of the caves.

Kuching has a population of over 260,000, and the name actually means 'cat'. The city retains much of its colonial charm and is built on the south bank of the River Sarawak. There are many temples, churches, historic buildings and markets.

On the corner of Satok Jalan and Tun Haji Openg is a unique market, called the Sunday market, which actually opens on late Saturday afternoon. The interior tribes such as the Dayaks bring their produce and stock to sell starting late on Saturday. They commence selling at their stalls again on early Sunday morning around 5 am. It is unique as there are fruit, vegetables and herbs that you may never have seen or will ever see again! You can see river fish in plastic bags alive in water, monkeys, lizards, wild boars, pigs, birds and flowers of all kinds. The quality is just incredible.

The Sunday market is the best place to see and eat Malay food. Some excellent cakes and sweets are sold here. There are many hawker stalls and restaurants that offer many different styles of food from Indian and Chinese to Indonesian and Filipino.

Sibu is Sarawak's second city and forms a pathway to the interior through the Rejang basin. In the centre of the city is a very exotic market, the Lembangan market, which has hundreds of stalls, many run by Iban traders, who sell snake and turtle meat, snails, wild fruits and fauna.

Sarawak is also famous for its bird nests and the collection of them is strictly licensed. They are collected from limestone caves and swallow houses. The most prized are the white nests, which are normally found in the coastal caves.

The main areas of revenue are based on mining, quarrying, crude oil production and gas. Agriculture and forestry are also beneficial.

The staple diet is rice with 90 per cent of the world's rice grown and consumed in Asia. In Sarawak, like many other cultures, a reverence is shown to the grain, and often its cultivation is celebrated in elaborate rituals, and the Gawai in Sarawak are no exception. Their own harvest festival, which is held at the very end of the planting cycle (every May–June), brings in the cultural, religious and social order known as ledoh to the Kayans. They gather in their longhouses throughout Sarawak and thank and bless the gods and spirits for a good harvest and pray for a better one next year.

If you are in town when this festival is in progress you are likely to be invited into a house and treated to traditional hospitality with food and drink. The latter is usually a very potent rice wine called tuak, a little like the Japanese Sake, and is called Lihing. If you are in the rural interior where there are longhouses, guests are expected to taste the wine and the food in each household, which could mean up to 20–30 times! The food can be glutinous rice, cakes, fruits, sweets or meat and rice cooked in bamboo.

Sali Ikan Merah Dengan Sayur Bayam

Grilled Red Snapper with Greens

Method

1. Slice the onion and place it with the ginger, chillies, turmeric, salt and sugar into a pestle and mortar or a food processor and pound to a fine paste adding 100ml coconut milk.

2. Top and tail the lemongrass, cut in half lengthways and remove the stalk. Slice very finely. Wash and remove the stalks from the spinach or mustard greens and cut into strips.

3. Remove the eyes, gills, scales, fins and intestines from the snapper. Cut three slits on each side of the fish, brush with oil and grill on each side for 5–6 minutes.

4. Put the paste into a suitable pan and bring to the boil with the lemongrass. Add the remaining coconut milk and all of the stock.

5. When the liquid is at a boil reduce the heat to a simmer for 5–8 minutes, then add the grilled fish and the greens. Cook for 10 minutes.

Measurements	Ingredients
70–80g	Onion (peeled)
2cm	Ginger (peeled)
2	Red chillies (deseeded)
1–2cm	Turmeric (peeled)
2.5g	Salt
2.5g	Sugar
400ml	Coconut milk
2 stalks	Lemongrass
200g	Spinach or mustard greens
2 × 350g	Whole red snapper
30ml	Vegetable or sunflower oil
150–200ml	Light fish stock or water

6. Check the seasoning and serve the fish on suitable plates, garnished with the sauce. Serve with plain boiled or steamed rice.

Malaysia

Chef's Notes

- If you would like to use fish other than snapper, use a small grouper or mackerel.

- You could use four fillets instead of whole fish but be very careful and do not overcook. Reduce the cooking times.

Undang Dengan Bawang Putih Cili Padi Kuah

Prawns with Garlic Chilli Gravy

Method

1. Top and tail the spring onions then cut into fine 5cm strips.

2. Place the shallots, garlic, ginger, turmeric and chillies into a pestle and mortar or a food processor and pound to a smooth paste. You may need to add a little water.

3. Pour the oil into a hot wok or suitable pan and stir-fry the paste until it is fragrant then add the prawns.

4. Stir-fry for 2 minutes then add half of the spring onions. Fry for a further 2 minutes.

5. Serve on a suitable plate garnished with the remaining spring onions.

Measurements	Ingredients
6	Spring onions
70g	Shallots (peeled)
4 cloves	Garlic
2cm	Ginger
1cm	Turmeric (peeled)
4	Red chillies
40ml	Palm oil
500g medium	Shelled prawns (with the central vein removed)

Chef's Notes

- If you find it slightly too dry you can add a little stock or water to the paste after you have fried it until it is fragrant. Do not allow it to burn and stir it constantly.

- It is very important to de-vein prawns as this is the area that contains the most harmful food-poisoning bacteria.

OTHER MALAYSIAN RECIPES

Ayam Goreng Enak

Savoury Fried Chicken

Method

1. Cut the chicken as for sauté (legs into 4 pieces, breast into 4 portions, all on the bone and discard the winglets and cage). Cut the onions, spring onions and chillies into fine slices and fry in the coconut oil until limp, then remove and keep hot. Save the oil.

2. Take the shallots, remaining spring onions, ginger and galangal and pound in a pestle and mortar or a food processor until a smooth paste has been achieved.

3. Place the chicken into the frying pan with the saved hot oil and continue to cook until the chicken is crispy and golden brown.

Measurements	Ingredients
1.5kg	Fresh chicken
100g	Red onions
8	Spring onions
4	Red chillies (deseeded)
60ml	Coconut oil
200g	Shallots (peeled)
3cm	Ginger (peeled)
3cm	Galangal (peeled)
500ml	Thick coconut milk
6	Kaffir lime leaves

4. Bring the paste, coconut milk and kaffir lime leaves to the boil in a suitable wok or pan. Add the chicken portions and stir to prevent sticking. Cook until all the liquid has almost completely evaporated.

5. Garnish with the onions, chilli and spring onions.

6. Serve with steamed rice.

Chef's Notes

• Some similar recipes call for you to marinate or rub the paste into the chicken, but this one is spicy enough without that.

Galangal

Galangal is often called aromatic ginger, but although it is from the ginger family they cannot be substituted for each other as they both have very different flavours and aroma. Galangal has a wonderful perfumed scent and aromatic flavour, whereas ginger has a much harsher scent and flavour. Galangal is used in many Malay and Nyonya dishes in combination with lemongrass. It is widely available in large supermarkets in the UK.

Ayam Pandan Daun

Shredded Chicken with Pandan Leaves

Method

1. Cut the raw chicken into thin strips. Grate the ginger and squeeze out the juice and keep to one side. Tie the two pandan leaves in a knot.

2. Pound the coriander seeds, star anise, sugar and white peppercorns in a pestle and mortar or food processor until a smooth powder has been achieved, then add the ginger juice to the powder.

3. Place the chicken strips in the ginger spice juice and marinate for 30–40 minutes, then drain keeping the liquid.

4. Heat a suitable wok or pan and pour the oil into the pan on a high heat. Cook the chicken until it is completely sealed.

5. Add the juice and bring it to the boil then stir in the coconut milk and the pandan leaves. Reduce, cooking the chicken until the sauce thickens. Correct the seasoning and remove the pandan leaves.

6. Serve with boiled rice (hot).

Measurements	Ingredients
750g	Fresh chicken
4cm	Ginger (peeled)
2	Screw pine leaves (pandan)
5g	Coriander seeds
1	Star anise
2.5g	Sugar
2.5g	White peppercorns
60ml	Oil
200ml	Thick coconut milk
600g	Rice (cooked)
	Salt

Chef's Notes

• If you cannot obtain the pandan leaves you can use bottled essence, available from Chinese or Asian food stores.

• Star anise can be substituted with aniseed.

Cili Padi Ketam

Chilli Crabs

Method

1. Take the crabs and remove the breast from the shell (underside), clean out the 'dead man's fingers' (gills) and sac. Cut into two. Mix the tamarind paste with 50ml water, strain the liquid and discard the leftover pulp.

Measurements	Ingredients
2	Crabs (blue swimmer crabs)
20g	Tamarind paste
1–2 stalks	Lemongrass

continued over →

2. Pound the lemongrass, shallots, garlic, galangal, ginger, turmeric, belacan and chillies in a pestle and mortar or place in a food processor until it becomes a smooth paste.

3. Heat the oil in a pan and fry the paste until it becomes fragrant. Add the tamarind juice with a little salt and sugar to taste.

4. Add the stock or water and bring to boil.

5. Add the crab meat and gently mix with the ingredients. The gravy should become slightly dry.

6. Serve hot straight from the pan with plain boiled rice.

Chef's Notes

- This recipe is a classic Nyonya dish.

- Lemongrass is very much like grass except it has a fleshy white base and you only use 10–12cm of that base. If you cannot obtain lemongrass use two large strips of lemon peel. It's not ideal but it will impart some flavour.

...continued	
100g	Shallots (peeled)
5 cloves	Garlic (peeled)
3cm	Galangal (peeled)
2cm	Ginger (peeled)
2cm	Turmeric (peeled)
20g	Belacan (shrimp paste)
12–15	Dried red chillies
80ml	Vegetable oil
5g	Sugar
5g	Salt
200ml	Light fish stock or water

Cucur Udang

Prawn Fritters

Method

1. Peel and finely chop the onion, prawns, spring onions, curry leaves and bean sprouts.

2. Mix the chopped ingredients in a suitable bowl with the turmeric powder and the eggs. Sieve the cornflour into the mixture to make a very thick batter.

3. Slowly add the hot water to the mixture, stirring until the consistency of thick double cream is achieved. You may not need all the hot water.

4. Heat the oil in a wok or fryer to 180°C. Scoop a portion of batter into an oil ladle and return it to the fryer. Repeat this process and do not overfill the fryer. This recipe will make 3–4 fritters.

Measurements	Ingredients
40g	Onion
200g	Prawns (peeled and with the central vein removed)
6	Spring onions
4–5	Curry leaves
20g	Bean sprouts
5ml	Fresh chives (chopped)
2.5g	Turmeric powder
2 medium	Eggs
30–40g	Cornflour

continued over →

5. Cook until the fritters are golden brown. Drain on dish paper and serve on a suitable plate with a covering of banana leaves, dishes of peanut or chilli sauce and a separate portion of rice.

...continued

100ml	Hot water
1lt	Vegetable oil
1	Banana leaf
100ml	Peanut sauce
100ml	Chilli sauce
	Salt

Chef's Notes

- **Safety Note:** Only fill one-third of any pan with oil when deep-frying. This will help to prevent the possibility of the oil spilling or boiling over when you add the ingredients to the fryer.

- The amount of cornflour (depending on the quality) could be a little less. Add water a little at a time when making the batter.

- You could add some fresh red chillies to give it a little kick if you are using the peanut sauce instead of the chilli sauce.

Danging Masak Merah

Beef in Red Sauce

Method

1. Cut the beef into either dice or slices. Set aside.

2. Pan roast the grated coconut in the oven until it is golden brown.

3. Boil the thin coconut milk in a suitable pan.

4. Pound the lemongrass, turmeric and chillies in a pestle and mortar or a food processor until a smooth paste, then mix with the beef and leave for 30 minutes.

5. Add the ginger paste and the coconut oil to the beef. Place the beef into the hot thin coconut milk and simmer until it is tender. Skim any debris from the surface.

Measurements	Ingredients
600gm	Beef (sirloin or rump)
30g	Grated coconut
30–40ml	Coconut oil
500ml	Thin coconut milk
2 stalks	Lemongrass
2	Turmeric leaves
20	Red chillies (no seeds)
250ml	Thick coconut milk
10g	Caster sugar
	Salt

6. Pour the thick coconut milk into the mixture and continue to simmer. The sauce should begin to thicken.

7. Add the seasoning and sugar to taste, simmer for a further 5–10 minutes or until the sauce is slightly dry. Remove from the heat.

8. Serve with Nasi Lemak or plain rice.

Chef's Notes

- The beef you use must be prime beef.
- You can reduce the amount of chillies if you wish.
- This dish is usually accompanied by diced cucumbers.

Ikan Bahan Dengan Kunyit Cili Padi

Fish Stuffed with Turmeric and Chilli

Method

1. Remove the scales, eyes and gills from the fish and then gut them.

2. To gut the fish make a cut from the stomach to 1cm from the head and remove all the innards. Run under cold running water to remove any debris and slime remaining.

3. Make three incisions across both sides (see Chef's Notes).

4. Remove the stalk and seeds from 6 chillies and roughly chop them. Peel and roughly chop the onions. Take the chopped chillies, onions, turmeric powder and 5g salt and place in a pestle and mortar or food processor and roughly blend to a paste.

Measurements	Ingredients
2	Red snapper
6	Red chillies (large)
140g	Red onions
5g	Turmeric powder
5g	Salt
80ml	Vegetable oil
Garnish	Ingredients
4	Spring onions
2	Red chillies
2 sprigs	Fresh coriander

5. Rub the fish with the paste and fill all the cavities and incisions with the remaining paste.

6. Heat the oil in a suitable wok or pan and fry the fish for 4–5 minutes on each side, trying to turn it only once.

7. Serve on a suitable plate and garnish with julienne of chilli, spring onion and sprigs of coriander.

Chef's Notes

- At stage 3, cut the thick part of the fish three times for even cooking and to allow the skin to shrink neatly for better presentation.

- You can also use mackerel as an alternative to snapper.

- This can be served either with rice or with slices of tomato, cucumber and lettuce leaves.

Kacang Panjang Goreng

Fried Long Bean

Method

1. Peel and remove the central vein from the prawns.

2. Slice the shallots and garlic, wash the long beans and then cut them into 8cm lengths. Remove and discard the seeds and stalk from the chillies and finely slice.

3. Pour the oil into the hot wok and fry off the shallots, garlic and chillies until they become fragrant.

4. Add the prawns and fry until they have changed to a pink colour. Then add the long beans and continue to cook and stir well for 3–5 minutes until the beans are cooked.

5. Season to taste.

6. Serve with Nasi lemak or plain rice.

Measurements	Ingredients
300g	Prawns
80g	Shallots (peeled)
1 clove	Garlic
300g	Long beans
1–2	Red chillies
40ml	Vegetable oil
500g	Nasi lemak or plain rice
	Salt

Chef's Notes

- An old Malay method to help remove the chilli burning or irritation to one's fingers and hands is to rub vegetable oil onto your hands, then leave for a minute or two then wash it off.

Long Beans

Long beans are stringless and a deep green colour and grow to around 30cm in length. They contain less flavour than other types of beans but cook more easily. They are normally used in curries, stir fries and soups. If you cannot find long beans use French beans as an alternative.

Kajang Goreng Daging Babi

Kajang Crispy Fried Pork

Measurements	Ingredients
2.5g	Salt
20ml	Dark soy sauce
60ml	Chicken stock
600g	Pork belly
100g	Red onion
6	Spring onions
2	Red chillies
2	Green chillies
200ml	Vegetable oil
2	Limes
20g	Sugar
	White ground pepper to taste
	Salt
40g	Cucumber (sliced)
12	Cherry tomatoes (cut in half)
500g	Rice (cooked)

Method

1. To make the marinade, mix 2.5g salt, dark soy sauce, chicken stock and white pepper in a suitable bowl.

2. Thinly slice the pork then blanch it in boiling water for 4–5 minutes. Place in the marinade for 35–40 minutes.

3. Drain, reserving both the marinade and pork.

4. Peel and slice the red and spring onions. Remove the stalks and seeds from the chillies and then cut into fine dice.

5. Heat the oil in a suitable wok or pan, add the drained pork and fry until crispy. Remove with a slotted spoon and drain on kitchen paper.

6. Pour off the remaining oil and then shallow fry all the ingredients (except the garnish and marinade liquid) for 2–3 minutes, then add the marinade and reduce for 2–3 minutes.

7. Add the pork. Cook for a further 1–2 minutes then serve.

8. Check the seasoning and serve with a garnish of sliced cucumbers, halved cherry tomatoes and a portion of rice.

Chef's Notes

- The key to this dish is to ensure that the pork is really crispy. It is up to you if you wish to remove the skin (rind) or not.

- Pork is rarely used in Malaysia, due to their religious beliefs, but can be found in Nyonya and Chinese areas.

Nasi Lemak

Coconut Rice

Method

1. Clean the rice and then drain. Very finely slice the ginger and shallots.

2. Cook the rice in the coconut milk (thick and thin combined) with the sliced shallots, the ginger, screw pine leaves, and add a little salt.

3. Serve the rice with sliced hard-boiled eggs, cucumber, peanuts and Sambal ikan bilis.

Measurements	Ingredients
250g	Rice (long grain) Basmati or jasmine
2cm	Ginger (peeled)
40g	Shallots (peeled)
100ml	Thin coconut milk
1	Freshly grated coconut or
400ml	Thick coconut milk (see Chef's Notes, p. 70)
2	Screw pine leaves
	Salt
4	Eggs (hard-boiled)
60g	Cucumber (diced)
30g	Peanuts
100ml	Sambal ikan bilis (anchovies in hot gravy)

Sambal Ikan Bilis

Anchovies in a Hot Gravy

Method

1. Pour the oils into a hot pan and fry the anchovies until golden brown then place on dish paper and keep warm.

2. Place the onion, chillies, shallots and garlic purée into a pestle and mortar or food processor and blend to a smooth paste. Pour half of the used oil into a hot pan and fry the paste until it becomes fragrant. Add a squeeze of lime juice.

3. Mix the tamarind paste with the water, strain off the liquid and discard the pulp. Mix the liquid into the paste.

4. Season with a little sugar and salt to taste. When thick, serve by pouring over the anchovies.

Measurements	Ingredients
120g	Dried anchovies
10	Dried red chillies (no seeds)
80g	Shallots (peeled)
5–10g	Garlic purée
100g	Onion (finely diced)
20g	Tamarind paste
50ml	Water
30ml	Sunflower oil
1	Lime
50ml	Vegetable oil
5g	Sugar
	Salt

Chef's Notes

- Nasi lemak is often eaten for breakfast in Malaysia, served with sliced cucumber, peanuts, deep-fried dried anchovies and sliced or quartered hard-boiled eggs.

- If you use fresh coconut, then squeeze out 400ml thick coconut milk from the grated coconut.

Nasi Impit

Compressed Rice Cakes

Method

1. Wash the rice in cold water, then wash the pine leaves and tie in a knot.

2. Bring the water to the boil, season with salt and add both the rice and the pine leaves.

3. Stir the rice occasionally. When the rice is cooked, drain from the pot and remove the leaves, then place into a mould or on a tray.

Measurements	Ingredients
300g	Jasmine rice
1–2 strips	Screw pine leaves (pandan leaves) *or*
4–5 drops	Pandan essence
500ml	Water
	Salt

4. Cover with a muslin cloth and then place another tray with heavy weights on top to compress the rice.

5. Allow this to cool and place in the fridge overnight.

6. Remove tray and cloth and cut the rice into cubes with a sharp wet knife.

Chef's Notes

- Nasi Impit is traditionally served with satay sauce (gravy) and is popular during festivals, especially the Hari Raya Festival.

Nasi Beriani Ayam

Chicken Biryani Malay Style

Method

1. Mix the diced chicken with the natural yoghurt and leave to marinate for 1–2 hours in the fridge.

2. Wash and soak the rice.

3. Remove the seeds and stalks from the chillies and chop into a purée with the garlic. Peel and chop the onions and spring onions into a very fine dice.

4. Mix the ground spices and water to form a paste. Mix the paste with the chillies, onions, garlic and spring onions.

5. Place the ghee into a wok or suitable pan, add the paste and fry. Stir the paste until it begins to smell fragrant then add the chicken (with yoghurt) and stir in well. Cook for 8–10 minutes.

6. Bring the stock to a simmer in a separate pan. Add this boiling stock to the chicken and then add the drained rice. Simmer for 5 minutes then reduce to a low heat and stir occasionally for 10–12 minutes. Check seasoning and that the rice is cooked.

7. Serve with a garnish of chopped coriander.

Measurements	Ingredients
700g	Diced chicken
100ml	Natural yoghurt
400g	Rice (long grain, jasmine)
6	Green chillies
6 cloves	Garlic
40g	Spring onions
100g	Onions
10g	Ground cumin
10g	Ground cinnamon
10g	Ground turmeric
2.5g	Ground cloves
50ml	Water
100g	Vegetable ghee (see p. 72)
1lt	Chicken stock
10g	Coriander (chopped)
	Salt

Chef's Notes

- This dish has a leaning towards the Indian influences found in Malaysia.

Ghee

This is Indian clarified butter, which unlike regular butter does not have the milky residue that will stick and burn under high heat. It also has a good rich flavour. It is also available in vegetable form.

Kari Kepala Ikan

Fish Curry

Method

1. Remove the scales and fins from the fish and gut them. Remove the head and cut up into 6–7cm portions on the bone.

2. Cut the shallots, onions and okra into rough dice. Wash and cut the tomatoes into quarters. Cut the ginger into very fine strips.

3. Mix the tamarind paste with 100ml water, strain the juice off and throw the remaining pulp away.

4. Mix the tomato purée, curry powder and chilli powder together with a dash of water to form a paste.

5. Fry off the fennel, black mustard seeds, cumin and curry leaves in the vegetable oil for 2–3 minutes then add the onions, shallots, ginger and garlic purée and continue to cook until the onions are soft.

6. Add the paste to the onion mixture and mix well. Continue to stir and cook the paste out until it releases its oil content (this could take 10–20 minutes). Do not move on until this occurs.

7. Now stir in the water and bring back to the boil for 5 minutes, then add the tamarind water, coconut milk and half the coriander. Cook for a further 5 minutes.

8. Add the okra, fish and tomatoes to the curry and correct the seasoning. Cook for 10–12 minutes at a simmer.

Measurements	Ingredients
2 × 700g	Red snapper
150g	Shallots
50g	Onions (peeled)
100g	Okra
8	Tomatoes
2cm	Ginger (peeled)
20g	Tamarind paste
20g	Tomato purée
150g	Curry powder (mild)
150g	Chilli powder
15g	Fennel seeds
15g	Black mustard seeds
10–14	Curry leaves
10g	Cumin
80ml	Vegetable oil
30g	Garlic purée
2lt	Water
500ml	Coconut milk (thick or thin)
20g	Fresh coriander (chopped)
1	Banana leaf
600g	Rice (cooked)

continued over →

9. Serve on a plate covered with a banana leaf, with rice, crackers, poppadoms and pickled vegetables.

...continued

8	Prawn crackers
4	Poppadoms (cooked)
120g	Pickled vegetables

Chef's Notes

- This is an excellent curry and the art to this is waiting until the paste has fully cooked out at which point the powders release the oil.

- This dish shows a heavy influenced from Indian cuisine but the addition of tamarind and coconut is very much Malay in style.

Pedas Manis Goring Sotong

Sweet Spicy Fried Cuttlefish

Measurements	Ingredients
3	Eggs
14 small	Cuttlefish
5	Bird's eye chillies
30g	Shallots
20g	Sesame seeds
1lt	Vegetable oil
300g	Rice flour
8 sprigs	Coriander
4	Red chillies (cut into fine strips)
1	Banana leaf
50g	Cucumber
100ml	Honey
	Salt and white pepper

Method

1. Separate the eggs and whisk up the whites with a little salt. Clean the fish and then place in the egg whites marinade for 15–20 minutes.

2. Remove the seeds and stalks from the bird's eye chillies and dice.

3. Peel the shallots and very finely chop them into dice.

4. Toast the sesame seeds under a grill or in a dry pan until they are golden brown.

5. Heat the oil into a suitable wok or pan.

6. Pass the fish through the rice flour and deep-fry until crisp. Remove with a slotted spoon onto kitchen paper, allowing any excess oil to drain off.

7. Blanch the banana leaf in boiling water for 1 minute, then refresh in cold water, and cut into round discs to line plates.

8. To prepare the garnish, wash and slice the cucumber, cut the chillies into fine strips and wash, and pick nice leaves of the coriander and reserve.

9. Take 40ml oil from the wok into a clean pan and sweat off the diced chillies and shallots, then add honey and sesame seeds and a ladle full of water (50–60ml) and bring back to the boil.

10. Add the fish to the sauce for a minute then check the seasoning and serve.

11. Garnish the fish with cucumber, banana leaf, julienne of chillies and coriander.

Chef's Notes

- If you have difficulty obtaining cuttlefish you could use squid instead.
- This recipe is a Nyonya dish from the coast of Malacca.

Okra Sambal Belacan

Ladies' Fingers in Sambal Belacan

Method

1. Wash the okra under cold running water then remove the stalks.

2. Mix the water with the tamarind pulp and the strain off the liquid and discard the remaining pulp.

3. Pour oil into a suitable wok over a medium heat and fry off the belacan for 2–3 minutes, then add the garlic purée. Cook until it smells fragrant.

4. Add the okra to the belacan and cook for another 2 minutes then add the fish stock and tamarind juice and simmer for 4–5 minutes.

5. Check the seasoning and serve with plain boiled or steamed rice.

Method (Sambal Belacan)

1. Remove all the seeds and stalks from the chillies and roughly chop.

2. Wrap the shrimp paste in tin foil and bake for 20 minutes at 180°C. It should then be smelling fragrant.

Measurements	Ingredients
500g	Okra
100ml	Water
20g	Tamarind pulp
200ml	Light fish stock
50ml	Vegetable oil
10g	Sambal belacan (see below)
5g	Garlic purée
200g	Prawns (peeled with the central vein removed)
300g	Jasmine rice (boiled or steamed)
	Salt
Sambal belacan	Ingredients
30	Red chillies
30g	Belacan (shrimp paste)
1	Lime (kalamansi)

3. Place the chillies and shrimp paste in a pestle and mortar or food processor and make into a smooth paste. Then mix in a squeeze of lime juice.

Chef's Notes

- Only use fresh, firm and crisp okra. The smaller ones are the best; the older ones become very waxy and are not nice to eat.

- Okra is from the hibiscus plant family and is an immature seedpod, mainly from Africa and India.

Nyonya Ince Kebin

Deep-Fried Spiced Nyonya Chicken

Method

1. Cut the chicken into pieces (legs into 2, breast into 4 portions on the bone). Discard the wings and cage.

2. Peel and roughly chop 110g shallots, 4 spring onions and the lemongrass stalks. Blend the chopped shallots and spring onions, lemongrass, chilli purée, candle nuts and belacan in a food processor or pestle and mortar until a smooth paste is achieved.

3. Rub and marinate the chicken with the blended ingredients for 2–3 hours.

4. Finely dice the remaining shallots, spring onions and chillies and then mix with the Worcester sauce and seasoning to make a dipping sauce.

5. Clean off the marinade and heat the oil in a suitable wok or pan, then deep-fry the chicken until it is golden brown, crispy and fully cooked. Remove from the oil with a slotted spoon and drain on kitchen paper.

6. Serve with a garnish of lettuce, cucumbers and dipping sauce.

Measurements	Ingredients
1 × 1.3kg	Fresh chicken
190g	Shallots
7	Spring onions
4 stalks	Lemongrass
20g	Chilli purée
5–6	Candle nuts
15g	Belacan (shrimp paste)
15	Bird's eye chillies (no seeds)
40–60ml	Worcester sauce
	Salt and pepper
1lt	Vegetable oil
8 leaves	Iceberg lettuce
60g	Cucumber (sliced)

Chef's Notes

- This is a hot dish from Penang. It is traditionally served on the bone to avoid it frying dry and tough. Keeping it on the bone will help it to remain moist and avoid it shrinking.

Nasi Pulut Wangi

Scented Glutinous Rice

Method

1. Wash the rice after leaving it to soak overnight, then drain. Steam the rice for 15 minutes and drain off any excess liquid.

2. Soak the prawns and Chinese mushrooms in water for approximately 30 minutes and then shred the mushrooms. Chop 3cm ginger, the shallots and celery into fine dice. Cut the chicken into fine strips.

3. Grate the remaining ginger and squeeze out the juice. Mix with the soy sauce, sugar, pepper, chicken stock and MSG or salt.

4. Heat the oil in a wok or suitable pan, and over a medium heat sweat off the chopped shallots and ginger for 1 minute and then add the celery until it softens. Add the chicken, stir and cook out for 3–4 minute (do not burn the vegetables).

5. Add the mushrooms and prawns to the pan then add the rice, mixing thoroughly. Add the ginger and soy sauce mixture to the pan and stir. Fold the mixture over ensuring all the rice has been coated by the liquid.

6. Check seasoning and serve in a suitable bowl.

Measurements	Ingredients
500g	Glutinous rice (soaked overnight)
50g	Dried prawns
6	Dried Chinese mushrooms
5cm	Ginger (peeled)
30g	Shallots
12cm	Celery
300g	Chicken (breast)
30ml	Soy sauce
10g	Sugar
2.5g	Ground white pepper
100ml	Chicken stock
	Monosodium glutamate (MSG) or Salt
40ml	Sesame oil

Chef's Notes

• Monosodium glutamate (or MSG) is used heavily in Asian cookery. It is a sodium salt of glutamic acid and occurs naturally in soy sauce. It can be made from wheat. It has little flavour of its own but helps to bring out the flavour of other ingredients. Too much MSG is not good for one's health.

• There are many grades of dried prawns and it is always better to get the superior brand. They are normally shelled, steamed and dried in the sun. If prawns are not available then use dried shrimps, but they have less flavour than the prawns.

Sagoo

Spiced Yellow Pumpkin

Method

1. Peel and finely chop the garlic. Peel and remove the seeds from the pumpkin and cut into 2–3cm dice.

2. Pour the oil into a hot and suitable wok or pan and gently fry the lentils, mustard seeds and curry leaves until the lentils are golden and the mustard seeds pop.

3. Add the garlic and fry for another minute. Add the ground spices and stir well to avoid sticking or burning.

4. Put in the pumpkin plus the water and coconut milk, which should be just enough to cover the vegetable.

5. Add salt, cover the pan and simmer until the pumpkin is half cooked. Sprinkle in the grated coconut and cook until the pumpkin is tender.

Measurements	Ingredients
5g cloves	Garlic
250g	Yellow pumpkin
20ml	Palm oil
30	Lentils
5g	Black mustard seeds
6	Curry leaves
10g	Ground coriander
5g	Ground cumin
2.5g	Ground turmeric
200ml	Water
100ml	Thick coconut milk
1	Coconut (freshly grated)
	Salt to taste

Chef's Notes

• Desiccated coconut can be used if fresh coconut is not available.

Rojak

Method

1. Pour the oil into a suitable pan for deep-frying.

2. Cut the tofu into slices, dust in cornflour and deep-fry until crisp. Top and tail the beans and cut into 4cm lengths. Peel and wash both the cucumber and radish and cut into thin strips. Fry and slice the tempeh, slice the papaya and cut the eggs into quarters.

3. Arrange all these ingredients and the bean sprouts on a suitable large plate.

4. Sieve all the flours, salt and baking powder, then whisk the eggs. Mix the egg and 250 ml coconut milk together and gradually fold in the flour, prawns, green chillies and diced shallots to make a thick batter.

Measurements	Ingredients
1lt	Vegetable oil
150g	Tofu
20g	Cornflour
150g	Long beans
1	Cucumber
1	Chinese white radish (mouli)
120g	Tempeh
250g	Papaya (hard)
4	Eggs (shelled and hard–boiled)

continued over →

5. Make sure there is just enough oil to cover the prawn cakes in the frying pan and carefully ladle in the mixture (approximately 60g each). Fry until golden brown on both sides. Remove and drain on kitchen paper, then arrange on the plate.

6. Mix the tamarind paste with 300ml water, then drain the liquid and discard the remaining pulp.

7. Place the nuts, belacan, garlic, shallots and dried chillies into a pestle and mortar or food processor and blend to a smooth paste. Then mix in the tamarind water and coconut milk and bring to the boil. Stir in the palm sugar, skim the surface to remove any debris and cook until it is thick. Spoon the sauce over the ingredients on the plate.

Chef's Notes

• This traditional dish has many variations and can be found throughout Malaysia. Some of the best Rojak can be found in Indian and Malaysia.

• Chinese white radish is often called mouli. It is a large vegetable, which looks like a very large white carrot.

...continued

150g	Bean sprouts (washed)
100g	Flour (plain)
100g	Rice flour
10g	Baking powder
3 medium	Eggs
250ml	Coconut milk (thick or thin)
250g	Prawns (chopped)
1	Small green chilli (finely diced, no seeds)
30g	Shallots (finely diced)
30g	Tamarind paste
250g	Roasted peanuts
10g	Belacan (shrimp paste)
4 cloves	Garlic
100g	Shallots (peeled)
8	Dried chillies (soaked)
300ml	Coconut milk (thick or thin)
20g	Palm sugar
	Monosodium glutamate (MSG)

Pulut Hital

Pandan Scented Glutinous Rice

Method

1. Wash the rice and then simmer for 1 hour with the tied up pandan leaves, until the rice is soft, then drain.

2. Bring the coconut milk gently to a simmer with a pinch of salt; do not split the milk by boiling it too rapidly.

3. Mix the rice and milk together, stirring in the sugar until it is all dissolved. Remove the pandan leaves and serve hot in a suitable bowl.

Measurements	Ingredients
300g	Wild rice
1–2	Pandan leaves *or*
2–4 drops	Pandan essence
500ml	Coconut milk (thick or thin)
	Salt
125g	Brown sugar

Chef's Notes

• If you do not wish to use wild rice you can always use green mung beans as a replacement.

Desserts

Malaysians do not normally serve desserts or puddings at the end of a meal, but if they do, a fresh fruit such as mango, papaya, rambutan or melon might be served.

They would usually have a hot or cold non-alcoholic drink with their main meal, which also reflects the majority of the population's aversion to alcohol because, as Muslims, their religion forbids the drinking of alcohol.

Pisang Kuih

Banana Cake

Method

1. Peel and purée the bananas and mix in the desiccated coconut and coconut milk.

2. Whisk the eggs and 125g sugar together until the mixture doubles its volume, then fold in the sieved flour. Add the banana mixture.

3. At this stage you can either spoon the mixture into cones made from banana leaves and place in a steamer and cook, then turn out and deep-fry until golden brown, or spoon into the hot oil and deep-fry until golden brown.

4. Once removed from the fryer, place on kitchen paper, roll in the remaining sugar and serve on a banana leaf.

Measurements	Ingredients
4	Bananas
70g	Desiccated coconut
200ml	Thick coconut milk
2	Eggs (small)
175g	Caster sugar
180g	Self-raising flour (sieved)
1lt	Vegetable oil
1	Banana leaf

Chef's Notes

• I have also seen this recipe used as a coating for whole bananas being deep-fried in the markets, but you should first coat the banana in rice flour to help to hold the batter in place.

Tauco Dan Undang Sup (Tauhu Titiek)

Tofu and Prawn Soup

Method

1. Cut the tofu into 3cm square dice. Place the candle nuts, onions, red chillies and belacan in a pestle and mortar or food processor and pound or blend until a smooth consistency is achieved.

Measurements	Ingredients
150g	Tofu
5	Candle nuts
120g	Onions (peeled)

continued over →

2. Fry off the paste in a hot pan with the vegetable oil until it smells fragrant. Place the bones and prawns into the pan and continue to fry for a further 2–3 minutes.

3. Add the fish sauce, stock and seasoning and bring to the boil. Skim any debris from the surface. Cook for 5 minutes.

4. Remove the bones and then add the tofu and half the coriander. Cook for a further 4–5 minutes at a simmer. Skim any debris from the surface.

5. Correct the seasoning then serve in suitable bowls, garnished with the remaining coriander.

Chef's Notes

- This is a Nonya-style soup. If you are unable to purchase threadfin fish bones, snapper is an acceptable replacement.

- Be careful with the seasoning, and only season after you have begun to simmer and cook the tofu. This is because the fish sauce is quite salty.

- It is best to purchase the fresh bean curd (tofu) from a Chinese or Asian supermarket.

...continued

2–3	Red chillies
10g	Belacan (shrimp paste)
40ml	Vegetable oil
100g	Fish bones (threadfin)
200g	Prawns (shelled and de-veined)
10ml	Fish sauce
800ml	Light fish stock (clear)
10g	Fresh coriander (chopped)
	Salt and ground white pepper

Santan Gula-Gula

Coconut Sweet

Method

1. Bring the palm sugar to the boil with the water and allow to cool.

2. Bring the thin coconut milk to the boil and remove from heat.

3. Mix the gelatine powder in with the hot thin coconut milk.

4. Add the thick coconut milk to the thin milk and allow to cool a little.

5. Whip up the double cream to the ribbon stage and then slowly fold it into the cream.

6. Whisk up the egg whites and the caster sugar until it is double its volume and then fold into the cream and milk mixture.

Measurements	Ingredients
80g	Palm sugar
30ml	Water
125ml	Thin coconut milk
15g	Gelatine powder
200ml	Thick coconut milk
100ml	Double cream
3 medium	Egg whites
125g	Caster sugar
1	Mango (sliced)
1	Papaya (sliced)
$\frac{1}{2}$	Watermelon (sliced)
	Salt

7. Very gently pour the mixture in to a suitable mould or dish and place in the refrigerator until it is set.

8. Turn out the dessert and decorate with slices of mango, papaya and watermelon and then pour the sugar syrup over the dessert and serve.

Chef's Notes

- You must ensure that the raw egg whites that you use are salmonella free; the eggs should have the Lion mark on them. It would be better to cook the eggs with boiling sugar as in the case of Italian meringue, but the Malay chef I observed making this dish used raw egg whites.

Sambal Kangkung

Spicy Greens

Method

1. Wash the kangkung and leave to drain, then cut into 5–6cm lengths. Mix the tamarind pulp with the water and then strain off the juice and throw the remaining pulp away.

2. Place the shallots, 1 garlic clove, tempeh, belacan, red chillies and anchovies in a pestle and mortar or a food processor and blend to a smooth paste.

3. Pour the oil into a suitable hot wok and fry the paste until it begins to smell fragrant, then add the kangkung, tamarind juice, soy sauce, the remaining anchovies and half the deep-fried garlic slices to the paste. Stir for 2–3 minutes, check the seasoning and transfer onto a suitable plate.

4. Garnish with the remaining slices of deep-fried garlic.

Chef's Notes

- You can substitute mustard cress or mustard greens for the kangkung and it works just as well with spinach.

Measurements	Ingredients
1kg	Water convolvulus (kangkung)
10g	Tamarind pulp
50ml	Water
50g	Shallots (peeled)
1 clove	Garlic
25g	Tempeh
25g	Belacan
4	Red chillies
5g	Dried anchovies
50ml	Vegetable oil
20ml	Light soy sauce
2 cloves	Garlic (sliced and deep fried)
10g	Dried anchovies (cut in half)
	Salt

Singapore 2

Duck in Lemon Sauce

SINGAPORE

Singapore is a tiny country lying at the bottom of the tip of Malaysia, some 137 kilometres north of the equator. Its wet season is from November to January and the driest time is from May to July. Singapore is not just a single island but is made up of 58 smaller islands within its territorial waters. It is officially known as the Republic of Singapore. This tiny island has grown, from its humble beginnings little more than 150 years ago, to become Asia's most dynamic city.

It has a tropical climate, with the temperature rarely dropping below 20°C, even at night. With its close proximity to the equator the country has plenty of sunlight throughout the year.

The whole island is approximately 616.3 square kilometres: 42 kilometres from east to west and 23 kilometres from the north to the south. The main population and built-up area is in the south of the island, mainly along the Singapore River. The river is termed 'a recreational river' with houses on the waterfront, restaurants for riverside dining and water sports.

When one mentions Singapore, many people immediately think of Sir Stamford Raffles and the hotel named after him. Some people also think that is when Singapore's history started, with Raffles' arrival! However, the history goes back much further to the thirteenth century, when it was a vassal state of the Javanese Majaphit Empire. Then, in the fourteenth century, the island became part of the Sumataran Sijayan Empire. It was called Temasek (which means 'sea town'). Legend has it that the Sri Vijayan prince, Sang Nila Utama, saw an animal that he mistook for a lion (probably a tiger), and from that day the island was called 'Singapura', which translated is 'lion city'.

The island could have remained relatively inconspicuous had it not been for Sir Stamford Raffles, who arrived in 1819. The British had a presence in the Straits of Malacca (Melaka) early in the eighteenth century when the East India Company set out to protect its interests from China to India, fearing the re-emergence of the Dutch, who were the major trading force for 200 years. Raffles set about turning Singapore from a tiny disease-ridden fishing colony into an influential trading port. He even ordered a small hill to be excavated to fill a low-lying side of the river so he could build a business quarter at that point on the river. That site is now the centre of Shenton Way, Singapore's answer to Wall Street. With a deep-water port, military and naval base, this tariff-free port soon attracted migrants, and Singapore grew.

The British remained until they surrendered Singapore to the Japanese in 1941. The British returned after the Japanese were defeated, but the country moved towards self-government and in 1959 Singapore joined the Malaysian Federation, but retained its own government, before becoming a Republic on 9 August 1965.

Singapore's inexorable growth since independence has not been paralleled anywhere in the world. This is due in part to Lee Kuan Yew, who was prime minister for 31 years until 1990. In less than a generation Singapore has become one of the most modern, sophisticated and vibrant cultures in the world.

The main industrial area is to the west of the island at Jurong. To the east is the modern housing of Beach Park and also one of the busiest international airports (Changi), making the city a jet age crossroads for Asia. Singapore is also connected to Malaysia by a 1-kilometre-long causeway to the mainland. Fifty per cent of the country's land is urban while parkland, plantations, reservoirs and open areas make up the other 40 per cent.

The main exports are rubber and tin. Other exports and industries include smelting, lumber, shipbuilding, oil refining, chemical products, food, tourism and banking. Only 1.7 per cent of the total land is used for farming, which means that most of the country's food is imported.

Singapore is one of the big four industrialised countries from south-east Asia that joined the International Monetary Fund (IMF), the others being Hong Kong, South Korea and Taiwan. Singapore has no major natural resources and built its wealth on one resource – its own people, who are hard working and goal orientated. It has one of the world's major oil refineries and distribution centres. It also supplies electronic components and is a huge and influential financial centre with great influence in the Far East.

Singapore is now home to 3,500,000 people. The ethnic diversity of the country is made up of 76.4 per cent Chinese, 14.9 per cent Malay, 6.4 per cent Indian and 2.3 per cent others. With Chinese being the largest group of inhabitants, Buddhism is prominent, with Islam, Hinduism, Christianity, Sikhism and Taoism also found.

There are four official languages spoken: English, Malay, Chinese and Tamil.

The feeling you get is one of cultural diversity, emanating from Singapore's people, cuisine and ethnic enclaves. The people think of themselves as Singaporeans. The identity is a marriage of influences from the Chinese, Arabs, Malays and Eurasians, who settled in the very early days of the Colony. There are still areas in Singapore occupied by certain ethnic groups with their own culture, festivals and religions, for example Chinatown, Arab Street and Little India.

The influences on Singaporean cuisine are as diverse as its people. I have therefore divided the following pages into Chinatown, Arab Street, and Little India, and have included a variety of recipes that encompass and reflect the cuisine of this country.

WHAT IS SINGAPOREAN CUISINE?

The cuisine has its origins in Malaysian, Indonesian, Indian and Chinese food. You will still find pockets of these authentic cuisines around the city. In this melting pot of food and cuisines Singaporeans do not necessarily think of what they are eating, but more about the taste. The usual food is a blend of numerous ingredients brought by the migrants who have settled here over the years, creating a unique culture and cuisine. Probably Peranakan or Nyonya food is the closest indigenous cuisine. Peranakan food is a mix of Chinese and Malay with other influences blended together to create its own unique, and extremely subtle food. Singapore's world famous food festival is held in July.

Here, as in Malaysia, the way in which food is eaten at the table is as varied as the food itself. One person may eat their rice with a spoon and fork, another with chopsticks, while yet another may eat with their fingers and no one thinks anything of it.

The one thing that the cuisine will do is tantalise your senses of smell, touch and sight, with satay grilling over hot coals, fish head curry simmering or the fragrance and sight of chilli crab.

CHINATOWN

Located close to the Singapore River, Chinatown is the historical home of the Chinese community and was the trading centre in the nineteenth century. As trade flourished, the community grew. One of the stunning sights in Chinatown is the Hindu Sir Mariamman Temple right in the heart of the enclave. Two of the things that you really notice about the area are the vibrant colours and friendliness of the people.

Another link in the cuisine chain in Chinatown is a number of herbal restaurants and physicians, who will prescribe you with the appropriate dishes to keep the yin and yang balanced within your body – black ants (that look like caviar), lotus roots, sea slugs, shark fins and scorpions, to name a few. The use of hot and cold foods helps to maintain balance and harmony within the body; one counters the other. Hot foods, like chillies, ginger and dense vegetables like carrots, stimulate the nervous system, appetite and blood circulation, but too much can cause inflammation and eczema. Cold foods include such items as seafood, bitter foods, citrus foods and leafy vegetables. Eating cold foods is

thought to counter toxic heat, fever and weight loss, but can cause diarrhoea and fungal infections. It is intriguing, though, as fish (cool) cooked with ginger and chilli (hot) does suggest a balance, and the fish would benefit from such a marriage. Interestingly, brown sugar is considered hot and white sugar cold, so there is a scientific conflict!

When the Chinese ask if you have eaten, it is best to understand that they are more likely asking you how you are. Indeed, eating is a way of life and the Chinese influence on the food is widespread; Europeans favoured the Hainanese Chinese as servants and cooks. It was Ngiam Tong Boon, a Hainanese Chinese, who is widely credited with inventing the world famous Singapore Sling. He also invented the Million Dollar cocktail, which was immortalised in *The Letter* written by Somerset Maugham.

As for the food, nearly all the regions of China are in one way or another represented in Singapore, from the Beijing and Shanghainese cooking from the imperial kitchens to the robust flavour from the north. The predominant food is from the southern provinces of Hokkien, Teochew and Canton.

The popular Hokkien food is characterised by dishes with oyster omelette or Popiah, which is a soft wheat spring roll. Hokkien food is predominantly made from pork, like braised pork in black soya sauce (Tau yew bak). Another contribution to the world of cooking is the yellow wheat noodles called Hokkien mee. This has transcended to dishes like Malay mee rebus and Indian goreng mee.

Teochew cookery is popular for its light soups, steamed seafood, fish balls and savoury porridge made with rice. One of the classic dishes or ingredients that has been incorporated by other groups is the Teochew fish ball. This again can be seen in dishes like Indian Rojak or a Malay Sambal. Another more popular dish, especially at breakfast time, is Teochew savoury porridge. This is a rice gruel that is eaten with other dishes.

Cantonese food has small neat portions and fruity flavours. Some of the most popular food is the Dim sum or little hearts, which are popular at lunch times or for a quick snack. Yet it can contrast well with the more hearty dishes like Sa poh, which are dishes cooked in clay pots, and roast meats such as roast pork and suckling pigs.

One thing to note is that the Chinese are very particular about anyone who points or gesticulates at the table using chopsticks, or leaves them sticking out or standing up in a bowl. It is regarded as very bad manners.

A food festival worth seeing is the Mooncake Festival in mid-September. Folklore tells how mooncakes were used to carry secret messages outwitting their Mongolian rulers, others say that it is an old Chinese legend of how magicians touched the moon.

ARAB STREET

Arab Street is in an area known as Kampong, and is also the centre of Singapore's Muslim community, displaying its architecture and culture. One of the best examples of this is the Sultan Mosque, built in 1824 with aid from Raffles and the East India Company as a result of the Johur Treaty, at a cost of $3,000. The Mosque has since expanded and has extensive grounds.

You can also see the Malay connection just by looking at the street names like Pahang Road, Jalan Sultan and Aliwal Street. This area is where Singapore's Malay Royalty were seated. Arab Street runs parallel with Little India and is separated by the Rochor River

Geylang Serai has been home for the Malay community since the floating village at the mouth of the Singapore River was removed in 1840. Everything Malaysian is there including cuisine, culture, arts and crafts. During the months of November and December the festival of Hari Raya Puas takes place when Muslims celebrate the birth of a new moon, at which time the streets are adorned with decorations and lights.

If you are looking for Muslim food you can enjoy tantalising Turkish or Mongolian oven-baked Mogul raan (baby leg of lamb). One story goes that a homesick tourist called John asked a helpful hawker for a sandwich. The friendly stallholder promptly took a French stick of bread (baguette) and filled it with minced onion and mutton. He then dipped it in egg and fried it until it was crisp. This was then called Roti John (John's bread) and locals took to it. It is more likely that it is an adaptation of the Muslim dish Murtabak, which is Asia's answer to pizza!

One of the great delights in Singapore is satay which is thought to derive from the Arab kebab, but again many versions developed over the years such as in Thailand (Nam jim satay), China (Satay chelop), Malaysia (Nyonya pork satay), Indonesia and a hawker version called Satay bee hoon.

LITTLE INDIA

This enclave runs from Lavender Street to Rochor Canal. It is believed that one of the reasons for the Indian community settling here was that the land was good for rearing cattle. Although the cattle have long gone, the area is still the centre of Indian commerce, culture and leisure. As you walk along the streets in Little India, the scent of the flowers, spices and herbs combine with the sights of the ladies in sarees. The atmosphere is awash with sounds of Indian music; you can hardly distinguish it from Mumbai or Delhi.

Little India is also where you will see strong traditions and religious fervour, especially around December–January, when Indian Hindu

followers pierce their bodies with skewers, spikes and hooks that carry kavadis during Thaipusum (birthday of Lord Murugan).

With the heady smells of spices you're never far from a good meal, no matter if it's a vegetarian meal that you want to eat with your fingers. The famous and popular Serangoon Road has excellent south Indian vegetarian restaurants, where you can have Masala dosa for a few dollars. You will often see the portrait of the money god Ganesh somewhere on the wall of the restaurant (normally behind the till) with a flower garland around it.

The southern cuisine is much more established than the northern Indian style of cookery. It is far more fiery than that of the north. Although cooks from both north and south use the same spices, such as coriander, fennel, cumin, cloves etc., the northern cooks tend to enrich their food with cream and yoghurt, and towards the end of cooking add chopped herbs, chillies and tomatoes, creating a thicker type of dish such as curry. Normally the northern Indians of Singapore tend to serve unleavened bread and baked naans. This compares to the southern Indian staple diet, which is more rice based and the dishes tend to be enriched with coconut milk. The heavier use of curry leaves and mustard seeds with the coconut milk gives it a more distinctive blend and taste than that in the north. The breads are slightly different in that they tend to be enriched with ghee as in the case of Roti prata.

It is worth pointing out that beef and pork will not be found in either northern and southern Indian cooking due to the religious beliefs imposed by Hinduism. The cow is sacred and worshipped, and pork is prohibited for Muslims. It is thought that the tradition that no pork or beef should be served in Indian restaurants was passed down from the Mughal Emperors, which conforms to both dietary requirements.

The Indian cooks of Singapore have been exposed to other styles of cuisine over the years due to the size of the country and interaction between the two cultures. The influence of the Indian cooks is far bigger than the size of the community. This has led to some interesting dishes and variations that have become favourites of the island, such as Fish head curry, which was invented in the 1950s by an immigrant from Kerala, Mee Goreng. It is made with fried wheat noodles, chillies, potato, bean sprouts, curry sauce and fish head. When the fish head curry was invented it spread like wildfire through the cheap restaurants of the time, known as banana leaf restaurants – places where you are presented with a banana leaf at the table and you eat all your food off the leaf and it is then discarded.

The traditional dish Rojak has some interesting additions, like Teochew (Chinese) fish ball, tofu (tauhu), and tempeh goring (tempeh is fermented soya bean) from Java, and battered eggs with your choice of dips, either sweet or fiery. Other variances are spicy potato samosas, a snack made with spring roll wrappers instead of the flaky pastry dough normally used.

Dining etiquette and eating has its own rules depending on the type and standard of the restaurant you are dining in. If you are eating with your

fingers you use only your right hand (never the left) and only the tips of your fingers should touch the food, the palm kept clean. You should wash your hands before and after your meal. This is not only for hygiene reasons, but also considered very polite.

In the slightly more upmarket banana leaf restaurants you will often get a row of bowls with warm water and soap for you to wash between dishes. You should only touch the food on your own plate and never a communal bowl of rice, for example. For this you should use a spoon in your left hand, which should be used only for this purpose.

In Chinese restaurants you are more likely to be presented with chopsticks, and these too have their own rules. The tips of the chopsticks should have as little contact with the mouth as possible and the sticks should not be licked or sucked as this is very impolite. If you would like larger mouthfuls, then use a spoon. Most restaurants will offer you a spoon and fork as well as chopsticks.

Singapore's astonishing culinary diversity can be best shown in its street food. Once the food hawkers roamed the streets selling their particular dishes but they have long since gone and have been allocated specific areas called food centres. The locals call them hawker centres, and they are both indoor and outdoor locations. Most women work in Singapore, so eating out is a family affair, with most home cooking done at weekends. This is where these hawker centres really come into their own. When you walk into a centre all your senses are bombarded. The smells of cooking are pervasive, your hearing is overwhelmed with chatter, chopping, frying and boiling pots bubbling and all the while your eyes are looking for a table while trying to catch a look at what is on offer at the photographs on each stall. Sharing a table is a common occurrence in such places. You must also place your order at each stall stating your table number and your selections. Some centres like Bugis Street, Lau Pa Sat, Clark Quay and Maxwell Road Market do become very busy.

A wide range and a veritable feast of cheap, tasty and quick meals from Chinese dishes to Indian curries are available – even a pizza or burger washed down with a tiger beer or traditional Chinese tea. The food in these centres very rarely disappoints, and dishes like Mee goring and Char kway teow are of an excellent standard and cheap in comparison to the over-priced five-star hotels.

Singaporeans love their seafood, consuming over 65,000 tonnes of fish, over 24 kilograms per person a year. You will no longer see the house on stilts 300–400 metres into the water from where the inhabitants would cast their nets to catch any passing shoals of fish. Restaurants are places where dreams are made if you are interested in seafood. Sea cucumber, chilli crabs and black pepper crabs along with some of the best lobsters are often found in tanks for you to choose from.

A typical dish will cost from as little as £1.50 to £2.00 with a good meal (two or three dishes and beer) for £5.00 or £7.00 and the phrase 'eating to your heart's content' probably comes from hawker centres.

Ayam Lemak Putih

Nyonya Chicken Curry Singapore Style

Method

1. Peel and chop the onion and garlic. Cut the galangal and ginger into thin slices and remove the root. Chop the lemongrass into large chunks, so they can be removed after cooking. Remove the wishbone on the chicken.

2. Place the onion, garlic, coriander, cumin, 200ml coconut milk and cream coconut in a pestle and mortar or food processor and blend until a smooth paste is achieved.

3. Heat the oil in a suitable wok over a medium heat and add the paste. Stir until it becomes fragrant.

4. Add the chicken, breast side down, and seal. Once sealed stir in the remaining coconut milk and other ingredients, and cook the chicken upside down for 40 minutes, leaving uncovered. It is advisable to turn the chicken every 15 minutes and stir the ingredients to prevent sticking or burning.

Measurements	Ingredients
100g	Onion
6 cloves	Garlic
3cm	Galangal (peeled)
2cm	Ginger (peeled)
2 stalks	Lemongrass
3.5kg	Whole chicken
40g	Coriander (ground)
15g	Cumin (ground)
700ml	Coconut milk (thick or thin)
40g	Cream coconut
80ml	Palm oil
4	Star anise
40ml	Fish sauce
	Salt

5. Remove the chicken and finish off the cooking in a hot oven for 10–15 minutes. Remove the lemongrass and star anise. Serve the chicken either in four or eight portions or whole with the sauce.

Chef's Notes

- Serve with plain jasmine rice and a dipping sauce, normally a thick soy-based sauce.

- This dish is not chilli hot and the chicken should have a crispy skin and a mild creamy sauce.

Chilli Crab

Method

1. Clean and cut up the crabs by cutting the crab in half lengthways. Open up the body by lifting the centre part and remove the gills. Cut off the legs and claws and crack open the claws and legs and remove the meat.

Measurements	Ingredients
750 – 1kg	Crabs
100g	Onions
4 cloves	Garlic

continued over →

2. Peel and chop the onion and garlic. De-stalk and remove the seeds of the peppers and chillies, then chop up roughly. Cut up the galangal and ginger into rough dice. Remove the root and chop the lemongrass into fine slices. Cut the lime leaves into fine strips. Toast the peanuts in a pan or under the grill until golden brown.

3. Place the chillies, belacan, lemongrass, galangal, ginger, peanuts, onions, garlic and caster sugar in a pestle and mortar or food processor and blend until a smooth paste is achieved.

4. Heat the oil in a suitable wok over a medium heat and then add the paste. Stir until it becomes fragrant.

5. Add the crab and fry for a few minutes then add the stock, half the lime leaves, the peppers and tomato sauce. Bring back to the boil and cook the crabs until they become bright red.

6. At this point add the beaten egg to the sauce. When it has curdled and cooked, place the crabs and sauce onto the plate, garnished with lettuce and finish with a sprinkling of kaffir lime leaves.

...continued

1	Red pepper (small)
4	Red chillies
8	Dried red chillies
3cm	Galangal (peeled)
2cm	Ginger (peeled)
2 stalks	Lemongrass
8	Kaffir lime leaves
40g	Peanuts
20g	Belacan (shrimp paste)
20g	Caster sugar
60ml	Palm oil
200ml	Chicken stock
50ml	Tomato sauce (ketchup)
1	Egg (medium, beaten)
8	Lettuce leaves

Chef's Notes

- This is possibly Singapore's most famous national dish.

- The quantities that I have given will make four starters or one main meal.

- The dish is hot with a slight sweetness to it, but you can alter this by reducing the chilli and sugar content.

Fish Head Curry

Method

1. Wash the fish head and blanch it in boiling water for 2–3 minutes then plunge into ice-cold water. Peel and chop the shallots and garlic. De-stalk and remove the seeds of the chillies, then chop up roughly. Cut up the ginger into rough dice.

2. In a separate pan bring 500ml water to the boil with a little salt and cook the aubergine and okra for 4–5 minutes at a simmer.

3. Place the garlic, shallots, chillies, turmeric, ginger and lemongrass in a pestle and mortar or blender and blend until a smooth paste is achieved.

4. Heat the oil in a suitable wok over a medium heat and then add the paste. Stir until it becomes fragrant. Mix the tamarind paste with the warm water then strain off the liquid and throw the pulp away, reserving the liquid.

5. Add the curry leaves and curry powder and stir in well. Cook for 6–8 minutes continuing to stir to prevent sticking or burning.

Measurements	Ingredients
1 large	Fish head (any non-oily fish head)
6	Banana shallots
10 cloves	Garlic
4	Green chillies
4	Red chillies
3cm	Ginger (peeled)
500ml	Water
1	Aubergine (small, cut into 8)
8	Okra
60ml	Palm oil
10g	Turmeric (ground)
50g	Tamarind paste
1	Lemongrass (chopped)
400ml	Warm water
25	Curry leaves

continued over →

6. Add the coconut milk and creamed coconut to the pan.

7. Add the fish head, okra and aubergine to the curry and cook out for 10–12 minutes.

8. Add the tomatoes, sugar and a pinch of salt and cook for 2 minutes.

9. Serve on a suitable plate with the aubergine, okra and tomatoes as a garnish, arranged around the plate.

...continued

40g	Mild curry powder
400ml	Coconut milk (thick or thin)
30g	Creamed coconut
2	Tomatoes (cut into quarters)
10g	Brown sugar
	Sea salt

Chef's Notes

- Since this dish was first cooked in the 1950s, dozens of different versions have developed.

- In Singapore, the cooks use a special curry powder for Fish head curry which is a blend of fennel, cumin, fenugreek, and husks from black garam dal.

- The fish head does look a little uninviting, but rest assured it adds an excellent dimension to a curry and is well worth a try.

Popiah

Spring Roll Hokkien Style

Method

1. Sieve the rice and plain flour, then place into a suitable bowl with the salt and eggs. Very carefully fold the ingredients together then slowly add the water and mix into a smooth paste, with as few bubbles as possible. Sieve if necessary to remove any lumps. Rest the mixture in a fridge for 30–60 minutes.

2. To cook the wrappers, wipe a non-stick pan with a little oil and place over a low heat. When the pan is up to temperature ladle a little of the mixture in and roll it around the pan like a pancake until the bottom of the pan is covered with a light mixture. Do not brown the wrapper. When the edges curl up turn over and cook for 2–3 minutes, then place on kitchen paper and allow to cool but do not allow to dry out. Place a sheet of kitchen paper on top and then a damp cloth on top of the kitchen paper.

3. Lay the wrapper out on a clean flat surface and then spread the hoi sin sauce or sweet black sauce over the wrapper. Then spread a little garlic purée over. Add a little sliced chilli over the centre. At this stage you can add a little of the chilli sauce or plum sauce (optional).

4. For the fillings, thinly slice the omelette, then blanch the sliced Chinese sausage in boiling water for 2 minutes. Keep the shallots, omelette, bean sprouts, crab meat, prawns, Chinese sausage, green beans and boiled egg warm. Add the lettuce and divide up the ingredients onto eight wrappers, then fold and roll them just like a spring roll.

5. This roll should be served immediately as the wrapper will go soggy. Garnish with lettuce leaves, deep-fried garlic and cucumber slices, with coriander leaves sprinkled over.

Chef's Notes

- The list for the fillings is endless. You can also use sliced pork, tofu, bamboo shoots, sweet potato or yam and so on. The Popiah batter will make around 24–26 wrappers.

- This dish is often left so the dinner guests can make up their own filling at the table.

Measurements	Ingredients
190g	Rice flour
20g	Plain flour
2.5g	Salt
5 medium	Eggs
450ml	Water
20ml	Sunflower oil (for frying)
50ml	Hoi sin (or sweet black sauce)
10g	Garlic purée
1	Red chilli (finely sliced)
50ml	Chilli sauce (optional)
50ml	Plum sauce (optional)
1	Omelette (thin)
50g	Chinese sausage (sliced)
100g	Shallots (sliced)
30g	Bean sprouts
40g	Bean sprouts (blanched)
50g	Crab meat
50g	Prawns (cooked and de-veined)
40g	Green beans (shredded and blanched)
1	Boiled egg (sliced)
8	Lettuce leaves (shredded)
8 leaves	Lettuce
20g	Deep-fried garlic (sliced)
40g	Cucumber slices
10g	Coriander leaves

Siew Mai

Pork Dumplings

Method

1. Peel the carrot and very finely dice. Trim and very finely dice the cucumber, bamboo shoots and spring onion. Soak the mushrooms in warm water then remove the stalk and very finely dice.

2. Mix the carrot, cucumber, bamboo shoots and spring onions together with the minced pork.

3. Take the garlic powder, 1 egg, sugar, salt, ground pepper, rice wine, sesame oil, cornflour and light soy sauce and mix them thoroughly with the pork.

4. Divide the mixture into 20–25 portions and place the mix into the centre of a wonton sheet and then brush the edges with beaten egg, bring the edges to the centre and press them together and press down slightly. This will then form a little dumpling.

5. Place all of the dumplings onto a steamer tray 2–3cm apart, and steam for 10 minutes.

Measurements	Ingredients
40g	Carrot
50g	Cucumber
30g	Bamboo shoot (tinned acceptable)
6	Spring onions
2	Dried Chinese mushrooms
200g	Minced pork
2.5g	Garlic powder
2	Eggs (1 beaten)
2.5g	Sugar
Pinch	Salt
Pinch	Ground white pepper
10ml	Rice wine
5ml	Sesame oil
10g	Cornflour
5ml	Light soy sauce

continued over →

6. Place the shredded lettuce leaves around the edge of the plate and the dumplings in the centre, garnished with slices of chilli and diamonds of spring onions. Serve hot.

Chef's Notes

- This dish is an excellent starter, and you will be surprised how many each guest will eat. This recipe should make between 20 and 25.

- You can use chicken instead of pork but it tends to be a little drier.

- The ingredients do vary and if you add chilli ensure that it is very finely diced.

...continued

Garnish	Ingredients
25	Wonton sheets
6 leaves	Iceberg lettuce (shredded)
2	Chillies (finely sliced)
4	Spring onions (cut into diamonds)

Singapore Three Shreds Fish

Method

1. Soak the mushrooms in warm water, then remove the stalks and discard. Finely slice the mushrooms, spring onions, carrot, shallots, chilli and ginger.

Measurements	Ingredients
4	Dried Chinese mushrooms
4	Spring onions

continued over →

2. Remove the scales from the fish (leave the head on) and clean out the insides. Make three incisions (1cm deep) on each side. Rub in 40ml rich soy sauce on both sides and then allow to marinate for 30 minutes.

3. Shred the chicken breast then coat with 2.5g cornflour, salt and pepper. Leave to marinate for 15 minutes.

4. Heat the sunflower oil in a wok on a high heat. Dry the fish and then add to the very hot oil and fry golden brown on both sides. Remove the fish onto kitchen paper and keep hot. Tip the excess oil from the wok.

5. Lower to a medium heat and fry the ginger and garlic purée. Stir and do not colour. Cook for 1–2 minutes then add the chicken until it is cooked.

6. Add the mushrooms and bean paste and fry for 2 minutes. Add the chicken stock, fish stock, the remaining rich soy sauce and rice wine and bring to a boil. Then add the fish to the mixture.

7. Once the fish is cooked remove to a plate and keep warm. Bring the sauce back to a simmer, mix the remaining cornflour with a dash of water and add this to the sauce to thicken.

8. Add the carrots, chilli, shallots and spring onions and cook for 2–3 minutes, then add the sesame oil.

9. Coat the fish with the sauce that also includes the garnish.

...continued

50g	Carrot (peeled)
30g	Shallots (peeled)
1	Green chilli (deseeded)
2cm	Ginger (peeled)
1	Red snapper or grouper
60ml	Rich soy sauce
150g	Chicken breast
12.5g	Cornflour
100ml	Sunflower oil
10g	Garlic purée
10g	Brown bean paste
130ml	Chicken stock
110ml	Fish stock (light)
20ml	Rich soy sauce
30ml	Rice wine
2.5ml	Sesame oil
	Salt
	Ground black pepper

Chef's Notes

• You can leave out the chilli if you wish. Use the freshest fish for the best results.

Prawns with Ginger

Measurements	Ingredients
700g	Prawns (medium to large)
4cm	Ginger (peeled)
30g	Shallots (peeled)
6	Spring onions
4 cloves	Garlic (peeled)
3cm	Ginger (peeled and grated)
50ml	Water
5g	Brown sugar
40ml	Sunflower oil
20ml	Oyster sauce
30ml	Rice wine
40ml	Sweet white wine
50ml	Light fish or chicken stock
10ml	Light soy sauce
5ml	Sesame oil
	Ground white pepper
	Salt

Method

1. Shell and remove the central vein from the prawns, but try to keep the heads on half of the prawns.

2. Very finely slice the ginger, shallots and spring onions, then chop the garlic.

3. Squeeze out the juice from the grated ginger, mix with water and add this and the brown sugar to the prawns. Leave to marinate for 30 minutes.

4. Remove the prawns from the marinade and fry in sunflower oil in a wok over a light heat, until the prawns change to a pink colour. Lift the prawns out with a slotted spoon and keep hot.

5. Fry the garlic, sliced ginger and shallots in the remaining oil until the shallots are limp.

6. Add the oyster sauce, rice wine, white wine and stock and bring back to the boil, then simmer. At this point return the prawns to the wok along with the spring onions. Cook for 1–2 minutes then add the light soy sauce and sesame oil. Cook for a further 2 minutes.

7. Serve hot with plain boiled rice.

Chef's Notes

- A simple dish to make but has plenty of flavour.
- You could remove all but four of the prawn heads and just use four for garnish, but the recipe is as I was served it at Clarke Quay.

Asam Prawns

Method

1. Shell and remove the central vein from the prawns. Mix the tamarind with 100ml warm water, strain off and reserve the liquid and throw the pulp away.

2. Remove the stalks from the chillies then put these and the shallots, garlic, candle nuts, turmeric and belacan in a pestle and mortar or blender and blend until a smooth paste is achieved. You may need to add a little of the remaining water at this point.

3. Mix the prawns and brown sugar, squeeze of lime, salt and pepper then leave to marinate for 30 minutes.

4. Heat the oil in a suitable wok over a medium heat, then add the paste and stir until the paste become fragrant.

5. Add the tamarind liquid and stock. Stir the liquid in well, then allow to cook out for 2–3 minutes.

6. Add the prawns and cook until they have turned a light pink colour.

Measurements	Ingredients
700g	Prawns (medium)
20g	Tamarind
200ml	Warm water
8	Bird's eye chillies
100g	Shallots (peeled)
4 cloves	Garlic
8	Candle nuts
5g	Turmeric (ground)
10g	Belacan (shrimp paste)
20g	Brown sugar
$\frac{1}{2}$	Lime (juiced)
50ml	Sunflower oil
240g	Light fish stock
20g	Coriander (chopped)
Pinch	Salt
Pinch	Ground white pepper

7. Finish with a sprinkling of chopped coriander. Serve hot with plain boiled jasmine rice.

Chef's Notes

• This is a simple dish, which should take 30 minutes to make. It is slightly fiery and you could adjust this by reducing the amount of chillies used.

Acar Campur Aduk

Pickled Vegetables

Method

1. Cut the long beans and snow peas into 3–4cm lengths and then blanch in boiling water and refresh in ice-cold water. Peel the shallots and cut in half.

2. Peel and thinly cut the carrots and mouli into strips. Cut the cucumber into thin batons.

Measurements	Ingredients
100g	Long beans
100g	Snow peas
100g	Shallots
150g	Carrots

continued over →

Remove the stalks and seeds from the chillies and then cut into thin strips.

3. Place the ginger, candle nuts, garlic, caster sugar and turmeric in a pestle and mortar or blender and blend until a smooth paste is achieved.

4. Heat a wok on a medium heat (no oil) and dry roast the mustard seeds until they start to pop open. When toasted add the oil and the paste, fry and stir well.

5. When the oil separates tip this excess off and add the vinegar. Stir in well. Add all the vegetables and remove immediately from the heat.

6. Place all the ingredients from the wok into a jar with a tight–fitting lid, but do not place the lid on until the vegetables have cooled.

7. Keep in a fridge until required.

Chef's Notes

- This is an excellent accompaniment to many dishes or you can use it as an appetiser.

- As long as the lid is sealed and the vinegar completely covers all the vegetables they should last a couple of weeks in the fridge.

...continued

100g	Mouli
125g	Cucumber
100g	Green chillies
100g	Red chillies
3cm	Ginger (peeled and roughly chopped)
6	Candle nuts
4 cloves	Garlic
5g	Caster sugar
5g	Turmeric
10g	Mustard seeds
40ml	Sunflower oil
250ml	Rice wine vinegar
100g	Bean sprouts
	Salt and ground white pepper to taste

Shark Fin Soup

Measurements	Ingredients
300g	Shark fin meat (off the bone and softened)
4	Dried Chinese mushrooms
20g	Carrot (peeled)
20g	Bamboo shoot (tinned acceptable)
20g	Shallot (peeled)
30ml	Sunflower oil
500ml	Chicken stock (light)
30ml	Rice wine

continued over →

Method

1. To soften the shark fin meat, soak overnight in salt water. Once softened, wash and shred the shark fin meat.

2. Soak the mushrooms in a little warm water. When softened, remove the stalks and discard, and thinly slice the mushrooms.

3. Very finely shred the carrots, bamboo shoots and shallots.

4. Pour the oil into a hot wok over a high heat and then add the vegetables and stir fry until the shallots have become limp.

5. Add the stock and bring to the boil. Remove any debris from the surface.

6. When the stock has come to the boil add the shark fin and cook for no more than 3 minutes.

7. Mix the rice wine with the arrow root or cornflour and add to thicken the soup slightly.

8. Finish the soup off by stirring in the oyster and soy sauce, then ladle into suitable bowls and serve.

...continued	
20g	Arrow root or cornflour
40ml	Oyster sauce
20ml	Rich soy sauce

Chef's Notes

• This soup is meant to be slightly thick and I prefer to use arrow root powder rather than cornflour as it tastes better. It also has no powdery aftertaste. Remember to add a little at a time.

• There is a dish that a friend had in a restaurant just off Clarke Quay, which replaced half of the shark fin meat with shredded chicken breast. It was just as good.

Oyster Omelette

Method

1. Clean the oysters, and pour any juice in with the water. Beat the eggs well and season.

2. Mix the rice flour, tapioca flour, and water together to form a batter.

3. Heat a pan over a high heat and add a dash of oil then add the batter. Count to 10 then add the eggs and cook until the eggs are almost cooked.

4. At this point make a hole in the centre of the omelette and add all the oil, then into the centre of the omelette add the garlic purée and cook for 30 seconds. Then add the oysters, soy sauce and rice wine and cook for 30 seconds.

5. Place on a plate and garnish with the parsley. Serve with a sambal or dipping sauce.

Measurements	Ingredients
8	Oysters (fresh and opened)
4	Eggs (medium)
20g	Rice flour
40g	Tapioca flour
150ml	Water
30ml	Sunflower oil
5g	Garlic purée
10ml	Rich soy sauce
20ml	Rice wine
4 sprigs	Parsley
	Salt and pepper to taste

Chef's Notes

- This is a very unusual and popular dish in Singapore. It is eaten at any time, night or day.

- It is often served with a hot and fiery sambal or a spicy soy sauce dip.

Chilli Sambal

Method

1. Chop up the chillies, garlic and prawns. Blend in a blender to form a smooth paste.

2. Heat a wok on a medium heat then add the palm oil, paste and tomato purée and stir and cook for 3–4 minutes. Then add the lime juice, brown sugar and check the seasoning with a little salt and pepper.

Chef's Notes

- This can be kept refrigerated in an airtight jar for up to two weeks.

Measurements	Ingredients
5	Bird's eye chillies
12	Red chillies
12	Garlic cloves
20g	Dried prawns, soaked
40ml	Palm oil
40g	Tomato purée
2	Limes (juice only)
20g	Brown sugar

Ling Meng Ya

Duck in Lemon Sauce

Method

1. Peel the shallots and ginger and finely dice. Peel the lemon zest, remove the remainder of the pith from the lemon and slice the lemon into rings.

2. Remove the skin from the duck breasts and cut into 2cm dice.

3. Mix the egg yolks, garlic, ginger, shallots, 30ml soy sauce and 30g cornflour together and completely coat the diced duck in the mixture. Leave for 90 minutes in a fridge.

4. Melt the butter in a suitable pan then add 10g cornflour to make roux. Heat the stock up to a simmer in a separate pan with the lemon juice. Then gradually pour the stock into the roux and stir until it forms a smooth sauce.

5. Bring the rice wine and palm sugar to the boil, so the sugar dissolves. Add the remaining soy sauce.

6. Pour the wine into the sauce. If the sauce is not thick enough add a little water to 40g cornflour and add to the sauce, stirring until it is a creamy consistency.

Measurements	Ingredients
50g	Shallots
3cm	Ginger
1	Lemon
4	Duck breasts
5	Egg yolks
5g	Garlic purée
50ml	Rich soy sauce
80g	Cornflour
50g	Butter
50g	Flour
100ml	Chicken stock
80ml	Lemon juice
40ml	Rice wine
20g	Palm sugar
10ml	Thick soy sauce
	Vegetable or sunflower oil for deep-frying

7. Heat a deep fat fryer to 180°C and deep-fry the duck until crispy. Remove onto kitchen paper and drain off any excess oil.

8. Place the duck on a serving dish, pour the sauce over and garnish with zest of lemon and rings.

Chef's Notes

• You can use chicken breasts instead of the duck if you wish. I have even been presented with whole chicken breast, with the sauce made with just cornflour in place of a roux.

• Serve with rice or noodles.

Zhi Ma Xia

Prawns with Sesame Seeds

Method

1. Peel and remove the central vein from the prawns and then butterfly them.

2. Remove and discard the stalk and seeds from the chillies. Chop the chillies and spring onions into a purée.

3. Mix together the ginger and garlic purée, spring onions, fish sauce, soy sauce, sugar, chillies, and wine. Place the prawns into the marinade, ensuring that they are all coated, and leave for 30 minutes

4. Remove the prawns and coat in the flour and then in the beaten egg. Remove any excess egg then coat in the sesame seeds.

5. Heat a deep fat fryer to 180 °C, and cook the prawns until golden brown. Remove onto kitchen paper and drain off any excess oil.

6. Decorate the serving plate with the garnish and serve immediately.

Measurements	Ingredients
16	Large prawns
6	Red bird's eye chillies
4	Spring onions
10g	Ginger purée
10g	Garlic purée
10ml	Fish sauce
10ml	Rich soy sauce
10g	Palm sugar
120ml	Sweet rice wine
125g	Rice flour
2	Eggs (beaten)
100g	Sesame seeds
	Oil for deep-frying
Garnish	Ingredients
4	Spring onions (cut into diamonds)

continued over →

Chef's Notes

- To butterfly prawns, cut a slit down the back, three-quarters of the way through, then with the palm of your hand press the prawns down and they should remain open.

...continued

4	Chilli flowers
4 sprigs	Parsley
4 leaves	Iceberg lettuce (shredded)

- This is excellent as a starter or main meal. If you find the prawns a little fiery use normal red chillies (2.5g) instead of bird's eye chillies.

Clay Pot Chicken

Measurements	Ingredients
400g	Jasmine rice
50g	Chinese sausage
50g	Shallots (peeled)
8	Dried Chinese mushrooms
2cm	Ginger (peeled)
2cm	Galangal (peeled)
4	Spring onions
750ml	Chicken stock
50ml	Oyster sauce
30ml	Sunflower oil
20ml	Sweet rice wine
10ml	Dark soy sauce
20ml	Light soy sauce
2.5g	Brown sugar
2.5ml	Sesame oil
600g	Chicken (diced)
5g	Coriander (chopped)
	Salt and pepper

Method

1. Wash the rice in cold running water. Peel and slice the Chinese sausage. Purée the shallots.

2. Soak the mushrooms in a little warm water. When softened remove and discard the stalks and thinly slice the mushrooms.

3. Thinly slice the ginger, galangal and spring onions.

4. Place the rice into a clay pot with 650ml stock and cook with the lid on for 20 minutes.

5. Mix the oyster sauce, sunflower oil, sweet rice wine, soy sauces, sugar and sesame oil together thoroughly. Add the chicken and the sausage to the marinade for 20 minutes, ensuring all the meat is covered.

6. Remove the lid from the clay pot and add the ginger, garlic, galangal, mushrooms and shallots. Cook for 5 minutes then add the remaining stock.

7. Add the chicken and marinade to the top of the rice. Replace the lid and cook on a low heat for a further 10–15 minutes. Check occasionally to ensure the rice is not burning.

8. Garnish the top of the chicken with spring onions and coriander.

9. Serve in the clay pot. Traditionally the pot is placed into a wicker type basket.

Chef's Notes

- The Chinese, Malay and Vietnamese believe that the clay pot is an important instrument in the cooking process, giving the right flavour to the dish. You can use any good sturdy casserole dish that has a tight-fitting lid for this recipe.

- There are numerous clay pot dishes from beef to shellfish, and they are very popular and cheap. The main and bulk ingredient is obviously the rice. The best clay pot dishes are cooked over charcoal and I believe that the clay pot does add that little extra something to the classic clay pot dish.

- Normally there are no accompaniments to the dish.

Tauhu Goreng

Fried Bean Curd

Method

1. Wash and peel the cucumber and cut into fine strips 4cm long.

2. Wash and cut the spring onions into fine strips 4cm long.

3. Deep-fry the bean curd until golden brown then drain and cut into 5cm squares. Make a cut in the side of the curd and stuff some with the cut bean sprouts.

4. Grind the peanuts to a fine powder in a blender.

5. Fry the shallots, garlic, spring onions, belacan and chillies in a little oil for 2 minutes then add the nuts, soy and tamarind. Stir and cook out for another 2–3 minutes.

6. Divide the remaining bean sprouts and the cucumber between four serving plates.

7. Place the bean curd on top of the bean sprouts and then ladle the sauce over. Serve hot.

Measurements	Ingredients
100g	Cucumber
4	Spring onions
500g	Bean curd
160g	Bean sprouts (washed)
200g	Roasted peanuts
50g	Shallots (peeled and sliced)
20g	Garlic purée
4	Spring onions (sliced)
10g	Belacan (shrimp paste)
5	Red chillies (sliced)
50ml	Sweet soy sauce
60ml	Tamarind water
4 sprigs	Coriander
	Oil for deep-frying

Chef's Notes

- This is the way most of the hawker stalls will serve this dish in Singapore, but you could just serve the curd without the filling placed inside.

Kembang Gempul

Sweet Coconut and Dumplings

Method

1. Season the rice flour with a little salt and slowly add hot water to bind and form a dough. Roll into small tight (2cm) balls.

2. Steam the balls for 10 minutes then re-roll them tightly again. Steam them again for 4–5 minutes then remove.

3. Bring the coconut milk, sugar and pandan flavouring to the boil over a medium heat and add a sprinkling of salt. Stir until all the sugar and salt has dissolved. Remove from the heat.

Measurements	Ingredients
500g	Rice flour
	Hot water
1200ml	Coconut milk
50g	Palm sugar
1	Pandan leaf *or* a few drops of pandan essence
	Salt

4. Divide the milk between four bowls and then add the dumplings. This can be served hot or cold.

Chef's Notes

- You may need to add more or less sugar, depending on your taste.

- You can also use demerara sugar in place of palm sugar.

Thailand 3

Clockwise from bottom left: Fish cakes, Catfish with coconut and turmeric, Hot and sour shrimp soup.

THAILAND

Thailand is the point at which two great cultural systems, Asia and India, meet. Both of these cultures have had a strong influence on Thai culture. Bordered by Malaysia to the south, Burma to the north-west, Laos to the north east and Cambodia to the south-east, Thailand lies on the edge of what used to be called French Indo-China.

As far back as 10,000 years ago, the earliest civilisation was believed to be that of the Mons in what is now central Thailand. They are believed to have brought the Buddhist culture from the Indian subcontinent. It is believed that around the ninth century there was a migration of people from central and southern China to eastern Cambodia, which is now Thailand. This migration may have been caused by the Mongolian invasion of China around the same time. As the Thai population grew, its people rebelled against the Khmer Empire, which was centered on Angkor Wat. The Thais then set up a new independent city of Sukhothai. Monks came from Sri Lanka and teachers from India. A succession of wars and an invasion by its neighbours led to the eventual fall of Sukhothai, and in 1350 the capital was moved to Ayuthya, which was further south. This magnificent city emerged over 417 years with 33 kings, 500 sumptuous royal palaces, temples, Buddhas and buildings that became the wonder of the East. Many can still be seen.

In the eighteenth century the Burmese constantly invaded the land and in 1767, after a lengthy siege, they breached the walls of Ayuthya and destroyed the capital along with the royal family.

A Chinese general called Taksin had seen the city destroyed and the people fleeing. He gathered his soldiers across the River Chao Phya from the estuary and set up a camp at Thonburi. It was here the nation of Siam was born. Taksin trained more and more soldiers, then he reinvaded, driving the Burmese back and out of the country. His life was ended by a group of his courtiers and a new Thai emperor, Chao Phya Chakri, became ruler and so began the dynasty that still rules Thailand today. The first three new kings rebuilt Thailand and expanded their territory to include Chiang Mai, with its hill tribes, of which a number still exist today. They then went on to the Laos/Burmese border, creating what is known as the Golden Triangle. As the area was drawn on a map it resembled the head of an elephant, which became the national symbol.

SIAM

Siam has remained an independent nation despite the numerous attempts by the French and British to take it over. Its monarchs King Mongkut and his son King Chulalonghorn modernised the kingdom, with the introduction of modern transport including the railways, and schools and universities. They even sent young Thais overseas to learn from the very best teachers and establishments of the day in order to bring back new ideas and help to shape their country. The reforms and ambitions of the people led to a bloodless coup in 1932, ending the absolute power of the king and a change of name for the country from Siam to Thailand, 'land of the free'. The capital is Bangkok. There has been a succession of military governments since.

The Thais love their monarchy and hold the king and queen in very high esteem, and treat them with great reverence. A custom that illustrates this is that, if a bank note falls to the floor, you must never place your foot upon it to prevent it from blowing away as this is considered a sign of great disrespect as the king's image is on the bank note. Although Thailand still has a constitutional monarchy headed by the king, it also has 76 provinces, each of which is sub-divided into amphoe (districts), tambon (sub-districts) and muban (villages). For the purpose of this book I have divided these provinces into Central Thailand, Northern Thailand, North-Eastern Thailand and Southern Thailand.

During the Second World War, Thailand was occupied by the Japanese, and the infamous Thai–Burma railway and the bridge over the River Kwai were built by 60,000 Allied prisoners-of-war. Later came the Vietnam War, which saw the USA military using areas of Thailand for rest and relaxation for troops.

Thailand has become a fascinating mix of East meets West, where the old and the new mix together. Even in the cities you can see religious traditions being carried out, with Buddhist monks accepting gifts of food, flowers and incense for the temple.

Thai culture can be divided into three areas: linguistic, court and traditional.

Language

The linguistic culture, or the Thai language, consists of monosyllabic words. The alphabet was created in 1283 by the Great King Ramkhamhaeng, who modelled it on the Indian Sanskrit and Pali alphabets through old Khmer characters. The Thai tonal language often confuses foreigners, as it can have five different tones, and therefore five different meanings, for the same word. Today the Thai language is a mix of several sources from Malay, English, Chinese, Khmer, Pali and Sanskrit.

Court culture

Court culture refers to the perfection, beauty and harmony of Thailand's fine arts of drama, music, architecture, literature and painting. In ancient times these were developed and supported by royal patronage and served the religion of Buddhism. The influences of the Indians, Khmers and the Mons merged over time into the unique style of Thailand.

Most Thai paintings and sculptures decorate and adorn the Buddhist places of worship. They are amazingly beautiful, often depicting the life, philosophies and stories of Buddha.

With a population of around 60 million, the main religion of Thailand is Buddhism (94.82 per cent), followed by Muslim (4.00 per cent), Christians (0.55 per cent) and other religions (0.63 per cent).

The architecture has evolved to encompass Indian, Khmer, Chinese and Burmese influences over the centuries and can be seen in the unique style of buildings with pointed towers, sloping rooftops and carved wood. The use of mother of pearl inlay, gilded lacquer and coloured glass all add to the stunning flamboyance of Thai buildings.

Traditions

Drama and dance, originally from India, was only ever seen in the royal palaces and courts. It evolved into a slow and graceful show with the use (in some cases) of masks and with the accompaniment of music.

The traditional culture comes from the family by bilateral descent. The young show respect for their parents, elders, teachers and the Buddhist monks who were the more educated in those days. The wat or Buddhist temple formed a large part in the community, not only as a place where the whole village could worship, but also where one could gain an education, receive rites or hold ceremonies, feasts and festivals.

The images of Buddha are sacred and any acts of sacrilege, even if committed by a foreigner, will be punished by imprisonment. On entering a temple you must be dressed correctly, no short skirts or shorts. You must remove any footwear and on no account can a female touch a monk, give things directly to him or receive anything back from him. As a sign of respect you must always remove your shoes or foot wear on entering someone's house.

Climate and revenue

Thailand has a tropical climate that ranges from 19°C to 38°C with a high humidity of 66 per cent to 88 per cent. The climate differs from the southern beaches to the northern mountains and hills. The hottest season is from March to May and the rainy season starts in June until October; from November to February it is much cooler.

Thailand's main sources of economic revenue are tourism, textiles, clothing, agriculture, tobacco, beverages and light manufacturing (jewellery and components). Thailand has natural resources of metals such as tungsten, tin, lead, rubber, natural gas, timber and fish. Their exports are rice, electronics, sugar, cassava, rubber, fish products, tin, textiles and handycraft.

Thai cuisine

Think of Thailand and you ultimately think of one of the most fragrant, spicy and colourful cuisines of the world.

Thailand's cuisine has been influenced by Burma (Myanmar), Malaysia, Cambodia, and its close proximity to China, Vietnam, Indonesia and India, which have all contributed over the centuries. Its cuisine has four basic tastes: salty, sweet, sour and pungent. It consists of an exciting mix of textures, temperatures and flavours, which can be addictive.

The influences that other countries have had on Thailand can be seen by the influx of Chinese migrants introducing the wok along with stir frying and deep-frying. Up until this point, it is thought, stewing, grilling and baking had been the usual traditional methods. Along with this came the use of Chinese ingredients such as bean sprouts, bok choy and cultivated fruits like papayas. The Indians introduced spices and curry leaves, and dishes similar to curry such as Kaengs. Ghee replaced coconut oil and coconut milk was introduced. Peanuts and fish sauce (Na´am plaa) made from anchovies can also be seen in Thai cuisine as well as some Vietnamese dishes. The Americans introduced whisky during the Vietnam War, and some recipes incorporate this spirit.

One of the most interesting facts I have come across is the answer to the question: when and where did the chilli come from? It is believed to have been brought from South America, possibly Mexico, in the 1600s by Portuguese missionaries who had become addicted to chillies just like Westerners of today.

Thai food always uses the freshest produce. It is harmonious and is characterised by a combination of lemongrass, galangal, garlic, kaffir lime leaves, tamarind, ginger, coriander and shrimp paste.

Thais use three different types of basil: sweet, holy (purple basil) and lemon. A wide array of chillies are used including bird's eye, jalapeno, bell and dried chillies.

The different types of rice used can be a little bewildering as you travel around the markets, where you will find stalls full of plastic bowls containing all varieties, grades and colours. The top rice is called fragrant Jasmine rice due to the fine aroma it gives when cooked.

Thai food can be hot and is noted for its fieriness, which is why rice is nearly always served, to help cool the mouth.

Thai food, like other cuisines, has regional differences and variations, but its cuisine used to have two variations: one principally for the court or

royal cuisine, and the other, the common cuisine eaten by the non-royals. Today this has all but disappeared and the ingredients and dishes have blended together. The high-class hotels do provide more decorative dishes, but they are essentially the same as those on the street, with some differences and variations in presentation.

Thailand has a very long coastline and also has the world's largest catch of fish. It not only provides its gourmets and diners with some of the freshest and most exotic fish, crabs, prawns, lobsters and shellfish available, it also has a large export industry.

When you stroll around the markets in Thailand you will see incredible displays of fish and luscious fruits like mangosteens, durian and lychees. The scent of basil, ginger and kaffir lime leaves fills the air, stimulating the cook's senses into action.

You can get food almost anywhere and at any time of day. When eating at food stalls, markets and local restaurants, it is best to remember that the social aspect of eating in Thailand is considered an occasion. The dishes served to you will normally be for two people as eating alone is considered very unusual, but as a foreigner (farang) it may be better to ask for small portions. Farang refers to Caucasians or white pepole, or things that are associated with them, such as Western food 'ahan farang'. It is thought that the word is derived from the way the Thais pronounce the French word 'français'.

The food is served and presented family style with rice, chicken (meat), fish and a soup dish in the centre of the table.

You will normally be given the option to eat with a fork and spoon as well as chopsticks. You would use the fork to move the rice onto the spoon; it is considered bad manners to place the fork in one's mouth. The chopsticks would normally be used for noodles and a separate ceramic soup spoon is used for soups. You will see Thais eating with their fingers. This is mainly for sticky rice desserts, were the rice is rolled into a ball with the right hand and eaten with any accompanying food.

Desserts or 'kanom' are not as popular when compared to Western cuisines, yet it is quite interesting to know where they came from. Constantine Phaulkon was the first minister to King Narai in the seventeenth century. The minister was killed during the revolution in 1688. Phra Petracha then became ruler of Siam. Constantine's wife, Marie, survived the revolution and was granted her freedom. She was of mixed race – Japanese, Bengali and Portuguese. As part of her duties she took on education and cooking in the palace. She used Japanese recipes that the Portuguese had taken to Japan to make cakes and sweets. This entailed the use of eggs in the recipes, never heard of before in Siam. These desserts became a favourite at the palace. Thus, Marie Phaulkon became one of the biggest influences on Siamese cookery.

One of the main things to remember if you are lucky enough to be invited to dine with Thais is always to place a portion of rice on your

plate first, then a spoonful of what you fancy around the rice. Never mix the meat and fish dishes together as this is one of the worst ways in which to insult your host. Always eat a spoonful of rice first, as in most places in Asia it is the most important part of the meal. It is considered polite to leave a little food on your plate to show your host that they have been generous in their hospitality. A traditional meal normally has a soup, a stewed dish, curry, and a salad, which are selected for variety and balance of flavours and textures.

There can be a confusing amount of condiments and dipping sauces accompanying the dishes as well as the normal fish sauce, ground nuts, soy sauce, puréed red pepper and fish sauce with sliced chillies, shallots and garlic.

It is normal when eating out in everyday restaurants that a single bill will be presented to the table. You will also be served by the younger members of the family that own the restaurant. As far as beverages are concerned, fruit juices and the range of teas are excellent, with Chinese tea being very popular. It is best remembered that when you ask for tea and coffee, you will normally receive tinned evaporated milk except in high-class hotels. Alcoholic drinks are freely available but are very expensive.

Equipment

The equipment used in most Thai kitchens (like most in Asia) is limited to a few essential items. One of the fundamentals of Thai cookery is the making of pastes that are the foundation to many recipes, and the use of a pestle and mortar are essential to this. There are two types. One is made from granite and is used for making pastes for curry and chillies (the pastes can be brought fresh in Thailand from the markets). The other is wooden and used for finer and gentler mixtures that may be used in salads. A coffee grinder is often used for grinding spices.

Bamboo steamers, pots and pans and round heavy wooden chopping boards, often made of tamarind wood, are used. A cleaver is used for all kinds of chopping, and a sharp carving knife is used for fruit carving.

However, the most important piece of equipment is the wok. In Thailand you will see many types made from brass and aluminium, but the favoured one is made from iron. The good thing about the wok is that it distributes the heat evenly and can be used for many methods of cooking, stir-frying, deep-frying, shallow frying, steaming, stewing, boiling and poaching.

It is best to prove the wok first by rubbing on a little oil and heating it over a flame until it is red hot so that it becomes black on the outside and non-stick on the inside. Clay pots (remember to soak in water first to prevent cracking), draining baskets, ladles and wire spiders are required for noodles, rice and for removing deep-fried foods from hot oil.

CENTRAL THAILAND

Central Thailand covers Kaeng Krachan National Park, Phetburi Provence in the west to Nakhon Ratchasima in the north, to the island of Ko Samet in the east and as far south as the island of Phuket.

Bangkok, or as the Thais call it 'Krungthep' meaning the city of angels, was established in 1782 when King Rama I made it the capital of Siam. The original Thai name for the city is the longest name in the world, containing 169 letters, and is over 200 years old. This is recorded in the *Guinness Book of Records*.

The city has developed into an over-populated, modern metropolis, with skyscrapers, luxurious hotels, restaurants, shopping centres, clubs and bars. Underneath this, however, you can glimpse the old Bangkok with its older architecture, arts, religious buildings and temples such as the Grand Palace and Wat Phra Kaeo with the incredible emerald Buddha, the old royal palace of Vimanmek mansion, which is the oldest and biggest teak building in the world, and the Wat Chetuphon built in the early sixteenth century which has 95 pagodas. The list of attractions in Bangkok is endless.

The over-population can have its side-effects; the heat, dust, traffic and noise can be hard to bear for some. A common sight is the famous Bangkok tuk-tuk or rickshaw from the eighteenth century that used to be drawn by humans. This gave way to the Japanese two-stroke powered engine, just after the Second World War. It is a cheaper and quicker way to get around than a normal taxi, although much scarier. Bangkok, translated, means place of the wild plum.

The city has a collection of canals and tributaries, which are used by fleets of craft from canoes and paddle boats to motor boats and rice barges. Today these are the quickest way to transport goods and people around the city, instead of the gridlocked roads.

Across the Chao Phraya River is the previous capital Thonburi, which is now the older part of the city.

A trip around the canals provides an interesting look into the past as there are large communities that live on them. As you travel along the canals and water streets you can see the residents swimming, playing, fishing, washing, swimming with their goods in plastic bags from one side of the canal to the other and, unfortunately, using the canals as their toilet and dust bin, but this is urban river life, Bangkok style.

Along the canals of the old city there are many temples or wats, which make it a very impressive sight.

The best part of life on the canals are the floating water markets. People with wide straw hats paddle wooden canoes loaded with all sorts of food for sale. You can even get hot food in some markets if you feel peckish. A number have sprung up just for the tourist, selling all sorts of trinkets and souvenirs.

The Wat Sai market is typical of this. The Bang Khu Wiang floating market in Thonburi is small and opens from around 6 am to 8 am, so you have to be early to see the bartering and selling of fruit, vegetables and many other items.

The best market and possibly the most photographed is south-west of Bangkok at Khlong Damnoen Saduak in the Ratchaburi Province, but again it is best to go as early as possible before the tours arrive.

In the central and southern parts of Thailand the curry dishes tend to contain more herbs and coconut milk to cool and soften the fieriness of the dishes.

Chinatown is one of the oldest parts of the city, located to the south-east of Bangkok. The Chinese communities were relocated 200 years ago by royal command so that the new city of Bangkok could be built on their land. Chinatown is a maze of narrow streets and there is a great assault on one's senses with the hustle and bustle of the crowds and the smells from the food stalls. Noodle sellers are everywhere, with people using their chopsticks to tuck into the bowl. Colourful sights abound from the vegetable and fruit food stalls, clothing and fabric stalls, to the sounds of the sellers trying to entice the public into bartering for a good deal or sale. You can buy almost anything you can think of from a snack of noodles to antiques in the Thieves Market. The hawker stalls selling noodles in Bangkok are everywhere, noodles are all they sell. They will normally have two or three different types of noodles (your choice) cooked in stock and served with beans, sugar, chillies, chicken or pork and fish sauce. The steaming bowls will be garnished with deep-fried anchovies, crushed peanuts and a ladle of stock.

During the ninth lunar month, which can be either September or October, the Thai-Chinese celebrate with a vegetarian festival that is centered around China town's largest temple, Wat Mangkon Kamalawat. The food is the best vegetarian food you can get in Asia.

The weekend market in Chatuchak on the Phahonyothin Road is very popluar and draws thousands of people. Again you can buy anything from a pet to kitchen utensils. You can visit the flower market, where you can buy wild orchids, roses and violets in abundance. Then there are stalls and dealers that will sell you all manner and grades of teas.

Food

It is very difficult to draw out recipes that come from Bangkok, because there is so much choice in this cosmopolitan city. Wherever you are in

the city you are not far from a food vendor or restaurant. Whether you want Japanese, Chinese, Indonesian, German, Muslim, vegetarian or Western, it is all here. In the famous Siam Square in Bangkok there are many restaurants and stalls selling food (but since my last visit there seem to be fewer hawkers in residence). One of the popular restaurant dishes of the area is Bon bon chicken noodles or Shanghai chicken noodles made with bean sheets and bean paste.

While Chinatown is the best place to get Chinese food, a little further along is Bangrak and Pahurat (districts) where you will see stalls and vendors selling turmeric, coriander, ginger and curry spices. This is the best place to get Indian food and not just the everyday Indian food that we are used to in the West. In addition, you can get southern Indian, northern Mongolian, and Indian food, and also some of the best Muslim cuisine.

The Bangkok night markets are still some of the best places to get Thai food but there are a number of restaurants that deal in the royal cuisine and these are centered around Silom Road, Convent and Soi Sala Daeng Roads. They are expensive, but worth the experience. Remember in Thailand the best food is not the prerogative of the rich, and you can eat just as well in the streets and markets.

The provinces

Seventy-six kilometres north of Bangkok is the UNESCO World Heritage Site of Ayutthaya, which was the Royal Siamese Capital from 1350–1776, until the Burmese invaded and destroyed the city. Previous to this it was a Khmer town and that influence can be seen in some of the architecture. Ayutthaya was a centre for trade with the English, Dutch and French in the West and the Japanese and Chinese in the East. It must have been an incredible sight to see the city in its full glory.

The new city is located where the province's three rivers, Chao Phraya, Lopburi and Pa Sak, meet. The city is also encircled by a canal. Among the sights you can find numerous stalls selling noodles and Thai fish cakes (Tod ma), which bear no resemblance to the bland stodgy types sold in the UK. They can be pungent, fiery and have a wonderful flavour. The cakes normally have garlic, red chillies, lemongrass, fish sauce, green beans, ginger and coriander as the main ingredients and they use any cheap fish available. The Tod ma fish cakes are often served with a sweet and sour cucumber relish, sprinkled with crushed peanuts. Afterwards you might try the crispy rice cakes!

Around the provinces in Central Thailand the food has many specialities and variations, but at the table there will be an abundance of rice in one form or another, such as plain boiled rice or rice noodles.

In Nakhon Pathom Province, which is approximately 60 kilometres to the west of Bangkok, is a good fresh fruit market, where you can buy some of the most inexpensive and tasty Khâo lāam (sticky rice, pressed and cooked in a section of bamboo cane).

Kanchanaburi in the Kanchanaburi Province is situated along the old invasion and smuggling route, once used by the Burmese and made famous in the Second World War by the Japanese army's inhumane treatment of the Allied prisoners. They were used to build the death railway, including the bridge over the River Kwai. Here a large number of food stalls, restaurants and hotels have established themselves. The food stalls sell Sôm-tam (spicy green papaya salad) and Khâo lãam (sticky rice).

In Chonburi Province, Pattaya has some of the best seafood restaurants in Thailand, although they are expensive compared to other parts of the country because of tourist patronage.

Pattaya was once a small fishing village and in the late 1950s it began to grow as a resort. This has brought the wrong type of tourist to Pattaya over the years, but there are some excellent beaches in and around the area and a good number of islands off the coast providing some of the best diving available. Pattaya also has around 12 golf courses.

Probably the two best restaurants in town are the King Seafood Restaurant and the Ruen Thai Restaurant, which are in the southern area of Pattaya. There are a number of restaurants that offer an unusual service to the customers. Outside, at the front of the restaurant keeping cool and fresh on ice are fresh fish, shellfish, vegetables, etc. You are given a basket to choose your own ingredients, and then you take the food inside to the chef who cooks it to your individual requirements. You are charged for the ingredients that you use.

Pattaya, like many towns in Thailand, has an interesting array of restaurants ranging from Muslim, Arabic, Pakistani and Indian to Western. Some bars offer food, beer and kick boxing, discos and other entertainment. Some of the best food can be found in vegetarian restaurants and should not to be overlooked.

Further down the coast near the Cambodian border is the province of Chanthaburi (300 kilometres or so from Bangkok). Chanthaburi is famous for its gemstones, hot peppers and excellent quality of fruits like durian, rambutan and mangos. The town is centred on the Chanthaburi River from where it takes its name. From the late 1800s up until 1975 it saw a continual influx of Vietnamese refugees fleeing religious and political persecution. This has resulted in Vietnamese food, like Chanthaburi noodles and fried noodles with crab, becoming a common sight on stalls and in restaurants around the town.

A little further on towards the Cambodian border is the province of Trat, which was built on wealth created by the gem market. Trat is famous for its Ko Chang National Marine Park. The province has numerous islands off its coast, together with some good beaches. There are many day and night markets around Trat, being close to the border, and that brings the inevitable plethora of food stalls and restaurants. Here the prices are much cheaper with a good supply of fish and seafood owing to its proximity to fishing villages and the coastline. You can see and try local

delicacies, such as deep-fried insects, lizard, snake and local beverages that claim to cure everything, or you can just have Khâo tôm (soup with rice).

If you travel south-east from Bangkok towards Malaysia to the Prachuap Khiri Khan Province you will come to Hua Hin, made famous in 1928 when King Rama VII decided to build a summer palace there. It has a much slower pace of life than Bangkok and is where a large number of Thais take their holiday. There are many places to see and eat fresh fish and seafood. The area around the pier has numerous restaurants and the Chatchai and Chomsin night markets are great places to try Tôm yum goong (spicy shrimp soup) or Nêung plaa râat phrik (steamed fish with chillies and garlic).

Tom Yum Goong

Hot and Sour Shrimp Soup

Method

1. Mix the tamarind pulp with 200ml of water, then strain off the liquid and reserve. Discard the pulp.

2. Peel the prawns and remove the central vein, leaving the tips of the tails intact (keep shells).

3. Remove and discard the stalks of the chillies and then chop up the fresh chillies and chilli powder, place in a pestle and mortar or food processor and grind to a smooth paste. You may need to add a little water. Wash and chop the coriander leaves.

4. Trim the mushrooms and rinse under cold water, drain and cut in half. Remove the root of the lemongrass and finely dice.

5. Wash and clean the prawn shells and then fry them off in the oil until they have changed to a deep orange colour, drain off any excess oil.

6. Bring the water to the boil and add the lemongrass, chilli paste and the prawn shells and cook for 10–15 minutes, then strain the stock and transfer into a clean pot.

7. Add the kaffir limes, mushrooms, prawns, tamarind water, fish sauce, sugar and half of the coriander to the stock, bring to a simmer for 2–3 minutes and serve.

Measurements	Ingredients
20g	Tamarind pulp
500g	Raw prawns (medium size)
2	Fresh red chillies (deseeded)
5g	Chilli powder
4–5 large sprigs	Coriander (chopped)
125g	Straw mushrooms
1 stalk	Lemongrass
20ml	Palm oil
1,500ml	Water
2	Kaffir limes
40ml	Fish sauce
5g	Palm sugar
Garnish	Ingredients
2	Kaffir lime leaves (cut into julienne)
4	Whole bird's eye chillies

8. Garnish with the remaining chopped coriander, julienne of kaffir lime leaves and whole chillies.

Chef's Notes

- If you cannot obtain fresh straw mushrooms, you can always buy the tinned variety from Chinese stores.

- If you find this soup a little fiery, you can omit the chilli powder.

- There are numerous variations on this dish and it even changes slightly from stall to stall. Some recipes call for the Thai sauce called Tom Yam. If you would like to give this recipe a little more flavour and bite, add 15g at stage 6.

- You can add or use crab, scallops or mussels in this dish.

Tom Yam Sauce

Nam Prik Pow

1. Fry 25g garlic purée and 30g chopped shallots in 30ml vegetable oil until golden brown then remove. Fry 25g chopped deseeded chillies until dark.

2. Place all in a food processor with 10g dried prawns, and blend to a smooth paste. Return the paste to the wok and continue to cook over a low heat, stirring the paste. Add 5–10ml fish sauce, 5g sugar and cook until it becomes thick, dark and a little oily.

Chef's Notes

- You can add more chillies or prawns if you wish. Every housewife, chef and restaurant has their own recipe or version of a chilli sauce/jam.

Tod Man

Fish Cakes

Method

1. Top and tail the green beans and finely slice. Remove and discard the stalk from the lime leaves and very finely shred the leaves.

2. Peel and remove the stalk from the spring onions and finely slice.

3. Mince the fish and then add the curry paste, beaten egg, kaffir lime leaves, green beans, fish sauce, spring onions and dust with half of the flour. Mix thoroughly together and season with a little salt.

Measurements	Ingredients
100g	Fresh green beans
4	Kaffir lime leaves
4	Spring onions
500g	White fish fillets
125g	Red curry paste
1	Egg (beaten)
15ml	Fish sauce

continued over →

4. Shape the mixture into 50g balls, then press them into 5cm-round circles. Dust them in the remaining flour and then fry in a suitable frying pan over a medium heat until each side is golden brown.

5. Drain on kitchen towel and serve with cucumber salad or 250ml dipping sauce.

...continued

Measurements	Ingredients
20g	Cornflour or rice flour
250ml	Vegetable oil
	Salt

Cucumber salad

Method

1. Wash and cut the cucumber into dice or quarters. Slice the red chillies and shallots.

2. Bring the water to the boil and add the sugar, vinegar and a little salt and mix well.

3. Place the ingredients into a bowl together in sections and pour over the liquid.

Chef's Notes

Measurements	Ingredients
200g	Cucumber
2	Red chillies
4	Shallots (peeled)
150ml	Water
20g	Palm sugar
15–20ml	Rice wine vinegar
	Salt

• The Thais normally use any firm white fish, such as king fish or cotton fish.

• Some recipes have no spring onions or just have puréed red chillies instead of the red curry paste. This is a good traditional recipe from Ayutthaya province.

Nam Prik Gaenh Phed

Red Curry Paste

Method

1. Place the dried chillies into a little warm water. Remove the stalks and seeds from all the chillies and cut into dice.

2. Peel the lime and cut the peel into fine dice.

3. Remove the root and cut the lemongrass into 5–6cm lengths and chop up. Peel and cut the shallots into dice.

4. Dry roast the coriander and cumin seeds until lightly toasted.

Measurements	Ingredients
10	Dried chillies
1	Lime
3 stalks	Lemongrass
80g	Shallots
10g	Coriander seeds
2.5g	Cumin seeds
12	Red chillies

continued over →

5. Place all the ingredients into a pestle and mortar or a food processor and blend into a smooth paste.

6. Cover and keep in the fridge, with tight-fitting lid.

Chef's Notes

- Placed in a oiled container with a tight-fitting lid, and covered with a little oil, this paste will keep for 6 weeks in a fridge.

- It will also freeze down well and can be kept for 3–6 months.

...continued

Measurements	Ingredients
3cm	Galangal
20g	Garlic purée
20g	Shrimp paste (kapi, belacan)

Kway Tiew Shanghai

Shanghai Bon Bon Chicken Noodles

Measurements	Ingredients
150g	Coriander (stalks, root and leaves)
5g	Ground white pepper
8 cloves	Garlic (peeled)
5g	Sugar
3cm	Ginger (peeled)
4	Chicken breasts
60ml	Vegetable oil
20g	Brown bean paste
5–10g	Chilli powder
20ml	Thick soy sauce
10ml	Fish sauce
20ml	Worcester sauce
5ml	Sesame oil
150ml	Water
8	Bean thread sheets
	Salt
Garnish	Ingredients
2	Red chillies (deseeded and sliced)

Method

1. Place the coriander, white pepper, garlic and sugar in a pestle and mortar or food processor and blend to a smooth paste. For the food processor you may need a little water.

2. Chop the ginger into a purée.

3. Cut the chicken into fine strips 3–4cm in length, then cook in a wok or suitable pan in a little oil. Add some water and cook out for 5–8 minutes, then drain. Keep covered and hot.

continued over →

4. Add the remaining oil to the clean wok and fry off the bean paste, coriander paste, chilli powder and ginger purée together until it becomes fragrant.

...continued	
4 sprigs	Coriander
2-3	Spring onion (sliced)

5. Stir in the soy, fish sauce and Worcester sauce and continue to cook and stir for 4–5 minutes. Then add the sesame oil and check the seasoning.

6. Bring the water to the boil. Cut the bean sheets into 3—4cm lengths and add to the water. Stir the sheets. When cooked, drain and keep hot.

7. Place the bean sheets onto plates with the chicken on top and bean sauce in the middle. Garnish with the sliced chillies, spring onions and coriander sprigs.

Chef's Notes

- Bean thread sheets are made from mung beans and are clear in colour. Brown bean paste can be purchased from most supermarkets or Chinese stores.

- I have eaten numerous versions of this in Bangkok's Siam Square, but I have not seen it elsewhere. You can try yellow noodles with this recipe and steamed chicken if you wish.

Gai Tom Ka

Chicken, Coconut and Galangal Soup

Measurements	Ingredients
3cm	Galangal (peeled)
1 stalk	Lemongrass
10g	Coriander leaves
2	Red chillies
150g	Chicken breast
500ml	Chicken stock
60ml	Fish sauce
2	Kaffir lime leaves
5g	Palm sugar
40ml	Lemon juice
250ml	Coconut milk (thick or thin)

Method

1. Finely dice the galangal, top and tail the lemongrass, remove and discard the root and finely dice it. Wash, dry and roughly chop the coriander. Deseed the chillies and chop them into a purée.

2. Trim the chicken breast and remove any fat. Cut into fine slices.

3. Bring the stock to the boil with the fish sauce, galangal, palm sugar, kaffir lime leaves, lemongrass, and lemon juice. Stir and skim any debris from the surface.

4. Add the chicken and coconut milk and simmer for 4–5 minutes, until the meat is cooked.

5. Add the chillies and half the coriander, then cook for 1–2 minutes.

6. Check the seasoning and serve with the remaining coriander.

Chef's Notes

- Adding the chilli so late will not allow the heat and fieriness of it to penetrate the soup. I often serve this soup if entertaining at home; it is excellent either in summer or winter.

Normai Pad Kai

Pork and Bamboo Shoots

Method

1. Remove any excess fat and sinew from the pork and cut into thin slices. Cut the garlic into a fine dice and slice the bamboo shoots into thin slices. Cut the straw mushrooms into quarters.

2. Peel the spring onions then wash and thinly slice them.

3. Break the eggs into a bowl and whisk them up and add a little seasoning and sugar.

4. Put the oil into a very hot pan and fry the garlic golden brown, then add the ginger and pork.

5. When the pork is almost cooked add the egg and stir-fry, then add half the spring onions, breaking the egg up. Then add the bamboo shoots, mushrooms, fish sauce and soy sauce.

6. Blanch the banana leaf in boiling water and cool in cold running water. From it cut out four round plate mats and divide the pork evenly and garnish with the remaining spring onions.

7. Check seasoning and serve with either rice or noodles.

Measurements	Ingredients
350g	Pork loin (boneless)
2 cloves	Garlic (peeled)
100g	Bamboo shoots (tinned acceptable)
100g	Straw mushrooms
6	Spring onions
2	Eggs
5g	Palm sugar
60ml	Vegetable oil
2cm	Ginger (peeled and chopped)
30ml	Fish sauce
50ml	Soy sauce (light)
1	Banana leaf
500g	Cooked rice or noodles
	Salt and ground white pepper

Chef's Notes

- You can replace the pork with chicken if you wish, it works just as well. Be careful how much salt you add, because the fish sauce is salty.

Kai Lahd Nah Khài Mee

Chicken, Bamboo Shoots with Egg Noodles

Method

1. Remove any excess fat and sinew from the chicken and cut into thin slices. Cut the bamboo shoots into thin slices. Cut the straw mushrooms into quarters.

2. Peel the spring onions then wash and thinly slice them.

3. Bring the water to the boil with a little salt and a dash of oil, blanch the noodles then refresh them under cold running water and drain.

4. Pour half the vegetable oil into a suitable wok and fry half the garlic and all the chicken until the chicken is cooked, then add the bamboo shoots, spring onions, mushrooms, fish sauce, soy sauces, sugar and seasoning. Cook for 2–3 minutes.

5. Add the stock and continue to cook for 5 minutes, and then thicken with a little cornflour and water solution. Add a little at a time, until the right consistency is achieved. Keep hot.

6. Place the remaining half of the oil in a pan or wok over a medium heat and then add the other half of the garlic and fry until golden brown. Then add the drained noodles, stir fry for 2–3 minutes then season with the sesame oil.

7. Place noodles on the plate, then add the chicken and bamboo shoots on top. Garnish with spring onions, lime, cucumber and coriander and serve.

Measurements	Ingredients
4	Chicken breasts
80g	Bamboo shoots (tinned acceptable)
60g	Straw mushrooms
8	Spring onions
500ml	Water
250g	Egg noodles (fine)
60ml	Vegetable oil
10g	Garlic purée
20ml	Fish sauce
30ml	Light soy sauce
30ml	Dark soy sauce
5g	Palm sugar
150ml	Chicken stock
20g	Cornflour
10ml	Sesame oil
Garnish	Ingredients
4	Spring onions (sliced)
1	Lime (sliced)
40g	Cucumber (sliced)
4 sprigs	Coriander

Chef's Notes

• The art to this dish is to make sure you drain off the noodles well and keep the wok moving to avoid them sticking to the pan. Don't get the pan too hot as they stick the moment you place them in.

• The egg noodles are often called Ba mee kūay tīaw. This dish is also popular in Bangkok.

Pad Thai

Thai Fried Noodles

Method

1. Deseed the chillies and very finely grind to a smooth paste. Peel and chop the spring onions. Soak the noodles in some warm water for 10–15 minutes, then drain.

2. Remove the central vein and shell the prawns, leaving the tail intact. Chop the prawns into small pieces. Beat the eggs in a suitable bowl. Take 25g of the peanuts and roughly chop.

3. Pour the oil into the pan and fry off the garlic and the chillies, then add half the chopped peanuts and all the eggs and stir the mixture well, ensuring the egg is well broken up.

4. Add the lime juice, fish sauce, sugar, and the fresh prawns and cook out and stir, until the prawns have changed to a pink colour.

5. Add the bean sprouts, half the coriander and all the noodles to the wok and stir fry for 3–4 minutes.

6. Serve garnished with the dried shrimps, peanuts, coriander and slices of lime.

Measurements	Ingredients
4	Red chillies
4	Spring onions
250g	2mm Flat rice noodles
16	Prawns (medium)
2	Eggs (medium)
50g	Dry roasted peanuts
30ml	Vegetable oil
10g	Garlic purée
30ml	Lime juice
30ml	Fish sauce
5g	Caster sugar
40g	Bean sprouts
10g	Coriander (chopped)
40g	Dried shrimps
1	Lime (sliced)

Chef's Notes

- This dish is sometimes considered the national dish of Thailand as it can be found everywhere from high-class restaurants to the market stalls. It can come in many variations: using fresh prawns and cooked minced pork combined; tofu; and additions of vegetables such as bok choy. If you wish to have minced pork in this dish, then add 150–200g and fry it off at stage 3.

Mūu Náam-man Hāwy Sen Yai

Pork Oyster Sauce with River Rice Noodles

Measurements	Ingredients
250g	Dried river noodles (Sen Yai) (see Chef's Notes)
300g	Tomatoes
6	Spring onions
150g	Onions (peeled)
2	Red chillies (deseeded)
60ml	Corn oil
300g	Minced pork
15g	Caster sugar
50ml	Oyster sauce
Garnish	Ingredients
	Curly endive lettuce

Method

1. Blanch the noodles lightly in hot water for 4–5 minutes until cooked and cool under running water, then drain.

2. Blanch, refresh, skin and deseed the tomatoes and then cut the flesh into concasse (small dice). Discard the rest of the tomato.

3. Peel and slice the spring onions and onions. Finely dice the chillies. Wash the lettuce.

4. Heat the oil in a suitable wok over a medium heat and fry the onions, garlic and the chillies until limp, then add the pork and stir fry until all white.

5. Add the sugar, concasse, half the spring onions and cook for 2 minutes, then add the noodles and oyster sauce and stir-fry for 2–3 minutes, making sure the noodles are thoroughly mixed, then serve.

6. Garnish with the remaining spring onions and top with the lettuce.

Chef's Notes

- River rice noodles are large broad flat noodles and if fresh can be sticky. They can be purchased dried from Chinese or Asian stores. You will require 400g fresh.

- This dish can also be served with prawns or chicken, but pork is the better option.

- This dish is from Pattaya. I was served from a little beach stall by two sisters and their elderly mother whose skill with the wok was incredible. All three would cook all day long without a break.

Khâo Mee Leang

Chicken and Yellow Noodles

Measurements	Ingredients
4	Chicken breasts
200g	Chinese cabbage
80g	Onion (peeled)
250g	Yellow noodles
50ml	Corn oil
10g	Palm sugar
60ml	Chicken stock
30ml	Oyster sauce
30ml	Soy sauce
10ml	Thick (sweet) soy sauce
10ml	Light soy sauce
10g	Cornflour

Method

1. Remove any skin, fat or sinew from the chicken and cut into 2cm dice. Wash and shred the cabbage and slice the onion.

2. Blanch the noodles lightly in hot water then cool under running water and drain.

3. Heat the oil in a suitable wok over a medium heat and fry the onions until limp, then add the chicken and stir-fry for 3–4 minutes.

4. Add the cabbage and continue to stir-fry for 4–5 minutes, then add the sugar, stock, oyster sauce and soy sauce and continue to cook for 2–3 minutes.

5. Add the noodles, sprinkle cornflour over the top, stir and cook for a further 2–3 minutes then serve.

Chef's Notes

- Chinese cabbage is also known as Tientsin cabbage or celery cabbage. You could replace it with bok choy or choy sam.

- This dish is from the Chatchai night market in Hau Hin and you can replace the chicken with diced fish, but add it at stage 5 to avoid the fish breaking up.

NORTHERN THAILAND

What is now northern Thailand is where the first true Thai kingdoms of Chiang Mai, Chiang Saen, Lanna, Nan and Sukhothai were founded. Chiang Mai is the northern capital of Thailand, and is 700 kilometres from Bangkok. The city was founded by King Mengrai on 14 April 1296. The king is thought to have started the building of the city walls and ramparts, some of which can be seen to this day. In 1556 the Burmese took control of the city for 200 years. 1775 saw the city recaptured by King Taskin and it has remained under Thai control ever since. The influence of the Burmese can be seen in the architecture of northern Thailand.

The rebuilding of the inner walls of the city was carried out by Kavila (appointed Lord of Lampang) in 1800. Chiang Mai became a centre for trade. When the railway came north from Bangkok around 1921, its silver trade, pottery, woodwork and weaving expanded. Chiang Mai's principal trade is now tourism; many traditional spiritual practices can be seen and participated in, such as yoga, traditional Thai massage, meditation and t'ai chi. Other activities include language classes, kickboxing and Thai cookery.

The north is deeply rooted in its culture, traditions and architecture, with its many temples and palaces still well preserved. The northern people call themselves 'khon meuang' (people of principalities). The northern provinces are home to approximately nine hill tribes who have their own cultures and traditions. The hill tribes are radically different to the low-land Thais and are a law unto themselves. Many women and children come down to Chiang Mai every evening to sell their trinkets to the locals and tourists. The hill tribes are called the Karen, Hmong, Mien, Akha, Lahu, Lisu, Lawa, Khamu and the Mlabri and have a combined population of around 935,000.

The northern provinces are dominated by the ancient principal city of Chiang Mai. Nestling in a valley 310 metres above sea level, it is the largest province, surrounded by mountains, including the highest peak in Thailand, Mount Doi Inthanon, which stands at 2,565 metres.

Beyond these high northern peaks the Thai, Burmese and Laos borders meet. It is also where the illicit opium trade still exists today and where most of the world's opium poppies are grown. The area is referred to as the Golden Triangle.

The climate of the north is cooler, averaging 25°C. This climate helps to produce some of the best fruit, vegetables and flowers in Thailand.

Unlike the modernisation and concrete of Bangkok, Chiang Mai has an abundance of rich green fields. Often a morning mist can be seen and the pace of life is much slower. Honking of horns, traffic problems or pollution seem very distant. The people are polite and helpful.

Chiang Mai is a spiritual place for pilgrims from all over the world; many visit the great temple of Wat Phra That Doi Suthep, which was built in the fourteenth century and rises 1,676 metres. There are 121 temples (wats) and religious places of worship within its city limits and over 300 around its province.

Many of the temples are decorated with great serpents (naga), which are said to have been invented in northern Thailand and to this day they are venerated by the people.

The city is surrounded by a neat square moat and parts of the old city walls, the best of which can be seen on the Moon Meuang Road (where the Chiang Mai cookery school is located) opposite Tha Phae Gate.

The population of Chiang Mai is estimated at one and a half million. Chiang Mai is located on the banks of the River Mae Ping.

If you visit, you will see many elaborately decorated houses and buildings. In many gardens you will also see little houses, perched on poles, called *san phra poom*. This is where you pay your respects to the spirits once or twice a year, or more in the case of something bad or drastic happening. You will see offerings of fruit and vegetables and burning incense sticks, and hear prayers to the spirits to come and enjoy their gifts.

The way to get around the cities of northern Thailand is by samlor (meaning three wheels); the motorised versions are commonly called tuk tuk and the non-motorised, three-wheel bicycle is commonly referred to as a samlor.

Northern Thailand's cuisine is different to other regions, with a heavy influence of chillies, sticky rice, red and green curries and featuring dishes such as Nam prik, Ba yon sausage and the marinated grilled chicken and pork dishes. The noodle dishes are quite superb in Chiang Mai and the variety and variations are amazing.

Northern Thailand's cuisine is rich, tasty and has many local and regional specialities, which cannot be said of other regions. Sticky rice in and around Chiang Mai is a very popular dish in various forms. The glutinous rice is mainly cultivated around Chiang Mai and has little value outside northern Thailand compared with the south where rice has more export value.

Chiang Mai sausage (Ba yon) was originally made by a pork butcher in the time before refrigeration came to Thailand. Raw meat had to be eaten the day it was slaughtered. This meant that if the butcher had a very quiet day he had to throw away his goods. So he experimented and came up with a recipe of pork, garlic, salt, chillies and sticky rice that was mixed together and then pressed and allowed to ferment and cure (Thai chefs describe this process as 'cooking') for three days. It is then sliced and wrapped in a banana leaf and served. It has become a famous Chiang Mai dish served with shallots, ginger, peanuts, spring onions and chillies. These days it is more often cooked on a griddle, for the tourist trade.

In Thailand, Chiang Mai is probably the best city in which to eat as it offers a great variety of quality food in its restaurants. There are some excellent vegetarian, Indian, Arabic and Muslim restaurants in downtown Chiang Mai. In one of its markets, the Anusarn market, you will find some excellent restaurants, stalls and hawkers selling all sorts of dishes and specialities from frogs legs with holy basil, to satay, and Chiang Mai noodles, all at very good prices. Uptown, around the area of Moon Muang Road is the Somphet market where you can eat or take away curries and fish cakes.

Along Moon Muang Road is the Chiang Mai cookery school, which offers budding chefs the chance to learn how to cook some modern Thai dishes. The school operates a very good Thai restaurant around the corner called The Wok. The area also offers trekking and jungle tours. Opposite the night bazaar off Chang Klan Road you can find the Sompet Thai cookery school office, which is run by Busara Boonmakham. Busara has an infectious passion for her native Thai food, especially the local Northern Thai dishes (see Useful Addresses, page 359) and she has a wealth of knowledge on the subject.

If you travel along the Mae Ping you can stop at a number of restaurants like the River Ping Palace, which offers good Thai food including freshwater fish dishes.

The food markets are some of the best with excellent fruit, vegetables, fish and meat. The fish and shellfish are normally sold from tanks or containers, running water is used for freshwater fish. The daytime and nightly haggling is always good-natured here and not like the unholy scrum often seen in Bangkok.

One of the most important ingredients in northern Thai cuisine is the coconut. Every part is used; the milk, oil and flesh for cooking, and the shells, which are made into ladles and spoons.

It would be easy to fill a book on the restaurants, hotels, guesthouses and stalls that offer food – you are never more than a few metres from food or drink in Chiang Mai.

The provinces

Lamphun Province is a small town surrounded by farms and rice paddies. Around a thousand years ago it was a very prosperous, sophisticated and important city. The city was established in about the ninth century by Queen Chamadevi, but it later became part of King Mengrai's kingdom of Lanna. Lamphun is reputed to be the oldest continuously inhabited town in Thailand.

In the second week in August a festival takes place to honour the gift of fruit, especially longans. Decorative floats are pulled along the streets, adorned with the brightly coloured produce.

Lampang Province along the River Wang is about 100 kilometres from Chiang Mai and was once the centre of the teak trade. Lampang is a quiet place with some magnificent teak temples and many describe the Wat Phrathaty Lampang Luang as the best temple in northern Thailand, showing the Lanna-style architecture.

Lampang is also the only place that you can see horse-drawn carriages, which are still used as public transport.

Chiang Rai Province is 180 kilometres north-east of Chiang Mai. Half of the border is separated from Laos by the Maekhong River, with mountains covering the other half separating Burma (Myanmar) from the rest of Thailand. Founded in 1262 by King Mengrai, Chiang Mai formed part of the Lanna kingdom.

The major source of income for the province is agriculture and tourism. In the mountains the illegal crop opium has been made from poppies. Attempts were made by the late Queen Mother to try to substitute the poppy crops.

Most of the visitors to the city of Chiang Rai are back packers, trekkers or tourists on day trips to the Golden Triangle or to the hill tribes.

There are many culinary influences and probably the biggest is from the Chinese. Dating from the fifteenth century, caravan routes travelling from Simao in China to Chiang Mai, Chiang Rai and Burma brought gold, musk, silks and other Chinese goods. Centuries on, Chiang Rai has many great Chinese restaurants that can be enjoyed today, offering dishes such as Yunnanese rice noodles and Khâo man rài (Hainanese chicken and rice).

Kamphaeng Phet Province, like many small towns and villages, is surrounded by a rectangular wall and is close to a river. Kamphaeng has a small night market and a number of wats (temples).

Sukhothai (meaning Dawn of Happiness) was Thailand's first capital city in the thirteenth century. It is now a UNESCO World Heritage site and is called Sukhothai Historical Site, with a second site at Si Satchanalai-Chaliang Historical Park.

The old capital was built on the east side of the River Yom with the new town on the west side. The historical site is surrounded by a moat, with three large city walls inside the moat. The array of temples is a sight to behold and well worth the trip. There are numerous restaurants, noodle and rice bars but the best place to see and eat food is the night market near the town centre.

Phitsanulok Province was the capital of Thailand for 25 years in the mid 1400s, under the Ayutthaya King Borom Trailokanat. The town is built on the banks of the River Nan.

Phitsanulok has many restaurants offering Thâwt man plaa (fish cakes) and Tôm khàa kài (chicken and coconut soup). There are also lots of stalls and shops selling noodles and rice.

Like many towns around Thailand there is a market but it is recommended that you get there early. There are several floating restaurants on the river that produce some good Thai food. It is a nice sight during the evening to see all the river boat restaurants lit up. Along the banks of the river there is a night market with a bit of a difference. A number of chefs and traders offer a side show and produce a dish called Phàk bung loi fáa, which roughly translated means 'flying in the sky morning glory'. The chef will stir-fry greens in a wok, with garlic, soy and bean sauce and then proceed to the throw the contents to a waiter who catches it on a plate and then serves it to the customer.

Tak Province is considered remote. It has often seen its border towns used as a traditional smuggling route for wood, and more recently guns, gems and drugs. The province has had its fair share of difficulties with Burmese and Karen refugees around Mae Sot.

Mae Hong Son Province is often referred to as 'The City of the Three Mists' and is around 350 kilometres from Chiang Mai. It is the crossroads for many ethnic minorities such as the Karen, Lahu, Lisu and the Pa Dong, whose women have elongated necks stretched by rings. Many of the hill tribes are concentrated into this region. Over 70 per cent of the area is covered by forest and mountains. There are many companies that offer treks to the hill tribes, where you can stay, eat and experience the way they live, but note, not all tribes are party to this. The main source of income is rice, with tourism as a growing market. Mae Hong is not a province that is known for great food.

Phrae Province is famous for two reasons, the first being that it produces the first rice crop in the area, which is started by the launching of rockets from towers in the Long and Sung men districts. The second reason is the indigo-dyed farmers' cotton shirts that are native to the province.

The capital of the province is Phrae, which has many old houses made from teak. Like other Thai cities and towns it is surrounded by a moat fed by the Yom River. The province still supports one of the few true hunter-gatherer tribes in Thailand. The Mabri are a true nomadic tribe, because when the leaves on their hut turn yellow they move on. The tribe are called the Mabri, but the Thai people call them 'phii thong leũang' which translates as 'spirits of the yellow leaves'.

Nan Province is remote and rural and relies on agriculture. However, only one-quarter of the land is cultivated; most of it is covered by monsoon forest. The main crops are sticky rice, corn, fruit, vegetables and tobacco. Nan Province shares its eastern border with the Laos province of Sainyabuli. Nan is home to many hill tribes, of which a few are very rarely seen outside the province. It has only really been possible in the last 20 years to gain access to the area owing to the 'banditry', and lack of roads in earlier times, but the banditry has disappeared and roads improved, opening up a very beautiful land with a patchwork of paddy fields and unspoilt valleys.

The climate produces some of the best chillies and oranges due to its more moderate conditions in the winter. The orange growers hold a orange festival in late December and early January which culminates in a parade.

Nan, or Nanthabuir as it was called in the 1300–1400s, was a powerful state and helped to form (along with Sukhothai) the new Thai nation in that period. The province became very prosperous during the fifteenth century, but the Burmese took over until they were forced out in 1786 and it remained independent until the province accepted governance from Bangkok in 1931.

Makheua Muang Salad

Eggplant (aubergine) Salad

Method

1. Cut the aubergine into 2cm large dice and then cook on a hot griddle, brushing regularly with hot palm oil.

2. Cut the shallots into slices. Deseed the chillies and chop into very fine dice. Peel the eggs and then slice. Wash and chop the mint

3. Peel and remove the root from the spring onions and then cut into diamonds

4. Mix the lime juice, syrup, fish sauce and the mint together.

5. Keep 8 slices of egg for garnishing and mix all the other ingredients together with the lime juice dressing.

6. Add the aubergine last and still warm.

7. Place into suitable serving bowls and garnish with sliced egg on top. Serve immediately.

Measurements	Ingredients
1	Aubergine (small)
40ml	Palm oil
40g	Shallots (peeled)
6	Bird's eye chillies
4	Eggs (hard-boiled)
6 sprigs	Mint
8	Spring onions
20ml	Lime juice
20ml	Sugar syrup
10ml	Fish sauce

Chef's Notes

• This dish is a simple recipe given to me by a local restauranteur from Chiang Mai.

• A good summer dish, but it is best to use baby aubergine as they are not as fibrous as the older and larger ones.

Nam Prik Ong

Pork and Tomato Dipping Sauce

Method

1. Wash and cut the tomatoes into half. Cut the garnish vegetables into bite-sized pieces, blanch lightly (until al dente) and refresh in cold water. Allow to drain.

2. Heat the oil in a suitable wok or pan and then add the red curry paste and cook until it becomes fragrant then add the pork and cook until it becomes dry, tipping off any excess oil. Add the palm sugar.

3. Add the stock and bring back to the boil. Add the tomatoes and the fish sauce and cook for 10 minutes.

4. Place the pork dipping sauce into a suitable bowl, and arrange the garnish vegetables around the plate. Serve.

Chef's Notes

- This is a simple traditional local family dish from the city of Chiang Mai in northern Thailand.

- When you are eating with chopsticks never leave them sticking up out of your food as it is considered very bad luck.

Measurements	Ingredients
8	Cherry tomatoes
40ml	Palm oil
150g	Red curry paste
200g	Minced pork
20g	Palm sugar
500ml	Chicken stock
100ml	Fish sauce
	Salt
Garnish	Ingredients
1	Baby aubergine
8	Okra
100g	Cucumber
4	Long beans
1	Green gourd
100g	Mustard greens

Sang Ka Yha

Mustard Greens

Method

1. Slice the shallots and garlic. Wash and shred the greens.

2. Bring 2 litres of water to the boil, add the garlic, shallots, shrimp paste and pork bones and bring to the boil for half an hour. Skim any debris from the surface.

Measurements	Ingredients
120g	Shallots (peeled)
750g	Mustard greens
2,100ml	Water
160g	Garlic (peeled)
50g	Shrimp paste

continued over →

3. Mix the tamarind with 100ml of water. Drain the water discarding the pulp.

4. You may either drain the stock off and discard the contents at this point or continue to the next stage leaving the stock with ingredients intact.

5. Add the tamarind water and the remaining garlic finely sliced and the shredded greens and continue to cook for a further 5 minutes, skimming off any debris.

6. Check the seasoning and then ladle into suitable bowls. Serve hot.

...continued

1kg	Diced pork bones (not bacon)
80g	Tamarind paste
	Salt

Chef's Notes

• The northern Thai use two types of shrimp paste, light and dark. The light is normally used for curry only. The dark is normally used for dipping sauces.

• Some recipes leave the bones in the soup and some don't, it all depends on the choice of pork bones and the cut size.

• The best pork bones to use would be pork rib bones cut into 5cm pieces.

Pla Rad Prik

Deep-fried Fish and Dipping Sauce

Method

1. Place the shrimp paste, shrimps, garlic, shallots, chillies and palm sugar in a pestle and mortar or food processor and blend until they become a smooth paste. Then mix in the lime juice and 20ml soy sauce (optional) to form a dipping sauce.

2. Lightly whisk the eggs in a suitable bowl and pour in 60ml light soy sauce.

3. Wash the fish and then gut and remove the fins and gills and dry it.

4. Wash and slice the aubergines.

5. Dip the aubergine slices in the egg batter and place in the deep-fryer (180°C) and fry until golden brown.

6. Dip the mackerel in the egg batter and place in the deep-fryer (180°C) and fry until golden brown.

7. Pour the sauce into a serving bowl and then place the bowl on a plate.

8. Place the mackerel on the plate next to the bowl of sauce then add the slices of aubergine and serve.

Measurements	Ingredients
50g	Shrimp paste (dark)
30g	Shrimps (peeled)
12 cloves	Garlic (small peeled)
40g	Shallots (peeled)
6	Chillies (deseeded)
50g	Palm sugar
50ml	Lime juice
20ml	Light soy sauce (optional)
2	Eggs
60ml	Light soy sauce
4	Mackerel (small)
2	Baby aubergine
2lt	Palm oil

Chef's Notes

• If you cannot obtain mackerel you can use pomfret or a small trout.

Plaa Meuk Phat Phet Tom Yam

Stir-fried Squid in Tom Yam Curry Paste

Method

1. Clean and prepare the squid by removing the sack and any slime and cut into rings.

2. Wash the basil and dry. Shred the basil and lime leaves.

3. Deseed the chillies and cut into julienne (fine strips).

4. Fry the paste in a hot wok with oil until it becomes fragrant.

Measurements	Ingredients
700g	Squid
8 sprigs	Sweet basil
4	Kaffir lime leaves
20	Red bird's eye chillies
80g	Tom yam paste

continued over →

5. Add the chillies, squid rings, basil and the lime leaves and stir-fry for 10–20 seconds

6. At this stage add the coconut cream, cook out for 1–2 minutes and then serve.

...continued

30ml	Palm oil
120ml	Coconut cream (extra thick coconut milk)

Chef's Notes

- You need the fresh coconut cream, not the block. If it is not available use 250ml thick coconut milk and boil it down to approximately 120–130ml.

- This is a rich and fiery dish from Chiang Mai.

- The fishmonger may clean out the squid if requested.

Yam Wun Sen

Spicy Vermicelli Salad

Method

1. Soak the noodles in water for 10 minutes then cut into manageable lengths. Place into boiling water for no more than a minute and then refresh under cold water and allow to drain.

2. Cut the onion and garlic into fine slices. Wash and cut the tomatoes in half then slice them. Drain and cut the mushrooms in half. Clean the snow fungus mushrooms and cut into 4–5cm pieces.

3. Peel the spring onions and cut into 2–3cm lengths. Deseed the chillies and cut into very fine julienne.

4. Place the noodles in a suitable bowl and mix in the prawns, squid, garlic, fish sauce, onions and spring onions. Mix in well.

5. Now add the tomatoes, mushrooms and half the coriander leaves.

6. Place the washed lettuce on the plate with a portion of the salad on top, sprinkle with remaining coriander and serve.

Measurements	Ingredients
100g	Glass noodles (vermicelli)
150g	Onion (peeled)
4	Tomatoes
30g	Straw mushrooms (tinned)
50g	Snow fungus mushrooms
8	Spring onions
2	Green chillies
16	Cooked prawns (shelled, ensure the central vein is removed)
150g	Cooked squid rings
5 cloves	Garlic (peeled)
50ml	Fish sauce
10g	Coriander leaves
4 large	Chinese lettuce leaves

Chef's Notes

- This is a common dish in northern Thailand and the combinations can vary using just prawns, prawns with minced pork and prawns and flaked fish.

- Do not overcook the noodles otherwise they will turn to a sticky glue. The glass noodles are made from mung beans and are used for soups, salads and spring rolls. If they are used in soups they are not normally blanched in the boiling water, they are usually soaked and cooked in the serving bowl just before the soup is served to the customer.

Yam Poon La Mai Ruam

Spicy Fruit Salad   *10 covers*

Measurements	Ingredients
1	Baby mango (unripe)
100g	Pineapple
1	Rose apple
1	Guava
100g	Cherry tomatoes
220g	Green grapes
50g	Sesame seeds
100g	Peanuts
100ml	Fish sauce
5g	Ground coriander
100g	Palm sugar
100g	Fried garlic (sliced)
100g	Fried shallots (sliced)
4	Bird's eye chilli (green, sliced)
10 sprigs	Chervil
	Salt

Method

1. Peel the mango, pineapple, apple and guava and cut into bite-sized pieces.

2. Wash the cherry tomatoes and grapes and cut in half. Remove the pips from the grapes.

3. Toast the sesame seeds and peanuts.

4. Mix the fish sauce, coriander and the sugar together to form a syrup.

5. Place all the ingredients into a suitable mixing bowl and gently fold together with the sugar and fish sauce mixture.

6. Decorate with picked chervil.

Chef's Notes

- This is a very unusual fruit salad, which is served at the end of a meal. It is an acquired taste, with fish sauce, chillies and garlic together with fresh fruit. The Thais I met in Chiang Mai loved this dish and would eat numerous portions of it.

- Save as much of the natural fruit juices as possible during the preparation, to add more flavour.

Prik Nam Pla

Fish Sauce with Chillies

Method

1. Chop the garlic. Finely slice the chillies.

2. Mix all the ingredients together.

Measurements	Ingredients
10g	Garlic (peeled)
2	Chillies (medium)
125ml	Fish sauce
20ml	Lime juice

Chef's Notes

- This dipping sauce is served as a condiment to noodle dishes and soups. There are a number of different chillies you can use, there is no hard and fast rule.

Sweet and Sour Sauce

Method

1. Dice the garlic and the chillies, then place in a food processor with the sugar, vinegar and 125ml water and liquidise until the ingredients are fully incorporated.

2. Boil the remaining water and add the liquidised ingredients, and the tapioca flour if required. Stir to prevent lumps from forming. Remove from heat and allow to cool.

Measurements	Ingredients
60g	Garlic (peeled)
4	Large red chillies
120g	Brown sugar
80ml	Vinegar
250ml	Water
5g	Tapioca flour to thicken (optional)

Chef's Notes

- You can use dried red chillies as an alternative. This is nice as a dipping sauce with spring rolls.

Khao Soi Gai Chiangmai

Chiang Mai Curry Noodles

Method

1. Place the fresh noodles in boiling salted water for 1–2 minutes then refresh under cold running water, and drain.

2. Deep-fry the dry noodles, remove when cooked and place on kitchen towel and keep hot.

3. Heat a little oil in a wok and fry off the red curry paste until fragrant. Then add the curry powder and continue to fry.

4. Incorporate the thin coconut milk and half the thick coconut milk, add the stock and bring to a simmer. Then add the drumsticks and cook for 15 minutes.

5. Pour the palm sugar into the wok and stir to dissolve the sugar. Add the soy sauce and the fish sauce. Cook for a further 10 minutes, stirring constantly.

6. Add the remaining thick coconut milk (keep a spoonful for garnish) and cook for a further 10 minutes.

Measurements	Ingredients
300g	Egg noodles (fresh)
8	Chicken drumsticks
100g	Dried egg noodles
2lt	Palm oil
150g	Red curry paste
10g	Mild curry powder
125ml	Thin coconut milk
125ml	Thick coconut milk
500ml	Chicken stock
60g	Palm sugar
50ml	Soy sauce
80ml	Fish sauce
Accompaniments	Ingredients
100g	Shallots (peeled)
50g	Pickled cabbage (chopped)

continued over →

7. Reheat the fresh noodles in hot water then place in serving bowls. Put the drumsticks on top and then the curry sauce. Garnish the top with the deep-fried noodles.

8. Serve the accompaniments in a separate bowl.

...continued

8	Spring onions (chopped)
4	Lime (cut into quarters)
8 sprigs	Coriander (chopped)

Chef's Notes

- This stew-soup dish originated in Chiang Mai, but has a Burmese influence.

- Some recipes call for the accompaniments to be stir-fried in oil with chilli or paprika powder. Some recipes also have minced pork in the recipe, but I believe this recipe reflects a good traditional Chiang Mai noodle curry.

- When writing this particular recipe, I had the choice of six different recipes from six entirely different sources, namely restaurants, schools, and chefs.

Gob Pad Krapow

Frog's Legs with Holy Basil and Green Beans

Method

1. Top and tail the green beans and cut into 3cm lengths. Peel and finely dice the shallots. Remove the stalk and deseed the chillies, then very finely chop them.

Measurements	Ingredients
200g	Green beans
30g	Shallots

continued over →

2. Pour the oil into a hot wok and add the frog's legs and cook over a medium heat for 1 minute.

3. Add the chillies and shallots and continue to cook for another minute.

4. Add the sugar and stir in the fish sauce.

5. Add a little water and then add the beans and the holy basil. Cook for 5 minutes until the meat is cooked.

6. Serve with plain boiled rice.

...continued

2	Chillies (1 x red, 1 x green)
40ml	Palm oil
16 pairs	Frog's legs
20g	Palm sugar
20ml	Fish sauce
30–40g	Holy basil leaves

Chef's Notes

• You should be able to obtain the frog's legs from any Chinese supermarket or store. If you do not wish to use frog's legs you can substitute them with chicken.

• I was served this dish with a colleague in the Anusarn market in Chiang Mai. It came without the chillies, shallots or the beans and it was excellent.

Nam

Chiang Mai Sausage

Method

1. Remove the fat and the rind from the pork in one piece. Then remove as much of the fat as possible and bring the rind to the boil in a pan of water for 20–25 minutes. Remove the rind from the pan and allow to cool. Remove any remaining fat and dice the rind. Dice the pork and then put the pork and rind through a mincer or food processor.

2. Cut the banana leaf into 30cm lengths and blanch in boiling water until limp, then refresh in cold water. The banana leaf must be very dry.

3. Remove the stalk and seeds from the large chillies and very finely dice the chillies.

4. Mix the chillies, pork, garlic, salt and rice together really well.

Measurements	Ingredients
500g	Pork (with rind)
1	Banana leaf
6	Chillies (large)
30g	Garlic purée
5g	Salt
60g	Cooked sticky rice
Garnish	Ingredients
8 leaves	Lettuce
10g	Ginger (cut into julienne)
8	Spring onions (cut into diamonds)
20g	Roasted peanuts
30g	Shallots (finely sliced)

continued over →

5. Make a sausage shape and roll in the banana leaves or in clingfilm. Either way it must be very tight when rolled up and should be tied at each end.

6. Allow to cure for at least three days in a refrigerator. Thais then eat it raw, but I recommend that you cook it, for the obvious health and hygiene reasons.

...continued

4 cloves	Garlic (sliced)
8	Small chillies (sliced)
10g	Coriander leaves
2	Limes (cut into wedges)

7. If you have wrapped the sausage in a banana leaf you can either place it on a char-grill or bake it in the oven, until cooked. If it is wrapped in clingfilm, you can part steam it and finish it under the grill or in a pan.

8. Once cooked, place slices of the sausage in a lettuce leaf and add your own filling from the garnish ingredients, then fold it up to eat.

Chef's Notes

- This is a very spicy sausage and I do recommend that it is cooked thoroughly before being consumed.

- Sticky rice or glutinous rice can be obtained from Chinese and Asian stores.

Sôm Tam

Green Papaya and Tomato Salad

Measurements	Ingredients
2	Papayas (unripe)
200g	Green beans (cooked)
200g	Carrot
2	Spring onions (peeled)
40g	Peanuts
3	Tomatoes
30g	Shrimps (dried)
Dressing	Ingredients
1	Red chilli (deseeded)
60g	Shallots (peeled)
40ml	Fish sauce
30g	Palm sugar

continued over →

Method

1. Peel the papayas, remove the centre seeds then cut or grate the flesh into long strips. Top and tail the beans and cut in half, lengthways. Peel the carrots and grate like the papayas. Cut the spring onion into diamond shapes.

2. Dry roast the peanuts and wash and slice the tomatoes. Soak the shrimps in a little water to soften.

3. Take the papaya and the carrots and gently pound in a pestle and mortar, do not break them up, just bruise them.

4. Place all the dressing ingredients into the pestle and mortar or food processor and blend until a smooth paste has been achieved.

5. Mix the carrot, papaya, spring onions, tomatoes, green beans and shrimps, and dress on to a plate or bowl, then pour the dressing over and serve with a sprinkling of toasted peanuts on top.

...continued	
20ml	Lime juice
10g	Garlic purée

Chef's Notes

- This is a popular salad in Thailand and the use of unripe papaya in this recipe is essential. The Thais eat unripe papaya as an alternative to the very sweet ripe papaya, as they often get very tired of it. It is also used unripe as a vegetable.

- This salad is so popular that you will see stalls with the words 'Sôm Tam' above, indicating it is probably the only dish that is made.

Phad Wun Sen

Egg Fried Glass Noodles

Method

1. Soak the noodles in water for 10 minutes then drain and cut in half.

2. Peel and cut the spring onions into 3–4 cm lengths. Peel and slice the onions. Wash each tomato and cut into 12 wedges. Cut the chilli into slices.

3. Pour the oil into a wok over a medium heat and add the beaten eggs. Stir to scramble the eggs while cooking.

4. Add the noodles, spring onions, onions, tomatoes, chillies, garlic and black pepper and fully incorporate them over a medium heat. Cook for 2–3 minutes. Keep stirring to avoid the noodles sticking to the pan.

Measurements	Ingredients
300g	Glass noodles
100g	Spring onions
100g	Onions
8	Tomatoes
2	Red chillies (deseeded)
50ml	Palm oil
5	Eggs (beaten)
20g	Garlic
5g	Black pepper (ground)
60ml	Fish sauce
100ml	Oyster sauce
15g	Palm sugar

5. Add the fish sauce and oyster sauce and pour the sugar around the edge of the wok and stir-fry so it coats evenly.

6. Serve when mixed well and very hot.

Chef's Notes

- This very quick dish is often eaten as a snack. You can add meat to this dish, such as cooked pork or chicken, to make an alternative.

Gai Phad King

Chicken and Ginger Stir-fry

Measurements	Ingredients
300g	Chicken
80g	Onion (peeled)
2	Red chillies (large)
12	Spring onions
70g	Young ginger (peeled)
60g	Chinese mushrooms
50ml	Palm oil
15g	Garlic purée
50ml	Oyster sauce
40ml	Fish sauce
40ml	Light soy sauce
20g	Light miso (soy bean paste)
100ml	Chicken stock

Method

1. Slice the chicken into thin strips, cut the onion into large dice, deseed the chillies and then slice them. Peel and cut the spring onions into 3cm lengths. Cut the ginger into julienne (fine strips).

2. Remove and discard the stalks from the mushrooms and then slice them.

3. Pour the oil into a wok over a medium heat then add the garlic and stir to prevent sticking. Do not allow it to burn. Add the stock, then the onion and cook for 1 minute then add the raw chicken and cook for 2–3 minutes.

4. Add the ginger and mushrooms and cook for a further minute and then add the oyster sauce, fish sauce, light soy sauce and light miso and cook for 2–3 minutes.

5. Add the chillies and the spring onions and stir-fry for a further minute, check seasoning and serve.

Thailand

Chef's Notes

- Young ginger is sometimes called green ginger.

- In Thailand miso is called soy bean paste, and is a protein-rich fermented paste made from soya beans and other ingredients, such as wheat, rice and barley. There are a number of varieties, from light brown, yellow, dark and even white, all with varying flavors.

- Remember to keep the preparation of raw meat, especially raw chicken, totally separate from other food to avoid cross-contamination.

Khao Meow Mamuang

Mango with Sticky Rice

Method

1. Soak the sticky rice in cold water for 4 hours.

2. Mix the thick coconut milk with the palm sugar and salt.

3. Steam the rice for 15 minutes on full heat. Remove and place in a suitable size bowl. Pour the coconut milk and sugar mixture over the rice and allow to fully absorb the milk. Leave for 1 hour.

4. To make the sauce, mix the coconut milk and palm sugar together.

Measurements	Ingredients
400g	Sticky rice
375ml	Thick coconut milk
175g	Palm sugar
2.5g	Salt
2	Ripe mangoes
Sauce	Ingredients
100g	Coconut milk (thick or thin)
25g	Palm sugar

5. Peel the mangoes and cut into suitable size dice and place on a serving plate. Add a portion of rice and pour the sauce over the mangoes and rice.

Chef's Notes

- The sticky rice is better prepared and soaked in the milk the day before. Use only the ripest mangoes, they must not be bruised or damaged.

- Some recipes suggest decorating with toasted sesame seeds or roasted crushed peanuts.

Khao Tom Goong

Prawns and Rice Soup

Method

1. Shell and remove the central vein from the prawns but leave the fan tail end intact. Peel and slice the spring onions and slice them.

2. Very finely slice the garlic and deep-fry until golden brown. Drain on kitchen paper and allow to go crispy.

3. Bring the stock to the boil and skim off any debris, then add the rice and simmer for 3–4 minutes.

4. Add the soy sauce, prawns, spring onions, salt and pepper and continue to boil for 2–3 minutes, removing any debris from the surface. Correct the seasoning.

5. Portion into suitable bowls and garnish with chopped coriander and a sprinkling of deep-fried garlic on top.

Measurements	Ingredients
200g	Prawns in shells (medium size)
8	Spring onions
10g	Garlic
1lt	Chicken stock
450g	Long grain rice (cooked)
60ml	Soy sauce
10g	Fresh coriander (chopped)
	Ground white pepper
	Salt

Chef's Notes

• The Thais consider soups such as this a healthy and cooling meal. This soup usually has an egg broken into it one or two minutes before serving and is eaten at breakfast. You may also see this soup served with chicken or fish.

Khaaw Neow Dum

Black Sticky Rice and Coconut

Method

1. Wash the rice and then put into the water. Bring to the boil and simmer for 25–30 minutes.

2. Add 450ml coconut milk, the sugar and coconut flesh and continue to boil for a further 5 minutes.

3. Divide into suitable bowls, decorate the top with a little coconut milk and serve.

Measurements	Ingredients
250g	Black sticky rice
1.5lt	Water
500ml	Thick coconut milk
300g	Sugar
100g	Fresh coconut flesh (grated)

Chef's Notes

- This is a very popular northern Thai dish. The rice is naturally black and the dish is very sweet. Adjust the sugar content as you wish.

- This is one of the few dessert dishes that could be served either hot or cold at the end of a meal.

Nam Prik Panaeng

Panaeng Curry Paste

Method

1. Place the coriander seeds, cumin seeds, cardamom pods and peppercorns in a pestle and mortar or food processor and grind to a fine powder.

2. Soak the chillies in some warm water for 10–15 minutes and then drain and chop roughly.

3. Chop the galangal, the lower third of the lemongrass and shallots.

4. Place all the ingredients into a food processor and turn into a smooth paste.

Chef's Notes

- If it is a little dry in the food processor add a dash of water. This recipe will make between 180g and 200g.

- Place in a slightly oiled container with a little oil to cover the top of the paste and with a tight-fitting lid. It should keep for 3–4 weeks in a refrigerator.

Measurements	Ingredients
10g	Coriander seeds
2.5g	Cumin seeds
3-4	Cardamom pods
5g	Black peppercorns
10	Dried red chillies (large)
4cm	Galangal (peeled)
4 stalks	Lemongrass
70g	Shallots
10g	Belacan (shrimp paste)
10 cloves	Garlic
1	Lime (zest and juice)
10g	Coriander (leaves, stems and roots)
20ml	Fish sauce
4	Kaffir lime leaf (chopped)

Kai Panaeng

Chicken Curry

Method

1. Pour 400ml thick coconut milk into a wok and cook until oil appears from the coconut. You must stir to prevent it from burning.

2. Add the curry paste and stir in. Cook until it smells fragrant then add the chicken, palm sugar and shredded kaffir lime leaves. Cook and simmer over a medium heat for 8–10 minutes then add the fish sauce.

3. Add the sweet basil leaves, stir in and take off the heat.

4. Serve with a spoonful of the remaining thick coconut milk, basil leaves and kaffir lime leaves as garnish.

Measurements	Ingredients
450ml	Thick coconut milk
120g	Panaeng curry paste (see Chef's Notes)
300g	Diced chicken
20g	Palm sugar
4	Kaffir lime leaves (Shredded)
30ml	Fish sauce
10g	Sweet basil leaves
8	Basil leaves
4	Kaffir lime leaves

Chef's Notes

- This curry should be thick and you will get coconut oil at the surface. If you don't like this, skim it off before serving.

- The coconut adds an excellent richness to the curry, which helps to temper the fieriness of the paste.

- Pork is also a common meat used in this curry sauce. Serve with steamed or boiled rice.

- For Panaeng curry paste see page 149.

Gaeng Khia Wan Gai

Green Curry with Chicken

Method

1. Slice the chicken breast into thin slices without any fat or skin.

2. Cut the aubergine into $1\frac{1}{2}$ cm dice.

3. Pour the thick coconut milk into the wok and cook until oil appears from the coconut. You must stir to prevent it from burning.

Measurements	Ingredients
500g	Chicken breast
100g	Aubergine
250ml	Thick coconut milk
100g	Green curry paste
30g	Palm sugar

continued over →

...continued

4	Kaffir lime leaves (cut in half)
250ml	Thin coconut milk
50g	Baby aubergine (pea size)
30ml	Fish sauce
30g	Sweet basil leaves
Garnish	Ingredients
2	Kaffir lime leaves (very finely shredded)
1	Large red chilli (sliced)
50ml	Thick coconut milk

4. Add the curry paste and stir in. Cook until it smells fragrant then add the chicken, palm sugar and the halved kaffir lime leaves. Add the thin coconut milk and all of the aubergines.

5. Cook and simmer over a medium heat for 8–10 minutes, then add the fish sauce and the basil leaves, continuing to cook and stir for a further 1–2 minutes. Check seasoning and serve.

6. Garnish with shredded kaffir lime leaves, sliced chillies and a spoonful of coconut milk.

Chef's Notes

• This is one of the most popular dishes from Thailand. The wonderful aromatic marriage of the spices and the rich taste of the coconut with the mild heat of the chillies is what I think Thai cuisine is all about.

• This recipe is from the northern provinces of Lampang.

• You can replace the chicken with pork if you wish.

• See Glossary for more information on aubergines.

Nam Prik Gaeng Kheo Wan

Green Curry Paste

Method

1. Roughly chop the shallots and the lower third of the lemongrass. Roughly chop the turmeric and galangal.

2. Pound the coriander seeds, cumin seeds and peppercorns in a pestle and mortar until a fine powder has been achieved.

3. Place all the ingredients into a food processor with a dash of water and process to a smooth paste.

Measurements	Ingredients
100g	Shallots (peeled)
3 stalks	Lemongrass
10g	Turmeric (peeled)
4cm	Galangal (peeled)
15g	Coriander seeds
10g	Cumin seeds
5g	Black peppercorns
10	Green chillies (medium to large)
2	Limes (juice and zest)

Chef's Notes

• To add extra flavour, dry roast the seeds and peppercorns and also wrap the shrimp paste in foil and roast for 10 minutes.

continued over →

- There are numerous green curry paste recipes; this particular one comes from a restaurant in Chiang Mai where I had to exchange my chef's apron for the recipe.

- Store in a slightly oiled container, with a little extra oil to cover the top of the paste, and cover with a tight-fitting lid. It should keep for 3–4 weeks in a refrigerator.

...continued

30g	Garlic purée
30g	Shrimp paste (belacan)
	Salt

NORTH-EAST THAILAND

The north-east of Thailand is known as Isaan, which is a term used for the 18 provinces within it. The region stretches as far north as Nong Khai to Surin in the south, close to the Cambodian border. It then stretches from Nakhon Phanom on the Laos border in the east to Khon Kaen to the west. This area is under-developed and the pace of life is much slower than elsewhere in Thailand.

The region's history is long, dating as far back as prehistoric times. The Undon Thani Province's cave drawings and the Bronze Age archaeological site date back some 2,000 years. Isana is a Sankrit name that comes from the Mon-Khmer kingdom that occupied the north-east of Thailand, pre-dating Angkor in Cambodia. Isana was the forebear of the Funan Empire, which ran between the first and sixth centuries.

The Funan Empire became part of the Chenla Empire which in the sixth to eighth centuries divided into upper and lower Chenla. Around the ninth century the powerful Angkor Empire took over Chenla and large parts of Thailand. The Isana region was more or less untroubled until the French came to Laos in the 1800s and was to a large degree self-governing. However, French intervention and the establishment of French Indochina forced the Thai king Rama V to mark out and specify its borders, which he did by making four self-governing states. These remained until 1933 when the states became provinces under the governorship of Bangkok. In 1940, a number of Indochinese communist leaders fled from Laos to Isana. Then, from the 1960s to 1982–83, the region became a centre of communist guerrilla activity. As the Thai economies began to grow in the early 1980s, drawing ever-increasing numbers of people to the provincial cities in search of prosperity, the authorities announced an amnesty that saw the disbanding of the communists.

The traditions, customs and culture of Isaan are still much in evidence. English is not spoken as widely as in other regions, but visiting is easy as the people are much friendlier.

The culture of this region of Thailand is a mix of Khmer and Lao (Laos) influences. The Khmer left numerous monuments across the region and Angkor Wat-style monuments exist in the provinces of Surin, Khorat and Buri Ram. Buri Ram has the largest stone temple, Prasat Phanom Rung. Along the Maekhong River many local people have their own Thai-Lao dialects and in some of the close border towns Khmer is widely spoken.

In Khon Kaen the best Thai silks in the north-east are produced. This is known as matmi silk.

The traditions of music and dance are very distinctive with the use of traditional instruments like bamboo and reed pipes and old-style three-string lutes giving a unique sound not found elsewhere in Thailand.

In the north-east the food is called 'aahāan isāan' and is distinguished by its aromatic biting and tangy flavours. Isaan food is found everywhere in Thailand. You do not have to go to elaborate restaurants to sample the cuisine; it is one of the least fussy and casual styles of dining in Thailand. I have heard it described as cheap, unfussy, casual, easy to eat and to cook, and some even call it Thai fast-food.

North-eastern Thai people, more than any one else in Thailand, eat with their hands, which is an art in itself. They will roll up balls of sticky rice and place a dent in the centre of the rice with their thumb, making it look like a spoon on the end of their three fingers. They then take a portion of the curry, put it in the centre of the rice and then place it in their mouths with precision. They also eat more sticky rice than anywhere else in Thailand. The north-eastern Thai people follow their traditions with dishes served on large enamel trays decorated with patterns of colourful flowers. The steamed rice is served in a Katib, which is a characteristic north-eastern-style wicker basket.

This cuisine is not as well documented as in the north or areas like Bangkok and Phuket. However, there are some notable dishes from this region, such as Kài yang (barbecued chicken with peppers and garlic) and a papaya salad called Sômtam, which is spiked with chillies, garlic and fish sauce. Khanom buang (crispy pancake with bean sprouts and shrimps) is often seen at festive times.

Nakhon Ratchasima Province is the largest province and is mainly famous for its excellent silk making. The best village for this is Pak Thong Chai. The capital is Nakhon Ratchasima (Khorat) which is 250 kilometres from Bangkok. Khorat has grown to become Thailand's second biggest city and has developed its industrial and manufacturing base since the late 1980s. It used to be an air base for the American air force during the Vietnam War, which once had an obvious influence on the city, but this has all but now gone.

Khao Yai National Park is the oldest National Park in Thailand, covering over 2,172 square kilometres, and is not only home to the mainland's largest monsoon rain forest in Asia, but also to many endangered and rare wild animals like the tiger, Malayan sun bear and the leopard.

Located in Khorat is the Thao Suranari monument. It is a Khmer-style stone shrine called Prasat Hin Phimai and has a 250-year-old banyan tree. Khorat celebrates the Thao Suranari Festival, that is the celebration of victory over Laos, with traditional dance, song and parades.

Khorat has numerous restaurants serving local dishes like Khorat noodles, Haw mok (ground fish curry custard, steamed in a banana leaf) and roast frog. There are some good fish restaurants but it is best to look for ones serving local freshwater fish dishes. The Manat Road night market is not that much of a spectacle, but it offers some good traditional local food.

Buriram Province is one of the larger provinces and was part of the Khmer Empire in the Angkor period. It has many excellent and impressive Angkor/Khmer monuments with the Phanom Rung being the most famous. Buriram is also the capital of the province. Just outside it is the Phanom Rung Historical Park, which holds the prasat's temple complex, and was built on the site of an extinct volcano. Constructed from the tenth to the thirteenth centuries, it has some of the best-surviving examples of architecture in Thailand. The construction of buildings and sculptures are incredible, with classic examples from Khmer and Indian religious architecture. Many buildings were built as places of worship. These boldly carved stone temples are dramatic examples of this period in Thailand history and development.

Chaiyaphum Province is located right in the centre of Thailand and has a small National Park called Taat Tohn.

The province used to supply elephants for logging, but when logging was banned, it supplied elephants for tourist 'elephant camps' at home and abroad.

Khon Kaen is north-east of Chaiyaphum and 450 kilometres from Bangkok. It is mainly a rural province where farming and the production of textiles are the main source of income and employment. Its silk and cotton products are some of the best in Thailand.

Although the province is rural, the city of Khon Kaen is the main centre for finance, commerce and for communications. Isaan has the biggest university in the north-east. The city has a good night market on Klang Meuang Road, which has admirable and first-rate fruit and vegetables. The inevitable food stalls and vendors abound selling ground Khai jiao mu sub (pork omelettes), Sôm-tam, sticky rice and congee.

Roi Et Province is built around a lake called Beung Phlan Chai. Silk and cotton are also produced here. There are a number of standing Buddhas, including the Wat Burapha standing almost 68 metres tall.

Undon Thani Province was once a small village that literally sprang up when the USA air force built a base there during the Vietnam War, due to its proximity to the Laos border. It still retains some of the American influences like KFC, steak and pizza houses as well as the coffee houses. There are some good Isaan stalls and restaurants selling Kài yang (grilled

chicken with peppers and garlic), Sôm tam, Khanom buang and numerous Undon noodle dishes. Undon is now an important transport link and agricultural market centre in the north-east.

Fifty kilometres east of Undon is the village of Ban Chiang, which has a general history stretching back over 2,000 years. At the edge of the village is the Wat Pho Si Nai that is now a UNESCO World Heritage Site. There is also a park at Ban Pheu that has prehistoric cave paintings.

Nong Khai Province borders Laos along the Maekhong River. It stretches 300 kilometres in length and is only 50 kilometres wide.

The capital is Nong Khai, which is 620 kilometres from Bangkok. It is also where the Thai–Laos Friendship Bridge has been constructed to take trade between the two countries. This is only the second bridge ever to be built across the river. The area was once a part of the Kingdom of Vientiane, until in 1827 a Thai lord established the city of Meuang Nong Khai under the king Ram III. During the late 1800s the area came under repeated attacks from the Jiin Haw (Yunnanese). A monument was erected in 1886 to commemorate the victories over them and this can be seen at the city hall. When the western part of Laos was partitioned off by the French in 1893, Nong Khai fell into insignificance until the friendship bridge was constructed. Now it is a stopping off point for people to visit Laos. The area has numerous wats (temples).

The Vietnamese and Laos influence on the local cuisine can be seen in the restaurants and street vendors' stalls with dishes like Pàw pía yuan (Vietnamese spring rolls), Phàt phèt (Maekhong freshwater fish stir fried with fresh basil and curry). A little of the French influence can also be seen with a dish like Kài lâo daeng (chicken cooked in red wine) along with other Thai dishes like Gai yang (BBQ chicken), Nu yang nam tok (waterfall beef salad).

There are several villages on the Maekhong flood plains which are surrounded by the banana, tobacco, tomato and vegetable plantations which cover this area.

There is a little town called Si Chiangmai that produces enormous numbers of rice paper spring roll wrappers. The French influence can be seen in the town with the many bakeries making baguettes and pastries.

Loei Province is linked to Laos along its northern border and then partly separated by the Maekhong River. The capital of the province is Loei, which is 518 kilometres from Bangkok. Loei has the lowest temperatures of Thailand in the cool season and the highest in the hot season.

The province is considered remote and holds little culinary interest, but it produces large quantities of cotton.

Numerous villages along the Maekhong River will serve you dishes with river shrimp, with chillies and lime. As far as development is concerned, the province has changed little over time. It is also home to the Nam Nao National Park, considered by many be the most beautiful and valuable park in Thailand.

Nakhon Phanom Province skirts the Laos border and Maekong River. It also has a large number of Vietnamese and Laos influences. The capital Nakhon Phanom has a strong ethnic Chinese community. There are numerous wats and some, like the Wat Si Thep, have unique murals on the walls. The capital's restaurants along the river serve large Maekong catfish. However overfishing of catfish is becoming a cause for concern.

Although the official religion of Thailand is Buddhism, Thais are essentially a carnivorous people and have a very unique way of looking at things. For example, the fishermen rationalise their fishing, believing that if the fish are so foolish as to get caught in their nets and die when the nets are pulled from the water, it is not the fisherman's fault and so what does it matter that the fish is eaten afterwards? The catfish can be served with Tôm yam or as a stir-fried dish with basil and green curry (Phàt phèt) or in the traditional clay pot with rice.

Another local delicacy is a beef and chillies dish called 'tiger tears' or 'crying tiger'. This is made with tamarind juice, fish sauce and bird's eye chillies or, as the Thais call them, 'bird shit' chillies. Some of the better Isaan food can be obtained along the Bamrung Meuang Road. There are a number of markets and towns like That Phanom along the Laos border and Maekong River where many market traders cross to sell their goods and the traditional art of haggling takes place.

Sakon Nakhon Province is mainly an agricultural province, but is famous for being the home of the two most famous Buddhist monks in the history of Thailand, Ajaan Man and Ajann Fan Ajaro. The two monks were ascetic thutong monks, who were believed to have attained the highest levels of meditation (vipassana). Both were very disciplined and abstained from any form of pleasure and spent many years at Wat Pa Sutthawat in the province's capital Sakon Nakhon. Sakon Nakhon is also home to Thailand's biggest natural lake, Nong Han.

Sakon is infamous for its trade in dog meat, which is still popular in this part of the country, although it is mainly limited to the Soh ethnic community in the Tha Lae district. The market there still sells and slaughters around 100 dogs a day. Dog meat is half the price of beef, which encourages this trade. With this in mind, it would be advisable to abstain from purchasing any curries, satay or any meat-based dishes from that district; it would more than likely contain dog meat. It is illegal in Thailand to buy and sell live dogs for dining purposes.

Yasothon and Mukdahan Province is rural and relies on agriculture, and superb scenery for its economy. It has numerous markets, especially in the Indochina market in Mukdahan. Culinary-wise, you can see the

French culinary influence with the Lao baguettes, and then the Vietnamese influences with the spring rolls and the rice soups for sale in the night markets.

Ubon Ratchathani Province is the largest province and the capital of north-east Thailand, some 556 kilometres from Bangkok. The province borders both Laos and Cambodia. The capital is situated on the banks of the Mun (moon) River, which is the second longest river in Thailand. The Mun and Chi Rivers were once part of the Khmer and Dvaravati empires, but after their decline, groups of Lao people settled there in the late 1700s.

Ubon is a centre for education, finance and communication. The city also holds a very famous five-day candle festival during October, which attracts people from all over Thailand. There is a procession during the evenings with floats, music and exquisite candles of all shapes, colours and sizes.

The province, like many other provinces, has impressive wats (temples), but one to mention is the Ko Hat Wat Tai, which is on an island in the middle of the Mun River to the south of the town.

The province is proud of its food and is considered to have some of the best Isaan food in north-east Thailand. For example, Hàw mòk, which is a curry of fish with thick coconut served in a banana leaf, or the local Lâap pèt, a spicy duck salad which is eaten with a local squash soup called Tôm fák. The locals also like the Lao-style grilled chicken, which is called Kài yang. The two large local markets also offer the sticky rice and baked items as well as Jók (broken rice) and Khâo tôm for breakfast.

This province also served as an American base during the Vietnam War.

Surin and Si Saket Provinces are scattered with wats from as far back as the eleventh century from the Angkor period. Surin is 450 kilometres from Bangkok. During the third weekend in November each year, the traditional round-up of elephants for trading is still held in Surin. The province is also famous for its silk weaving.

Culturally, Surin has an interesting mix of customs and dialects from Laos, Khmer, Thai and the Suay people.

Si Saket is a smaller province than Surin but has more Khmer ruins and there is a much more laid back and relaxed feel to the place.

Just across the border in Cambodia are the ruins of Khao Phra Wihaan, a major Angkor site. It was started by Rajendravarman II in the tenth century and was then built over during the next 200 years by successive kings.

Haw Mok

Steamed Curried Fish

Method

1. Cut the banana leaf into four pieces, each 12cm square. Cover a 10cm inverted bowl with a banana-leaf sheet then cut around the edges and staple the sides together to form a bowl. Repeat this three more times.

2. Pick the basil leaves from the stalks. Skin, debone and thinly slice the fillets. Finely shred the kaffir lime leaves and cabbage. Chop the eggs finely.

3. Place the tapioca flour in with 50ml coconut milk and stir over a medium heat.

4. Mix the curry paste, the remaining coconut milk and fish sauce together in a suitable bowl then mix in the tapioca mixture.

5. Add the lime leaves, eggs, basil and peanuts.

6. Gently fold in the fish and leave for 15-20 minutes.

Measurements	Ingredients
1	Banana leaf (optional)
100g	Thai basil
500g	Red snapper (fillet)
4	Kaffir lime leaves
100g	Chinese cabbage
2	Eggs (hard-boiled)
20g	Tapioca flour
150ml	Thick coconut milk
20g	Red curry paste
30ml	Fish sauce
50g	Ground peanuts
1	Red chilli
12 large sprigs	Coriander

7. Place cabbage at the bottom of the banana-leaf cups, divide the fish mixture equally and then steam for 20 minutes. It may rise slightly during cooking.

8. Decorate the tops with julienne of red chilli and coriander sprigs.

Chef's Notes

- This north-eastern dish, like most Thai dishes, varies between stalls, restaurants and chefs. I have seen all of the ingredients of this dish puréed and left for 30 minutes to allow the curry paste to fully penetrate the mixture and then steamed. I prefer the recipe above because you can taste the food without the full fieriness of the red curry paste.

- If you cannot find any banana leaves you can use any type of tea cup or bowl.

Khai Jiao Mu Sub

Ground Pork Omelette with Coriander

Method

1. Peel and slice the shallots and spring onions.

2. Whisk the eggs in a suitable bowl with the of water and fish sauce.

3. Add the minced pork, shallots, spring onions and mix together well.

4. Heat 30ml oil in a suitable pan and when hot pour in one-quarter of the mixture and fry. When cooked on one side turn over and continue to fry until cooked.

5. Repeat this process three more times.

6. Decorate with chopped coriander and slices of chilli.

Measurements	Ingredients
40g	Shallots
4	Spring onions
4	Eggs (medium)
30–40ml	Water
5–10ml	Fish sauce
200g	Minced pork
120ml	Sunflower or palm oil
15g	Coriander (chopped)
1	Chilli

Chef's Notes

- This is a typical Isaan dish. You could replace the chicken with pork or fish. You could also replace the meat with tofu or a mixture of mushrooms if you wish.

- Serve with hot rice.

Gai Yang

BBQ Chicken

Method

1. Peel and very finely dice the galangal, garlic and lemongrass.

2. Mix with the coconut milk, oyster sauce, chilli sauce, Thai yellow curry powder, palm sugar, sesame oil and white pepper.

3. Make sure the chicken is dry then lightly make three slits in the thighs with a sharp knife.

4. Cover the whole of the chicken and marinate overnight, or if you are short of time allow the marinade to penetrate for at least for 30 minutes.

5. Place on a charcoal grill and cook until golden brown and the juices run clear from the meat when cut with a knife.

Measurements	Ingredients
50g	Galangal
50g	Garlic
15g	Lemongrass
200ml	Coconut milk
50ml	Oyster sauce
50ml	Chilli sauce (see below)
30g	Thai yellow curry powder
20g	Palm sugar
15ml	Sesame oil
2.5g	Ground white pepper
4	Chicken thighs

Chef's Notes

- This traditional Isaan dish can be seen all over Thailand and is often cooked by street traders over burning coals with marinated chicken on street corners, enticing their customers with the wonderful cooking aroma. It is a very easy dish, but it is best to allow the chicken to marinate overnight for the best results.

- As an alternative you could cook this in the oven, 200°C (gas mark 6) for 20–25 minutes.

Chilli Sauce

Method

1. Remove the seeds and stalks from the chillies and roughly cut up the flesh, then soak in 50ml warm water.

2. Place the rest of the ingredients into a blender or processor and blend to a smooth paste.

3. Place the paste into a suitable pan and then gently cook over a medium heat for 10 minutes or until it becomes thick. Allow to cool before using. If you require a sweeter chilli sauce, add a further 10–20g sugar.

Measurements	Ingredients
4	Large red chillies
60ml	White wine vinegar
60g	Caster sugar
10g	Garlic purée
2	Coriander roots
1	Large shallot (peeled)
10–15ml	Fish sauce
2.5g	Salt

Nu Yang Nam Tok

Waterfall Beef Salad

Method

1. Peel the onions and finely slice. Deseed the chillies and cut into fine strips.

2. Cook the beef as you prefer, well cooked, medium, etc.

3. When cooked and while it is still hot, cut the beef into thin 2cm strips.

4. Place the chilli paste, tomatoes, red chillies, red onions and the beef into a suitable bowl and mix together.

5. Place the lettuce onto a suitable plate, put the beef on top and sprinkle with the rice.

Measurements	Ingredients
3	Red onions
2	Red chillies
4 x 180g	Sirloin of beef
20g	Nam prik pow (chilli paste)
4	Tomatoes
250–300g	Mixed lettuce leaves
120g	Roasted ground sweet rice

Chef's Notes

• You can garnish with chilli flowers and extra tomatoes if you wish.

Khao Tom Goong

Rice Soup with Prawns

Method

1. Shell and remove the central vein from the prawns.

2. Wash and slice the celery and slice the 10g garlic.

3. Sweat off the sliced garlic in oil until it just starts to colour then pour in the stock and bring to the boil.

Measurements	Ingredients
16	Large prawns
75g	Chinese celery (khunchai)
10g	Garlic
10ml	Vegetable oil

continued over →

4. Add the celery and the pepper and stir, then add the rice and bring back to the boil, skimming any debris from the surface.

5. Add the fish sauce.

6. Add the prawns and cook until they begin to turn pink.

7. Portion out into four bowls and garnish the top with deep-fried garlic and chopped coriander.

Chef's Notes

- Chinese celery (khunchai) looks like coriander but has a very different taste that resembles celery. If you cannot find it substitute with normal celery.

- Khao tom is eaten as a staple diet for breakfast in Thailand. It can be eaten and made with or without shrimps. The soup can also be made with chicken, pork or fish. It must always be made with pre-cooked rice.

...continued

500ml	Light fish stock *or* water
2.5g	Ground black pepper
175g	Jasmine rice (cooked)
30ml	Fish sauce
4 cloves	Garlic (thinly sliced and deep-fried)
10g	Coriander (chopped)

Udon Kŭaytĭaw

Udon Noodles

Method

1. Crush the peanuts and keep to one side.

2. Mix the Japanese vinegar, caster sugar, red pepper flakes and bean sprouts with the noodles.

3. Heat the oil with the garlic until it starts to colour, then pour over the noodles. Garnish with peanuts, bean sprouts and coriander.

Chef's Notes

- You can substitute apple cider for Japanese vinegar.

- Thai noodles are made from a number of different types of flour – rice, soya and mung bean. Egg noodles use mung bean flour.

Measurements	Ingredients
50ml	Japanese vinegar
40g	Caster sugar
30g	Red pepper flakes
200g	Fresh bean sprouts
800g	Udon noodles (cooked)
100ml	Sunflower *or* vegetable oil
20g	Garlic (diced)
Garnish	Ingredients
40g	Roasted peanuts
20g	Bean sprouts
30g	Coriander

Isaan Moo Manao

Isaan Lime Pork

Measurements	Ingredients
5	Dried chillies
60g	Shallots
4	Spring onions
380g	Minced pork
120g	Pork liver (sliced)
60ml	Chicken stock
30g	Ground rice
10g	Fresh coriander (chopped)
30ml	Fish sauce
30ml	Lime juice
Garnish	Ingredients
5g	Picked fresh mint
160g	Long beans
150g	White cabbage (shredded)
150g	Cucumber (sliced)

Method

1. Ground the dried chillies to a fine powder. Peel and slice the shallots and spring onions.

2. Mix together the minced pork, liver and the chicken stock. Bring to a boil and then simmer in a suitable pan.

3. When the pork is cooked, add the rice, chillies and chopped coriander.

4. Mix in the fish sauce and lime juice.

5. Serve garnished with mint leaves, long beans, large cucumber slices and shredded cabbage.

Chef's Notes

• This dish is traditionally served cold with the garnish raw.

Kai Yang-Khao Neow

Peasant BBQ Chicken with Sticky Rice

Method

Measurements	Ingredients
30g	Garlic (peeled)
10g	Ginger (peeled)
2 x 800g	Whole small chickens
100ml	Fish sauce
100ml	Dark soy sauce
30ml	American whisky
30ml	Coconut milk (thick or thin)
5g	Ground white pepper
15g	Coriander (very finely chopped)
10g	Salt

1. Purée the garlic and the ginger.

2. Remove the wish bone, cut off the claws at the first joint, place the chickens on their backs and insert a large knife through the neck end and out of the vent, cutting through the back bone and rib bones, and flatten out.

3. Put fish sauce, soy sauce, garlic, whisky, coconut milk, pepper, coriander, ginger and salt into a mixer and blend thoroughly and then rub the mixture into the chicken and marinate for at least 1 hour, or preferably overnight.

4. Cook over hot coals or a grill for 30–40 minutes turning regularly, until the juices run clear.

5. Split each cooked chicken in half and serve with sticky rice.

Sticky Rice

Method

1. Take 400g Thai glutinous rice and cover with water, then wash it and drain off the milky coloured water. Repeat this a number of times until the water becomes clear. Cover the rice with fresh water and place in the fridge overnight.

2. Drain off the rice and place in a muslin cloth. Transfer to a steamer on full boil and cook for 20 minutes. Take out of the steamer carefully and remove muslin. Serve.

Chef's Notes

• Kai yang is basically barbecued chicken and is very much the food of the streets.

• This recipe is Isaan from the north-east. Versions differ from one cook to another. The Bangkok style is more complex and fussy.

• I have seen this dish baked in a pre-heated oven as opposed to BBQ or grilled.

• Sticky rice or a simple green salad should accompany this dish.

Khao Man Gai

Boiled Chicken and Steamed Rice

Method

1. Pre-soak the rice in water, then wash and drain off the milky coloured water. Repeat this a number of times until the water is clear. Cover the rice with fresh water and place in the fridge overnight.

2. Place the chicken into the cold stock and bring to the boil. Then reduce it to a simmer for 35–40 minutes until the chicken is cooked. Skim off any oil that appears and keep.

3. Once cooked remove the chicken and allow to cool slightly. Cut into slices and keep hot. Keep the stock.

4. Purée 10g garlic and finely slice 25g ginger. Roughly chop the 20g coriander root.

5. In a dish place in a little of the chicken stock and gourd. Bring to the boil then simmer until it is cooked. Keep it hot to one side, finished with a little chopped coriander.

6. For the rice, take the reserved oil from the chicken and heat in a suitable pan. Sweat off the garlic purée, sliced ginger and coriander then pour in the rice, season and stir. Add some of the reserved chicken stock to the pan and bring to a boil. Simmer for 10–12 minutes until cooked. Drain and serve.

7. For the sauce, chop 10g garlic, 10g ginger, 5g coriander root and chillies. Mix them together with the thick soy sauce, preserved soya beans, sugar and vinegar. Serve in a small dipping bowl.

8. Put the chicken slices on a plate with rice and sliced cucumbers and sprinkle with coriander leaves. Serve with the gourd and dipping sauce separately.

Measurements	Ingredients
350g	Glutinous rice
1 x 1.2kg	Chicken (oven ready)
4lt	Chicken stock
10g	Garlic
25g	Ginger
100g	Gourd (diced 2cm)
20g	Coriander root
Sauce	Ingredients
10g	Garlic (peeled)
10g	Ginger (peeled)
5g	Coriander root
10g	Bird's eye chillies
25ml	Thick soy sauce
20g	Soya beans (preserved)
15g	Caster sugar
25ml	Rice vinegar
Garnish	Ingredients
150g	Cucumbers (washed, peeled and sliced)
10g	Coriander leaves

Chef's Notes

- This recipe can be altered by using duck as a replacement for the chicken.

- Steamed glutinous rice is a staple food in Isaan cuisine and therefore is the base for meals such as this one.

Kaeng Khua Saparot

Shrimp, Pineapple and Holy Basil

Method

1. With a small knife remove the eyes of the tomatoes. Then place the tomatoes in boiling water for 10 seconds and then immediately into cold water, then remove the skin, deseed and cut the flesh into small dice. Cut one-third off the top of the pineapples and scoop out the flesh. Remove the core and discard. Dice the flesh. Reserve the shell for service and for presentation.

2. Shell and remove the central vein from the prawns. Roughly chop the chillies.

3. Pour the oil into a wok or suitable pan and fry off the garlic purée over a medium heat, then add the basil. Spoon out the garlic and the leaves and keep to one side.

4. Fry off the curry paste until it is fragrant, add the thin coconut milk, fish sauce, diced tomatoes, lime juice, sugar and pineapples. Mix the ingredients and bring to a simmer for 5 minutes.

5. Add the thick coconut milk and then the prawns and simmer for 4–5 minutes. Add the kaffir lime leaves, chilli and the basil and garlic mixture.

6. Serve the curry in the pineapple shell with hot jasmine rice as an accompaniment.

Measurements	Ingredients
6	Tomatoes
4	Baby pineapple
20	Large jumbo prawns
4	Bird's eye chillies
50ml	Palm oil
10g	Garlic purée
20	Holy basil leaves
40g	Red curry paste
250ml	Thin coconut milk
40ml	Fish sauce
1	Lime (juice only)
20g	Palm sugar
250ml	Thick coconut milk
4	Kaffir lime leaves
350g	Jasmine rice (cooked)

Chef's Notes

- This dish will have a good reddish colour. It is creamy with the pineapple giving a sweet but sharp contrast.

- Serving this dish in pineapple shells is very eye-catching as an alternative to plates.

Pak Dtom Gkati

Cooked Kale with Prawns and Coconut

Method

1. Shell and remove the central vein from the prawns. Wash and cut the kale into 2–3cm pieces.

Measurements	Ingredients
400g	Prawns
400g	Kale

continued over →

2. Peel the shallots and cut into very fine dice. Cut the lime leaves in half length-ways.

...continued

3. Bring the coconut milk to the boil in a suitable pan and add the shallots. Simmer for 2–3 minutes then add the kale and chard or spring greens and simmer for a further 10–12 minutes until all the greens are cooked.

4. Season with salt and pepper and add sugar to the soup. Add the prawns and lime leaves cook for a further 2–3 minutes.

5. Serve into four warmed soup bowls. Garnish with half a lime leaf in each bowl, chillies and coriander.

100g	Shallots
2	Kaffir lime leaves
400ml	Coconut milk
200g	Chard *or* spring greens
5g	Palm sugar
	Salt
Garnish	Ingredients
4	Red chillies (made into flowers)
10g	Coriander (chopped)

Chef's Notes

- Isaan food is very simple, quick and uncomplicated. Most dishes take no longer than 10–12 minutes to make.

Jok Moo

Porridge Rice with Egg and Pork Meatballs

Method

1. Cut the ginger and spring onions into julienne and keep to one side for garnish.

2. Bring the stock to the boil.

3. Season the minced pork and roll into small uniform balls and immerse in the boiling stock. Simmer until cooked. Remove and keep hot.

4. Add the rice porridge to the stock a little at a time on a low heat stirring constantly until a runny consistency has been achieved and the porridge is cooked.

5. Correct the seasoning and portion into hot bowls.

Measurements	Ingredients
30g	Ginger (peeled)
6	Spring onions
650ml	Chicken *or* vegetable stock
300g	Minced pork
4 medium	Eggs
400–500g	Instant rice porridge
5g	Ground white peppercorns
	Salt

6. Place the meatballs back into the porridge and then crack one egg into each bowl and allow them to cook (see Chef's Notes).

7. Garnish the porridge with the ginger and spring onions and serve.

Chef's Notes

- You can just use hot water if you so desire in place of stock.

- I would recommend with this dish that it would be better to lightly poach the eggs first or ensure that they are from salmonella-free flocks, and that you also ensure the eggs are cooked in the porridge before serving to guests.

- This is a popular dish eaten at all times of the day and is very substantial.

Moo Grob

Crispy Fried Pork with Chillies

Method

1. Score the pork belly and then rub in salt. Leave for 30 minutes then brush off any excess salt and cut into strips or leave whole.

2. Peel and finely dice the shallots. Blanch and skin the tomatoes, remove the core, then cut into small dice.

3. Top and tail the chillies and remove the seeds, then finely slice into suitable sizes.

4. Place enough oil to be able to deep-fry the pork in a pan. Heat and cook until the pork is golden brown and crispy. Remove, drain onto kitchen paper and keep warm.

Measurements	Ingredients
300g	Pork belly
100g	Shallots
4	Tomatoes
2	Red chillies
2	Green chillies
10g	Garlic purée
10g	Ginger purée
10g	Coriander root

continued over →

5. Pour off any excess oil from the pan and sweat off the garlic, ginger and shallots, then add the chillies, coriander root, diced tomato and fry for 1–2 minutes. Add the wine, stock, fish sauce and soy sauces and bring all the ingredients to the boil, then reduce to a simmer.

6. Add the pork and cook for a further 8 minutes.

7. Check the seasoning then portion into suitable plates or bowls and garnish with the chopped coriander leaves.

8. This dish is best served with steamed rice.

...continued	
20ml	Rice wine
60ml	Vegetable or chicken stock
30ml	Fish sauce
15ml	Light soy sauce
30ml	Dark soy sauce
20g	Coriander leaves (chopped)
	Salt
	Vegetable oil

Chef's Notes

• If you cannot find any coriander root, supplement with chopped coriander.

• Please note the pot or pan should never be more than one-third full of oil.

• This dish is simple but can be fiery. Thick soy sauce adds sweetness to the dish and mellows the spice a little.

• The fish sauce adds that authentic flavour and extra protein. Fish sauces are somewhat of a bewilderment to many uninitiated chefs, but as with soy sauces there are numerous varieties that differ from country to country and sometimes area to area. Fish sauce is made by layering small fish in tanks with salt between each layer. It is left to ferment for 3 months. The liquid is then decanted, normally into earthenware pots in the sun. The pots and sun help to remove bad odours but some may argue this point. This is the best grade of fish sauce. The next grade is when the liquid is pressed out. The worst grade is when water is added and the liquid is decanted.

Tom Khing Kai

Ginger and Lemongrass-flavoured Chicken

Method

1. Peel and purée the ginger, garlic and the galangal. Peel and finely slice the shallots. Cut the stalks off the bottom of the lemongrass and crush it. Cut the kaffir lime leaves into a fine julienne after removing the stalk.

2. Remove the stalks and seeds and cut the bird's eye chillies into thin slices. Dry roast the dried chillies a little in a suitable wok or pan then crush them in a pestle and mortar with the juice from the limes and coriander root.

Measurements	Ingredients
3–4cm	Ginger
3 cloves	Garlic
3–4cm	Galangal
100g	Shallots
2 stalks	Lemongrass
2	Kaffir lime leaves

continued over →

3. Bring the stock slowly to the boil and simmer, then add the lemongrass stalks.

4. Pour the oil into a suitable wok and then add the garlic, ginger, galangal, shallots and bird's eye chillies and cook until fragrant.

5. Add the ingredients from the wok to the stock. Cook for 2 minutes.

6. Add the dried chillies, lime juice, bamboo shoots and the coriander root. Then bring back to the boil, add the chicken and simmer for 10–12 minutes. Remove the lemongrass stalks then add the fish sauce and check for seasoning.

7. Portion into suitable bowls.

Chef's Notes

• If you cannot find any coriander root, supplement with chopped coriander.

• No extra garnish is required for this dish.

...continued

8–10	Bird's eye chillies (green)
8–10	Dried red chillies
3	Limes (juice only)
20ml	Palm oil
1lt	Chicken stock
50g	Bamboo shoots (sliced)
400g	Diced chicken
40–60ml	Fish sauce
20g	Coriander root
	Fresh ground black pepper

Dtom Gkati Bplah Doog

Catfish with Coconut and Turmeric

Method

1. Peel the shallots and cut in half. Remove the stalk from the lemongrass.

2. Roughly dice the turmeric, onion, galangal and lemongrass and then pound in a pestle and mortar or food blender until smooth paste is achieved.

3. Gut the fish and then remove the head and retain it. Cut the fish into 150g portions, either in steaks or diced.

4. Heat the oil in a pan and then add the paste and cook out until fragrant, stir and don't allow to burn. Add the coconut milk and cook out for 2–3 minutes.

5. Add the salt and sugar and fish head and boil, reducing the milk by one-third.

Measurements	Ingredients
8	Small shallots
2 stalks	Lemongrass
10cm	Turmeric (peeled)
1	Small red onion (peeled)
2.5cm	Galangal (peeled)
1 x 1kg	Catfish (or carp)
30–40ml	Coconut oil
900ml	Coconut milk (thick or thin)
10g	Sea salt
5–10g	Palm sugar
50ml	Fish sauce
10g	Chopped coriander

6. Remove the fish head and add the fish portions to the milk and slowly cook on a low heat, adding the fish sauce. This should take 10 minutes; ensure an even cooking is achieved.

7. Serve on suitable plates and dress with a little chopped coriander.

Chef's Notes

- Many people from the north of Thailand rely on fish such as catfish and carp as well as frogs that they catch with nets, baskets and rods from the paddy fields and freshwater rivers. This dish was served to me in the province of Ubon Ratchathani in a restaurant on the Moon River with a paddy field to the side, where you could see the fish swimming.

- The dish has very subtle flavours of turmeric and coconut that are often used with fish in Thailand.

- Coconut helps to reduce the heat in many dishes, helping to prevent the lips tingling and the mouth numbing.

- If you cannot obtain fresh turmeric, substitute with 20–30g powered turmeric.

- Like numerous curries, this sauce is better made the day before.

SOUTHERN THAILAND

Southern Thailand is often referred to as the Thai Malay peninsula, which has the Indian Ocean on one side and the South China Sea on the other, and covers an area from Trang on the Andaman Coast down to the Malaysian border, then up to the Gulf of Thailand. Southern Thailand also shares part of its northern border with Myanmar (Burma).

Southern Thailand is made up of some 14 provinces: Krabi, Nakhon Si Thammarat, Chumphon, Narathiwat, Pattani, Phang Nga, Phattalung, Phuket, Ranong, Satun, Songkhla, Surat Thani, Trang and finally Yala. These states occupy some 70,715 square kilometres. The topography is varied, including paddy and vegetable fields, mountains, jungles, beaches, lakes, waterfalls, caves and islands of all shapes and sizes.

The most prominent tourist attraction in the south is the island of Phuket located in the Andaman Sea.

There are two rainy seasons in the south. From May through until September is the main monsoon period, which brings heavy rain to the west coast. The east coast suffers heavy rain from November through to February.

The dense tropical rain forest and jungles give the south a humid and hot climate. Three of Thailand's main exports that come from the south are tin, coconuts and rubber. They also harvest large numbers of pineapples and cashew nuts.

There are large concentrations of the ethnic Chinese in many of the provincial state capitals while the general population of Muslims live in the more rural areas. The further south you travel and the closer you get to Malaysia, you will find more Muslims and exquisite mosques. You encounter a change of culture and religion. This also affects the food and cuisine, as the further south you go, the more lamb and mutton is eaten rather than pork. Yet in other areas of Thailand, lamb or mutton is not really seen or enjoyed.

The people of this region are known as Thai pàk tâi, and are mostly seafaring people. If you travel down either coast you will see the highly decorated and colorful fishing boats bringing back their day's catch. The great consequence of this is the predominance of seafood in the diet. Southern Thais can enjoy seafood all year round.

The close proximity to a Muslim country like Malaysia and its Islamic culture together with Chinese and Malay descendants has resulted in some of the finest cuisine produced anywhere in Asia. It draws on numerous spices from Indian and Malay cuisine such as cinnamon, cardamom, cumin and turmeric, combined with traditional flavours like lemongrass, galangal and chillies. This has created a style of cuisine that is not only unique but also very tasty.

The sultry taste of the south is often pungent and slightly sweet. Many of the specialities of the region can be very hot on the tongue. The influence of Malaysia on southern cuisine can be seen in the extensive use of turmeric for example, the favourite dish Gaeng leuang or yellow curry is a spicy coconut and bamboo shoot soup with fish. It is a rather sour and spicy hot soup. Then you have the famous Massaman curry, which is a very popular dish spiced with kaffir lime leaves, ginger, nutmeg or galangal, cardamom, cayenne pepper, paprika, coriander, vinegar and fish sauce.

One of southern Thai's best loved dishes is Gaeng tai pla, or better known by Westerners as fish viscera curry. It is made from chillies, shrimp paste and fermented fish viscera, turmeric, peanuts, bamboo shoots and grilled fish. This is not a typical curry; it is hot and has a strange taste.

One of the most attractive dishes I've seen in the south is called Khao yam. It is made from strips of vegetables common to that region, served on fragrant rice with lemongrass, peanuts, green beans, bean sprouts and sour mango, and garnished with kaffir lime leaves, chilli pepper, lime and a piquant sweet and sour sauce.

The Chinese influence can be seen in the many noodle dishes like Khanom jiin naam yaa and Khanom chin, white noodles soaked in nam ya, a sort of curry paste made from puréed fish that is very flavoursome. One of the great pleasures in the south is the fact that nearly all restaurants will serve you with a helping of vegetables 'nam prik', free of charge with your order. Roti is a staple food in the south. It is unleavened bread fried and used as a dip when you have a seafood curry, or it can be stuffed with spices, onions and different meats.

Vegetarian cooking in Thailand is still very important. Meat was very scarce in times past. It was also very difficult to get fish unless you lived on or near the coast, although dried fish was available. The absence of refrigeration was also a factor in the lack of meat and fish inland. Large sections of the population remain vegetarians today and believe it to be a healthy lifestyle.

The provinces

Chumphon Province, the state capital is around 500 kilometres from Bangkok and the translation from Thai is meeting place. There are a number of islands close to Chumphon, the most famous being Koh Samet, but from a Thai chef's point of view, the most important is Ko Rang Kachiu. This is called 'bird's nest island'. It is restricted to protect the swiftlets' nests, which are collected for gourmet chefs. Chumphon Province is not known as a place for its cuisine but, intriguingly, it has many side-street stalls selling southern delicacies. Chumphon is also famous for its princess fingernail bananas, which are small, slender and relatively cheap.

Ranong Province is possibly the least populated region in Thailand with some 80 per cent covered in forest and nearly 70 per cent being mountainous. Its economy is based on mineral extraction, partly due to the rainfall of the region. Crops of cashew nuts, coconuts, rubber and fishing also support its infrastructure. The capital of the province is Ranong, and is small in comparison to other state capitals. Ranong is separated from Burma by the River Pakchan. The Hokkien Chinese influenced the capital as they were the first settlers to the area and this can be seen still in the architecture. The province is better known for its gems, waterfalls and hot springs than its cuisine.

Phang Nga Province is the main departure point for Phuket. Other islands off the coast, such as Krabi and Surin (marine park), are sometimes restricted due to the 'chao leh, choa nàam' or sea gypsies. These islands' villages hold traditional ceremonies on full moons in March. Around this area, including the Similan Islands, are some of the best diving areas in the world. This is why the town and region is dominated with dishes like Nàam yaa (fish curry) and Khao tom pla (rice soup with fish).

Phuket Province – also known as the Paradise Island – is often referred to by the tourist industry as the 'pearl of the south' nestling in between the Andaman Sea and the Indian Ocean. The island is about the same size as Singapore. It was once known as Ko Thalang. The island has developed a culture a little different from the mainland, which is partly due to its colourful history.

Phuket is on the main trade routes between Indian and China and derived its wealth from tin, rubber and cashew nuts, as it still does today. Numerous Western nations traded with Phuket including the Portuguese, Dutch, French and English. Many of these traders left

173

cultural influences on Phuket, the biggest of these being the Chinese and the Portuguese. These influences mixed with the southern Thais and the indigenous Chao naan people, which makes for delightful Indo-Portuguese, Chinese and colonial-style influenced architecture. The largest population is Thai Muslims (35 per cent).

Not all the visitors were so friendly. The Burmese tried to invade the island in 1785, but were repelled by the island's most famous heroines, Thao Thep Kasatti and Thao Sisunthon, who gathered the islanders together and beat off the invaders.

Phuket is blessed with many palm-fringed beaches with powdery sand, surrounded by island-dotted seas and magnificent bays. It has superb seafood, which makes it a magnet for tourists. There are around 30 islands off the coast of Phuket. Some are large enough to sustain fishing communities, coconut and rubber plantations while many others contain caves supporting swiftlets and the prized birds' nests. The island has a temperature of 21–34°C all year round and the wettest month is September, but the rain normally only lasts 1–2 hours. The hottest months are November through to April. This allows the terrain to develop mini-microclimates over the island, as it is very varied, comprising of a mountain, with rocky beaches, sandy beaches, hills, tropical forests and vegetation, and cliffs of limestone. There are plantations of rubber, cacao, cashew nuts, pineapples and coconuts, and paddy fields, which make it one of wealthiest provinces in Thailand.

The most important date for Phuket as far as food and cuisine goes is the first day of the ninth month of the Chinese calendar year (normally in late September or early October). At this time the Chinese descendants of Phuket commit themselves to a nine-day diet of vegetarian cuisine. The festival also takes place in other Thai towns, such as Trang and Krabi. There are numerous temple offerings, firecrackers, and colorful parades during this event. The most extraordinary part is the first day of the festival, which is marked with a parade of white-clothed people performing incredible acts of self-mutilation under a self-induced trance. Walking over hot coals, pushing iron rods through parts of their body and piercing the skin, tongue and mouth with skewers, knives and spears, in fact any sharp object that they can find! This is all undertaken in the belief that the participants are able to purify the body and spirit through the regimen.

The town centre is well known as the best place to obtain good authentic Phuket food, which is a mix of Straits Chinese, Malay and Thai cookery, and the food costs much less than in the tourist areas. Here they serve the best known dishes, such as Khanōm jiin nàam yaa phukèt, which is Chinese noodles with a puréed fish curry sauce, green beans, cucumbers and a side dish of vegetables. Variations exist on well-known dishes, such as Kari mai fan, which is a version of the Malay dish Laksa using noodles and Khài plaa mòk, a version of Hàw mòk, which is steamed egg and fish in a curry sauce, wrapped in a banana leaf.

If you would like to try something different then the sea cicadas of Phuket could be what you are looking for. They can only be found on Mai Khao Beach to the north of the island. They are a kind of mollusc locally called cicadas (Chakkachan thale), which are plentiful on Mai Khao Beach but not so abundant anywhere else. The oval-bodied shellfish live in the powdery sand and are almost the same colour. They have short legs and look a bit like a crab. They are best cooked by deep-frying in oil in a batter, and are often served as a salad. They are exotic and a delicacy and are served in restaurants around Phuket.

In Surat Thani Province the most famous city is called Chaiya and it is one of the oldest cities in Thailand. It is believed the city dates back as far as the Srivijave Empire. Surat Thani is a small trading area for rubber and coconut and is used as a stopping point on the way to Ko Samui. People arrive at the bus station and meet at the pier, and the locals miss no opportunity to bring their stalls to the Ban Don area. The local food stalls will offer things from baked chicken on rice to mango and sticky rice and an array of seafood, such as oysters and prawns with limes and chillies.

Ko Samui is Thailand's third biggest island measuring 247 square kilometres. It is surrounded by 80 other much smaller islands, which together were called Muu Ko Samui, but this reference is almost forgotten.

Six of these islands are inhabited. These islands are Ta Pao, Pha-Ngan, Ta Loy, Ma Ko and Taen.

Ko Samui's once tranquil and unpopulated environment was first inhabited by the islanders of Hainan, which is now part of China. The islanders' culture is a little different from those of the mainstream Thais and they like to refer to themselves as Chao samúi.

The island has changed over the last 20 years with the building of the airport and the ferry buses transporting holidaymakers to and from the island. Most of the population is in the town of Na Thon, on the western part of the island. One major road encircles the island. Ko Samui has two waterfalls and a number of wats (temples).

A big part of the island's economy is the export of coconuts, which were first farmed by the islanders of Hainan over 150 years ago.

To get to eat some real island cooking you will have to go a little further inland, as most of the restaurants are owned by Thais from Bangkok and not the native islanders. The native food is distinctive in that the obvious use of coconut is very evident. Fruits like durian, langsat and rambutan, cultivated on the island, are in abundance.

The food offered around the island varies, but the seafood is excellent. With its mixture of spices it can be hot, but it can be toned down if you ask. Spicy dishes common to the area include Khao tom kung (mild rice soup flavoured with shrimp), Khaw yam (spicy rice salad) or Tom khlong (salted fish boiled with tamarind and onions), a nice little spiced

soup. One of the more unusual ingredients used in southern Thai cookery is the seeds of the sa-tor (parkia speciosa) tree. These can be eaten raw, boiled or even fried with other ingredients like shrimps, a dish which is very popular. The Gai tom ka (chicken, coconut cream and galangal soup) and sticky rice with mango and coconut milk are common in restaurants and bars around the island.

Nakhon Si Thammarat Province is mainly composed of rugged mountains and forest, and until recently was the last bastion of the Thai communists. The economy of the northern coast is built upon fishing and shrimp farming. The central plains produce mainly rubber, rice, coffee and fruit from plantations with the wonderful mangosteen being the dominant fruit of the region.

Nakhon Si Thammarat became an important centre for culture and religion during the early Thai kingdoms. For example, classical dance and the art of shadow play all came from this region. Dance masks and puppets made from buffalo are still made in the region.

This area is often neglected by tourists due to its proximity to the busier island of Ko Samui. It has a relaxed atmosphere and a great reputation for fine cuisine and handicraft and is especially known for its basketware.

The food in this part of Thailand is influenced by the Chinese and Indian populations, for example you can see street traders serving Khâo mók (chicken biryani) and on the next stall you can eat Roti klûay (banana pancakes). There are numerous Hokkien-style restaurants and noodle shops. In the centre of the town is a bazaar (Bovorn Bazaar) and an open-air resturant that specialises in the traditional Nakhon cuisine. They serve Kaeng tai plaa (a spicy fish curry), Khanõm jiin (curry noodles and vegetables) and the southern-style spicy rice salad called Khâo yam. All over the city you will find many vendors selling the famous roti. The most famous of the dishes is the Roti klûay, for which the vendors use only the freshest of banana and purée to order. Other roti dishes include roti with curry, roti with egg or chicken, the variety is endless. The occasional vender can offer Khanõm jíip, which translated means chicken and shrimp dumplings.

The Khao Luang National Park is in the centre of the province and covers 570 square kilometres. The park still has wild leopards, tigers and elephants along with fruit orchards, and waterfalls.

Phattalung Province is over 840 kilometres from Bangkok and is thought to be in the realm of the ancient Sri Vijaya Kingdom, which has been long forgotten. Only a few hallowed hills remain today. Phattalung is one of the few provinces in the south that thrives by growing rice.

The provincial capital Phattalung is small in comparison with other provincial capitals and has a population of around 34,500, with a large Chinese community. This province is not really known for its cuisine but has slight variations on dishes such as Khâo yam (rice with peanuts, kaffir lime leaves, coconut and shrimps) and Kài yâang. A southern Thai

favourite which comes from this province is a snack called Klûay chap (deep-fried banana). In the town, the shop Mair Daeng sells this and other sweeter and saltier versions.

Well over 20 varieties of banana are sold and eaten in Thailand. The two main ingredients in desserts in Thailand are coconut and banana. The most commonly used banana variety is called Klûay namwa, which is the small, sweeter type. The most common dessert eaten all over Thailand is called Klûay buat chee. All you need to do to make this is slice the banana and bring it to the boil with coconut milk and serve it warm.

If you have a real sweet tooth, then try the candied banana (Klûay namwa cheuam). Make a sugar stock syrup and bring the whole or sliced banana to the boil and remove from the heat. The banana (Klûay namwa) will turn a very pale reddish colour. Serve warm.

Another part of the ancient Sri Vijaya Kingdom, Songkhla Province is 950 kilometres from Bangkok and has a population of around 86,000. The name Songkhla is thought to come from the lion-shaped mountain opposite the harbour. Today it is called Khao Daeng.

The area has become Westernised over the last few years largely due to the multinational oil company workers.

The inland sea of Thaleh Sapor or Songkhla Lake as it is also known, is where the famous black tiger prawns are found, but they have been over fished and it is now illegal to gill-net fish for the prawns.

There are still enclaves of old Malay, Portuguese and Chinese architecture around the back streets and the waterfront. The waterfront and pier are bustling areas where you will see the local fishermen unload their day's catch and begin to set up their boats for the following day's work. You can see some fantastic fish and seafood for sale here.

Unlike Phattalung, Songkhla is famed for its excellent seafood cooking, which comes from the diversity of the traders. The ethnic mix of native Thais, Chinese, Malay and Muslims is well reflected in the food. As with many of the night markets and hawker centres, Songkhla's is located near the old train station with tables and chairs laid out by the stall holders anticipating the arrival of their customers.

Another bustling and famous place in the province is Hat Yai, 50 kilometres from the Malay border. It is effectively the major city of the south, with commerce, entertainment, and shopping and is the centre for culinary excellence with offerings from the Andaman Sea and the Gulf of Thailand. Exotic dishes like bird's nest soup, shark fin soup and charcoal grilled squid are amongst the many offerings. You can indulge in roti, dal, biryani and curried crab (Muslim style), Chinese noodles, dim sum or dishes such as Khâo nâa pèt (Chinese roasted duck) or perhaps Malay dishes like Rojak and Nasi. Although there are many Chinese, Malay and Muslim eateries, there are also some excellent Thai restaurants. In Hat Yai, there are a small number of night markets

offering fresh food. Hat Yai is also famous for a single street called Snake Street where you can have a live snake killed at the table. Its blood is mixed with a rice wine as a drink, its heart is eaten raw, and the meat is then used for the soup.

Krabi Province is composed of up to 150 islands and hundreds of years ago this area used to be a great hideout for the Asian pirates. Today it belongs to the Hat Noppharat Thraa-Ko Phi Phi National Marine Park. The province's major income comes from tin, rubber and palm oil. The provincial capital is called Krabi, which is on the banks of the Krabi River. It is an expanding city with a growing population of around 20,000 people. The city is 180 kilometres from Phuket and 1,000 kilometres from Bangkok. The best food around this area is found on Saphaan Jao Fah or the big pier. The food stalls are larger, selling a range of Thai desserts with dishes like Sangkaya gab kannoon (jackfruit custard) cooked in banana leaves, or sticky rice with mango (Kah niew mamung). The main delights are the seafood, with traders selling Thai shrimps with straw mushrooms cooked in peanut oil and fish sauce. Lemongrass, Thai basil and shrimp soup is particularly pleasant. One vegetarian dish from a Chinese stall that is worthy of note is the Tao Hou or fried tofu with a sweet nut sauce. It is excellent.

From as far back as the first century but especially in the seventh and twelfth centuries Trang Province was an important centre for trade for ships travelling to and from Trang and the Straits of Malacca. During the the reign of the Sri vijaya Empire, the great cultural and trade centres were Nakhon Si Thammarat, Surat Thani and Trang. They served as a safe port and transit area for the east coast and Sumatra. It was also a common port for the western traveller at the time of the Ayutthaya period.

The city of Trang is often called the 'the city of waves' as it has the best surfing waves in Thailand. They come with Robinson Crusoe-style beaches of long white sand and crystal clear waters. This area is one of the best-kept secrets in Thailand and has very few tourists.

Trang is famous for its Khanōm jiin or the Chinese noodle curry of which there are a number of choices in which to dip your noodles! For example, your choice can be Kaeng tai plaa, which is a spiced mixture of green beans, fish sauce, bamboo shoots, fish and potato. Náam yaa is a very spicy ground fish and not for the faint hearted, or Náam phrík, a lightly spiced, sweet peanut sauce. Then you can have a choice of sweet pickled vegetables, or just freshly grated fruit like green papaya.

Satun Province is the southern-most province and shares its border with Malaysia. This province was part of the Malaysian province of Kedah before 1813. At this time a number of Malay provinces paid tribute to the then Siamese state. The treaty of 1909 released parts of these areas to the British.

Satun is not famous for its cuisine in reality but more for its Ko Tarutao National Marine Park, and immigration port. Its population is 22,000 and there are approximately 51 islands off its coastline.

Yala Province is often referred to as the cleanest city in Thailand, even with a population close to 70,000. It is one of the fastest developing provinces, with its main income coming from rubber. It also produces large numbers of coconut and banana. Yala is also a mainly Muslim state, with most of the Muslim population in the more rural areas with a large Chinese community in the city. There are large areas of jungle and mountainous regions in the province.

Because Yalas is close to Malaysia, its culture and cuisine is heavily influenced. For example, fish is cooked in pandan leaves and the spicy dish rendang can be found on menus. Also other obvious dishes like Chinese dumplings, Jók and the Muslim roti are in abundance.

The town of Betong is famous for its flavoursome chicken, which is used for a local speciality called Kái betong.

Pattani Province is much smaller, with just over 41,000 people, but it is not as clean as its neighbour Yala. It also borders Songkhla and Narathiwat Provinces, with its northern coastline facing the Gulf of Thailand. Its main claim is that it was one of the first trading ports established by the Portuguese in 1516, followed by the Japanese, Dutch, and then the British. Pattani is known more for its weekend tourist and holiday trade than its cuisine, although there are some traditional fishing villages along the coast like in Hat Talo Kapo where you can eat really nice fresh seafood from local vendors.

Narathiwat Province is possibly one of the smallest provincial capitals in Thailand. It has a culture and architecture all of its own, Many of the buildings are made of wood, and these can be hundreds of years old. Every year in September the town shows off its culture with music and dance, traditional boat races and crafts. The fishing boats are colourfully decorated and are called 'reua kaw-lae'.

Narathiwat is another province that is not really known for its cuisine, but with a large proportion of its inhabitants being Muslim, many spicy curries can be found. The night market has numerous stalls selling Khâo kaeng and Khâo yam, along with Malay noodles, curry and rice dishes.

Tod Man Poo

Crab Cakes

Method

1. Combine the egg, curry paste, mustard powder, garlic, coriander, lemon juice, fish sauce, white breadcrumbs and chilli together, then fold in the crab meat. You may need to add a little water to bind.

Measurements	Ingredients
500g	Crab meat
1	Egg
15g	Yellow curry paste

continued over →

2. Divide the paste into 8 even balls.

3. Press each ball into a 'cake' shape (4cm dia) and lightly dust in flour.

4. Pre-heat the deep-fryer or wok to approximately 180 –190°C.

5. Place the cakes into the fryer one at a time to avoid lowering the fryer temperature by adding too many at once. Fry for 6–8 minutes or until a golden colour.

6. Remove from the fryer onto kitchen paper and serve hot, with salad garnish or dipping sauces.

...continued

2.5 g	Dry mustard powder
2 cloves	Garlic (puréed)
10g	Coriander (chopped)
5ml	Lemon juice
10ml	Fish sauce
150g	White breadcrumbs
1	Red chilli (finely diced)
60g	Plain flour or cornflour

Chef's Notes

- Extreme caution must be observed when deep-frying in a wok.

- This simple crab dish recipe is from Songkhla and is best prepared with fresh crab the day before. This will allow the spices to penetrate.

- You may also purée the crab, press the paste onto a skewer and deep-fry then serve with dipping sauces. This method can be seen on a number of hawker stalls along the quay side, with communal dipping bowls (not recommended due to hygiene and cross-contamination).

Kluay Buat Chee

Bananas in Coconut Milk

Method

1. Peel each banana and cut into four equal quarters. Bring the coconut milk and sugar to a simmer and stir in the coconut cream and salt until it completely dissolves.

2. Add the bananas and simmer for 1–2 minutes then remove from the heat and allow to cool slightly.

3. Divide equally and serve warm.

Measurements	Ingredients
4	Bananas
300ml	Coconut milk (thick or thin)
75g	Coconut cream
100g	Palm sugar
2.5g	Salt

Chef's Notes

- This dish is a very popular Thai dessert from the Pattalung Province.

- It is very sweet, which may require a little adjustment on the amount of sugar added.

- You can use demera or brown sugar, but the best results are with palm sugar.

- For variations on this theme, you can use sweet potato, taro or even pumpkin.

Sangkhayaa Gab Kanoon

Thai Custard with Jackfruit

Method

Measurements	Ingredients
330ml	Coconut milk (thick or thin)
2 x 15cm strips	Banana leaves
3	Eggs (beaten)
2	Egg yolks
40g	Palm (or brown) sugar
10g	Cornflour
200g	Jackfruit (chopped)

1. Bring the coconut milk to the boil with the strips of banana leaf. Allow to cool and remove the strips.

2. Whisk the whole eggs, yolks, sugar and cornflour together until fully incorporated.

3. Then pour the coconut milk slowly onto the mixture.

4. Pour the mixture back into the pan, add the jackfruit and bring almost to a simmer.

5. Transfer the mixture to a heat-proof dish with a lid and steam for 30–40 minutes. You may transfer the mixture into four smaller dishes and cook in a water bath (165°C, 325°F, Gas Mark 3) for 20–30 minutes, if you do not have a steamer.

6. Serve hot or cold.

Chef's Notes

- This recipe is from Pattalung in southern Thailand.

- You can use pumpkin instead of jackfruit, but instead of chopping the pumpkin, just carefully remove the top and remove the seeds and fibrous centre. Pour the mixture into the pumpkin, and continuing from stage 5, replace the top and steam. This dish is called Sangkhayaa fak thawng.

- This dish was popularised by Marie Phaulkon in the late 1600s, when she introduced desserts using eggs.

Khao Pad Songkhla Prik Gung

Tiger Prawns with Chillies and Rice

Measurements	Ingredients
1	Red pepper
1	Onion
2	Spring onions
2	Red chillies
400g	Black tiger prawns
2.5g	Caster sugar
20ml	Light soy sauce
30ml	Coconut oil
15g	Garlic purée
20ml	Fish sauce
500g	Jasmine rice (cooked)
10g	Coriander (chopped)

Method

1. Peel and slice the pepper, onion and spring onions. Deseed the red chilli and very finely chop.

2. Peel and devein the prawns. Mix the sugar into the soy sauce until dissolved.

3. Pour the oil into a wok and place on a high heat. Add the garlic and cook until it begins to colour. Add the prawns and stir.

4. Pour in the fish sauce and light soy sauce and stir.

5. Add the chillies, onions and red pepper and cook for 1 minute.

6. Add the rice and stir until the rice is fully incorporated.

7. Just before serving add the spring onion and chopped coriander.

8. Serve hot.

Chef's Notes

- This is a dish using the famous black tiger prawns of Songkhla Province. This dish and variations of this recipe are quite common around the province.

- If you cannot obtain these prawns you can substitute them with tiger prawns.

Gung Kratiem

Tiger Prawns with Garlic

Method

1. Peel and devein the prawns. Peel and chop the garlic.

2. Heat the wok and oil over a high heat. Add the garlic until it begins to colour, then add the prawns and cook out for 2–3 minutes. Add the soy and fish sauces.

3. Dust over the sugar and add the stock. Cook and reduce by half.

4. Dress the plate (or four plates) with the garnish ingredients.

5. Place the prawns on the plate and then pour the sauce over the prawns.

6. Serve immediately.

Chef's Notes

• This recipe is a light starter for any Thai menu.

• This dish is from the Songkhla Province, which is famous for the black tiger prawns.

• If you cannot obtain these prawns you can substitute them with tiger prawns.

Measurements	Ingredients
16	Black tiger prawns
4 cloves	Garlic
40ml	Palm oil
20ml	Light soy sauce
20ml	Dark soy sauce
20ml	Fish sauce
2.5g	Caster sugar
75ml	Fish stock
Garnish	Ingredients
4	Red chilli flowers
30g	Cucumber slices
8	Lettuce leaves (Chinese)
4	Spring onions (sliced)
	Coriander leaves

Roti

Measurements	Ingredients
400g	Wheat flour
75ml	Water (ice cold)
2.5g	Salt
5g	Caster sugar
15g	Clarified butter
1	Egg (beaten)
60ml	Sunflower oil

continued over →

Method

1. Placed the sifted flour onto a clean surface and make a well. Add the water, salt, sugar, butter and the beaten egg into the centre and mix the flour into the liquids to make a dough.

2. Knead the dough until it is smooth and soft. Divide into balls approximately 75–100g each.

3. Very lightly roll the balls in oil and place on a tray and rest for 3–4 hours.

4. Roll the balls as flat as possible with the palm of your hand, shaping them into a flat round disk. If using a filling, add it now. See stage 4 Roti Mataba method below.

5. Heat a griddle pan to a high heat and pour over a little oil. Place the Roti on to the griddle pan when smoke appears. Press down every now and then to ensure even cooking. Turn over when golden brown.

6. Remove the Roti from the pan and serve.

7. To serve as a dessert, warm the condensed milk and dust the Roti in sugar and serve.

...continued

Roti Mataba	Ingredients
5g	Cumin seeds
5g	Dried chillies
10g	Coriander seeds
20g	Garlic purée
100g	Shallots (chopped)
2.5g	Curry leaves
20g	Madras curry powder
200g	Minced chicken
2	Red chillies (cut into fine strips)
1	Egg (beaten)
20ml	Clarified butter
Roti dessert	**Ingredients**
60ml	Condensed milk
10g	Caster sugar

Method Roti Mataba

1. Toast the cumin, dried chillies and coriander seeds. Then place into a pestle and mortar with the garlic, shallots, curry leaves, madras powder and a little salt. Pound until a smooth paste is achieved.

2. Fry off the paste until it becomes fragrant, then add the minced chicken and cook out.

3. Add the finely sliced chillies and then stir until fully incorporated. Finally add the beaten egg, stirring until cooked.

4. Cool and then add to the centre of each Roti at stage 4. Flatten out and place the filling in the centre, flattening the edges. Then lift up the edges to make a square pouch or pocket. Ensure the pocket is well sealed. Then continue to stage 5.

Chef's Notes

- For an Egg Roti, beat an egg and halfway through cooking at stage 6, roll or brush the hot Roti in the egg and continue to cook.

- For a Banana Roti, add banana purée to the centre of each Roti at stage 2. Flatten out and place the filling in the centre, flattening the edges. Then lift up the edges to make a square pouch or pocket. Ensure the pocket is well sealed. Then continue to stage 5.

Khao Tom Madt

Banana with Sticky Rice

Method

1. Soak the rice overnight in water. Drain well. Peel and cut the bananas into slices

2. Blanch the banana leaf in hot water then plunge it into ice-cold water. Cut the leaf into four 12cm x 20cm pieces.

3. Bring the coconut milk to a simmer and add the sugar and salt and dissolve, then stir in the rice and cook over a slow heat. Keep stirring over a low heat until all the milk is absorbed. Stir in the bananas.

Measurements	Ingredients
175g	Sticky rice (glutinous rice)
4	Bananas
$\frac{1}{2}$	Banana leaf
500ml	Coconut milk (thick or thin)
60g	Caster sugar
	Salt

4. Allow to cool, then spoon the rice equally into the banana leaves. Tie the leaves securely and place into a steamer for 20 minutes and then serve immediately.

Chef's Notes

• This again is one of the more popular desserts in Thailand. It is also very filling and sweet.

• If you do not like or want to use banana, you can use mango instead.

Kaeng Phanaeng Kai

Chicken Curry Malay Style

Method

1. Place all the paste ingredients (page 186) in a pestle and mortar or food processor and blend to a smooth paste.

2. Peel and chop the onion. Skin and cut the tomatoes into concasse (small dice). Remove the root of the lemongrass and finely chop. Shred the lime leaves.

3. Blend 50g peanuts, tomato purée, fish sauce, sugar and 100ml coconut milk together and keep separate.

4. Brown off the chicken in a suitable wok, then remove and keep hot. Add the curry paste to

Measurements	Ingredients
100g	Onion
4	Tomatoes
1 stalk	Lemongrass
4	Kaffir lime leaves
60g	Roasted peanuts
20g	Tomato purée
20ml	Fish sauce
20g	Palm sugar
300ml	Coconut milk (thick or thin)

continued over →

the remaining oil and cook out until fragrant (do not burn).

5. Return the chicken and continue to cook for 4–5 minutes. Add 150ml coconut milk, the nut purée, lemongrass and chicken stock. Place a lid on top of the wok and slowly cook out for 45 minutes. You could transfer this to a clay pot (or casserole dish) and leave in the oven for 45 minutes on a medium heat.

6. Remove the lid and add the kaffir lime leaves, coriander and half of the basil and cook out for a further 10–15 minutes, until dry in texture.

7. Garnish with the remaining peanuts, basil and spoon 50ml coconut milk over the top of the curry. Serve with plain boiled or steamed jasmine rice.

Chef's Notes

- This dish should be slightly dry, a red and brown colour and spicy. You can use beef or lamb instead of chicken and I have even seen quarters of boiled eggs in with this curry.

...continued

700g	Chicken (cut up on the bone for stewing)
30ml	Sunflower oil
100ml	Chicken stock
10g	Coriander (chopped)
20g	Holy basil (chopped)
Panaeng Paste	**Ingredients**
60ml	Sunflower oil
8	Red chillies (stalk and seeds removed)
15 cloves	Garlic (peeled)
4cm	Ginger (peeled)
1	Red pepper (diced)
5g	Shrimp paste
5g	White peppercorns
5g	Ground coriander
2.5g	Ground cumin
2 stalks	Lemongrass (chopped)
20ml	Fish sauce
8	Spring onions (chopped)

Kaeng Matsaman

Moslem Curry

Method

1. Place all paste ingredients into a blender and purée to a fine paste.

2. Peel and dice the onions. Chop the peanuts. Place the bay leaves, cassia bark and chilli into a string muslin cloth and tie securely.

3. Pour the oil into a suitable wok and seal and brown the beef over a high heat. Add the onions and brown. Stir in the Matsaman paste and garlic cook until fragrant, then add the stock.

4. Stir continually and add the bay leaves, cassia bark, chilli, sugar and a pinch of salt. Bring to the boil and simmer for $1\frac{1}{2}$ hours, reducing the liquid by half.

5. Remove the muslin cloth and add the coconut milk and half the peanuts. Continue to cook for 15 minutes at a simmer.

6. Garnish with the remaining peanuts and serve with plain boiled jasmine rice.

Measurements	Ingredients
100g	Onions
70g	Peanuts
4	Bay leaves
1 x 5cm	Cassia bark
2	Whole chilli peppers
50ml	Sunflower oil
500g	Beef (diced)
500ml	Beef stock
15g	Brown sugar
200ml	Coconut milk (thick or thin)
20g	Garlic purée
	Salt
Matsaman paste	Ingredients
2	Kaffir lime leaves
3cm	Ginger or galangal (diced)

continued over →

Chef's Notes

- You can either use chicken, beef, lamb or prawns in this curry.

- A lot of the traditional curries made by the Thai housewife or street trader are pounded in a pestle and mortar with no recipes or measurements. The paste is made by a combination of instinct, taste and experience and the unique freshness of the ingredients.

- The further south you go towards the Malay border, the more Muslim restaurants and food stalls you will see and one curry you will see a lot of is Mussaman (masaman or matsaman), especially in Yala and Satun Provinces.

...continued

10g	Ground nutmeg
2.5g	Ground cloves
5g	Mace
5g	Cardamom powder
2.5g	Cayenne pepper
20g	Ground coriander
2.5g	Ground caraway seeds
10g	Paprika
30g	Shrimp paste
10ml	Vinegar
10ml	Fish sauce

Nam Prik

Hot Chilli

Method

1. Destalk the chillies and peel and chop the garlic cloves.

2. Place all the ingredients into a blender and purée until a very fine paste is achieved.

3. Place in a sterilised jar with a tight-fitting lid and keep until required.

Measurements	Ingredients
100g	Bird's eye chillies
4 cloves	Garlic
30ml	Lemon juice
5g	Brown sugar
15ml	Fish sauce
10g	Shrimp or anchovy paste

Chef's Notes

- You can use Nam prik on rice, noodles, fish and raw vegetables in Thailand. The recipe for nam prik will, without a doubt, differ from book to book and chef to chef, no two chefs I have met have used the same one!

- You can serve this with any savoury dish and it will mature with age, as long as you have sterilised the jar and sealed it correctly. This is due to the acid content of the paste.

- If you add 30g tamarind, 200g grated green mango mixed with 70g smoked minced herring and a dash of Tabasco to the Nam prik and roll it into very small balls, you have a savoury snack. You can replace the tamarind and mango with green olives if you wish.

Khao Yam

Rice Salad

Method

1. Cut the lemongrass, red pepper and chilli into very fine strips. Cut the green beans, mango and cucumber into fine strips. Wash the bean sprouts.

2. Fry off the onion in sunflower oil until golden brown and crispy. Drain onto kitchen towel and allow to cool.

3. Mix all the other ingredients together and serve cold.

Chef's Notes

- This southern salad is an excellent addition to any menu – refreshing, slightly spicy and full of flavour.

- Sometimes you may come across the vegetables cut with a ribbed knife to add to the attractiveness of the dish.

- The vegetables do vary, for example with carrots, sweetcorn or prawns, etc. Sometimes there may not be as many items in the dish as I have included above.

- You may also serve a sweet and sour sauce with this salad if you wish.

Measurements	Ingredients
1 stalk	Lemongrass
1	Red pepper
1	Red chilli
40g	Green beans
1	Sour (green) mango
30g	Cucumber
20g	Bean sprouts
50g	Onion (peeled and diced)
20ml	Sunflower oil
5ml	Sesame oil
10ml	Fish sauce
2	Kaffir lime leaves
40g	Peanuts (roasted or toasted)
400g	Jasmine rice (cooked)

Gaeng Leuang

Yellow Curry Paste

Method

1. Remove the stalk and chop the lemongrass. Deseed the chillies and peppers and roughly chop with the galangal and ginger.

2. Place all the ingredients into a blender and purée into a smooth paste.

3. Use as required.

Measurements	Ingredients
1 stalks	Lemongrass
2	Yellow scotch bonnet chillies
2	Yellow peppers
3cm	Galangal (peeled)

continued over →

Chef's Notes

- For a **soup** place half of the curry paste into a wok with 20ml oil and fry until it becomes fragrant. Add 300ml of coconut milk (thick or thin) and 500ml fish stock and cook for 10 minutes then add 250g diced grouper or snapper (fried and drained) and continue to cook for 2 minutes. Add coconut strips and bamboo shoots. Garnish with very fine strips of chilli, coriander and kaffir lime leaves. Serve.

- For a **curry** add the paste to the hot wok and stir until the paste has released the oil. Add 700g meat (chicken, beef or lamb on the bone) and cook out on a medium heat for 5 minutes, stirring to prevent burning and sticking. Add 500ml coconut milk (thick or thin), peanuts, chopped coriander, 30g palm sugar and a dash of rich soy sauce. Cook for a further 10 minutes. Serve with jasmine rice and vegetable accompaniments.

...continued

2cm	Ginger (peeled)
10g	Turmeric powder
5g	Ground coriander
5g	Ground cumin
10g	Shrimp paste
15ml	Fish sauce
20g	Holy basil
30ml	Coconut oil

Kao Tom Pla

Rice and Fish Soup

Method

1. Destalk and finely slice the lemongrass and galangal. Destalk and deseed the chillies and then very finely dice. Quarter the mushrooms. Remove the roots from the spring onion and cut into diamonds.

2. Bring the chicken stock, lemongrass, galangal and kaffir lime leaves to the boil and reduce to a simmer. Skim the surface for any debris.

3. Add the coconut milk and the fish, mushrooms and lime juice. Cook for 1–2 minutes.

4. Add the fish sauce, chillies, rice, spring onions and half the basil. Bring back to a simmer.

5. Skim the surface for any debris and serve hot, garnishing with any remaining basil.

Chef's Notes

- This is dish comes from the Phang Nga Province in southern Thailand. The cuisine is dominated by the sea.

Measurements	Ingredients
1 stalk	Lemongrass
3cm	Galangal or ginger
3	Birds' eye chillies
60g	Straw mushrooms
400ml	Chicken stock
2	Kaffir lime leaves
300g	Coconut milk (thick or thin)
400g	Fish fillets (sliced)
20ml	Lime juice
20ml	Fish sauce
150g	Jasmine rice (cooked)
8	Spring onions
10g	Basil (chopped)

- You can use any white fish for this dish, for example pomfret, snapper or grouper.

- This is easy to prepare and takes minutes to cook. Again the ingredients can vary depending on the chef's interpretation and area you visit.

Gai Tom Ka

Chicken and Coconut Milk Soup

Method

1. Finely slice the lemongrass and galangal. Destalk and deseed the chillies and very finely slice.

2. Bring the stock and coconut milk to the boil. Then add the sliced chicken, lemon grass, kaffir lime leaves and galangal. Simmer for 10 minutes.

3. Add the chilli and half of the coriander leaves, the lime juice and the fish sauce. Simmer for another 2–3 minutes, skim the surface and then serve hot, garnished with the remaining coriander.

Chef's Notes

- This is a very simple dish with the fragrance of the kaffir lime and lemongrass and the sharpness of the chilli and lime juice.

Measurements	Ingredients
1	Lemongrass stalk
3cm	Galangal (peeled)
1	Red chilli pepper
400g	Chicken stock
200g	Coconut milk (thick or thin)
150g	Chicken breast (cut into slices)
4	Kaffir lime leaves
20g	Coriander leaves
30ml	Lime juice
40ml	Fish sauce

OTHER THAI RECIPES

Pla Duk Pad

Golden Fried Catfish

Measurements	Ingredients
75g	Onion
2 cloves	Garlic
50g	Spring onions
20g	Coriander
1	Red pepper
6	Birds' eye chillies
40ml	Palm oil
600g	Catfish meat (with skin on)
20ml	Lime juice
20g	Brown sugar
20ml	Fish sauce

Method

1. Peel and slice the onions, garlic and spring onions. Chop the coriander. Deseed the peppers and chillies and cut into strips.

2. Heat the oil in a suitable wok and then add the catfish, and cook until crispy and golden brown. Remove from the wok with a slotted spoon.

3. Add the onions, shallots and garlic and cook until just starting to colour, then add the sliced red pepper and chilli. Cook for 1–2 minutes then add the lime juice, sugar and fish sauce. Stir until the sugar has dissolved.

4. Stir in the coriander and add the catfish. Cook for a further 1–2 minutes.

5. Serve with jasmine rice.

Chef's Notes

- This is a dish from the Lamphun area in northern Thailand.

- If you cannot obtain catfish, you could use firm white fish meat, like pike or carp. You could change the dish to use monkfish or similar.

Khao Pat Gai

Fried Chicken and Rice

Method

1. Peel and slice the spring onions. Purée the garlic cloves. Cut the snow peas in half and cut the broccoli into small florets.

2. Pour the oil into a hot wok and add the garlic and then the chicken strips. Seal the chicken well, do not burn the garlic or allow the chicken to stick.

3. Next add the soy sauce and the fish sauce and stir well.

4. Add the vegetables and continue to stir. After 2 minutes add the rice; stir well.

5. Sprinkle the sugar and spring onions and stir for a further 2–3 minutes. Serve hot.

Measurements	Ingredients
40g	Spring onion
4 cloves	Garlic
50g	Snow peas
70g	Purple broccoli
30ml	Palm oil
600g	Chicken (cut into 6cm strips)
30ml	Soy sauce (rich)
20ml	Fish sauce
600g	Jasmine rice (cooked and dry)
10g	Palm sugar (or brown)

Chef's Notes

• This dish is from one of the many small restaurants in southern Thailand, somewhere around the beach area of Ko Samui.

• You could replace the chicken with fish; and add a squeeze of lime or lemon to enhance the flavour.

Sotong Sambal Jagung Muda

Stir-fried Squid and Chilli

Method

1. Clean and dress the squid by removing the head and tail. Throw away the skin, the sack and the quill. Cut the body into three and lightly score the flesh by criss crossing it with a sharp knife and wash.

2. Place all the paste ingredients into a pestle and mortar or blender and purée until they become a smooth paste.

3. Cut the corncobs in half lengthways. Deseed the chillies and cut lengthways then in half.

4. Place the oil in a suitable wok and add the paste and cook over a high heat until it smells fragrant.

5. Add the squid and stir-fry until the squid begins to curl. Add the corncobs, the fish sauce, chillies, kaffir lime leaves and the basil. Stir and cook for 2–3 minutes over a high heat.

6. Serve hot with jasmine rice.

Measurements	Ingredients
700g	Fresh squid
24	Baby corncobs
4	Red chillies
40ml	Sunflower oil
30ml	Fish sauce
4	Kaffir lime leaves
20g	Sweet basil leaves
400g	Jasmine rice (cooked)
Paste	Ingredients
2.5g	Salt
6–8 cloves	Garlic
100g	Shallots (diced)
10	Red chillies

Chef's Notes

• This dish has its origins in the south of Thailand but you can obtain different versions in many central parts of Thailand, such is their love of seafood.

Gai Tua Lisong Khaeng

Chicken and Peanut Curry

Method

1. Place the peanuts and 10ml oil into a blender or pestle and mortar and blend into a fine smooth paste.

2. Remove the stalk and finely chop the lemongrass.

3. Pour the remaining oil into a suitable wok and place over a high heat. Stir in the red curry paste and reduce the heat to a very low flame. When it becomes fragrant add the chicken. Stir while cooking.

Measurements	Ingredients
260g	Roasted or toasted peanuts
30g	Palm oil
1 stalk	Lemongrass
30g	Red curry paste
600g	Diced chicken
400ml	Coconut milk (thick or thin)

continued over →

4. Add the coconut milk and nuts. Cook for a further 3–4 minutes then add the fish sauce, kaffir lime leaves and sugar. Cook for another 2–3 minutes.

5. Add three quarters of the basil leaves and stir for 1 minute. Garnish with the remaining basil and serve hot.

...continued

30ml	Fish sauce
4	Kaffir lime leaves
30ml	Palm sugar
10g	Sweet basil (chopped)

Chef's Notes

• This is a spicy dish and is best served with boiled rice. It originates from the streets of Chiang Mai in the north of Thailand.

Thai Satay

Method

1. Cut the beef and pork into small dice and the chicken breast into thin strips.

2. Place into a pestle and mortar or a blender the lemongrass, 10 shallots, garlic, ginger, turmeric, tamarind water and palm sugar, and blend to a fine paste. Divide into three separate containers.

3. **In the first container** for the beef, add the ground coriander and a pinch of very finely chopped coriander leaf, the condensed milk and 30ml coconut milk. Carefully thread the beef on the wooden skewers and then allow to marinate in the mixture overnight.

4. **In the second container** for the pork add 20ml sweet soy and a pinch of finely chopped coriander. Place the pork onto the skewers and allow to marinate in the mixture overnight.

5. **In the final container** for the chicken stir in the melted butter and place the chicken on skewers and then marinate for approximately 6 hours.

6. Cooking satay is always best outdoors over a very hot charcoal fire, but if this is not possible then use a grill. Cook until golden brown on all

Measurements	Ingredients
500g	Beef (fillet or sirloin)
500g	Pork tenderloin
500g	Chicken breast
1 stalk	Lemongrass (chopped)
20	Shallots (peeled)
4 cloves	Garlic
3cm	Ginger (peeled)
5g	Turmeric powder
20ml	Tamarind water
30ml	Palm sugar
15g	Ground coriander
10g	Coriander (chopped)
30ml	Condensed milk
400ml	Coconut milk (thick or thin)
60ml	Sweet soy sauce
20ml	Clarified butter
60g	Cucumber (sliced into quarters)

continued over →

sides, basting in coconut milk during cooking. This will keep the meat moist during cooking.

7. Serve with bowls of quartered shallots, cucumber, limes cut in half, sliced chillies, coriander leaves and sweet soy sauce. Serve with peanut sauce.

Satay Sauce Method

1. Place the chillies, peanuts, shallots, chilli powder, palm sugar, sweet soy, tamarind water and curry paste into a blender or pestle and mortar and blend to a smooth paste.

2. Pour the oil into a suitable wok and fry the paste until it becomes fragrant. Then add the coconut milk, stir and bring to the boil.

3. As the milk boils skim the surface for debris and excess oil. It is normal to have a little oil on the surface, but not an excessive amount.

4. Simmer until a thick consistency is achieved.

5. Serve either hot, warm or cold.

Chef's Notes

• This is the traditional Thai way to serve satay and will vary from north, east, south, and west. In Muslim areas you will not see pork and it is very impolite to ask for it due to their religious beliefs. This recipe is from a chef in Pattaya.

• I would suggest that if you serve satay ensure each person has their own bowl of peanut sauce and not a communal one.

• There are many differing satay sauces, hot ones, fiery ones and downright boring ones. This one is a mix of hot and spicy.

...continued

4	Fresh limes (cut in half)
6	Red bird's eye chillies (sliced)
6	Green bird's eye chillies (sliced)
1pkt	Kebab or satay skewers
	Salt
Satay sauce	**Ingredients**
4-5	Bird's eye chillies (de-stalked)
150g	Roasted or toasted peanuts
125g	Shallots (peeled)
2.5g	Chilli powder
40g	Palm sugar
10ml	Sweet soy sauce
20ml	Tamarind water
30g	Red curry paste
30ml	Palm oil
500ml	Coconut milk (thick or thin)
	Salt

Moo Pad King

Fried Pork with Ginger

Measurements	Ingredients
10	Chinese dried mushrooms
4 cloves	Garlic
2	Red chillies
50ml	Sunflower oil
400g	Pork tenderloin or loin (sliced)
6cm	Ginger (peeled and finely sliced)
70g	Onion
70ml	Chicken stock
10g	Palm sugar
30ml	Fish sauce
30ml	Light soy sauce
30ml	Dark soy sauce
4	Spring onions
4 sprigs	Coriander
4	Chilli flowers to garnish

Method

1. Soak the mushrooms in warm water and slice when soft. Chop the garlic finely, remove the stalk and deseed the chillies. Remove the roots from the spring onion and cut into diamonds. Cut the onion, and the chillies into 2cm slices.

2. Heat the oil in a wok over a high heat, add the garlic and fry until it is golden brown, then add the pork and seal well.

3. Add the ginger, mushrooms and the onion and continue to cook and stir for 3–4 minutes.

4. Add the chicken stock and sugar and stir until the sugar has dissolved. Do not allow the sugar to stick.

5. Next add the fish sauce, soy sauces and the chillies. Stir in well and continue to cook for 3–4 minutes, then add all the spring onions. Stir.

6. Place in a dish or on a plate and garnish with coriander sprigs and chilli flowers. Serve hot with rice.

Chef's Notes

- This dish reminds me of a story I was told while I was in Thailand. Generally Buddhists refrain from eating meat in varying degrees, but as a general rule most avoid pork. This may be because Buddha accepted a meal to avoid insulting a man who had offered him a meal containing pork. Buddha realised the man was acting in good faith and he decided to eat it. Buddha fell ill after eating the meal and died.

- This dish is quick and easy both to prepare and cook. It originates from the Songkhla region of southern Thailand. You can substitute chicken for pork.

Pad Ga Pow

Stir-fried Chicken with Holy Basil

Method

1. Destalk and deseed the pepper and chillies, and cut into slices.

2. Place the peppercorns, garlic and shallots into a pestle and mortar or blender and blend to a smooth paste.

3. Heat the oil in a suitable wok, add the chicken and cook ensuring that the mince is broken up. When the meat is sealed add the paste and cook well stirring all the time.

4. Add in the fish sauce and sugar, continue to cook for 2–3 minutes, stirring continuously.

5. Add the pepper, chilli and the basil and continue to cook and stir for a further 1–2 minutes.

6. The meat should be cooked, portioned onto the plates and garnished with sprigs of basil and chilli flowers.

Measurements	Ingredients
1	Red pepper
2	Red chillies
5g	Black peppercorns
30g	Garlic purée (made fresh)
50g	Shallots (finely diced)
20ml	Palm oil
500g	Minced chicken
40ml	Fish sauce
30g	Palm sugar
20g	Holy basil leaves
4	Holy basil sprigs and red chilli pepper flowers

Chef's Notes

• This dish is taken from a stall holder around one of the famous markets in Bangkok, called Patpong.

• You can use pork for this dish in place of the chicken.

Moo Manao

Lime Pork with Kale

Method

1. Either pan fry or grill the pork until it is cooked, then remove, slice thinly and divide evenly onto serving plates or dishes. Keep hot.

2. Cut the kale (including the stalks) into 5–6cm lengths and steam until cooked. Arrange over the pork.

Measurements	Ingredients
400g	Boneless pork loin steaks
4	Kale stalks
2	Limes

continued over →

3. Remove zest and then segment the limes keeping any juice for the sauce.

4. To make the sauce peel and very finely dice the garlic. Destalk and deseed the chillies and very finely dice them.

5. Mix all the sauce ingredients together until the sugar has dissolved. At this stage, either warm the sauce or serve it cold, garnished with the lime zest and segments.

6. Pour the sauce over the pork and kale and serve.

...continued

Sauce	Ingredients
6 cloves	Garlic
2	Red chillies
10–20g	Palm sugar
50ml	Fish sauce
50ml	Lime sauce
10g	Coriander (chopped)
10g	Parsley (chopped)

Chef's Notes

- This recipe is a sweet and sour sauce. It is a very spicy dish, and you may adjust the amounts of garlic and chillies contained in the recipe.

- The dish is from a restaurant in Bangkok that I visited with Chef Timo Ruess, the former head chef of the Bangkok Hilton, and his wife Nancy.

Pak Dtom Gkati

Kale Cooked in Coconut Milk

Method

1. Peel and purée the shallots.

2. Peel, and remove the central vein from the prawns.

3. Cut the kale (including the stalks) into 5–6cm lengths and clean under running water.

4. Place the coconut milk into a suitable saucepan, bring to the boil and then reduce to a simmer.

5. Add the shallot purée and stir. Add the kale and continue to cook for 13–14 minutes.

6. Add the salt and sugar and stir until dissolved.

7. Add the prawns and cook for 2–3 minutes then serve with boiled jasmine rice.

Measurements	Ingredients
70g	Shallots
600g	Prawns (medium)
4	Kale (large stalks)
400ml	Coconut milk (thick or thin)
2.5	Sea salt
5–10g	Palm sugar

Chef's Notes

- You must ensure that you remove the central vein from the prawns and only use the freshest available.

Gaeng Jued Tao Hou

Bean Curd Soup

Method

1. Bring the stock to the boil and simmer. Cut the bean curd into 1cm cubes or triangles.

2. Cut the spring onions into diamonds. Peel and slice the shallots into thin rings. Cut the root off the lemongrass and crush the bottom of the stalk.

3. Add the shallots, spring onions and the lemongrass stalk to the stock. Cook for 2–3 minutes then add the soy sauce and the fish sauce. Bring back to a simmer.

4. Add the bean curd and simmer. Serve hot in suitable bowls.

Measurements	Ingredients
600ml	Vegetable stock
150g	Bean curd
4	Spring onions
40g	Shallots
1 stalk	Lemongrass
20ml	Light soy sauce
40ml	Fish sauce

Chef's Notes

- Vegetarian food is very popular in the West but it has been a way of life for thousands of years in Asia. Buddhists believe that doing without meat is a way of respecting the Creator.

- This dish cannot be regarded as totally vegetarian due to the fish sauce.

- This dish is from southern Thailand on the borders of Songkhla.

- Soups such as this are used to cleanse the palate and offset the heat of the chilli. It is traditional that each diner should have a bowl of clear soup.

Pad Tao Hou Tau Saus

Fried Bean Curd with a Nut Sweet Sauce

Method

1. Cut the bean curd into 1cm triangles and lightly dust in cornflour, then tap off any excess flour. This will give a crispy coat when deep-fried.

2. Place the peanuts into a grinder and grind to a smooth paste.

3. Bring the vinegar to the boil and stir in the salt and sugar until it begins to thicken slightly. Add the chilli, then add the peanuts and stir until thoroughly mixed.

Measurements	Ingredients
500g	Bean curd (tofu)
100g	Cornflour
50g	Roasted peanuts
70ml	White vinegar
2.5g	Salt
60g	Palm sugar (or brown sugar)
2.5g	Chilli powder
4 sprigs	Coriander

4. Remove from the heat and serve in a suitable bowl.

5. Heat the deep-fryer (180°C), then add the bean curd one at a time. Be careful not to overload the fryer or allow the temperature to drop too much.

6. Fry the bean curd until it is golden brown, remove and place onto kitchen paper to remove excess oil.

7. Place on a suitable serving dish, garnish with coriander and serve with the sweet peanut sauce.

Chef's Notes

• This recipe is from Krabi and has a sweet sauce to accompany the bean curd. It can be used as a snack, starter or a main course alternative.

• Be careful when deep-frying any food. Only fill the fryer two-thirds full with oil.

Laab

Spicy Beef Salad

Method

1. Remove the stalks from the chillies and chop the flesh. Peel and chop the shallots and garlic.

2. Pour the oil into a suitable wok and put it on a high heat. Fry off the beef, stiring well to break up the mince.

3. When the mince is cooked, add the shallots, garlic, chillies and fish sauce. Stir in well.

4. Add the herbs and rice flour and stir until it is fully incorporated.

5. Allow to cool, then divide and wrap in the lettuce leaves and serve with the garnish.

Measurements	Ingredients
8	Bird's eye chillies
80g	Shallots
20g	Garlic
40ml	Groundnut oil
500g	Minced beef
30ml	Fish sauce
20g	Coriander (chopped)
10g	Parsley (chopped)
50g	Ground rice flour
12	Lettuce leaves
Garnish	Ingredients
	Lettuce leaves (chopped)
	Coriander sprigs
	Red chilli slices

Chef's Notes

• This dish can be used as a starter. Instead of lettuce you can also use chicory, Chinese lettuce or flat leaf lettuce.

• The northern Thais who work in the country prefer water buffalo to beef.

• If you wish to make your own roasted ground rice flour take 50g Jasmine rice and dry roast it in the wok (no oil) until it becomes a light yellow colour, then remove from the heat and cool. Grind it a few times in a good coffee grinder.

• This dish is eaten in many restaurants in the north.

Po Pia Hat Yai

Shrimp and Lychee Spring Roll

Method

1. Shell the prawns and remove the central vein. Then slice in half length ways. Blanch and refresh the lime zest.

2. Roughly chop the lychees and keep separate.

3. Take a spring roll wrapper and fold over one corner towards the centre. Place half a prawn with some chopped lychees, a leaf of basil, some noodles and lime zest over the top. Season the prawns with a little salt and pepper.

4. Roll the spring roll wrapper over once and then seal the edges with the beaten egg and then fold inwards towards the centre. Continue to roll over to make a cigar shape.

5. You may at this point brush the whole spring roll with a little egg. This will give a bit more of a crunch to the roll.

6. Heat the deep-fryer to 180°C, then add the spring rolls one at a time. Be careful not to overload the fryer or allow the temperature to drop too much.

7. To make the nut dipping sauce, bring the vinegar to the boil and stir in the salt and the sugar until it begins to thicken slightly. Add the chillies, and peanuts to the sauce and stir until thoroughly mixed together. Remove from the heat and serve in a suitable bowl.

8. Fry the spring rolls until golden brown, then place onto kitchen paper to allow any excess oil to drain away.

9. Place on a suitable serving dish and garnish with the coriander. Serve with the sweet peanut sauce.

Measurements	Ingredients
6–8	Large prawns
1	Lime (zest)
6–8	Lychees (peeled)
12	Spring roll sheets
12	Sweet basil leaves
50g	Vermicelli noodles (cooked)
1 medium	Egg (beaten)
2.5g	Black pepper (ground)
2.5g	Salt
Nut Dipping Sauce	Ingredients
70ml	White vinegar
2.5g	Salt
60g	Palm sugar (or brown sugar)
2	Red chillies (destalked, deseeded and finely chopped)
50g	Roasted peanuts
4 sprigs	Coriander

Chef's Notes

- This recipe is from Hat Yai in Thailand. There are many different fillings for spring rolls. This one is a little unusual due to the inclusion of lychees.

- Tinned lychees can replace fresh if necessary, but drain them really well first to avoid problems when frying.

Lahb Gai

Chicken Salad

Measurements	Ingredients
$1\frac{1}{2}$	Green pepper
120g	Red onions
120g	Green shallots
200g	Rice
10	Dry red chillies
250ml	Chicken stock
700g	Minced chicken breast
40ml	Lemon juice
20g	Mint leaves
60g	Green beans (chopped)
50ml	Fish sauce
20g	Coriander (chopped)
12	Fresh crisp lettuce leaves

Method

1. Peel and slice the pepper, onions and shallots.

2. Roast the rice in a very hot clean pan, with no oil. Stir until it almost has a burnt look. Remove quickly into a coffee grinder or a pestle and mortar and pound until a powder has formed.

3. Then pound the chillies.

4. Bring the stock to the boil and add the minced chicken and stir well. Allow to cook well then add the lemon. Allow the chicken to cool a little.

5. Add the onions, shallots and mint leaves and stir in well.

6. Next add the chillies, rice, beans and fish sauce and really stir well.

7. Finally add the coriander, place onto the lettuce leaves and serve immediately.

Chef's Notes

- This dish is very popular in eastern Thailand. It is robust and spicy and can be served with lettuce or boiled rice. Traditionally it is served with sticky rice, a favourite in north and eastern Thailand.

- If you do not wish to try the roasted rice flour, you can use plain rice flour and carefully toast it in a dry pan first.

Phad Mii Korat

Noodles, Chicken and Broccoli

Measurements	Ingredients
40g	Red onion
250g	Purple broccoli
50ml	Palm oil
10–20g	Chilli powder
30g	Palm sugar
600g	Diced chicken
500ml	Chicken stock
100g	Rice sticks (Sen Yai or river rice noodles)
30ml	Fish sauce
15g	Preserved soya beans (tinned)
30ml	Sweet soy sauce
1	Lime (cut into wedges)

Method

1. Peel and dice the onions.

2. Trim the broccoli and cut into florets. Pour the oil into a suitable wok and heat.

3. Add the onions, chilli, palm sugar and then the chicken and stir well. Do not burn or allow the ingredients to stick to the wok.

4. Bring the stock to the boil in a separate pan then add to the wok and return to the boil.

5. Add the rice sticks and stir well to prevent them sticking together. Lower the heat.

6. Add the fish sauce, soya beans and soy sauce and allow to cook for 3–4 minutes, then it should be ready to serve.

7. Serve with crispy vegetables and lime wedges.

Chef's Notes

- Dried noodles are known as rice sticks and are made from rice flour. They are normally made in Chantaburi, but the rice sticks used to come from Korat.

- This dish is a perfect dish to compliment Sôm tam which is green papaya and tomato salad (see page 144).

Vietnam 4

Clockwise from top left: Catfish noodle soup, Hué pancakes, Deep-fried wontons.

VIETNAM

When one thinks of Vietnam, the war with America, made famous by numerous films and books in which capitalist America fought against the communist Viet Cong between 1965–1973 probably comes to mind.

Two great rivers, the Red River Delta in the north and the Mekong Delta in the south, divide Vietnam. The two deltas are divided by a central belt of mountains and the eastern coastline (3,451 kilometres long) which runs the length of the country along the South China Sea with magnificent beaches and isolated coves.

Vietnam is a stimulating and beautiful country, with its rich civilisation and friendly people whose welcoming nature enchants visitors.

Travelling through the country is much easier than 20 years ago when the borders were shut to the outside world. The Vietnamese people have been very protective of their independence for 2,000 years. However, they welcome foreigners as guests, and are extremely friendly. The country's shape reminds you of two rice baskets hanging on a pole, which represent the fertile rice lands in each delta area. Here you can see paddy fields full of women wearing conical straw hats for protection from the sun while working on the rice plants. Many women cover their arms and hands with gloves and even wear a scarf over their face under the hat. This is because Vietnamese women believe white skin is a sign of wealth and beauty and to tell a woman she has a nice tan is a great insult.

Yet throughout Vietnam's history, both its geography and destiny have travelled hand in hand. With the 3,500 kilometres of coastline, lush paddy fields, deltas and valleys, its landscape has great appeal to potential conquerors; mercenaries, traders and kings, emperors and numerous foreign powers have been tempted to try to claim control of the Vietnamese people and their country for their own means. Although Vietnam has seen the passage of influences, it also increased the people's desire for independence. However, numerous foreign influences have also helped to shape its architecture, culture, religion, politics and cuisine.

The history of Vietnam can be traced as far back as half a million years from the earliest Palaeolithic hunter-gathers. Four thousand years ago saw the cultivation of the Red River Delta and the birth of the first Vietnamese nation. Before the first millennium BC there were Bronze Age settlements in what is Hanoi region today.

The third century BC saw an invasion by a Chinese warlord, starting both the Vietnamese struggle against numerous foreign invaders and centuries of Chinese dominance as China ruled and influenced the north.

Indian culture shaped central Vietnam with the Champa Hindu Kingdom from the fourth to the seventeenth centuries introducing agriculture, trade and fishing with Indians, Arabs and Chinese. Over the

centuries the kingdom thrived, despite the many battles against the Chinese north and the Khmer Empire in the west. The kingdom built many marvellous Champa temples; some still remain at My Son and Po Klong Garai, but many were destroyed by B52 bombers during the war.

As China became more and more influential, so did the Vietnamese desire for independence. This all came to a head in the Bach Dang River Battle around the tenth century, which ended Chinese dominance and gave independence to the Vietnamese people for the first time in over a thousand years.

By the end of the century the country was united by the warlord Dinh Bo Linh, although he paid tribute to China.

The Le Dynasty that ruled from the eleventh to the thirteenth centuries helped to stabilise the country and establish a Confucian system of politics. The capital moved to Thang Long, which is now Hanoi. During the Le Dynasty, the ruler Le Thong Tongs (1460–97) managed to push the Champ Kingdom further south and he introduced civil and criminal codes, which were the basis of Vietnamese law until the nineteenth century. During the sixteenth to eighteenth centuries much of central Vietnam around the Hue area was ruled by the Nguyen clan, with the Trinh ruling Hanoi. By the end of the seventeenth century the Nguyen clan had taken over the Mekong Delta area. The most successful uprising against the Trinh and Nguyen's rule was the Tay Son Rebellion by ethnic minorities and peasants in 1771, which then allowed a return to Chinese rule.

Vietnam as we know it today was established during the Gia Long's Nguyen Dynasty in 1802 and lasted until 1945. Under this rule rebellions were brutally suppressed and political power centralised. Missionaries and foreign traders were then accused of creating discord and the borders were closed to all foreigners for a time.

The French were expanding their territories in Indochina after repeated and successful assaults on Saigon, Danang and the Mekong Delta, southern Vietnam (Cochinchina), central (Annam) and north (Tonkin) by the mid-nineteenth century. By 1887 the French had established French Indochina, which consisted of Vietnam, Laos and Cambodia.

In 1925 Ho Chi Minh founded the Revolutionary Youth League and worked tirelessly to achieve a free Vietnam, by getting other revolutionary leaders and groups to work together. The French influence lasted until 1954, with a brief period during the Second World War which saw the Japanese invade and take control. The period after 1945 saw anti-colonial feeling and much unrest as the French tried to return. This continued until 1954 when the Geneva Accord divided the north and south along the seventeenth parallel. This renewed old tensions between the north and south. Almost a million displaced people moved south while the supporters of a free Vietnam moved north. As tension rose, this led to a call to hostilities and ultimately to the American-Vietnam War that claimed the lives of 57,000 American soldiers and

over 3 million Vietnamese. Vietnam is now emerging from the years of the Vietnam War, the Cold War, and the nearby Cambodian War. In 1994 the USA lifted its trade embargo, and the first visit ever made by an American President, Bill Clinton, took place. Vietnam has since joined the Association of South East Asian Nations (ASEAN).

Vietnam's climate is diverse, created by a wide variety of altitudes. Although much of the country is located in the sub-tropics it can range from frosty winters in the hills of northern Vietnam to the tropical warmth of the Mekong Delta. This owes much to the fact that over a third of the country is 500 metres above sea level. Vietnam has two monsoons, the first runs from October to March with cold wet winters blowing from the north-east. Then from May to October comes the south-western monsoon, bringing moist winds from the Indian Ocean and the Gulf of Thailand to the whole country (except mountainous areas). July and November experience occasional unpredictable typhoons, which develop and hit the central and northern areas of the country with devastating effect.

Vietnam covers an area of 326,797 square kilometres. This is larger than Italy but a little smaller than Japan. Vietnam shares its borders with China, Cambodia and Laos. Three-quarters of the country is mountains and hills. The forests that once covered Vietnam have been removed, through deforestation and war with only 20 per cent left by 1995. The government has banned any deforestation and has began a re-forestation programme, which saw 30 per cent coverage in 1998.

The population of Vietnam is almost 78 million of which 84 per cent is ethnic Vietnamese, 2 per cent ethnic Chinese, with the remainder made up of Champ and Khmer and a further 50 ethno-linguistic groups. The northern mountains of Vietnam are where the remaining hill tribes and minority communities live.

The main religion in Vietnam is Mahayana Buddhism and the largest sect is the Mahayana Zen Buddhist. Other practising religions are Theravada Buddhism, Confucianism, Taoism, Ancestor worship, Caodaism, Catholicism, Protestantism, Islam and Hinduism.

The Vietnamese were not influential architects like their neighbours the Khmer who built the great city and temples of Ankor Wat in Cambodia. Most of the buildings tended to be wooden structures, some of which still remain around Hue. The Champ kingdom constructed most of the stone buildings. There are pagodas and temples that were built several hundred years ago but most buildings tend to be new. The tradition of worshipping one's ancestors has left memorials and graves that date back many centuries. However, most of the memorials are for the Vietnamese who died in the French and American conflicts.

CUISINE

Vietnam can trace its cuisine back to migrants from China, Indonesia, Thailand and Mongolia and this has led to a wonderful diversity of dishes. It has evolved from the ten centuries of Chinese rule and has brought not only art and architecture but also an impact on kitchen equipment like the wok for stir frying, deep-frying and steaming. The use of chopsticks also developed. Please be warned, leaving chopsticks vertical in food at any time is a very bad omen and means there will be a death. It is really frowned upon. Rice is the staple food of Vietnam. The most common type of restaurant in Vietnam is the rice and noodle shop called com-pho.

China introduced foods like soy sauce, noodles and bean curd. Another influence has come from the introduction of the Buddhist religion. This has led to a wonderful vegetarian cuisine, with an incredible variety of dishes. One old proverb in Vietnam suggests that 'One should learn to eat before one learns to talk' (hoc an, hoc noi). The thirteenth century saw the Mongolian army invade and introduce beef to the north with specialities like Mongolian hot pot (Lau), beef cooked seven ways (Bay mom), and Pho bo, a beef and noodle soup that can be purchased for less than a dollar or a few dong, the Vietnamese currency almost any where in the country.

Surrounding countries like Cambodia, Laos and Thailand have contributed with the introduction of herbs and no meal is complete without one or two herbs in each dish. The introduction of Indian spices into Vietnamese dishes and curries has been introduced over a period of time.

It appears that around the time of the sixteenth century, traders and explorers brought new foods such as tomatoes, potatoes, peanuts and corn to Vietnam in exchange for valuable spices like black pepper and cinnamon. Interestingly enough, some ingredients still retain the name of the country of origin, for example, Holland peas refers to snow peas and French or Western bamboo shoots refers to asparagus.

More recently major influences from France and the USA have changed some eating habits. The old style of Imperial cuisine was once widespread, but is now more limited to a small handful of chefs like Master Chef Madame Ha, who serves this style of cuisine at her restaurant, TinhGai Vien in Hué. The cuisine serves many sophisticated small courses, which are lavishly presented: the more courses and the wider the variety, the wealthier the family. Even the poor and peasant households would have many dishes at meal times and the meal times would vary. It is reputed that the chef would have to be able to cook 2,000 dishes as the king would have up to 50 dishes served at meal times.

Today, however, the influence of France and the USA has led to the Vietnamese eating three times a day, starting with breakfast at 6–7 am. Dishes sold might be sticky rice (Xoi), or a rice gruel called chao or

congee with fish or meat or even noodle soup (Pho) with meat. Lunch will start at around 11 am. Most workers go home for lunch, but in the cities some will stay at work and eat from a street vendor or street café. A typical meal would be noodle soup again, pickled vegetables, or meat cooked barbeque style, all served with rice.

Dinner is where the whole family will sit down together for a meal, and is similar to lunch. It is a communal gathering. There will be a soup with a little meat, followed by the fish, meat or eggs and then the rice. The rice will be placed in the centre of the table first and the other dishes around the table. There will normally be dipping sauces of some description.

Chopsticks will normally be used, but often spoons will be available. Custom dictates that you would take rice to your bowl first and then take a portion of each of the protein dishes on the table. If you are a guest at a family or business dinner you may find that other guests place the best portions onto your plate as a way of honouring you. Never spear your food with the chopsticks and it is expected that you lift your bowl close to you and eat with the chopsticks. The Vietnamese find it rather peculiar if you try to eat with chopstick from a great distance.

Most restaurants will have spoons and forks available. Chopsticks for kings, emperors and nobles in ancient times would only be made of wood from the Cay Kim Gao tree. This is due to the fact that if any poison touched the sticks, the sticks would turn black. If there is a spoon (for soup), the Vietnamese sip from the spoon and never place it into their mouths. It is best to remember that when passing plates, in fact anything, use both hands and nod politely when passing the item. When the food has finished, the remaining soup liquid would normally be added to the rice and eaten. When you have finished and you wish to pass a compliment, it is appropriate to say Long num, which means delicious. It is best also to remember that it is customary to feed guests, even if they are not hungry, until they are almost bursting, so make sure you are very hungry if invited to dinner

While dining or entering a house, one must remove one's shoes, never show the soles of your feet and remove any hat to elders and guests.

It is rare that a dessert is served, but fresh fruit would be available. Sweets are eaten as a snack rather than a course.

The French have had a huge influence since the days that they built the old trading port and central market for all of Indochina and Saigon, now called Ho Chi Minh City, which they called the Paris of the Orient. French colonialists introduced bakery items such as baguettes, which are baked twice a day and sold by street vendors. Butter, milk, yoghurts and café au lait, along with French pastries, are all extremely popular. The Americans introduced a passion for ice cream and whisky. Although through the centuries the Vietnamese cuisine has been influenced by new styles of cooking, ingredients and national cuisines, it has, on the whole, assimilated the influences into its cuisine rather than be taken over or dominated by one influence, thus keeping its unique Vietnamese character.

So what makes the cuisine so different from its neighbouring countries and what are the general regional differences?

When you first look at the cuisine, the ingredients lemongrass, garlic, chillies, mint, basil and coriander are all used in Thai and Malay cookery, but Vietnamese cuisine has a more subtle delicate flavour and rarely has the fire of Thai cuisine or depth of spiciness of Malay. Shallots, bean curd, kale, Chinese cabbage, chives, bean sprouts and bamboo shoots are all used. Many dishes see combinations of greens incorporated into them, but you will almost never see cornstarch-thickened sauces.

The flavouring that gives the Vietnamese cuisine its distinctive taste is Noc mam or Vietnamese fish sauce. It is made in similar ways to other fish sauces, except it uses more anchovy. The fish are laid in wooden caskets and salted between each layer then pressed and fermented for three months. Concrete caskets are more commonly used these days. The liquid is then drained off from the bottom of the caskets, and then poured back and fermented for a further three months. After these final three months it is decanted and, just like a good wine, the first pressing, which is dark in colour, is the most prized by gourmets. It will usually carry the words 'thuong hang' or 'nhi' indicating that it is the best grade. Subsequent pressings will have had water added and will be a little less expensive.

The Noc mam will replace salt at the table and sometimes this is used as a dipping sauce. If you add sugar, chillies, garlic and a dash of lime and rice vinegar you will have Nuoc cham, a hot sauce that can be added to spice up any dish or salad. As a general rule Vietnamese cuisine is light, using very little fat or oils, full of flavour, lovingly prepared, and healthy for anyone who is diet conscious.

Vietnamese cuisine has three distinctive regions with their own style and traditions. These are the north, south and central areas of the country.

In general terms the north has been influenced primarily by China, using the wok to deep-fry and for stir fries, congees, soups and stews. Because the climate is cooler and drier, this affects the cuisine in several ways. Fewer herbs, vegetables and spices are used, as fewer are available due to the inhospitable climate. Black pepper is a common spice added for flavour. During the winter in the north you will see the Mongolian influence on the cuisine, with the increased gathering of the family around a big charcoal-heated table, brazier-cooking wafer-thin beef along with vegetables in a broth, similar to Chinese pot cooking. Wafer-thin beef is placed on top of thin noodles and boiling stock will be poured over these ingredients. Green chillies, onions, lemon, coriander and mint will be added to create Hanoi's famous Pho bo, which is the north's comfort food to keep out the winter chill.

Through the nineteenth century Hué in central Vietnam dominated the once imperial kingdom, which is now demonstrated in its food. Elsewhere

in Vietnam, food is served in a small number of large bowls. In the central region around Hué, the food is served in much smaller bowls and portions. These are then spread out on the table creating the impression of a royal banquet, which characterises and replicates the once-famous sophisticated imperial cuisine. Hué is also famous for its sausages called nems, vermicelli soups and rice cakes that are very tasty.

One of the characteristics of the cuisine of central Vietnam is the use of a shrimp sauce that replace the Vietnamese fish sauce. It is made in the same way, but the fish is replaced by shrimps. It has a strong aroma and taste that some people dislike. The region also grows western vegetables such as asparagus, potatoes and cauliflowers.

The fertile soil of the tropical south yields a wonderful abundance of tropical fruit and vegetables. The cuisine is much simpler than those of the two other regions. Spicier dishes with an Indian flavour and curries are seen mainly in the south. The curries can be served with either rice or noodles. Fruits such as pineapples, durian and dragon fruits are plentiful, along with sugar cane and coconuts. Stir frying and shorter methods of cooking are more popular than stews. The use of the French style of skill for cooking is preferred to the wok.

A novelty from the south is a vegetable platter that accompanies grilled food and a spicy peanut dipping sauce. You take a small piece of grilled meat and place it in the centre of a lettuce leaf together with herbs and wrap it up, then dip it in the sauce and eat it. Much to my embarrassment a resident Westerner from Manchester politely pointed out this method to me as he could see me struggling with the food. He was soon to become an in-law of the street café owner in Saigon in which I was dining. The vegetable platter will often have raw vegetables and unripe mango, star fruit and banana, as well as other fruit.

The Vietnamese, like their neighbours the Chinese, consume tea, both black and green varieties, at all times of the day. You can also see fresh refreshing coconut milk and sugar cane drinks being sold on the streets in plastic bags with ice and numerous other teas made from flowers like lotus, rose and chrysanthemum. Vietnam now grows coffee beans in the central highlands and when ordering coffee one should remember that the Vietnamese like their coffee very strong. So unless you want your taste buds doing somersaults, request it watered down. If you ask for it to be white you will get a third of your coffee with condensed milk of some description. Vietnam does export beer, called Saigon beer.

Another drink is snake wine in which there are several pickled snakes actually in the rice wine, which is supposed to be an aphrodisiac. A variation on this is to have a poisonous snake (the more poisonous the better) killed in front of you, then its blood, beating heart and gall bladder tipped into a glass. You are then expected to drink it down in one gulp! The meat is a little like chicken and a good source of calcium and protein.

I have divided this chapter on Vietnam into the following areas: north-east, north-west, north central, central south central and the Mekong Delta.

NORTH-EAST VIETNAM

The capital for the north and the country as a whole is Hanoi, a city of over $3\frac{1}{2}$ million people located on the Red River Delta, which has been the site of a major settlement for over a thousand years and can trace its origins as far back as the Neolithic period.

The emperor Ly Thai set up his capital in 1010 and named the city Thang Long, translated as city of the souring dragon. Hanoi remained the capital through the Le Dynasty until 1788 when Nguyen Hué, who founded the Tay Son Dynasty, overthrew the Le Dynasty. The emperor Gai Long then decided to move the capital to Hué and Hanoi was relegated to a regional capital. In 1831 the emperor Tu Duc renamed the city Hanoi, which means 'city in a bend in the river'. The French kept Hanoi as the capital city until 1953.

Hanoi is the capital of the Socialist Republic of Vietnam and since the early 1990s has seen the benefits of opening up to the tourist and foreign travellers with shops, restaurants and foreign investment. Hanoi has lagged behind when compared to Saigon. Much of the investment has gone south. This was because foreigners were not really welcome and were given a hard time. But the north-east is catching up, with better roads, hotels, restaurants and infrastructure.

The atmosphere is very different to that of Saigon. The pace of life is slower and there is less traffic and pollution than its southern counterpart. Parks and trees are a pleasant addition. The city is created around the Hoan Kiem Lake (lake of the restored sword), where you can see Tai Chi being practised early in the morning. The legend of the lake has it that Heaven gave Emperor Ly Thai To a sword which he used to drive the Chinese back to China. On returning he went boating on the lake and a giant golden tortoise or turtle grabbed the sword, returning it to its owners.

The old quarter is the centre of a variety of crafts. It seems that each of the 36 streets is home to a differing trade such as textiles, tin, silver and goldsmiths or oriental medicines established in the thirteenth century. Silk painting has been practised in Vietnam since the thirteenth century along with lacquerware, which came from China in the mid-fifteenth century, and is often inlaid with mother of pearl, egg shell, silver and gold. Most of the fine silk sold in markets in Hanoi is produced in a village called Van Phuc about 8 kilometres south-west of Hanoi.

Most of the ancient buildings and monuments were destroyed by French troops in 1894 and then the American bombing during the Vietnam war destroyed many parts of Hanoi. The Long Bien Bridge (1888–1902), which was designed and built by the same architect who built the Eiffel Tower, still spans the river. Although it was bombed many times by the Americans during the war the Vietnamese managed to repair it. The bridge is now only used by pedestrians and non-motorised vehicles. Bach

Ma Temple, which is dedicated to the guardian spirit of Thang Long, was built sometime in the ninth century.

The French quarter is like stepping back into 1930s Parisian streets. The opera house was the climax of French architecture in Hanoi and where Ho Chi Minh declared independence in 1945. Ho Chi Minh's Mausoleum is sited by Hanoi's largest lake, Ho Tay.

For centuries the populace have considered themselves to be scholars and artisans in comparison to their southern countrymen. For example, a temple of literature was constructed in 1070 to honour men and scholars and to mark their achievements. The temple displays some very rare architecture.

A favoured pastime is visiting the famous water puppets. The art is over a thousand years old and little known outside Vietnam. The art of puppeteering started with the workers in the rice paddies in the countryside. Farmers used to carve the puppets out of wood from the fig trees and model them on local characters and animals, using them to teach the audience the legends and stories of Northern Vietnam. It soon became an attraction for courtly entertainment and is now a major attraction at the municipal water park.

Until recently the movement and supply of food was difficult if not impossible for the northern Vietnamese in comparison with the south and this resulted in a culinary desert. But this situation is rapidly changing, with an explosion of new cafés and restaurants. The cuisine is nowhere near as exciting or accomplished as central or southern Vietnamese cuisine.

In the central area of Hanoi on the banks of the Red River is the Sam Son seafood market, a huge market with restaurants. Some of the best seafood and river fish can be purchased here. It is best to note that in the markets of Vietnam, just like in Cambodia, all food is normally sold live. This includes chickens, pigs and goats, fish, shellfish and eels, because there is no refrigeration. Once selected the fish are normally killed and prepared. It is also worth remembering that if meat is sold it has probably been freshly killed a few hours ago. You might come across caged dogs and bears around this market.

Mo and Buoi markets also sell live meat. The most interesting part of the markets is watching local characters who have travelled on their bikes or motorbikes, bringing their own hard-earned produce to barter and sell. It is normally left to the women to do the selling.

The influence from China can be clearly seen in the cuisine of the north-east, with combinations of chicken and crab for fillings and soups, bean curd and soya beans, and the use of Chinese herbal medicine.

The coastline, rivers and tributaries throughout Vietnam have been a good source of protein through the ages. Fish like snakehead fish, tailapia, eel, carp and catfish are mainly used and are often farmed. You may use

bass, carp or perch if available. Dishes like snapper with turmeric and dill appear in restaurants in Hanoi along with prawn rolls with minced beef, shrimp soup with noodles, and slow braised beef. The Chinese and Mongolian influences can be seen in the cooking of aubergines, beef with noodles, beef stew, stuffed cabbage soup, duck congee, grilled pork, pork ball and tofu soup and spring rolls with pork and crab.

Just 25 kilometres south-west of Hanoi is a little village called So that produces noodles. The village makes its own flour from cassava and yams instead of wheat to give the noodles their distinctive flavour.

Much of the architecture and many buildings of So have fallen into disrepair and replaced by concrete. This town is small and still developing. It is dominated by the three summits of the Tam Dao Mountains. There are a number of hill tribes still living in the hills. Women of the Tay, Dao and Mong hill tribes still cap their teeth with silver or gold. They believe that the flash of metal makes their smiles more beautiful, even graceful. They also think it shows their wealth and status and protects the teeth. There are numerous restaurants here and many have the same dishes on the menus, but you will find an abundance of venison, fish and squirrel. I tried on a number of occasions to determine if they were wild or farmed, but I just received a yes to all my questions and a smile. One dish I did enjoy was a small pheasant roasted with ginger, garlic and soy with a sprinkling of five spice.

Haiphong is the third most populated city with over 1,668,000 people, but still has a slow pace of life for a ferry port. The French created a major port there from a small village in the late 1800s and, surprisingly, it still has some fine colonial French buildings. Haiphong was one of the primary causes of the war against France. When the French bombarded the native areas in Haiphong some 6,000 inhabitants were killed. It also has some history from the American war when it was bombed and the harbour was heavily mined by the Americans, trying to prevent supplies from the USSR reaching them.

Since the late 1970s the port has seen a large migration of boat people and in particular fishermen, who have taken most of the fleet with them.

Den Kiep Bac is a temple on the way to Halong Bay. It is dedicated to General Tran Hung Dao (1228–1300) and held in reverence second only to that of Ho Chi Minh. The general defeated 300,000 Mongol warriors around the 1280s. The temple was erected the year he died and also honours other notables from his family. It was built where he died.

Halong Bay is principally divided into two sections or districts – Bai Chay on the west side and Hon Gai on the east side. It is a main port and the major export is coal. Halong city, which is the capital of Quang Ninh Province, has a rather unpleasant reputation and it is best to miss this out, if you are visiting the area.

The sinking limestone plateau (ethereal karsh formations) have given way to the creation of some of the most spectacular geological sights on

the planet. Halong Bay in the Gulf of Tonkin became a UNESCO World Heritage Site in 1994, although this plateau continues 100 kilometres up to the Chinese border with countless bays, grottoes and over 3,000 islands, all of outstanding beauty such as Bai Tu Long Bay, Van Hai and Van Don islands and Quan Lan island, to name a few.

The name Ha long translated mean 'where the dragon descends into the sea'. Legend has it that a dragon ran down into the sea and his tail made waves that carved out the bay and land. Over the years there have been reports from sailors and fishermen that monsters like the Loch Ness monster have been seen around the area.

The seafood around the coast is excellent, as one would expect. Most of the hotels in Bai Chay and Hon Gai have restaurants and you will see house specialities like white fish in a caramel sauce or jellyfish and shrimp salad as well as spring rolls and deep-fried cuttle fish with garlic and fish sauce.

You can eat on a number of floating restaurants, but the best one (so I was told) was the Xuan Hong, which is a fish farm and restaurant combined. You pick your own fish from the baskets and then they are cooked for you.

Mong Cai is the furthest border crossing in north-eastern Vietnam. It shares the border with China. The markets and town are considered to be a free-trade zone by Vietnam and China. The Chinese were good neighbours and friends to Vietnam during the American and French wars. But in 1979 the Chinese army crossed the border and attacked the Vietnamese who were already fighting the Khmer Rouge. The Khmer Rouge were close allies to the Chinese. The Vietnamese had also taken anti-capitalist measures against the Chinese living and working in Vietnam, which heightened the tension. The invasion lasted 17 days and cost the lives of over 20,000 Chinese troops who were badly mauled by the hardened Vietnamese troops. Today the border is booming and the hostilities seem to have been put to rest.

Lang Son and Cao Bang (capital of Cao Bang Province) offer no real culinary significance. Although Lang Son has many restaurants, all offer similar fare. Cao Bang is home to numerous lakes and the highest waterfall in the country being some 53 metres high. There are a number of local villages like Tay whose inhabitants still keep to their traditional way of life.

Cá Chiên

White Fish in a Caramel Sauce

Method

1. Peel and finely chop the onion and garlic. Top and tail the spring onions then slice into diamonds.

2. Cover the fish fillets in a little salt and plenty of black pepper and leave to marinate for 10 minutes.

3. Place the sugar into a thick bottomed saucepan over a medium heat and cook until a nice brown colour has been achieved. Add the fish sauce and water and stir rapidly to dissolve the sugar evenly with no lumps.

4. Simmer sauce for 5 minutes on a low heat.

5. Add the onions, garlic and spring onions and cook for 2 minutes then add the fish fillets, ensuring they are well coated in the sauce. Place a lid on the pan and cook for 5–6 minutes then remove and serve.

Measurement	Ingredients
1	Small onion
2 cloves	Garlic
10	Spring onions
600g	Prime white fish fillets (no bone or skin)
60g	Sugar
20ml	Fish sauce
100ml	Water
5g	Freshly ground black pepper
	Salt

Chef's Notes

- The same recipe can be used for shrimps.

- This recipe is best served either with a simple salad or plain boiled rice.

Thịt Heo Nướng Vói

Grilled Pork

Method

1. Mix the soy, sugar, ginger, galangal, garlic and spices together thoroughly.

2. Remove any fat or sinew from the pork then very thinly slice into strips. Add the pork to the mixture you have just made and marinate for 45 minutes.

3. Preheat a griddle or grill and place the pork slices on to cook for 6–8 minutes.

4. Wrap the pork with the coriander, mint and vermicelli in the lettuce leaf.

5. Place on a serving dish and serve immediately or just place the individual ingredients on a serving plate and allow your guests to make up their own.

Chef's Notes

- This is a nice summer starter, and it is good to allow your guests to make up their own rolls.

- You could add a little hoisin sauce to the recipe for more sweetness and flavour.

Measurements	Ingredients
200ml	Soy sauce
10g	Brown sugar
5g	Ginger (finely chopped)
5g	Galangal (finely chopped)
5g	Garlic (finely chopped)
2.5g	Cinnamon
2.5g	Ground star anise
300g	Pork tenderloin
4	Coriander leaves
4	Mint leaves
300g	Vermicelli (cooked)
8	Fresh lettuce leaves

Baw Baw Bò Kho

Beef Stew

Method

1. Cut the beef into 3cm dice.

2. Peel and finely dice the lemongrass and onions. Blanch, deseed and cut the tomatoes into 1cm dice. Peel the carrots and cut into 2–3cm dice.

3. Mix together the soy, chilli, garlic, ginger, sugar, lemongrass, five spice, fish sauce, 70g onion and marinate the beef in the fridge for 1 hour.

4. Remove the beef and strain off a little of the liquid. Heat the oil in a clean pan and cook until brown.

5. Add the remaining onions and cook for 3–4 minutes then add the tomatoes and continue to cook for a further 4–5 minutes. Add a little of the marinade and the water. Add the carrots and black pepper, bring to the boil and simmer for 1 hour.

6. Chop the basil leaves and add half to the meat and cook for 5 more minutes then check the seasoning. Serve with a sprinkling of the remaining basil.

Measurements	Ingredients
700g	Chuck or topside of beef
1 large stalk	Lemongrass
120g	Onions
2	Beef tomato
400g	Carrots
10ml	Rich soy sauce
40ml	Dark soy
10g	Garlic purée
2.5g	Chilli powder
30g	Ginger
15g	Brown sugar
10g	Five spice powder
50ml	Fish sauce
50ml	Vegetable oil
4 sprigs	Basil leaves
1lt	Water
	Black pepper

Chef's Notes

• There are numerous versions of this beef stew. Some add sweet potatoes and bay leaves. Some recipes include curry powder, beer and even whisky.

• Best served with French bread or large noodles.

Choa Boi

Rice Soup with Chicken and Seafood

Method

1. Shred the chicken into bite-sized segments. Remove the central vein from the prawns then split them length ways.

Measurements	Ingredients
220g	Cooked chicken
230g	Shelled prawns (4cm long tail)

continued over →

2. Peel and slice the spring onions and onion. Wipe the mushrooms and chop very roughly.

3. Part cook the rice in boiling water with salted and a dash of oil until just cooked. Then drain under cold running water and reserve.

4. Place the tapioca into cold water and stir until they are all on the bottom of the bowl, and then drain.

5. Bring the stock to a simmer and add the ginger, mushrooms and rice.

6. In a separate pan heat the oil and start to cook the onions. As they go limp add the prawns and crab meat. The prawns should turn pink and curl. Keep stirring gently.

7. Add the tapioca and simmer for 15 minutes. As the tapioca turns transparent add all the other ingredients except the spring onions and coriander. Check seasoning. Remove from the heat and stir. Serve with a sprinkling of coriander and spring onions.

...continued

4	Spring onions
50g	Onion
30g	Pigs' ear mushrooms
230g	Jasmine rice
110g	Tapioca pearls
3lt	Chicken stock
10g	Ginger purée
150g	White crab meat (cooked)
30g	Coriander
30ml	Vegetable oil
10g	Black pepper
	Salt

Chef's Notes

- To make the chicken stock bring a $1-1\frac{1}{2}$ kg chicken covered by $\frac{1}{2}$ inch water and one large onion, 10g salt, 4 peppercorns and a 2cm crushed piece of ginger to the boil. Simmer for 90 minutes, skimming any scum and debris from the surface. Remove chicken and strain the stock. Remove meat from the carcass, and keep to one side.

- There are a few variations on this recipe, some add white fish and scallops but this recipe is the best example. It can be a soup or a one-bowl meat, it is up to you. The rice should be well cooked and look almost split for this dish.

Phở Bó

Beef Pho

Measurements	Ingredients
50g	Shallots
1	Lime
30g	Coriander
10g	Mint
10g	Parsley
20g	Spinach leaves (baby)
3 medium	Red chilli peppers
90ml	Nuoc Mam (fish sauce)
20g	Garlic purée
225g	Rice noodles (5mm size)
10ml	Lemon juice
1 stalk	Lemongrass
10ml	Peanut oil
3lt	Beef stock
4	Ginger slices
1 (3cm)	Cinnamon stick
200g	Rump steak (very thinly sliced)
100g	Bean sprouts
8	Spring onions
	Salt

Method

1. Peel the shallots and cut into rings. Cut the lime into six wedges. Finely chop the coriander, mint and parsley separately. Wash and cut the spinach into strips.

2. Top and tail the chillies, remove the seeds and very finely slice.

3. Mix the fish sauce with the garlic. Soak the noodles in warm water for 20 minutes and drain. Soak the shallots in lemon juice for 20 minutes. Remove the stalk from the lemongrass and crush the bottom. Bring some salted water to the boil with a dash of peanut oil.

4. Bring the stock to the boil with the lemongrass, ginger, cinnamon stick, and boil for 40 minutes allowing the ingredients to infuse. Strain and place back on the stove and simmer. Discard the strained ingredients.

5. Add the fish sauce and garlic and simmer. Add the sliced beef and cook for 1–2 minutes. Add the noodles to the boiling salted water and cook.

6. Have four heated bowls ready and divide the noodles into each bowl, then the spinach and lay the beef strips on top. Ladle in the beef stock over this and serve immediately.

7. Arrange the chillies, herbs, shallots, bean sprouts, lime and spring onions neatly on a serving plate and allow your guests to help themselves.

Chef's Notes

- Pho differs slightly from place to place, for example, street stalls may have oxtail, but in a slightly upper class restaurant you may have diced sirloin or on the rare occasion fillet of beef.

- The rice noodles (broad size) are often called rice sticks or Banh Pho.

- If you like your beef rare or medium just place the wafer-thin beef raw on top of the spinach and noodles and add the boiling hot beef stock. It should be just right.

NORTH-WEST VIETNAM

This area of Vietnam has some of the best scenery in all of Asia. In fact this often-remote corner of Vietnam is almost another country. It offers the visitor many diverse experiences, from the more rural cultures and scenes to the dramatic mountain ranges down to the lush fertile valleys and hills. There is little western influence in this area, which is not surprising due to the difficulties, discomfort and hard work of getting there. This area is dominated by hill tribes where one must be sensitive in dress and behaviour. Dropping litter, taking photographs, wearing shorts and not removing one's footwear are disrespectful. The area is inhabited by the Montagnards (White Thai, Black Thai and H'mong).

The rice terraces make for spectacular sights especially around Sapa in the Lao Cai Province. Mai Chau in the Hoa Binh Province is possibly the closest area to Hanoi where you will see hill tribes. It is not really a village or a town but a collection of small hamlets and farms where you can find the small huts of the White Thai tribes. It is believed that they are descendants of the hill tribes from northern Thailand and Laos who migrated there long ago. If you trek for several days you could see other tribes from Xa Linh village, which is inhabited by the H'mong tribe. Mai Chau also has a local popular market held on Sundays. Like many hill tribes they still hunt birds, frogs, snakes and other animals, and will either eat or sell them. They will often grow fruit and vegetables in little plots of land close to the house such as soy beans, bamboo shoots, mangos, bananas and other tropical fruits.

Son La Province is dominated by the Song Da Reservoir, and is about 200 kilometres long. The capital of the province is Son La and it has a population of 61,500. It is tucked away and has some dramatic views of the Karst Mountains. The area is populated by the White Thai, Black Thai, Muong and Meo ethnic tribes. The area and town is known for its infamous French prison which was feared by the Vietnamese people and bred hardened resentment against French rule.

If you go to the high plateau you will see beautiful tea, coffee and mulberry plantations, and dairy farming in progress. The delicacies from

the hill tribes around Son La are mainly goat dishes with noodles, simple rice noodle soups and rather bitter bamboo shoots. One dish consists of congealed goat's blood and nuts.

Moc Chau, south of Son La, has been a centre of dairy farming since the 1970s and supplies most of the milk for Hanoi. It has a population of over 113,000 and the area is home to numerous hill tribes.

Yen Chau is an area of agriculture that produces excellent fruit, such as bananas and custard apples, and has a reputation for prime mangoes.

Dien Bien Phu (in the Lai Chau Province) is populated by 545,000 inhabitants and is the site of the decisive battle in 1954 in which the Vietnamese overran the French garrison in the town, with 13,000 French troops killed or captured and 25,000 Vietnamese killed or wounded. The battlefield has been turned into a museum. The area is a tourist site and many French tourists visit the town.

Sapa is an old hill station that was constructed in 1922. With a population of 36,000 it is the most popular destination in north-west Vietnam. It is a very beautiful little valley that is often shrouded in a mist and is very cold in the winter months of January and February. Sapa is fast becoming a tourist town and this is having a damaging effect on the rural and cultural villages and hill tribes around the area, like the Dzao and H'mong. Sapa also has a popular market on Saturdays that brings in people like the Red Dzao and H'mong tribes. The area is dominated by the Fansipan Mountains with Vietnam's highest peak (3143 metres). Again the region is not really famed for its cuisine and caters more for the tourist.

Bac Ha is a real highland town with loud speakers echoing the Vietnamese virtues (some may call it propaganda). It has a population of 70,000 and is slowly becoming a little like Sapa. As in many parts out of the city the supply of electricity is patchy. This area is home to many hill tribes like the Kinh, who are ethnic Vietnamese, Thai, Thulao and the Xa Fang to name but a few. Around Bac Ha the hill tribes are very friendly and if you are invited to eat it is difficult to say no as it is part of their culture. So if you are lucky enough to be asked don't turn your nose up at the food you are given. It can often be new-born chickens in soup and internal organs of chicken and pork, and the sight can turn even the most hardened diner's stomach.

On the occasion of a wedding, a pig is ceremoniously washed and killed, then cooked, and every single piece is eaten, including brains, ears, etc.

The markets around Bac Ha are well worth a visit, where you can see the traditional trading of live animals taking place – pigs, goats and horses. You may see the unpleasant sight of poor old Rover (dogs) for sale in the markets of Can Cau and Bac Ha.

Gỏi Bao Tử Heo

Salad of Pig's Stomach

Method

1. Wash and peel the carrots and cut into 5cm pieces (batons). Wash the cucumber and cut the same as the carrots. Peel the onion and cut in two. Wash and deseed the pepper and slice. Wash the sugar beet with salt and then clean it again with cold running water. Then mix beet and cucumber together with half the sugar and allow to stand for a while then drain off the excess water.

2. Remove the central core from the shrimps then split them lengthways.

3. Fry off the pork loin and then cut into thin slices. Then fry off the peanuts and keep hot.

4. Wash out the stomach very well in cold running water. Place into a pan and cover with water. Add some salt and bring to the boil, removing any debris from the surface. Cook for $1\frac{1}{2}$ hours and then cool and slice.

5. Mix the fish sauce, vinegar, lemon juice, sugar, garlic, shrimps, cucumber mix and pepper together.

6. Divide the mix up onto four plates and then top with pork, stomach and peanuts.

Measurements	Ingredients
100g	Carrots
100g	Cucumber
100g	Onions
1	Red pepper
2	Sugar beet (peeled)
20g	Sugar
250g	Peeled shrimps
250g	Loin of pork (boned)
30ml	Peanut oil
200g	Peanuts
150–200g	Pork stomach
20–30ml	Fish sauce
10ml	Sweet white rice vinegar
1	Lemon (juice only)
10g	Garlic purée

Chef's Notes

- This is one of the more palatable recipes I came across. You can serve this salad with fried shrimp fish cakes.

Súp Bóng Cá

Fish Bladder Soup

Method

1. Soak the fish bladder in hot water for 2–3 hours, then squeeze it out and boil until it swells again. Clean off any rough bits and cut it into very fine strips.

Measurements	Ingredients
100g	Fish bladder (any white fish)
150g	Pork bones
20g	Ginger purée

continued over →

2. Bring the water to the boil and add the bones, ginger, fish bladder, rice wine and rice.

3. Take the bladder out after 8 minutes, drain and keep warm. Continue to cook the soup for a further 30–40 minutes.

4. Take the egg and a pinch of salt and cook in a bowl over a pan of boiling water until it becomes like a sloppy scrambled egg. Keep warm.

5. Separately mix the fish bladder with the sliced onion and then add a ladle of soup and yam bean powder and mix well. Return this to the soup.

6. Add the eggs, sesame oil, and crab to the soup. Check seasoning.

7. Serve immediately garnished with chopped coriander.

...continued

20ml	Rice wine
50g	Jasmine rice
1	Egg
50g	Onion (sliced)
10g	Yam bean powder
5ml	Sesame oil
500g	Crabs
5g	Black pepper
3 lt	Water
10g	Coriander leaves (chopped)
	Salt

Chef's Notes

- This soup isn't as bad as it sounds, but you could use chicken bones or veal if you can afford it. The pork bones here tend to be far too salty.

- Life in Vietnam as elsewhere in Asia revolves around the street cafés. People just sit and relax with a tea, Coke, beer or whatever they fancy. They watch, chat and let the world go by. It is quite possible as I have found that you may end up in deep conversation with a total stranger at your table over a bowl of soup.

Vit Congee

Duck Congee

Method

1. Cut the duck breast into fine slithers 1cm x 3cm thick. Peel and chop the spring onions and shallots.

2. Drain the rice and add to the stock then slowly bring the rice and stock to the boil.

3. Simmer with the ginger, garlic, shallots and spring onions and cook down for 1 hour 30 minutes until it is mushy and looks like porridge. You must stir to avoid the rice sticking and burning.

Measurements	Ingredients
2 x 200g	Duck breast (cooked)
4	Spring onions
20g	Shallots (peeled)
150g	Jasmine rice (soaked in cold water)
1.5lt	Good chicken stock
5g	Ginger (chopped)

continued over →

4. Add the cooked duck and cook for a further 20 minutes. You may need to add a little more stock or water if you simmer it too fast. Stir in the rice wine, sugar and peanuts, and add the chilli oil.

5. Cut the wonton sheets in half at an angle and deep-fry with the rice sticks until they puff up. Remove and drain on to kitchen paper.

6. Finely slice the garlic cloves and shallots and deep-fry in the vegetable oil to a golden brown colour, then drain on kitchen paper so they become crispy.

7. Divide the duck congee into four bowls and add the garnish to the side of each bowl.

Chef's Notes

- This dish can be a substantial meal in itself, and takes the northern winter chill away.

- If you do not want duck you can substitute chicken breast if you wish.

...continued

20g	Garlic purée
10ml	Chilli oil
30ml	Rice wine
10g	Sugar
Garnish	**Ingredients**
8	Wonton sheets
50g	Noodles (rice stick)
3 cloves	Garlic (peeled)
4	Shallots (peeled)
50g	Peanuts
20ml	Vegetable oil
	Oil for deep-frying

NORTH CENTRAL VIETNAM

This is probably the poorest region of Vietnam, stretching from just north of Ninh Binh to just south of Dong Hoi. It has little culinary significance other than it produces rice. Many tourists, on their way to or from Hanoi to Hué in Central Vietnam, tend to leave out this part of Vietnam.

Historically, north central Vietnam dates back to the tenth century when the capital of the whole country was in Hoa Lu. The area had magnificent temples mixed with the rural landscape of paddy fields and limestone cliffs. During the American war the carpet-bombing destroyed much of this region along with temples and buildings.

Thai Binh is where you will find the Keo Pagoda, which is thought by many to be an excellent example of Vietnamese architecture and carving with its wooden bell tower, which is dedicated to Buddha. It is also dedicated to a monk who is reported to have cured the Emperor Ly Thanh Ton who ruled from 1128–38.

Further south you come across Ninh Binh with a population of around 50,000. What is remarkable about this area is the rock formations at Tam Coc that protrude out of the rice paddies, similar to the rock formations at Halong Bay. The name Tam Coc translates as 'three caves' – one can visit the caves by a boat that also goes into them.

Close to Hoa Lu is the Kenh Ga floating village, where everyone lives on a boat of some kind. The village is on the Hoang Long River and with the mountains in the background it only adds to the enduring images that you will have when you leave this area. The river is the lifeblood of the village, its waters provide for food, water, washing and transport. The village people spend most of their lives cooking, eating and sleeping on their boats in and among the river village. You will have to go some way on the Mekong Delta to see village life like this. You will see dishes like carp with coconut, chilli and cinnamon, then there is peanut and lemongrass with deep-fried eel.

Cuc Phuong National Park, established in 1962, covers 222 square kilometres of tropical forest and was opened and dedicated in 1963 by Ho Chi Minh. Generally the wildlife, flora and fauna have suffered in recent years. The government has been trying to conserve and protect its precious reserves. This park is probably one of the most important with over 2,000 species of flora, over 1,800 insects, 70 mammals, and nearly 80 species of reptile, and that's not including birds and bats! The park's ecofriendly rangers can arrange trips for just a day to three days' trekking in the jungle, to visit native tribes. The park also has been trying to re-introduce species back into the wild with captive breeding programmes. One of the places of interest at the park is the endangered primate rescue centre that has save some primates from extinction.

Thanh Hoa is the capital of the province of the same name. The highway is littered with bomb craters from the war. The province is where the Lam Son uprising in 1418–28 was led by Le Loi and his Vietnamese army who managed to rid the country of the Chinese rulers.

Vinh is a port city and is the capital of Nghe An Province. The obliterations of the US air force bombings during the war left only a couple of buildings standing, and due to the high loss of aircraft and air force pilots they then decided to bombard the port from the sea with the US navy, reducing it to rubble. Most of the buildings are made of concrete, which makes it look like a cold place. The area is also prone to typhoons on a regular basis. The Viet Minhs scorched earth policy has done little for the soil around Vinh. A huge fire also destroyed Vinh. In all it is probably not worth staying too long around this area, although the port is the start of the Ho Chi Minh trail where war materials were transported.

Just north of Vinh is the little village of Kim Lien. This is where Ho Chi Minh was born in 1890. His old house is now a shrine, with its own museum close by.

Dong Hoi is a fishing port north of the de-militarised zone, which was bombed regularly by the Americans. Dong Hoi is also the capital of the Quang Binh Province, and significant archaeological finds have been unearthed from the Neolithic period. Close by is the Phong Nha cave, formed around 250 million years ago, which is now a UNESCO World Heritage Site. Thousands of metres of underground caves full of stalagmites and stalactites can be seen.

Luon Xáó Vói Sa Vá Lac

Peanut and Lemongrass Scented Eel

Measurements	Ingredients
600g	Eel fillets
2 stalks	Lemongrass
1	Lemon
2cm	Galangal (peeled)
10g	Brown sugar
50g	Cornflour
	Vegetable oil for deep-frying
15ml	Rice wine
5ml	Anchovy essence
100ml	Chicken stock
100ml	Fish stock
40ml	Nuoc Mam (fish sauce)
30g	Peanuts (roasted and chopped)
10g	Arrow root powder
10ml	Sesame oil

Method

1. Cut the eel fillets into neat strips 4–5cm x 2cm.

2. Remove the dry outer leaves of the lemongrass, cut in half, remove the root, and cut into very fine strips. Extract the juice and zest from the lemon.

3. Grate the galangal and squeeze the juice out. Throw away the left over fibres.

4. Mix two teaspoons of lemon juice with the galangal juice and half the sugar and soak the fillets in this marinade for 15 minutes. Remove and pat dry, lightly dust in the cornflour then carefully drop them in the deep-fryer and fry until golden brown. Remove onto kitchen paper and keep hot.

5. Bring to the boil the remaining sugar, rice wine, anchovy essence, stocks and fish sauce. Remove any debris from the surface, then add the lemongrass and boil for 10 minutes.

6. Place the fillets and half of the peanuts into the simmering stock for 2 minutes to take on the flavour.

7. Remove onto serving plates. Mix a little water with the arrow root powder and stir into the stock a little at a time. Thicken until it coats the back of a spoon, then whisk in the sesame oil.

9. Serve the fillets on to suitable serving plates and spoon the sauce over with a sprinkling of the remaining peanuts.

Chef's Notes

- Eels are popular throughout Vietnam.

- Serve this dish with plain rice rather than noodles.

- You could use the same sauce with snapper or bass.

Cá Chép Nâu Vói Núóc Daù

Freshwater Carp with Coconut, Chilli and Cinnamon

Method

1. Remove the scales and wash and dry the carp. Remove the zest from the lemon and extract the juice. Keep the zest separate. Mix the lemon juice and the sugar together and brush over the carp.

2. Place the lemongrass, galangal, peppercorns, garlic, chillies, cinnamon stick, cloves and shallots in a pestle and mortar or a blender and grind until a rough consistency is achieved.

3. Place this mixture into a suitable pan or wok and fry off without any oil until it smells fragrant. Stir to prevent burning. Then add the fish sauce.

4. Add the coconut milk and stir, then add the carp and cook for 15–20 minutes at a simmer with a lid on.

5. Remove the fish carefully and rapid boil the sauce for 4 minutes to reduce then ladle the sauce over and garnish with zest of lemon and chopped coriander.

Measurements	Ingredients
2–2.5kg	Carp (gutted)
1	Lemon (juice and zest)
10g	Sugar
1 stalk	Lemongrass
2cm	Galangal (peeled)
2.5g	Peppercorns
2 cloves	Garlic
1	Red chilli
2cm	Cinnamon stick
4	Cloves
2	Shallots
30–40ml	Nuoc mam (fish sauce)
150ml	Coconut milk (thick or thin)
20g	Coriander (chopped)

Chef's Notes

- For this recipe I feel that you should remove the fish scales, as they are not nice in this sort of dish.

- You may also use catfish or any firm fish as a replacement.

- Remember to have a spoon at the table to allow your guests to remove the flesh otherwise they will use chopsticks, which is unhygienic when they are eating with them.

Ca Tre Mi Sup

Catfish Noodle Soup

Method

1. Peel the ginger and cut into fine strips. Mix with the pepper and 20ml fish sauce, marinate the fillets in this sauce for 20 minutes, then remove. Soak the rice sticks in warm water for 20 minutes and drain.

2. Grind the shallots, shrimp paste, turmeric, lemongrass and curry powder in a pestle and mortar or a blender until a smooth consistency is achieved.

3. Fry off the paste with no oil until it smells fragrant, stir to prevent burning. Then add the remaining fish sauce.

4. Stir in the stock and bring to the boil and then simmer and remove any debris from the surface.

5. Add the rice sticks and cook for 3–4 minutes then add the diced fish and simmer for a further 5 minutes.

6. Add the coriander and check the seasoning.

7. Ladle out the soup into four pre-warmed soup bowls, and serve with a squeeze of lime.

Measurements	Ingredients
3cm	Ginger
5g	Black pepper (fresh ground)
50ml	Nuoc mam (fish sauce)
60g	Rice sticks
4	Shallots
10g	Shrimp paste
5g	Turmeric
1 stalk	Lemongrass
2.5g	Curry powder
2lt	Chicken stock
400g	Catfish fillets (diced)
20g	Coriander
1	Lime (cut into 4 wedges)

Chef's Notes

- You may use any firm fish as a replacement for the catfish.

CENTRAL VIETNAM

From the Ben Hai River to Chu Lai in the Quang Nam Province is the area of Central Vietnam which is both historically and culinarily important. For me this area of Vietnam is the most interesting and as far as Vietnam's cuisine goes is unsurpassed.

From the years 1954 to 1975 the Ben Hai River, and five kilometres on either side, was the demarcation zone, called the demilitarised zone (DMZ), between the north and south. This area saw lots of action during

the American war. In 1956, Ho Chi Minh's government agreed to the cease-fire and the creation of the DMZ as a temporary measure, effectively dividing the country in two.

Nationwide elections should have taken place by 1956 and never did. This narrow piece of land – only 50 kilometres long, spilt the country from Huong Lap in the east on the Laos border, to the beaches of Cua Tung in the west. The area just south of the DMZ saw some of the most famous and bloodiest battles of the Vietnam War. Places that have gone down in history include Hamburger Hill, the Rockpile, and Quang Tri to name a few.

This part of central Vietnam is terribly poor, the land is barren and next to nothing grows here. The populace lives off selling tourists drinks and cards and most worrying of all collecting war relics and selling them on either to tourists or to dealers for next to nothing. Over 5,000 people have been killed or injured since the end of the war, collecting or stepping on unexploded ordinance like mortar shells, artillery rounds and worst of all phosphorus shells, that burn on exposure to air. This area is still littered with mines and dotted with bomb craters. If you ever visit the DMZ never pick up anything. As one guide said, if it has not been touched or removed by the locals, it means they are afraid to disturb it! Leave well alone and watch your step. You can hire guides and four-wheel drive motor vehicles to take you to most of the battlegrounds and bases. This area is home to hundreds of thousands of missing in action soldiers (MIA) on both sides of the conflict.

Dong Ha is just south of the DMZ and was once home to the South Vietnamese army but was attacked in 1968. The town is part of the Quang Tri Province and has a population of over 62,000. Quang Tri has a population in excess of 15,000 and is 12 kilometres south of Dong Ha and almost 60 kilometres north of Hué. Quang Tri used to have a citadel and was a very important citadel city, but in 1972 the USA and the Southern Vietnamese obliterated the area because the North Vietnamese overran the whole province as part of the Eastertide offensive. It is reported that the South Vietnamese suffered over 5,000 casualties to retake the city in hand-to-hand combat. If you are interested in the war you can see the actual Vinh Moc tunnels that were used by the North Vietnamese. These tunnels were constructed originally to escape the heavy American bombardment inflicted on the locals in 1966. The Viet Cong saw the potential of these tunnels and made a massive base underground. They were so big and elaborate that tonnes of armaments were transported through the 2.8 kilometres of tunnels to the nearby port. The tunnels took 18 months to construct and similar tunnels were built elsewere around the country during the war.

The battlefield of Khe Sanh at the Khe Sanh combat base saw 500 USA soldiers and 10,000 North Vietnamese die. Today USA MIA army teams regularly visit the site. The Huong Hoa Khe Sanh is famous for their excellent coffee plantations.

Other famous sites include Camp Carrol, Dakrong Bridge, Aluoi and the Con Thien firebase.

The ancient citadel city of Hué is at the hub of Vietnamese cuisine in central Vietnam and is situated on the tranquil banks of the Perfume River. From 1802 to 1945, Hué was the Imperial City of the Nguyen Dynasty and for centuries the centre for culture, religion and education under thirteen different emperors. Despite the ravages of war the city still has a regal air and many of the palaces, citadels, pagodas and imperial mausoleums are in excellent condition. In 1993 the complex of monuments in Hué were designated an UNESCO World Heritage Site.

In 1968 Hué was the site of one of the bloodiest battles of the Vietnam War (the Tet offensive). The American commanders at the time were concentrating their resources on the relief of the troops at Khe Sanh, and the North Vietnamese troops walked around the defences of Hué, and straight into the city. They remained there for 25 days in which time they rounded up some 3,000 civilians in house-to-house searches and executed Hué's uncooperative population, from names on a well-prepared list. These included monks, priests, travellers and intellectuals, all of whom were either burned alive, shot or clubbed to death and buried in mass graves around the city. The Americans together with South Vietnamese took just over ten days to dislodge the North Vietnamese in bitter hand-to-hand and house-to-house fighting. Over 10,000 people lost their lives here in Hué, mostly civilians caught up in the fighting.

It is here in Hué many years after the war that a former American veteran is reputed to have said to a former Viet Cong officer that, 'America never lost a battle in the entire war', and the VC officer replied, 'That is absolutely correct, but that is irrelevant, is it not?'

As you walk along the Perfume River, you begin to understand why Hué is the third most visited city in Vietnam. The quiet streets and the sedate pace of life here is most noticeable. You can watch the children jumping off the banks into the river, swimming and playing, while a little further upstream you can see a man and his wife fishing with nets from his little boat for their dinner or for the market. Along the river the beautiful coloured dragon boats are moored. Just before sunset, you can sit and drink a freshly made sugarcane drink that comes in a plastic bag with a straw, bought from a street vendor. The people here are very proud of their city and love to talk to you about what you must see and do during your time in Hué, either on foot or cycle. This shows in the streets around Hué, as they are much cleaner. At around 12 midday until 2pm everywhere just seems to stop for a siesta. Even the street traders just get their cardboard out and go to sleep next to their carts on the pavement. But as elsewhere in Vietnam the day starts at 5am as the sun rises with the sounding of lorries, bikes and car horns bibbing.

Emperor Gia Long commenced construction of the great citadel the Forbidden City or Purple City in 1804. Then a citadel within a citadel, it was constructed with 6-metre high walls and covers 2.5 kilometres in

length. The ramparts are encircled by a 30-metre moat that is 4 metres deep. It has ten fortified gates all reachable by a bridge.

The inner Purple Forbidden City was for the exclusive use of the emperor. The only servants allowed were eunuchs, not able to threaten the royal concubines. This was almost entirely destroyed during the Tet offensive.

The inner citadel is where the nine holy cannons are located. These are the symbolic protectors of the place. Cast in 1804 from the brass that was taken from the Tay Son Rebels, the 5-metre long cannons each weigh 11 kilograms and have a bore of 23 centimetres. The cannons have never been fired. Four cannons representing the four seasons stand on ornate wooden carriages at the Ngo Mon gate. The Nguyen Dynasty ended on 30 August 1945 when the emperor Bao Dai abdicated to a delegation from Ho Chi Minh's Provisional Revolutionary Government.

One of the biggest attractions is that of the Imperial Palace and the Emperors' Tombs just south of the city. The palace and tombs indicate that the emperors lived in great opulence. The longest-reining Nguyen Emperor was Tu Duc (1848–83) and he is reputed to have lived a life of luxury. He had 104 wives and many more concubines, but he never fathered any offspring. This is thought to have been as a result of contracting smallpox as a child, which made him sterile. Tuc Duc stood only 1m 52cm tall. He had a lake constructed with a small island in the middle with a boat landing from which he and his empress used to race two dragon boats. On occasions he also used to hunt small game on the island, but his chief interest was sitting among his concubines or wives and writing poetry.

He built himself a tomb, but decided not to use it. No one knows exactly where he is buried, as all 200 of the courtiers and servants were beheaded on his burial. This was to protect him and his reputed treasure from grave robbers. The tombs of his empress, mother and a number of other emperors are on the site. The palace and tombs are in superb condition and a number of buildings are made of wood.

Tu Duc was a fussy eater and even demanded that his morning cup of tea was made with the dew and water collected from lotus leaves on his lake within the walled imperial palace.

Long before the French master chefs of the modern day began to include a 'Menu degustation' in their establishments, Tu Duc insisted on a menu and cuisine entirely different from the common person. This was a very tall order for the chefs of the time because Hué was not known for its agriculture, and food was not really transported as it is today. The chefs had to be very creative and show a great deal of resourcefulness. They began to refine the dishes to be very small, delicate, sophisticated, colourful and well presented. It is reputed that a chef needed to have a 2,000-dish repertoire from which approximately 50 would be served to the emperor. The dishes and the experience became an art, eating ritual, sensory pleasure and a sign of intellectual meaning, similar to those experiences of the Chinese banquets and Japanese tea ceremony.

Today the Imperial cuisine menu would consist of around 12 dishes including soup, spring rolls, and shrimp farce wrapped around a sugar cane and grilled. Hué's famous pork sausage, which is minced pork, shrimp, vegetables and fish sauce, is steamed until cooked, and then grilled until golden brown and served with a garnish of herbs and crispy salad. Another local speciality are small crisp rice cakes.

The menu would have meat like beef wrapped in betel leaves. In most markets you will see betel nuts for sale, which are from the beautiful betel palm tree. The nut is in reality the seed, and it is meant to be chewed like tobacco. You must not swallow the nut, as this would cause gastric problems. The chewing causes you to produce more saliva than normal and it creates a hot sensation. As you walk along the pavements you will notice black stains which were made by betel chewers' spit. The stains also discolour the teeth. You can substitute betel leaves with vine leaves and pepper leaves also are some times used.

The menu would also normally contain a glutinous rice of some description and fresh fruit.

You may still get some of these dishes served to you in other parts of Vietnam but the main different is the size of the portions, complexity and presentation of the food. For example, rice may be cooked and served in lotus leaves or banana blossom and glutinous rice may be served in a box made from banana leaf.

The size of the kitchen brigade was enormous, with the labour intensive requirements that the food, dishes and the emperors required. The number of chefs needed would have been seen as an impressive luxury.

A few lucky chefs today have been passed down the skills, techniques and recipes of the cuisine from Imperial households. The more modern chefs of Hué are trying to reproduce the Imperial cuisine in the hope of restoring it to the heights of past glory, rather than cashing in on its increasing popularity.

The general day-to-day food on the streets, restaurants and cafés of Hué is much the same as elsewhere in Vietnam but you will tend to see the hawker stalls more spread out, rather than in one or two places. The cuisine is generously flavoured with coconut, herbs and spices, but not to the excess of Thai cuisine.

Markets on the other hand are excellent for local cuisine with specialities like eggy pancake called Banh khoai and a soup and noodle dish called Bun bo Hué. Food products at market are of a very high quality with dragon fruits, mangoes, asparagus, gourd, cabbage, spring onions, chillies and garlic in abundance. Ducks and chickens are sold from cages and are handed over with their feet tied, then secured to the handlebars of the purchaser's bicycle and taken off for dinner.

Shrimps (prawns) along with catfish, snakefish and eels are all still alive in large bowls, covered with nets to prevent them jumping out, ready for you to choose the fish you want.

In Hué you can see the strong influence of the French with bread and cakes for sale. Food vendors sell French bread (baguettes) freshly baked daily and sold toasted with BBQ pork, herbs, crispy salad vegetables and chilli sauce, or spread with a soft pork pâté. You can also see spaghetti, pâté and prepared meats on menus.

Because of the cooler climate and hilly terrain the more temperate vegetables and fruit like asparagus, carrots, cauliflowers, potato, plums and strawberries are grown along with tea plantations. Growing crops like rice in this area is not really possible because of the climate.

Many inhabitants who live closer to the rivers, streams and the sea still support themselves through fishing.

The hill tribes of the Central Highlands have a number unusual customs and rituals. One is teeth filing, which has all but disappeared. Filed teeth were seen as a sign of maturity and beauty. Painful as it was, teenagers on a fixed day would bathe in the stream, then put on their best clothes and lie on their backs in the village's communal house, while someone would file their upper teeth down almost to the gums with an iron blade or stone. Burnt banana would be pressed against the gums and stubs to prevent bleeding. A pig would be slaughtered as an offering to the gods, with music and dance to celebrate the coming of age of the teenagers. During this process the victims were not allowed to eat or drink any alcohol, but it may have helped to distract from the intense pain.

Further south is the port city of Danang, which in the eighteenth century was an important trading port after Hoi An silted up (see below). It lies halfway up the coastline and is not really a place of culinary heritage or that interesting, although it is a nice place to stop over after a long trip from Ho Chi Minh City (Saigon). The coastline is famous for the China Beach, with long stretches of white sand and uncrowded beaches. Some parts are being developed into tourist resorts.

The present site of Danang is where the Kingdom of Champa began in the second century. It lasted to the fifteenth century. The kingdom stretched from Danang to what is now Nha Trang and Phan Rang. The kingdom had very good trade relations with India and slowly became Indianised by converting to Hinduism and taking on the language and art.

The kingdom was in an almost constant state of war against the Khmers and Vietnamese, due to their attacks on passing ships and merchants. By the seventeenth century the kingdom had completely disappeared and been overrun by the Vietnamese. Danang has a Champ museum, with some of the best Champ art and artefacts in the world. Just outside Danang on the way to Hoi An is the major Champ site of My Son, now a designated UNESCO World Heritage Site. The site was considered to be one of intellectual and religious significance, and also thought to be the counterpart of other important sites like Angkor (Cambodia), Ayutthaya (Thailand) and Bagan (Burma Myanmar). Occupied from the fourth to the thirteenth centuries, most of the temples are dedicated to

Champ Kings and some parts were left unfinished. Although the site has been repeatedly pillaged over the centuries by the Khmers, Chinese and the Vietnamese, most of the damage was caused by the American bombing during the war, which destroyed and damaged many of the monuments. All but 20 of the 68 monuments around the site remain.

Other sites around Danang are the Hai Van Pass, a mountain pass on the way to and from Hué. This pass was an old French Fort and was the dividing line between the Champ Empire and Vietnam. The spectacular views over the mountain are breathtaking. There are some excellent seafood restaurants dotted around Danang if you are prepared to search them out.

The Marble Mountains are five hills made of marble and named after the five elements. These are Fire (Hoa Son), Water (Thuy Son), Earth (Tho Son), Metal (Kim Son), and Moc Son (wood). Over the centuries the mountains have been home to Champ Hindu priests who built altars and shrines for worship, Buddhist monks and Viet Cong battalions, due to the natural layout of the caves. The biggest one is Thuy Son, a popular pilgrimage during the silver moon (or full moon days).

My favourite place for food and a look into the past of Vietnam is the little sleepy and attractive village of Hoi An, 30 miles south of Danang. Once an important trading port between the sixteenth and eighteenth centuries, it was considered a modern-day Melaka during this period, in which the majority of Hoi An's wealth was made.

It was a well-established trading port centuries before the West came to trade with the Chinese and Japanese, who would wait for the winds to blow them to Hoi An and then stay for the spring, until the southerly winds in the summer would blow them home.

There is some evidence that the Arabs and the Persians traded in Hoi An. From the second to the tenth centuries the village was in the heartland of the Champ Kingdom, serving as a trading port. Then in 1307 the Champ king married the Vietnamese Emperor's (Tran Dynasty) daughter and gave the Quang Nam Province as a present. When the king died his successor refused to accept this and war broke out and continued until the early part of the fifteenth century. Later, Hoi An's port was a calling point for the Dutch, Portuguese, English, Japanese, Chinese and even the Americans. Many Vietnamese ships also sailed to ports all over Vietnam, Thailand, Java and Indonesia from Hoi An. During the Tay Son Rebellion in the 1770–80s Hoi An was destroyed, but was quickly restored and rebuilt.

Hoi An merchants would trade in silk, spices, paper, lacquer, pearl, tea, porcelain and other merchandise. Many of the old merchants' houses which were made from hard wood are now open to the public as living museums. The mother of pearl inlay is some of the finest examples in Vietnam, if not Asia.

It was during the late nineteenth century that the Thu Bon River (or Hoi An River) began to silt up and become far too shallow for the great

merchant ships to navigate, and that ended the golden era for Hoi An as a major trading port. The trade then shifted to Danang, further up the coast.

Now the sleepy village is becoming a stopping off point for many of the tour operators. The ancient streets and temples have come through the onslaught of Vietnam's recent history rather well. There are over 800 buildings that have been identified as being of historical significance in the town; many are rarely seen around Vietnam today. The streets are remarkable little gems of history on their own, with the house and shop frontages mixed with eclectic architectural styles, which gives a feeling of genuine living history. You have the feeling that you will see a Dutch, French or Japanese sailor or merchant walk around the next corner trading with the locals. History is everywhere in Hoi An; for example, the Chinese assembly hall built in the late 1780s, or the 400-year-old Japanese wooden bridge built to join the Japanese area to the Chinese quarter in 1543. The pagodas and the French colonial houses and streets at the end of the village, together with the ancient waterfront, are all still very much the hub of village life. Much of its traditional culture is still evident as you wander around the streets, with their markets and crafts, although the craftwork is mainly for the tourist market.

I found the food here to be impressive. Raw ingredients such as fish are of superb quality. Even before the catch is landed, there is a frenzy of activity on the wharf. A small boat is manoeuvred alongside the fishing boat, then the catch is lowered down in small round bamboo baskets and rowed to the shore, where a crowd of women is ready to squabble and haggle over the price of the catch. Some of the locals jump onto the boats to start haggling for the best deals even before the catch has landed. You will only see the women haggling and dealing on the market stalls and it is a great sight to see this customary process taking place.

During the quiet periods waiting for merchandise to be transported to the larger vessels, the women will moor their boats close to the wharf, and ask if you wish to take a trip up and down the river for a small fee.

As you walk around the market the atmosphere is very friendly, with the locals often just wanting to talk to you, out of courtesy. They show immense pride in their identity and village.

Hoi An is well known for its fabrics, especially cotton. As you walk down towards the bottom end of town, you will hear the constant noise of sewing machines. You can have a suit made to measure, made by hand within a few hours, or an entire new wardrobe overnight for a few pounds.

Hoi An's only slight drawback is the constant failing of the electricity supply during the evening, but this is compensated for when the locals bring out candles and lanterns. The Hoi An Legendary Night or lantern festival is on the fourteenth day of every lunar month, i.e. full moon. From around 5.50 until 10 pm the streets are lit with colourful lanterns and local food, music, games and dance add to the celebrations.

One of the biggest impressions left on me was how clean the village and surrounding areas were and this ultimately shows in the food and whole eating experience. The vegetables and fruit are of excellent quality, as one has come to expect in Asia, and with this being a local port and market, the quality is even better. Fruit and vegetables are picked early in the morning as the dew is beginning to form, carefully loaded into the bamboo baskets and transported to market by boat, bicycle, motorbike or a small van on the rare occasion.

The local food cooked and served here is on the whole impressive. Each restaurant I indulged in had its own little twists, but the standard was always good. While in Cambodia, I had the good fortune to be introduced to a very nice lady called Cathy Foscatti, a guide from the company 'Intrepid'. We talked about the food in Vietnam, Thailand and Cambodia for several hours. Kathy was very knowledgeable and gave me a list of restaurants to visit on my travels in Vietnam. She particularly raved about two small local restaurants in Hoi An called the White Lantern and in particular Miss Ly (22 Nguyen Hue), whose specialities were a dish called the white rose and 'deep-fried wonton'. The white rose dish is made with minced pork, garlic, chilli, peanuts, black pepper and rice wine wrapped in either Banh trang, which is the Vietnamese equivalent to ravioli, or sheets of Cao lau, and then shaped like a rose. I visited Miss Ly's restaurant a couple of times, but she would not divulge exactly what she wrapped the meat in! Chefs are often very secretive. You can, however, wrap them either in rice flour wrappers or wonton sheets as a last resort.

The deep-fried wonton dish is made from minced pork and black pepper folded into a wonton sheet and deep fried, placed on a lettuce leaf and garnished with sauté vegetables and sweet and sour sauce. Wonderful!

The speciality in Hoi An is a dish called Cao lau. This is a noodle made from the water drawn from the Ba Le Well and used in the authentic preparation of the noodles. The Well itself is reputed to date from the Champ Kingdom. The slightly doughy noodles are mixed and served with bean sprouts, croutons, greens, herbs and slices of pork, and finished with broken crispy rice paper. According to the locals this dish can only be authentic and called Cao lau if the noodles are made with the water from the Well.

One of the better places I have eaten in was at the Faifoo Restaurant, which served Cau lau noodles. The Fu Kien Restaurant, which also serves Vietnamese food, is in a delightful old building just up from the market.

There are few food hawker stalls in Hoi An, possibly due the large number of excellent and reasonably priced restaurants in which you can just watch the world go by, without the constant hassle of peddlers trying to sell you books and cards as happens in Hanoi and Saigon.

Bánh Bao Bánh Vạc

White Rose

Method

1. To make the Vietnamese Bánh trang (ravioli paste), mix the flour and water to make a batter. Fill a steamer two-thirds full of water and stretch a cheese (muslin) cloth tightly over the top. Wait until the water is boiling, then brush the top of the cheese cloth with oil and carefully pour a ladle of the batter over the top. The water will then drain through and the batter will form a sheet of ravioli on top. Place a lid on top for a couple of minutes, then remove the lid and carefully remove the sheet with a pallet knife or fish slice. Repeat the process until the batter has all gone.

2. Slice the garlic very thinly and then deep-fry until golden brown and drain on kitchen paper.

3. Remove the stalk and de-seed the chillies. Purée 1 chilli and then cut the second into very fine slices.

4. Dissolve the sugar with the rice wine vinegar and heat gently. Reserve until required.

Measurements	Ingredients
2 cloves	Garlic
2	Whole chillies
30g	Sugar
60ml	Rice wine vinegar
100g	Minced pork
20ml	Fish sauce
20 sheets	Banh trang
100g	Roasted peanuts (chopped)
	Black pepper
Banh Trang	**Ingredients**
220g	Rice flour
800ml	Water
	Salt
	Oil for brushing

5. Mix the minced pork with the chilli purée, black pepper and fish sauce. Roll the meat into little balls (2 pence size), then place a ball into the centre of a ravioli sheet and very gently and carefully pinch the sheet into a little 'purse' shape, then flatten it slightly to look like a bud. Repeat this until all the meat and sheets have gone.

6. You can at this stage either place into a steamer or boiling water to reheat and cook the pork.

7. Place on a serving plate and spoon over the rice wine and sugar sauce. Finish with a sprinkling of garlic, chilli and peanuts and serve.

Chef's Notes

- If you do not wish to make the rice sheets fresh you can obtain them from any good Asian supermarket.

- This is my interpretation of the famous 'Miss Ly's White Rose' dish from Hoi An.

Thịt Heo Mè Đậu Phong

Pork Slices with Sesame Seed and Peanuts

Method

1. Remove any sinew and fat from the pork loin and slice thinly.

2. Slice the garlic very thinly and then deep-fry until golden brown. Drain on kitchen paper. Remove the stalk, deseed the chilli and slice. Peel and slice the cucumber.

Measurements	Ingredients
600g	Pork tenderloin
2 cloves	Garlic
1	Chilli
60g	Cucumber
10g	Sesame seeds

continued over →

3. To make the sauce, take the tamarind paste and mix it with the water. Drain and reserve the tamarind water. Discard the pulp.

4. Then slice the garlic clove and sauté in the peanut oil until soft, and with no colour. Add the yellow bean sauce, chilli, lemongrass, tamarind juice, coconut milk, sugar, peanuts, and a pinch of salt. Cook and stir for 4–5 minutes.

5. Place the pork slices in the marinade for 1–2 hours then remove. Coat in sesame seeds and place either under the grill or on a griddle for 3–4 minutes, until cooked.

6. Serve with a dusting of deep-fried garlic, cucumber and peanuts.

Chef's Notes

- This is a very simple but very tasty dish I was served in Hoi An.

- You could replace the pork with veal.

...continued

50g	Roasted peanuts (chopped)
Peanut marinade	**Ingredients**
20g	Tamarind paste
40ml	Water
1 clove	Garlic
1	Chilli
20ml	Peanut oil
120ml	Yellow bean sauce
1 stalk	Lemongrass
125ml	Coconut milk (thick or thin)
5g	Sugar
220g	Peanuts
	Salt

Ram Tôm

Deep-fried Spring Rolls

Method

1. Moisten the rice sheets with a damp cloth. Remove the central vein from the prawns. Peel the spring onions, remove the roots, cut them in half widthways and then lengthways.

2. Lay the sheets out and place two prawns and a spring onion on each of the spring roll sheets.

3. Roll the sheet tightly once. Brush the rice paper all around the edges with the egg white. Then fold in both sides and brush again. Now roll up tightly and brush the spring roll in egg white and place in the pre-heated deep fat fryer.

4. Fry until golden brown, then remove onto kitchen paper to drain.

5. Serve with pickled vegetables.

Measurements	Ingredients
8	Rice paper sheets
16 medium	Shelled prawns
8	Spring onions
1	Egg white
40g	Pickled vegetables
	Oil for frying

Chef's Notes

- This is a speciality from Hoi An. A number of local restaurants served this dish.

- The pickled vegetables are blanched and marinated in rice wine vinegar and sugar.

Hoành Thánh Chiên

Deep-fried Wontons

Method

1. Cut the tomatoes into 8 wedges and remove the seeds, leaving just the leaf shapes. Peel the cucumber and cut in half lengthways and remove the seeds, then cut into thick slices. Peel the onion and cut in half. Remove the root and then cut into wedges approximately the same size as the tomatoes. Peel and cut the carrots and spring onions into slices at an angle. Peel and cut the pineapple into 4 small slices.

2. Mix and fully incorporate the minced pork, black pepper, five spice and fish sauce. Roll the pork into small balls the size of a 2 pence piece.

3. Lay the sheets out and place the ball of meat just off centre towards the corner of the sheet. Then lift and bring the corner just past the centre, wet the edges with a little water and press firmly down ensuring no air bubbles are in the pocket and it is well sealed.

4. Place the wontons into a preheated fat fryer and fry until golden brown. Once cooked place for a few moments onto kitchen paper and allow to drain.

Measurements	Ingredients
2	Tomatoes
60g	Cucumber
1	Onion
1	Carrot
4	Spring onions
80g	Pineapple
400g	Minced pork (minced twice)
5g	Black pepper (fresh ground)
Pinch	Five spice
20ml	Fish sauce
8	Wonton sheets
30g	Vegetable oil
100g	Sweet and sour sauce
8	Lettuce leaves
	Oil for deep-frying

5. Pan fry the pineapples in a little oil until they have begun to caramelise, then remove and keep warm.

6. Pan fry the rest of the vegetables in a little oil for a few minutes, drain off any excess oil and then add the sauce and cook for a further 2–3 minutes.

7. Place a lettuce leaf on a suitable plate then a pineapple ring on top of the lettuce leaf and then the wonton followed by a spoonful of sweet and sour vegetables.

Sweet and Sour Sauce

Method

Sauté the garlic purée in the oil. Then add the sliced shallots, carrot, pepper, chilli and sugar. Cook for 2 minutes then add the rice wine vinegar and tomato sauce and boil for 2–3 minutes, then thicken with a little water and cornflour.

Chef's Notes

- This is an excellent recipe and dish. I first had it in Hoi An at Miss Ly's restaurant and then the following day around the corner at another restaurant.

- The recipe is as authentic as it is possible to get.

Measurements	Ingredients
20g	Garlic purée
15ml	Oil
40g	Shallots (peeled and diced)
30g	Carrot (peeled and diced)
1	Red pepper (deseeded and chopped)
1	Red chilli (deseeded and chopped)
30g	Brown sugar
100ml	Rice wine vinegar
30ml	Tomato sauce
5g	Cornflour

Mỳ Mêm Tôm Ran

Stir-Fry Noodles with Shrimps and Vegetables

Measurements	Ingredients
100g	Carrots
60g	Choi sam lettuce or baby green spinach (including stems)
350g (medium)	Peeled shrimps
50ml	Vegetable oil
60g	Spring onions
400g	Thin yellow noodles (cooked)
2.5g	Black pepper (fresh ground)

Method

1. Peel the carrots and cut into 7cm x 1.5 cm strips. Blanch and refresh in cold water. Wash and shred the spinach. Wash and peel the spring onions, removing the root. Cut off any excess green stalk, then cut in half widthways.

2. Trim and peel any roots and leaves from the choi sam and cut into thick strips.

3. Remove the central vein from the shrimps and leave whole.

4. Pour oil into a wok over a high heat.

5. First add the vegetables and cook for 2–3 minutes, then add the noodles and shrimps and stir until all the shrimps have gone a nice pink colour.

6. Check the seasoning and serve.

Chef's Notes

- A nice quick dish from Hué.

- The noodles used here are yellow 'thin' noodles. Just soak them in cold water for 20 minutes then blanch in boiling salted water and refresh under cold running water.

Cháo Tõm

Shrimp Mousse on Sugar Cane

Method

1. Deseed and very finely dice the red chilli. Ensure that the cane is peeled.

2. Dry roast the rice grains in a pan until all the grains are golden brown, then grind them in a coffee grinder or pestle and mortar until a flour has been achieved.

3. Squeeze out any excess water from the prawns and place them in a clean bowl, with a beaten egg, chilli, fish sauce, pepper, sugar and a pinch of salt. Stir vigorously and add the rice flour a little at a time.

4. Dip your fingers into the oil and mould the paste around the sugar cane, making sure it is really tight to the cane, leaving the ends of the cane free.

Measurements	Ingredients
1	Red chilli
8	Sugar cane sticks (10cm long)
30g	Long grain rice
450g	Minced prawns
1	Egg (beaten)
15ml	Fish sauce
2.5g	Black pepper (freshly ground)
5g	Brown sugar
2.5g	Rock salt
30ml	Vegetable oil

continued over →

5. Grill over a charcoal heat until crispy golden brown.

6. Garnish the plate with cooked vermicelli, vegetables and herbs.

Chef's Notes

- I first had this dish in Hué and this recipe is an adaptation of it.

- The cane bursts with sweetness when you bite into it.

- You can also serve a sweet and sour sauce with chilli and coriander leaves as a dip.

...continued

Garnish	Ingredients
450g	Rice vermicelli (cooked)
8	Spring onion (cut into slices)
2	Shallots (peeled and cut into slices)
50g	Cucumber (peeled and cut into slices)
10g	Coriander (washed and picked)
10g	Mint (washed and picked)
8 leaves	Lettuce

Bánh Khoai (Xeo)
Hué Pancake

Method

1. Peel spring onions and cut into slices. Cut the mushrooms in half (can be used whole if small).

2. Mix together eggs, water, pepper, fish sauce, sugar and rice flour until a smooth batter has been achieved. Strain the mixture through a muslin cloth.

3. Pour 10ml oil into a suitable frying pan, heat, tip out any excess oil and ladle in a spoonful of the batter. Roll the pan quickly to make a thin even pancake. Make sure it is evenly distributed then add some mung beans, prawns, pork, mushrooms, spring onions and bean sprouts. Put a lid on and turn the heat down to medium for 3 minutes then add the herbs. Repeat with the remainder of the pancakes.

4. Cook for a further 1 minute, then serve flat on a plate with a lettuce and salad garnish.

Measurements	Ingredients
4	Spring onions
100g	Straw mushrooms
2	Eggs
180ml	Water
5g	Black pepper (fresh ground)
20ml	Fish sauce
5g	Caster sugar
200g	Rice flour
40ml	Sunflower oil
50g	Mung beans (fresh or tinned)
100g	Peeled prawns (cooked)
4 x 57g	Pork tenderloin strips (cooked)
100g	Bean sprouts

continued over →

Chef's Notes

...continued

8	Basil leaves
4	Wild betel leaves
5g	Coriander
5g	Mint

- Traditionally the pancake was poured onto a flat steamer and scraped off and folded with the filling in the centre, but today the pan is used.

- This recipe is seen around the streets in Hué and other versions of omelette will be seen in most parts of Vietnam, but always served open faced.

- The Xeo is a large pan used in southern Vietnam for making omelettes, but in Hué and central parts it is called Khoai and is smaller.

- Some recipes I have seen in Saigon have coconut milk and even curry powder added.

SOUTH CENTRAL VIETNAM

The capital city of the south is called Quang Ngai. In Quang Ngai Province there is a population of 108,000 living on the banks of Tra Khuc River, 15 kilometres from the coast. The area is known for its large water wheels and for the region's excellent beaches, which are some of the very best in Vietnam. The countryside is dotted with little villages, rice paddies, palm trees and vegetable and fruit plantations, making it picturesque.

This has always been a stronghold for resistance and support for the Viet Cong during the French and American wars. The My Son district just 15 kilometres north of Quang Ngai is where the appalling My Lai massacre occurred in 1968, when American soldiers carried out the brutal slaughter of hundreds of civilians, including women and children.

The city is also noted for a dish called Com ga – boiled chicken with steamed rice over the boiling chicken, which will slightly colour the rice yellow, and served with egg drop soup and pickled vegetables as a side dish.

Nearby are the ruins of Cha Ban, the capital of the Champ Kingdom for almost 500 years. The city was enclosed by a huge wall and at the centre lies the tower of brass. The Khmer, Vietnamese and Chinese attacked the capital repeatedly. In 1471 the Vietnamese, led by the Vietnamese emperor Le Thanh Ton captured the capital, including all the Champ royal family and court. This cost the lives of over 60,000 Champs in what was to be the city's last great battle.

The eldest of the Tay Son brothers also ruled the city during the Tay Son rebellion. The second eldest Tay Son brother, Nguyen Hue, declared himself emperor Quang Trung in 1788 and subsequently led the greatest military campaign against a Chinese army of 200,000 troops and defeated

them as they invaded Vietnam near Hanoi in 1789. Quang Trung died at the age of 40 in 1792 and was succeeded by the Nguyen Dynasty.

On the way south to Nha Trang are numerous little beaches, towers and ruins from the Champ era.

Nha Trang is the capital of the Khanh Hoa Province, which has 71 islands off its coast and boasts possibly the best beach in Vietnam. The city is eight hours north of Saigon and is surrounded by green hills, a 6-kilometre beach of golden sand and the glorious clear turquoise waters of the South China Sea. The best and driest season is from June to October, the rainy season is from October to November.

The beach lies between two rivers and there is a fishing fleet of over 10,000 junks and trawlers which support the province and Phu Yen next door. The sight of the fleet leaving the port each night with the twinkling of their lights disappearing in the distance is wonderful. Then in the early morning after a hard night's work they return with their catch of tuna, mackerel, lobster, abalone, prawns and snapper, which are deposited on the quayside ready for distribution to local markets and beyond. You will also see little basket boats dotted about the fleet, which are made of woven bamboo strips covered with a type of tar, making them waterproof. These transport goods and people up and down the port.

Exports from Nha Trang consist of coffee, coconuts, cashew nuts and salt.

Nha Trang has a cluster of ninth-century Champ towers and a Buddha standing 14 metres tall overlooking the town.

Naturally with a fishing fleet in full swing and a beach, there is no shortage of superb food on offer. In fact, it is a haven for seafood. Dishes like roasted cuttlefish, steam boiled fish in salted soya beans, baked squid and roasted crab are delights to enjoy in the bars, coffee shops, cafés and restaurants dotted along the beach front and its side streets.

Just off the coast is the island of Salangane. Here they harvest swifts' nests twice a year, which are required for making bird's nest soup and traditional medicine. The red nests are the most highly prized and the annual production is about 1,000 kilograms, making them very expensive.

Further south is Cam Ranh Bay, a military naval base since the early 1900s when it was occupied by the Russians, Americans, Japanese and sometimes the Vietnamese themselves. Moving south along the National Highway you will see many fields of dragon fruit growing on large concrete stakes, encouraging the stems of the fruit tree to grow upward and then over, like a green upside-down mop, with the dragon fruit growing on the branches (stems). They look a great sight as they ripen into a bright red and purple colour. The flesh is white speckled with black dots and it is full of juice that tastes great on a hot day.

The area is famous for its production of grapes, dragon fruit, prickly pear and cacti, mainly due to the difficult dry soil in this area.

Phan Theit is even better known for its production of Nuoc mam (fish sauce). Built along the Phan Thiet River it has a population of 168,000 and is becoming used to increasing tourism, due to the Mui Ne Beach beaches and four brick towers at Phan Rang and Thap Cham. These Hindu temples were built in the thirteenth century and called Po Klong Ghirai, which means dragon.

The area of the central highlands in the west borders Cambodia and Laos. This part of Vietnam is home to many of the ethnic minority groups or Montagnards (French for Highlanders) as they are collectively called. The area is dominated by the Truong Son mountain range. Its scenery, streams, lakes and waterfalls, cool climate and tranquillity set this area apart from the hustle and bustle of Hanoi and Saigon. The land is very fertile and made from a red volcanic soil, making it excellent agricultural land. Many of the forests have disappeared due to the American war or logging. Much of this area was closed to foreigners before 1992, possibly due to lack of central government control.

Along the border 150 kilometres from Ho Chi Minh City is the Nam Cat Tien National Park, which stretches over Song Be, Dong Nai and Lam Dong provinces; and is home to a number of very rare animals. One of the rarest creatures is a mammal called the Jarvan rhino. Other creatures like the rare wild oxen called the Gaur, jaguars, birds, monkeys and a small number of elephants all live in the flora and fauna of the park.

Between Ho Chi Minh City and Dalat are the towns of Bao Loc and Di Linh that are famous for the production of silk and tea. There are numerous waterfalls around the area but one of the great sights close by is the magnificent 90-metre high Dambri waterfalls. The Dan Nhim Lake is 9.3 square kilometres, and was built in 1962–64 as part of the war reparations by Japan. This hydroelectric dam supplies much of the southern area.

Dalat, formally an old French hill station, has a romantic atmosphere, partly due to the city being the honeymoon capital of Vietnam. The city became known as the 'city of eternal spring' during the French colonial days when it was discovered by Dr Alexandre Yersin. He encouraged the colonials to spend time in the cooler temperatures away from the baking heat of the Mekong Delta. Set in a beautiful green region dotted with lakes, waterfalls and forests it's not surprising it is so popular with tourists. The city's French district and the old governor's residence both add to the old colonial feeling one gets as you walk around the city. There are many artists applying their paint to canvas, drawn by the beauty and many differing scenes along with the calm atmosphere of the city.

Another attraction is the summer palace constructed in the 1930s by Emperor Bao Dai. Set in a pine grove, the palace has virtually been unchanged over the years. There are numerous pagodas and churches across the city representing the religious diversity from Catholic and Protestant to the Buddhist places of worship.

Around Dalat other industries such as floral and agricultural production thrive and the products are distributed all over Vietnam. The city was spared the ravages of the American war, falling to the north Vietnamese without a fight in 1975.

Over 5,000 ethnic hill tribe people make up the 130,000 people living in Dalat. There are also numerous tribes around the province that still try to live by their traditions, although in today's society that is becoming increasingly difficult.

The food here as one would expect is dominated by the superior quality of the freshly picked fruit and vegetables like tomatoes, cucumbers, lettuce, peas, carrots, artichokes, beets, squashes and yams and fruits such as strawberries, blackberries, grapes, plums, mulberries, apples and peaches just to name a few of the wonderful abundance of produce that you can see and purchase at the central market and at the Thien Vuong pagoda.

For vegetarians there are a number of dishes like Canh rau, a mixed vegetable soup, or Cà-tim tuyêt ngon, an aubergine dish with green pepper and olives finished with rice crackers, followed by a dessert of mung bean cake. Look for the words Com Chay, which mean vegetarian food.

The best way to enjoy the food of Dalat is not in the hotels or the touristy restaurants but in the street market on D Nguyen Thi Minh Khai, which is a big open food market. All of your senses are aroused: you hear the clatter of woks, the cleavers chopping on wooden blocks, while the aroma of the spices and herbs cooking delights the nose and stimulates the palate, and the sight of the simmering clay pots on the hawker stalls and the grilling chicken on semi-permanent stalls all adds to the pleasure of sitting in the cool evening air and sampling the cuisine along with a cold drink.

Some of the more unusual types of dishes cooked in the market of Dalat are pork, chicken, catfish and eels, for example Cà khô dry (boiled catfish) is a simple dish, then there is Luö xào lãn (eels in spices) cooked in coconut milk, onions, peppers and herbs. You will also see many of the traditional dishes like spring roll, Pho, papaya salad and prawn on sugar cane (Chao tom).

On the way to Ho Chi Minh City (Saigon), are Pleiku and Kon Tum. Pleiku is where the American involvement started in the Vietnam War. Up until 1965, the Americans had military observers in Vietnam who were not involved in combat. Then the Viet Cong bombed the base at Pleiku killing eight of the American observers, which provoked President Johnson into involving more troops into the conflict.

The town of Kon Tum is home to a number of hill tribe people. The town is a nice colourful place and remains relatively unspoilt. The town was destroyed by heavy American bombing in 1972, but was thankfully rebuilt soon after. Just outside the town, within walking distance, are several little montagnard villages that you can walk through, but it is best not to be too intrusive and to behave with respect towards the people of the villages.

Ho Chi Minh City (Saigon)

This 300-year-old city has an official population approaching 5 million, although it is more likely to be approaching 7 million, and covers 2,029 square kilometres.

Saigon is actually a small district within the centre of Ho Chi Minh City, but most people in the south tend to use the name Saigon. It is best remembered that officially (especially in the north) it is better to use Ho Chi Minh City when having to deal with any officials.

Its history dates back to when Chinese merchants begin to settle there in 1778. The French invaded in 1859 and made it the capital until 1975 when the North Vietnamese unified the country.

I have seen many things as a seasoned traveller, but nothing prepared me for this city. It is a living being that never sleeps any time of the day or night, there is the constant hustle and bustle of daily life on every street and corner. One moment you can see a businessmen trying to strike a deal, then a poor cripple (broken back and no legs) pushing himself along on a wooden cart with a tin for donations.

The capital is the industrial heart of Vietnam providing 30 per cent of the country's industrial output and 25 per cent of its trade. The investment and increase in trade dramatically increases with more and more foreign investment heading for the capital as it opens up to world trade. Even the USA ended its embargo in 1994.

As you walk around the city, you can see the classical colourful buildings with music coming from the guesthouses, smell the aroma of street food barbequing and feel the buzz of café life emanating from the tables, while motorcycles fly around each street and corner. Then you turn into the next street and find high-rise apartment blocks, pot-holed roads, fermenting drains, old men leaning against the wall or asleep on their cyclos (three-wheeled pedal-powered rickshaws). Many of this older generation were stripped of their citizenship after the American war, and placed into re-education camps as capitalist sympathisers for many years. These men cannot go back to their former professions as writers, doctors, lawyers and teachers, nor can they afford a proper home or to start a business because they no longer hold an official residence permit and without one they are prohibited from officially even being in the city. Turn around the next corner and you are back to a beautifully decorated pagoda or temple with people praying, grass and trees and overcrowded shops, bars and street entertainers trying to earn money.

There are numerous ways to travel around the city – on foot, cyclos or motorbike taxi. I walked around the large part of the city from early morning to late afternoon taking in the sights, sounds and atmosphere it provides. Motorbikers would constantly pull up beside me. No sooner would I get rid of one, another would pull up, and ask 'Where are you from?' (in English). 'England', I would reply, then they would say

something like, 'Manchester United good team' or 'my uncle lives in London [Manchester or Liverpool]', and try to keep up as I walk. Then they would say, 'Where are you going?', I reply something like, 'Ben Thanh Market' and they say, 'Come on I take you there', like I was a long-lost friend. But I had heard some other travellers say they had a lot of hassle due to not agreeing a fee before they got on the bike and that most were not licensed by the government. But it's an easy way for the bikers to earn extra cash.

One of the most frightening things I tried while in the city was crossing the road. It is truly a terrifying experience. I was waiting for quite a while at the kerbside looking for a gap in the flow of traffic. I just could not work out the flow, as the signs indicated one way, yet the traffic was flowing in all directions. The traffic lights worked, but rarely did anyone take notice of them whatever the colour. They did take notice, however, when a police officer or someone dressed in a military uniform was on the corner of the road.

The next thing I witnessed was an old lady standing beside me (she must have been in her 70s) carrying two baskets on either end of a pole, and she just stepped out and kept walking through the traffic in a straight line. The traffic just curved around her missing by inches. I thought there must be some order within this chaos. I focused on the lamppost on the other side of the four-lane road and stepped out and just kept walking calmly at one speed until I reached the other side. The vehicles just passed within inches, and I truly thought I would be splattered like a fly on a windscreen and never make it across. I discovered the art very quickly: never run, hesitate or change speed and the vehicle drivers will compensate for you and try to avoid hitting you.

If you are fit enough, then walking around the city is a great way to experience the sights and food, just pack plenty of water and a camera. The people here are very accommodating and friendly, always willing to help if you are struggling with directions or need a little help.

Sitting in the Saigon Café just off the corner of D Pham Ngu Lao and D De Tham, you can see all the life, culture and diversity of Ho Chi Minh City pass by your table as you drink a glass of Saigon beer. What these people carry on their bikes is incredible, I even saw two guys on a 50cc motorbike carrying a 3 × 3 metres square pane of glass. People deliver all sorts of merchandise, even uncovered blocks of ice to shops in 80°C heat. The pace of life is not as hectic as you'd think from seeing the madness and speed of the traffic, but is still faster than anywhere else in Vietnam.

You could spend two weeks in Ho Chin Minh City and still miss something worth seeing or doing. One of the more interesting things in and around the centre are the The People's Committee Building (Hotel de Ville City Hall) with the statue of Ho Chi Minh. The building was built in 1901–08. It has a very elegant French style and design. Once a hotel, it is now the home of the People's Committee. It has a wonderful interior with chandeliers, but it is not open to the public. It is a popular landmark and a

large statue of Hoi Chi Minh is just outside the building. Then there is the imposing French-style GPO building. The Reunification Palace, once the site of the South Vietnamese government, was built in 1966 and called the Independent Palace. The palace looks very modern and is open to the public. There are many features including a helicopter still on the landing pad, tunnels and a war room used by the South Vietnamese.

The Xa Loi Pagoda was built in 1956 and was the site of numerous self-immolations in opposition to the Diem regime (South Vietnamese Government). The interior shows the life of Buddha in pictorial form.

During 1877 and 1883 the Nôtre Dame Cathedral was constructed in the heart of the city. It stands 40 metres high with iron spires. A statue of the Virgin Mary is sited in front of the main entrance, yet there are no stained glass windows. The original ones were the casualties of the Second World War. There are many museums – the War Remnants Museum, History Museum, Fine Arts museum, Ho Chi Minh Museum, Ho Chi Minh Military Museum. The list is endles.

The one place I could not find the time to visit was the famous Binh Soup Shop. This was the secret headquarters of the Viet Cong in Saigon. They planned all their attacks right under the noses of American troops, eating in the restaurant before and especially during the Tet offensive in 1968.

The southern part of Vietnam is much wealthier than the north, and this shows in the cooking. The south has sweeter and spicier dishes with, on the whole, more ingredients. Coconuts and sugar cane add to the sweetness and chillies add to the heat, with the fish sauce adding the Vietnamese flavour and nutrition.

In Ho Chi Minh City they have their own twist on the traditional northern dish Pho. The soup is called Mee quang and consists of lettuce leaves, strips of cucumber, bean sprouts, cooked rice noodles and herbs all placed into a bowl and then a highly flavoured hot stock is poured over the ingredients. The stock is made from pork, chicken, shrimp paste and fish sauce. The dish is then topped off with crushed roasted peanuts. There are a number of restaurants that offer a feast called Bo bay mon; translated it means seven beef dishes that are cooked in different ways, but the beef is always wafer thin and cooked by pouring boiling water or stock over it. The dishes may start with the heaviest first, like a sort of fondue, and finish with a soup.

While in the city I was recommended (by Kathy from Intrepid) to visit two restaurants, Lemongrass and Huong Lai. Lemongrass was wonderful with live traditional Vietnamese music and an excellent menu. Huong Lai was also good. The best way to experience the food of any country you visit is to eat where the locals eat. One of the best experiences I had was in the Ben Thanh market. Here they have a little food section in the shape of a square. Some very nice ladies took the time to try to show me what went into the dishes I pointed at. The market is very crowded and hot. I became a sort of attraction especially when I asked them to stand

together for a quick photo on the digital camera. When I showed them the photo, it became a real show, with screams of laughter and girls giggling. The food here was excellent, the stalls were clean and well kept and the food was very fresh. I visited on several occasions and it was always great eating with the locals.

As the night draws in the atmosphere becomes a little more excited when the streets become more lively with food stalls and restaurants selling the world's best crispy spring rolls, roasted rice crackers coated in sesame seeds, satays flavoured with lemongrass and peanut sauce, fish cakes of various descriptions and pork with noodles flavoured with fish and soy sauce. The enormously popular Cha ca or fish cakes, BBQ chicken or egg dishes are always just a few metres away in any direction. There are many vegetarian restaurants and it is not hard to find one around the city, especially in the Pham Ngu Lao area. Much of the vegetarian influence comes from the Buddhist religion. Many Buddhists are strict vegetarians and during the first and fifteenth days of a lunar month food stalls and market stalls all serve vegetarian food or the same dish but without meat. For four days of the month Buddhists are required not to eat any animal products, and even the famous fish sauce is prohibited.

It is not surprising then that the Vietnamese have developed a vast range of foods and dishes to combat any hunger for meat dishes, by using substitutes like bean curd, fermented beans like (tempeh), coconut milk, and various mushrooms and nuts. There is always a profusion of fruit available.

The people of Ho Chi Minh City love their food and are proud of their cuisine but one of the more disturbing incidents I encountered was when I enquired what meat I was eating in a street café. It was just a little bit chewy and neither pork nor chicken. So, I asked the owner to write down what I was eating, and he wrote down the words 'thit cay'. When I next visited Paul (from Manchester) I asked him and the café owner what it was. Much to my horror, I discovered it was dog. Yes, Rover can end up on the menu!

I had a long and difficult discussion with the chef/owner over the eating of cat, dog, rat and snakes. The question I was asked was, 'Where do your rats back home live?' In the sewer systems and drains, I replied. And 'Where do your cats, dogs and snakes live?' In homes and kept as pets, went my reply!

I was astonished by the response that came back, 'Well, our cats, dogs, rats and snakes are in the fields, living off the corn, vegetables and wild life and not in the sewers feeding on rubbish, so to us they are considered as game.' Paul said that they do not think of them as pets but rather as we would consider pigeon, duck, deer, wild boar, venison and eels. Most of these delicacies are in the north or deep south, mainly in the countryside. Most Vietnamese do not like these meats.

Snake is now a rarity due to the laws protecting its sale. One of the countryside delicacies is a rodent that looks like a rat, called chuot dong,

but is not a rat and lives in the rice paddies. I am told that its meat is just like chicken, but I never had a chance to indulge in that particular delicacy.

The Vietnamese do eat frog's legs, snails and the occasional deep-fried cricket, although snails and crickets are not the norm in an average Vietnamese restaurant.

There are a number of markets located in Ho Chi Minh City, where you can observe daily life for the average Vietnamese. There is the Thai Binh market, Ben Thanh market close to the Rex Hotel which was built in 1914, and the Huynh Thuc Khang street market.

Around Ho Chi Minh City are a number of interesting sites including the Cu Chi tunnels in the district of the same name. The population numbers 200,000, but during the war, it had a population of only 80,000. This town was famous for its huge network of tunnels, built over 25 years from the late 1940s. The 250 kilometres of tunnels helped the Viet Cong control large parts of the countryside during the war. At its height the tunnel system stretched from the capital to the Cambodian border. The tunnels are only 30 kilometres from the city and are in parts 20 feet high, with living quarters, trap doors, kitchens, command centres and hospitals. The tunnels also served as weapons stores and factories. The Americans tried numerous different tactics to combat the tunnels' effectiveness, but failed to make any difference to them even when they repeatedly bombed, gassed and burned the whole area. It was only at the end of the war that an enormous carpet-bombing campaign destroyed the tunnels and killed many people.

The tunnels were repaired and are open to the public. Tunnels at Ben Duco and Ben Dinh are also open together with the Cu Chi war history museum.

Tay Ninh, capital of Tay Ninh Province, is home to the religious order Caodaism. The unusual holy structure called the 'Holy See' was constructed between 1933 and finished in 1955.

The temple at Cao Dai is very different and is a wild display of the Cao Dai pantheon, and features murals of Victor Hugo, Sun Yat and Nguyen Binh Khiem, the Vietnamese poet.

There are the usual mountains, pagodas, parks, waterfalls and mangrove swamps around the Ho Chi Minh area.

There are 14 islands off the coast 180 kilometres south of Vung Tau in the South China Sea, called the Con Dao Islands. The Malays called the islands Pulau Kundur, but they were also occupied by the Khmer, and the (British) East India Company who built a fortress on the Con Son Island around 1702. The British occupation ended when soldiers who were recruited from Indonesia massacred the English. It also earned a bad reputation in the hands of the French who used it as a prison. This reputation persisted when the South Vietnamese government used it for the same purpose. The island now houses the Revolutionary Museum, and produces teak, and fruits such as coconuts, mangoes and grapes.

Cà-Tim Tuyệt Ngon

Aubergine Supreme

Method

1. Remove the stalk from the aubergine, peel off the skin and cut into 2cm dice. Peel the celery and onion and cut into 2cm square dice. Deseed the pepper and cut into 2cm square dice.

2. Steam and cook the aubergine until tender. This should take 10 minutes.

3. Sauté the onion, pepper and celery in the butter until tender then add the aubergine. Cook for 2–3 minutes.

4. Add the hot chilli sauce and the Worcestershire sauce.

5. Next add the olives and the cheese, stirring for 1–2 minutes to avoid sticking.

6. Put all the ingredients in a baking dish, sprinkle the cracker crumbs on top, and bake for 20–30 minutes at 180°C (gas mark 6).

7. Serve when golden brown.

Measurements	Ingredients
4	Aubergine (medium)
2 sticks	Celery
70g	Onion
1	Red pepper
50g	Butter
5ml	Hot chilli sauce
10ml	Worcestershire sauce
200g	Olives
220g	Cheese (grated)
20g	Cracker crumbs

Chef's Notes

- This recipe is a complete throwback to the American war, with butter, cheese and Worcestershire sauce.

- The recipe comes from a vegetarian street café in Ho Chi Minh City.

Cà Khộ

Dry-boiled Catfish

Method

1. Wash and clean the fish, remove the head and fins, then cut into four pieces.

2. Put the sugar and water into a pan and heat. Stir until the sugar has dissolved and a syrupy texture achieved.

3. Cool the mixture slightly and brush over the fish

Measurements	Ingredients
800g	Catfish (on bone)
40g	Brown sugar
60ml	Water
4 cloves	Garlic
1lt	Light fish stock

continued over →

fillets until it has all gone. Then place into a suitable ovenproof dish.

4. Peel and slice the garlic cloves and deep-fry until golden brown. Drain onto kitchen paper.

5. Mix the stock with fish sauce, pepper and a little salt then pour over the fish.

6. Place the dish into the oven and cook uncovered for 30 minutes. Ensure you baste the fish occasionally. When cooked serve in oven dish.

7. Garnish with sliced cucumber and deep-fried garlic and serve with plain boiled rice.

...continued	
30ml	Fish sauce
30g	Black pepper (freshly ground)
60g	Cucumber (peeled and deseeded)
600g	Jasmine rice (cooked)
	Salt

Chef's Notes

- If catfish is not available, you can use carp or any firm white fish.

- This dish is cooked in the market at Dalat on the top of a stove. You could cook it in the oven at 180°C (gas mark 6) for 20 minutes with a little greaseproof paper on top.

Luö Xào Lãn

Eels in Spices

Measurements	Ingredients
1kg	Skinned eels
1 stalk	Lemongrass
100g	Shallots (peeled)
2	Red peppers
100g	Soya beans (cooked)
50ml	Vegetable oil
30g	Garlic purée
10g	Black pepper (freshly ground)
10g	Mild curry powder
400ml	Thin coconut milk
200ml	Thick coconut milk
20ml	Fish sauce
5g	Basil (chopped fresh)

Method

1. Remove the head and fins from the eels, then cut into 7–8cm lengths on the bone.

2. Top and tail the lemongrass, cut in half lengthways, then remove the stalk and finely chop. Slice the shallots, and deseed the peppers and cut into quarters and then slice.

3. Chop the soya beans and then fry in a little oil in a wok. Add the garlic, shallots, peppers, lemongrass, black pepper and curry powder. Stir and cook until the shallots have gone limp then add the thin coconut milk and reduce by one-third.

4. Add the thick coconut milk and bring back to the boil, then reduce to a simmer and skim any debris from the surface. Add the fish sauce.

5. Add the eel chunks and continue to simmer until a nice thick sauce is achieved.

6. Stir in the basil and serve immediately.

Chef's Notes

- This dish can be served off the bone, but leave the cooking of the boneless eels until as late as possible as they will only take 3–4 minutes.

- If you cannot obtain eel fillets or whole skinned eels, you may like to use trout.

- In Dalat this was served with a bowl of rice rather than noodles.

Mực Dôn That

Roasted Cuttlefish

Method

1. Remove the insides and clean the cuttlefish well. Mince up the pork together with the prawns and any pieces from the cuttlefish and season with a little pepper.

2. Fill the cavity of the cuttlefish with the filling and seal each end with cocktail sticks.

3. Whip up the egg white and dip each fish parcel in the egg and roll in the wheat flakes. Place in a preheated deep fat fryer and cook until golden brown (220°C, 453°F). Drain on to kitchen paper.

4. Blanch and refresh the tomatoes then peel, remove the seeds and roughly dice the flesh to produce approximately 100–150g.

5. Fry the onions and garlic in oil in suitable saucepan, then add the tomatoes and cook until completely broken up. Add the sugar, black pepper, salt and fish sauce.

6. Place the sauce on the plate with the deep-fried cuttlefish on top.

Measurements	Ingredients
500g	Cuttlefish
120g	Pork mince
180g	Prawns (shelled)
1	Egg white
100g	Wheat (flakes)
250ml	Tomatoes
50g	Onion
2 cloves	Garlic (chopped)
20ml	Vegetable oil
20g	Caster sugar
10g	Fresh black pepper
10ml	Fish sauce
	Salt
	Lettuce
	Oil for deep-frying

Chef's Notes

- You can serve rice or a salad with this dish, either is acceptable.

Gà Cari

Stewed Chicken Curry

Measurements	Ingredients
250g	Potato
100g	Carrot
100g	Onions
4	Spring onions
50g	Mouli
100g	Pigs' ear mushrooms
50ml	Oil
500g	Breast of chicken (diced)
50g	Long green beans
20g	Curry powder (mild)
200ml	Chicken stock
5g	Freshly ground black pepper
10–20g	Cornflour

Method

1. Peel and slice the potatoes, carrot, onions, spring onions and mouli. Wipe and clean the mushrooms and roughly chop them all.

2. Heat the oil in a suitable frying pan or wok. Add the chicken and seal over a high heat. When sealed add the potatoes, carrot, onion, mouli and beans. Cook for 3–4 minutes then stir in the curry powder.

3. Add the chicken stock, bring to the boil, then simmer for 10–12 minutes with a lid on. Add black pepper and a little salt.

4. Add the mushrooms and half the spring onions and cook for a further 8–10 minutes.

5. Mix a little water with the cornflour and pour into the curry, stirring continuously until the sauce coats the back of the spoon. Correct seasoning and serve. Garnish with the remaining spring onions.

Chef's Notes

- If you boil the stock too much and it reduces just add a little water.

- Serve with a bowl of rice and dipping sauce.

- This is a very mild curry and it shows the influences from India and the West in its ingredients.

Thịt Nứớng Mì Đậu Phọng

Fried Pork with Noodles and Peanuts

Method

1. Wash the spinach well then finely slice it. Place a pot of water on the stove to boil.

2. To prepare the garnish, cut the mouli and carrots into 5cm x 1cm strips. Remove the root from the bottom of the spring onion and cut in half.

3. Bring the sugar and the rice wine to the boil and simmer. Add the chillies, spring onions, mouli and carrots and allow to cool.

4. Pour the oil into a wok over a high heat and add the pork. Stir-fry for 2 minutes then add the spinach, and peanuts and cook for 2 minutes.

5. Place the cooked noodles into boiling water for 1—2 minutes and then drain and place on the serving plate. Then add the pork slices.

6. Serve the garnish including the syrup separately.

Measurements	Ingredients
140g	Spinach
30ml	Vegetable oil
500g	Sliced pork (3cm x 6cm)
100g	Roasted peanuts (crushed)
200g	Rice noodles (cooked)
Garnish	Ingredients
100g	Pickled mouli (Chinese white radish) and carrot
4	Spring onions
20g	White sugar
230ml	Rice wine
8	Bird's eye chillies (crushed)

Chef's Notes

- The garnish is served separately but is poured over the dinner once it has been served.

- This dish is very popular for breakfast in the Ben Thanh market in Ho Chi Minh City.

Thịt Nứớng Giá Mì

Pork, Bean Sprouts and Noodles

Method

1. Peel the carrots and cut into thin ribbons. Peel and very finely slice the garlic and deep-fry until golden brown. Cut the root off the spring onions, then cut into 3–4cm strips.

2. Pour the oil into a wok over a high heat and add the pork. Stir-fry for 2 minutes then add the noodles and toss and cook for a further 1–2 minutes.

3. Add the bean sprouts, carrots and spring onions, toss and stir, then add the fish sauce and black pepper. Cook for a further 2 minutes, then add the deep-fried garlic and stir in.

4. Serve with a sprinkling of sliced spring onions on top.

Chef's Notes

- This was one of the dishes I discovered while having lunch in the centre of Ho Chi Minh City.

Measurements	Ingredients
200g	Carrot
2 cloves	Garlic
30ml	Sunflower oil
400g	Sliced pork (3cm x 6cm)
300g	Yellow noodles (cooked)
30g	Bean sprouts
8	Spring onions
20ml	Fish sauce
	Fresh ground black pepper
Garnish	Ingredients
4	Spring onion (sliced)

Com Chiên Gá

Fried Rice with Chicken

Method

1. Remove the stalks then clean the mushrooms and slice them. Remove the stalks and deseed the peppers and then cut the peppers and onions into $2\frac{1}{2}$cm square dice.

2. Heat 50–60 ml butter in a suitable pan, then add the chicken and cook over a high heat for 4–5 minutes until the chicken is completely sealed.

3. Then add the onions and peppers, cook for a further 3–4 minutes.

4. Add the peas and the mushrooms and stir, cooking for 3–4 minutes until the chicken is completely cooked. Keep hot.

Measurements	Ingredients
200g	Chinese mushrooms (fresh)
2	Red peppers
175g	Onions (peeled)
170ml	Clarified butter
600g	Chicken (diced $2\frac{1}{2}$cm square)
120g	Peas (petite pois)
600g	Fragrant jasmine rice (cooked)
	Salt and pepper

5. Pour the remaining butter into a wok over a high heat. When the butter has reached a high temperature add the rice and stir and toss until the rice is hot.

6. Check the seasoning and serve immediately. Tip out a small bowl of rice in the centre of the plate then spoon the pork mixture on top and serve.

Chef's Notes

- Note that the rice must be well drained and as dry as possible to prevent the fat spitting.

THE MEKONG DELTA

The most southerly region in Vietnam is an area called the Mekong Delta. It has lush jungles, tall grass and mangrove swamps, creating a beautiful landscape. A visit to the delta provides a good opportunity to explore, observe and experience traditional rural life in Vietnam.

The delta has formed due to the silt deposits that have been carried down the huge Mekong River (4,500 kilometres) over the centuries and still continues to this day. Its delta is one of the biggest in the world. The river has two tides and at its lowest point in the dry season no boats can travel up or down the river. The river starts its journey on the Tibetan plateau, flowing through China, then in between Burma and Laos, along the Thai border with Laos, through Cambodia where at Phnom Penh it branches into the lower (Bassac) and upper (Tien Giang) rivers. It then carries on into Vietnam, branching into several tributaries leading into the gulf of the South China Sea, hence the name Mekong, meaning 'river of the nine dragons'.

The area is sometimes referred to as the breakfast basket of Vietnam, or as most people call it, the rice bowl. Most of the area is used to cultivate rice, which is enough to supply the whole country and still export large amounts. The Mekong actually accounts for over 40 per cent of the rice production. Vietnam is now the second largest producer of rice in the world after Thailand. As you travel through the myriad canals in the area you can see simple thatched-roof houses and rice fields still being worked by means of water buffalo, and teams of peasant women hard at work planting seeds by hand. Irrigation is still done by hand with bamboo woven baskets, moving water from the river or canal into the fields. Fish are then added to the paddies and are farmed along with the rice.

Fruit orchards do rather well here too, producing excellent results. Also grown are sugar cane and coconuts.

The many rivers and waterways are the arteries of life for the Mekong Delta and its people who live and work along the river. It stretches from the southern central highlands to the gulf and provides an incredible range of fresh fish and crustaceans such as abalone, shrimps and oysters all year round. But it does have natural dangers, especially in the Hau Giang River where there are estuarine crocodiles. They are becoming a little scarce in some southern parts of the Mekong Delta.

Living in this area is challenging due to the constant threats of flooding. The people of the delta have built traditional bamboo houses on stilts to try to avoid the floods. They have, over the centuries, built canals to travel along instead of roads as these tend to get washed away or turned into impassable muddy tracks during the rainy season and any flooding. There are a small number of roads up on high banks, but these are very expensive to build. In the Mekong Delta you can either travel by a cart pulled by cycle or motorbike, or by riverboat.

Once part of the Khmer Kingdom in the eighteenth century, the Mekong Delta became part of Vietnam. The Khmer Rouge decided in the 1970s to begin a campaign to take it back. This was done by killing and wiping out small villages. This action prompted the Vietnamese to quickly invade Cambodia in 1979 and remove the Khmer Rouge from power. The inhabitants along the delta are Vietnamese although there are pockets of ethnic Chinese and Champs.

The capital city of Tien Giang Province is Mytho and it has been a trading centre on the Mekong for centuries, but is now one of the poorest cities in Vietnam. It is renowned for its vermicelli soup dish Hu tieu my tho, which is more like a broth garnished with pork, chicken and seafood, either fresh or dry, with the broth served on the side. Vinh Long, the capital of the Vinh Long Province, is a smaller town and this is where many travellers on the Mekong tend to get boats to other destinations, such as islands, and organised trips to orchards and animal farms (snakes, etc). There are some nice riverside eateries. One journey worth taking is an early morning trip to the floating market, although it is not as good as in Thailand, but still worth a look. You need to travel by boat to Cai Be early to see the big boats come in and watch the smaller ones come alongside to sample the produce hanging over the sides. Then the negotiating starts.

Tra Vinh is bordered by the Mekong branches of Tie and the Hau. It has a population of over 70,000 and there are over 300,000 ethnic Khmers living in the province. There are numerous Khmer pagodas and monasteries throughout the province. The Khmers themselves are followers of the Theravada Buddhist movement.

Cantho is the capital of Cantho Province and the main area for transportation. It is also the cultural, economic and political centre in the Mekong Delta. The population is growing, as well as the area's importance.

Most of the economy is based on rice and Cantho's rice husking mill provides most of the local industry. One can see why, with the river and canal system connecting most of the other major areas to the city, it is the hub of the delta. The markets here (especially the central market) are colourful and very lively. The fruits are well worth seeing with most of the sellers arriving by boat to sell their produce. There are some excellent floating markets on the delta such as Cai Rang, Phung Hiep, and Phong Dien. It is best to get a boat and just slowly travel among the other craft early in the mornings to get a good look and enjoy the atmosphere.

Here along the waterfront you can sit in one of the many restaurants, bars and cafés and have a choice of any one of the local Mekong Delta delicacies, such as frog's legs with banana, frog's legs with lemongrass, carp cooked in coconut milk, or giant river prawns with chilli and coriander, and then wash it down with a little snake wine. You can get deep-fried snake but they are becoming endangered. Some parts of the delta are suffering from an increased rat population, which is destroying the rice paddies due to the lack of the rat's natural predator, the snake.

Further south is Camau, capital city of Camau Province. None of the land was cultivated until the seventeenth century. This was probably because the land is not that hospitable. The area is mainly swampy and full of rather large mosquitoes. It is an area for bird lovers and naturalists, which is why I gave the area a wide birth. The main speciality is the shrimps that they farm in ponds and the mangrove swamps.

Close to the Cambodian border lies the riverside commercial town of Chau Doc. One of the interesting features here are the floating water houses; they are built on old metal oil drums. The occupants also farm fish under their boats in nets made from metal. The fish are allowed to breed, swim and eat relatively naturally, the occupants of the house feed them on whatever they have left over. Most of these floating houseboats are where the Bassac River meets the Mekong. The farming produces 15,000 tonnes of fish, which are exported. The farming production represents 15 per cent of Vietnam's total seafood output.

Right on the Cambodian–Vietnamese border is the little town of Ba Chuc. This town is the site of one of the most terrible atrocities in Vietnam's history. It happened between 12–30 April 1978, when the Khmer Rouge crossed the border and began their slaughter of the entire town, some 3,157 people. It is believed that only two people survived the massacre. The pagoda called The Skull Pagoda is home to the skulls of the victims. Close by is a temple that has a photographic collection of the atrocities that occurred.

On the Gulf of Thailand lies Ha Tien, which is a little different from the other parts of the Mekong Delta due to the formations of limestone and splendid caves. The area is better known for its black pepper and seafood. The area also produces items made from turtle shells. The surrounding area has numerous pagodas, tombs and temples. There are islands where the locals collect the swifts' nests crucial to making bird's nest soup.

Phu Quoc island is 45 kilometres west of Ha Tien and is in the shape of a tear drop. The island is claimed by Cambodia but the Vietnamese also lay claim to it and have a large military presence at the north tip of the island. The island is reputed to have some of the best beaches anywhere in Vietnam. The island produces pepper crops rather than rice, and also some of the best Nuoc mam (fish sauce), which is exported around the world. Most of the islanders make a living from the sea. The island has a prison that is still used. The French set up the prison, then the Americans housed Viet Cong prisoners there during the war. It was nicknamed Coconut Prison.

Cá Trê Khóm

Catfish and Pineapples

Measurements	Ingredients
10g	Tamarind paste
30ml	Water
1	Lime
400g	Catfish fillets
1	Baby pineapple
40ml	Palm oil
200g	Bamboo shoots
200ml	Fish stock (light)
100g	Chicken stock (light)
40ml	Fish sauce
10g	Sugar
10g	Mint (chopped)

Method

1. Mix the tamarind paste with the water, then strain and discard the pulp, keeping the water. Zest the lime and extract the juice.

2. Cut the fish into 3cm square dice.

3. Peel the pineapple and cut into dice.

4. Heat a suitable wok and add the oil, fry off the bamboo shoots for 1 minute then add the pineapple and stir. Cook for 2–3 minutes. Tip off any excess oil and add the stocks and bring to a boil, then reduce to a simmer.

5. Add the fish sauce, tamarind water, sugar and diced fish and simmer for 4 minutes.

6. Add half the lime zest and half the juice together with half the mint. Continue to cook for 2 minutes.

7. To serve, ladle into a suitable bowl and garnish with the remaining lime zest and mint.

Chef's Notes

- This is a typical southern dish.

- Serve noodles or rice with this recipe.

- You can use carp, trout or any freshwater or saltwater white fish.

Cá Rút Xương Dút Lò

Roast Snake Head Fish

Method

1. Soak the mushrooms and vermicelli in warm water.

2. Remove the fins and gut the fish. From inside the cavity, snip the bone at the tail end and then the head end. Carefully prise out the back bone to form a boneless cavity inside the fish.

3. Mince the shallots, red pepper, garlic, sugar, spring onion and half the black pepper to a purée.

4. Rub this mixture over the inside and outside of the fish.

5. Cut the vermicelli into short strips and very finely cut the mushrooms into strips. Mix them with the egg yolk, black pepper, salt and the minced pork.

6. Fill the cavity with the pork stuffing and secure with a cocktail stick.

7. Oil a suitable roasting dish, lay the fish in the centre and pour some more oil over the top of the fish. Place in a pre-heated oven (190°C, 375°F, gas mark 5) for 10 minutes then baste and cook for a further 10 minutes, then remove.

8. Cut the lime in half lengthways and squeeze one half over the fish. Cut the other half into wedges as a garnish. Serve with a sprinkling of deep-fried shallots.

Measurements	Ingredients
20g	Chinese dried mushrooms
50g	Vermicelli (rice)
800g	Snake head fish
60g	Shallots (peeled)
1	Red pepper
20g	Garlic purée
5g	Brown sugar
20g	Spring onions (peeled)
5g	Ground fresh black pepper
1	Egg yolk
	Salt
200g	Minced pork
50ml	Oil
1	Lime
20g	Shallots (deep-fried and sliced)

Chef's Notes

- You could use a fish such as tailapia if you cannot obtain snake head fish.

- Serve with a salad or fried rice.

Cua Xào Chua Ngọt

Crabs in a Sour Sauce

Method

1. Peel and slice the onions. Slice the pickled onions in half. Remove the stalk and deseed the pepper and cut into quarters and then slice.

2. Place the bean powder into a suitable bowl with vinegar and half the black pepper, soy sauce and sugar.

3. Fry off the garlic, peppers and onions in hot oil in a suitable wok. Try not to brown.

4. Add the crab meat then tip off any excess fat and add the pickled onions and vinegar mixture. Cook for 2–3 minutes.

5. Check the seasoning and add all the coriander and toss in the wok.

6. Serve immediately with rice.

Measurements	Ingredients
70g	Onions
50g	Chinese pickled onions
1	Red pepper
20g	Yam bean powder
20ml	Rice wine vinegar
2.5g	Freshly ground black pepper
20ml	Rich soy sauce
20g	Brown sugar
20g	Garlic purée
30ml	Oil
600g	Crab meat
10g	Coriander (chopped)

Chef's Notes

- Freshwater crabs are highly prized in southern Vietnam for their sweet taste. You find them in lakes, rivers, streams and ponds.

- The original recipe I was given calls for the crabs to be cooked in the shell after a little bit of cleaning and preparation. They are cut into six and fried as in stage three above. I think this way is a little easier.

Chán Êch Chiê Ăn Vói Chuói

Frog's Legs and Banana

Measurements	Ingredients
1	Green pepper
2	Green chilli
20g	Garlic purée
20ml	Fish sauce (Nuoc mam)
5ml	Sesame oil
20ml	Rice wine
50ml	Vegetable oil
8 pairs	Frog's legs
4 small	Bananas
Batter	Ingredients
1	Egg white (beaten)
250ml	Ice cold water
2.5g	Baking powder
200g	Self-raising flour
	Salt and a little white pepper
	Oil for deep-frying

Method

1. Remove the stalk and deseed the green pepper and chilli then cut into fine strips.

2. Mix together the garlic, one of the chillies, fish sauce, sesame oil, rice wine and 20ml vegetable oil. Place the frog's legs into the marinade for 2–3 hours.

3. Pour the remaining vegetable oil into a wok and place over a high heat. Add the frog's legs and cook, stirring to prevent sticking and burning.

4. Add the pepper and remaining chilli, stir and cook until limp.

5. For the banana batter, mix the beaten egg white, water, baking powder, salt and flour until it is nice and smooth.

6. Peel the bananas and cut each one into four, then dip into the batter and place into a preheated deep-fryer. When golden brown remove onto kitchen paper.

7. Serve the frog's legs with the banana fritters.

Chef's Notes

- This is a simple recipe from a street café in the Vinh Long on the Mekong Delta.

- The art to the light batter is make the water ice cold and use it straight away.

- The recipe was exchanged for a biro pen with a well-known UK hotel logo on.

Thit Bó Xaó Núrong Sả

Beef and Lemongrass Kebabs

Method

1. Top and tail the lemongrass, cut in half lengthways, remove the stalk, and cut into dice. Roughly chop the shallots and galangal.

2. To make the marinade, place the lemongrass in a blender and blend for 2–3 minutes then add the fish sauce, shallots, shrimp paste, sugar, sesame seeds, black pepper and galangal and blend to a fine smooth paste.

3. Trim the beef and cut into 1cm x 6cm strips, then marinate the strips of beef in a bowl (2–3 hours minimum) or overnight in the fridge ensuring you clingfilm the bowl.

4. Thread the meat onto a skewer, rubbed with nut oil, until half the skewer is full.

5. Then grill over a charcoal heat turning every 2 minutes. You can alternatively use a salamander until a light golden brown.

6. Serve immediately.

Measurements	Ingredients
1 stalk	Lemongrass
3	Shallots (peeled)
2cm	Galangal (peeled)
20ml	Fish sauce
10g	Shrimp paste
10g	Dark brown sugar
10g	Sesame seeds
2.5g	Fresh ground black pepper
450g	Rump, sirloin or fillet of beef
40g	Nut oil
12	Skewers (wooden) soaked in cold water

Chef's Notes

- I have eaten this dish in both the north-west and central Vietnam. The recipe can be also be served with a dipping sauce and salad or even rice or eaten in a baguette.

- Alternatively you can remove the beef from the skewers and serve with a salad of yellow noodles, carrot strips, Choi sam lettuce or baby green spinach (including stems), spring onions, and black pepper (fresh ground).

- To prevent the wooden skewers from burning while cooking wrap the ends in tin foil.

OTHER VIETNAMESE RECIPES

Gá Khô

Chicken and Ginger in Caramel sauce

Method

Measurements	Ingredients
4cm	Ginger (peeled)
4	Spring onions
30ml	Vegetable oil
600g	Diced chicken (on the bone)
50ml	Water
20ml	Fish sauce
Caramel Sauce	**Ingredients**
150ml	Water
140g	Palm sugar
20g	Shallots (sliced)
30ml	Fish sauce

1. Grate the ginger, squeeze out the juice and keep to one side discarding the pulp. Slice spring onions into diamond shapes.

2. Seal the chicken in a suitable pan, then remove onto kitchen paper and wipe out the pan to remove any trace of oil. Place the pan back on to a high heat and add the water, fish sauce, ginger juice and the chicken. Cover with a lid and bring to the boil then reduce to a simmer. Skim any debris from the surface.

3. To make the caramel sauce, bring the water and palm sugar to the boil and simmer, add the shallots and continue to simmer until it turns to a dark caramel colour then vigorously whisk in the fish sauce to ensure there are no lumps.

4. Take 60ml caramel sauce, add to the chicken and stir. Cook for 20 minutes at a simmer.

5. The chicken should be nice and golden. Spoon onto serving plates and garnish with the remainder of the sauce and spring onions.

Chef's Notes

- This is a simple northern recipe, which is less complicated than some of the southern recipes I have come across.

- The ginger gives a wonderful tang to the taste, and the palm sugar sweetens that sharpness.

- You can either use it as a starter or a main course dish.

- The chicken is traditionally left on the bone as I have done, but you can use boneless chicken if you wish.

- The Vietnamese believe that both ginger and lemongrass help to cure a cold.

Cá Nửóng Vói Nửọc Sôt Gửng

Tailapia Grilled with Ginger

Method

1. From the sauce ingredients thinly slice the ginger then grate into fine strips Squeeze out the juice and keep to one side discarding the pulp. Mix the juice with the rice wine.

2. Soak the mushrooms in warm water then remove the stalk and finely slice.

3. Top and tail the lemongrass, cut in half lengthways, then remove the stalk and cut into dice. Cut the stem ginger into fine strips.

4. Purée the shallots then mix with the lime and sugar. Cut three incisions on each side of the fish and rub the shallot mixture into the fish. Marinate for 1–2 hours.

5. Wipe off the marinade with a cloth. Mix the vegetable oil with the sesame oil and then pour over each side of the fish. Place under a pre-heated grill and cook until golden brown, approximately 8–10 minutes.

6. Bring to the boil all the sauce ingredients except the cornflour. Mix the cornflour with a little water then add a small amount at a time, stirring rapidly until it thickens slightly. Add the ginger strips, dill and spring onions.

7. Place the fish onto a suitable serving dish and spoon over the ginger sauce.

Chef's Notes

- The Vietnamese serve whole fish at banquets and special occasions.

- The fish farmed in the house river boats are normally catfish, tailapia and carp. Any of these fish would suit this recipe.

Measurements	Ingredients
40g	Shallots (peeled)
20ml	Lime juice
20g	Sugar
600g	Tailapia (gutted and descaled)
20ml	Vegetable oil
10ml	Sesame oil
4cm	Ginger (peeled and cut into strips)
10g	Chopped dill
8	Spring onions (cut into strips)
Sauce	Ingredients
4cm	Ginger (grated)
50ml	Rice wine
4	Chinese mushrooms (dried)
1 stalk	Lemongrass
3cm	Stem ginger
50ml	Fish stock
20ml	Fish sauce
5g	Garlic purée
1	Red chilli (sliced)
10g	Cornflour

Sủỏng Kho

Pork Ribs in Caramel Sauce

Method

1. Chop the ribs into 4–5cm lengths.

2. Place the shallots into a blender with fish sauce, sugar, a pinch of black pepper and blend until a smooth purée has been achieved.

3. Place the pork ribs on a tray and cook under a preheated grill until golden, ensuring an even brown colour has been achieved.

4. Place the pork and the purée ingredients into a suitable pan, bring to the boil and the simmer for 10 minutes with a lid on.

5. To make the caramel sauce, bring the water and palm sugar to a boil and simmer. Add the shallots and continue to simmer until it turns to a dark caramel colour. Vigorously whisk in the fish sauce to ensure there are no lumps, then add the chilli.

6. Take 80ml caramel sauce and add to the ribs and stir. Simmer for 20 minutes.

7. The pork ribs should be nicely golden. Spoon onto serving plates and garnish with sauce, spring onions and coriander.

Measurements	Ingredients
1kg	Pork ribs (younger the pig the better)
100g	Banana shallots (peeled)
40ml	Fish sauce
10g	Palm sugar
2.5g	Ground black pepper
4	Spring onions (cut into diamonds)
10g	Coriander (chopped)
Caramel Sauce	Ingredients
150ml	Water
140g	Palm sugar
20g	Shallots (sliced)
30ml	Fish sauce
1	Red chilli (sliced)

Chef's Notes

- I came across this dish at a restaurant in Hanoi while I was waiting for the bus back to Ho Chi Minh City. I also had the same dish the night before, but with large prawns instead of pork. For a nice deviation, just add a little squeeze of lime when you add the fish sauce to the sugar syrup.

- The younger pig ribs are better and easier to chop into short lengths.

- The caramel sauce has a good flavour with the added hotness of the chilli.

Chả Cá Chiên

Fish Cakes

Method

1. Cook and mash the potatoes. Peel the outer leaves from the lemongrass and cut in half then finely dice. Blanch, refresh and deseed the tomatoes then cut into dice.

2. Remove the stalk of the red chilli and then deseed and finely cut into dice.

3. Steam the fish fillets and break up into flakes, removing any bones and skin.

4. Place the flesh into a bowl with the potato, beaten eggs, fish sauce, coconut milk, chilli, tomatoes, pepper, pinch of mint, coriander and lemongrass. Gently mix the ingredients until well incorporated. The mixture should be able to hold its shape when you squeeze it in your hand.

5. Dip your hand lightly in a little oil and take a small 50–60g dollop of the mixture and shape and roll it into a ball. Repeat this process until all the ingredients have been used.

6. Place the little balls into a preheated deep-fryer (230°C, 425°F). When golden brown remove onto kitchen paper to drain.

7. Serve with lettuce, spring onions and herbs.

Measurements	Ingredients
250g	Sweet potato
1 stalk	Lemongrass
2	Tomatoes
1	Red chilli
300g	Pomfret fillets (or cod)
2 medium	Eggs (beaten)
30ml	Fish sauce
20ml	Thick coconut milk
2.5g	Black pepper (ground)
2.5g	Mint (chopped)
5g	Coriander (chopped)
30ml	Vegetable oil
	Rice flour
Garnish	Ingredients
4	Lettuce leaves
4	Spring onions (trimmed)
8	Coriander and mint sprigs

Chef's Notes

- If you feel the mixture is too wet just add some rice flour until it holds its shape.

- The Vietnamese do this dish really well. You can flatten the balls with the palm of you hand and shape into cakes, if you choose.

- You can use the cakes as snacks, starter or main course items.

- If you cannot find pomfret you can use cod or any good meaty white fish.

- The Vietnamese also believe that eating a fish head will bring good luck. This is why they often present fish with their heads on.

Dipping Sauces and Condiments

Fish Sauce Dip

Nuoc Mam Cham

Method

1. Place all the ingredients into a saucepan and bring to the boil, then allow to cool and serve.

Measurements	Ingredients
50ml	Coconut milk (thick or thin)
40ml	Fish sauce
10ml	Rice wine vinegar
10g	Sugar
10g	Garlic purée
5ml	Lemon juice
1	Red chilli (chopped finely)

Soy Sauce Dip

Nuoc Tuong Ot

Method

1. Place all the ingredients into a bowl. Mix well and let stand to infuse for 15 minutes, then serve.

Measurements	Ingredients
60ml	Soy sauce
20g	Roasted peanuts (chopped)
10g	Shallots (sliced)
10g	Garlic purée
5g	Brown sugar
1	Red chilli (chopped finely)
10ml	Lime juice

Tamarind Dipping Sauce

Nuoc Cham Me

Method

1. Work the tamarind paste into the warm water. Strain off the water and place to one side then discard the pulp.

2. Place all the ingredients into a bowl. Mix well and let stand to infuse for 15 minutes, then serve.

Measurements	Ingredients
60g	Tamarind paste
20ml	Fish sauce
5g	Palm sugar
1	Red chilli (chopped finely)
50ml	Warm water

Hay Vịt Tiềm

Duck Nut Soup

Method

1. Remove any fat from the duck and fry in a wok over a high heat with the nut oil until golden brown. When cooked remove and drain onto kitchen paper.

2. Chop the nuts. Bring the stock to the boil and skim any debris from the surface. Reduce to a simmer then add the nuts and duck and cook for 1 hour.

3. Wash and clean the fruit, then add to the soup and allow 4–5 minutes for the fruit to heat through. Check seasoning and serve immediately.

Measurements	Ingredients
750g	Diced duck
30ml	Nut oil
450g	Mixed nuts (peanuts, almonds and pecans)
300g	Chicken stock
60g	Logan berries
40g	Lychees (pitted)
	Salt and black pepper

Chef's Notes

- You can replace the duck (vịt) with chicken (gà) if you're looking for an alternative.

- To intensify the flavour you can dry roast the nuts.

Sừờn Nứờng

Charcoal Grilled Pork

Method

1. Peel the shallots then purée them. Mix the shallots, garlic, fish sauce, oil and the sugar together until the sugar has dissolved.

Measurements	Ingredients
70g	Shallots
20g	Garlic purée

continued over →

2. Marinate the pork chops in this mixture in the fridge, covered with clingfilm for 90 minutes, then remove them and wipe dry.

3. Place them onto a preheated charcoal grill and cook for 10–12 minutes, turning regularly until golden brown and cooked through.

4. Serve with jasmine rice and cucumber slices.

Chef's Notes

- You can also serve a sweet and sour salad as a side garnish, or pickled vegetables.

- You will see many families cooking this dish in Ho Chi Minh City outside their shop or house in the street, with their charcoal burning away. As the family members come home they drive their motorbikes right into the front room of the house and chain them up!

- If you do not have a charcoal burner use a grill.

...continued	
40ml	Nuoc mam (fish sauce)
20ml	Oil
30g	Brown sugar
8	Pork chops (2 per person)
Garnish	Ingredients
400g	Jasmine rice (cooked)
40g	Cucumber (peeled and sliced)

Ga Ướp Quế Nướng

Chicken Scented with Cinnamon

Method

1. Peel and finely dice the shallots. Mix together the pepper, salt, cinnamon, garlic purée and sugar, and rub this mixture really well into the chicken, front and back, and allow to stand for 15 minutes.

2. Mix any left-over spice with the oil and place the chicken in the oil. Cover with clingfilm and marinate for 2 hours in the fridge.

3. Remove the chicken from the marinade and allow to drain for 10 minutes, allowing the excess oil to run off.

4. Place the chicken portions onto a preheated charcoal grill and cook for 20–25 minutes over a medium to low heat, turning regularly until golden brown and cooked through.

Measurements	Ingredients
50g	Shallots
2.5g	White pepper (ground)
5g	Salt
2.5g	Cinnamon
20g	Garlic purée
30g	Brown sugar
4 portions	Chicken (see Chef's Notes)
200ml	Oil

Chef's Notes

- For the chicken portions you can either have baby chickens and get the butcher to cut into spatchcock or use breast or leg left on the bone with two incisions cut across the portion to allow even cooking. Either of these options is normal for this recipe.

- This dish is normally served with sweet sticky rice in bowls.
- If you do not have a charcoal burner use a grill.

Bắp Cải Nhồi Thịt

Stuffed Steamed Cabbage

Method

1. Remove the root fibres on the spring onions then blanch and refresh the spring onion and cabbage leaves in cold running water.

2. Pat the cabbage dry and then season.

3. To make the stuffing, dice the shallots and mix with the garlic and pork and season with the salt and pepper.

4. To make the sauce, blanch and refresh the tomatoes, peel and remove seeds then cut into dice.

5. Heat the oil in the pan and add the tomatoes over a medium heat for 12 minutes. Season then add the boiling stock. Add the chilli sauce and simmer for 2–3 minutes then purée in a blender. Bring back to the boil and mix a little cold water with the cornflour and add a little at a time until the sauce is thick enough to coat the back of the spoon.

6. Divide the stuffing onto the cabbage leaves. Roll the cabbage over once to cover the stuffing then tuck in the ends and roll once more. Tie securely with a spring onion to prevent it from coming undone. Place into a steamer basket and steam for 25–30 minutes, then remove and keep hot.

7. Pour the sauce onto the serving dish and then add the cabbage parcel and serve immediately.

Measurements	Ingredients
16	Spring onions
12	Chinese cabbage leaves
	Salt and pepper
Stuffing	Ingredients
100g	Shallots (peeled)
10g	Garlic purée
400g	Minced pork (minced twice)
	Salt and black pepper
Sauce	Ingredients
4	Tomatoes
20ml	Oil
250ml	Vegetable stock
20ml	Chilli sauce (sweet)
	Salt and black pepper

Chef's Notes

- For a vegetarian option, replace the minced pork with bean curd or cooked mashed soya beans, weight for weight. This will be called Bắp cải nhồi dậ hủ.

- You can serve hot plain or coconut scented rice with this recipe.

- It is possible to use Chinese lettuce if you cannot obtain the Chinese cabbage.

Thịt Gà Xớ Voi Đậu, Nấm Và Bắp

Chicken with Mushrooms, Baby Snow Peas and Corn

Measurements	Ingredients
100g	Onions (peeled)
200g	Snow peas
100g	Spring onions
50ml	Vegetable oil
600g	Chicken (cut into strips 1.5cm x 4cm)
16	Baby corn
200g	Chinese mushrooms (fresh)
20ml	Rich soy sauce
2.5g	Black pepper
	Salt

Method

1. Slice the onions and top and tail the snow peas. Remove the stalk from the spring onions, then cut in half and split in halves again.

2. Pour the oil into a suitable wok over a medium to high heat, add the onions and sauté for 3–5 minutes.

3. When the onions are just beginning to go limp add the chicken and stir. When the chicken is almost cooked through add the other vegetables and stir well. Cook for no more than 5–6 minutes.

4. Pour in the soy sauce and season. Toss and stir for a minute then serve immediately.

Chef's Notes

- This recipe is from a stall in the main market in Hué. An old lady, who was dressed in her conical hat and traditional pyjamas, ran the stall. She must have been near her late 70s and would put many a qualified professional chef to shame the way she handled the wok and produced this dish with total ease.

- Serve with noodles or rice.

Rau Trộn Đủ Thừ

Mixed Vegetable Salad

Method

1. Peel and slice the cucumber and shallots. Wash and finely shred the cabbage.

2. To make the dressing, simply mix all the dressing ingredients together.

3. Place all the vegetables in a suitable bowl and pour on some dressing and season. Serve.

Chef's Notes

• Serve as an accompaniment to meat and fish dishes.

Measurements	Ingredients
1	Cucumber
4	Shallots
1 small	Chinese cabbage
Dressing	Ingredients
50ml	Rice wine vinegar
30ml	Sunflower oil
50ml	Rich soy sauce
20g	Brown sugar

Rau Trộn Ngọt Và Chua

Sweet and Sour Salad

Method

1. Clean the radish, carrots, shallots and beans and cut the celery into 5cm lengths and peel. Shred the lettuce.

2. Mix the dressing ingredients well until the sugar has completely dissolved. Marinate the radish, carrots, shallots, baby corn, celery and green beans in this mixture for $1\frac{1}{2}$–2 hours.

3. Place the lettuce, sliced cucumber and marinated vegetables into a bowl and mix together. Serve when required.

Chef's Notes

• Serve as an accompaniment to meat and fish dishes.

Measurements	Ingredients
50g	Radish (baby)
50g	Carrots (baby)
50g	Shallots (peeled)
50g	Green (long) beans
50g	Celery
50g	Baby corn
Garnish	
8 leaves	Lettuce leaves
60g	Cucumber (peeled and sliced)
Dressing	Ingredients
120ml	Water
120ml	Rice wine vinegar
50g	Caster sugar

Thịt Gỏi Tôm

Pork and Shrimp Salad

Method

1. Slice the pork into thin strips then place into a bowl of boiling stock. Cook for 3–4 minutes, then keep to one side. Remove the pork when you are ready to add it to the other ingredients.

2. Ensure that the shrimps have been shelled and remove the central vein.

3. Toss the pork, shrimps, fish sauce and salad together and divide into four equal portions. Sprinkle with herbs and serve.

Measurements	Ingredients
500g	Pork tenderloin
1lt	Chicken stock
250g medium	Shrimps
20ml	Nuoc mam (fish sauce)
100g	Sweet and sour salad
5g	Mint (chopped)
5g	Coriander (chopped)
	Salt and ground white pepper

Chef's Notes

- For sweet and sour recipe see page 278.

- It is much easier to place the meat in the freezer for 60 minutes, and then slice it. The meat will hold its shape much better.

Chào Báo Ngư

Abalone Soup

Method

1. Cut the abalone into thin slices and wash them well. Wash the rice and then drain it well.

2. Bring the chicken stock to the boil and reduce to a simmer then add the rice. Cook for 10–12 minutes.

3. Peel the shallots and slice thinly.

4. Season the pork mince then roll into tight little balls the size of one pence pieces, then add them to the stock along with the shallots. Cook for 10 minutes.

5. Add the abalone and fish sauce, cook for a further 3–4 minutes and skim any debris from the surface.

Measurements	Ingredients
230g	Abalone
50g	Rice
1.5lt	Chicken stock (light)
70g	Shallots
220g	Minced pork
30ml	Nuoc mam (fish sauce)
10g	Coriander (chopped)
2.5g	Fresh ground black pepper
	Salt

6. Check seasoning and add the coriander. Ladle into suitable bowls and serve immediately.

Chef's Notes

- I have been searching for a simple and easy to follow recipe for this sea creature for a number of years and this is it!

- I managed to persuade a chef from a restaurant in Hoi An who spoke good English to part with this recipe. I have had to adapt it slightly, but it is easy to follow and tasty.

Gà Nâ˙u Bia

Chicken Cooked in Beer

Method

Measurements	Ingredients
80g	Shallots (peeled)
30g	Garlic purée
700g	Chicken on the bone (cut into large dice)
40ml	Vegetable oil
500ml	Saigon beer
60g	Cocktail onions (peeled)
20g	Wheat flour
250ml	Chicken stock
4 small	Eggs
20g	Coriander (chopped)
	Black pepper and salt

1. Purée the shallots, then mix with the garlic purée, pepper and salt. Rub this into the chicken and marinate for 1 hour in the fridge covered with clingfilm.

2. Heat the oil over a medium heat then add the chicken, and fry to a golden brown colour.

3. Tip off any excess oil, then add the beer and cocktail onions. Continue to cook for 10 minutes with a tight-fitting lid.

4. Add the wheat flour to the chicken and stir in the chicken stock. Cook for a further 10 minutes.

5. When the chicken is cooked season the stock and break the eggs carefully into it. When the eggs are soft poached, transfer onto the serving plates with the chicken portions and keep hot. Reboil the stock and quickly reduce a little, then add the coriander and stir. Spoon the sauce over the chicken and the eggs.

6. Serve quickly and hot.

Chef's Notes

- This is normally served with a crusty French baguette, although you could serve a bowl of plain rice. The dish has its origins in the American war.

- This was one of the first dishes I saw when I visited the backpacking quarter of Saigon.

Gỏi Sứa Chay

Salad of Sea kale

Method

1. Wash and cut the sea kale into small bite-size segments. Drain the soya beans. Peel, deseed and slice the cucumber. Peel and slice the onion. Peel the carrot and pepper then cut into matchsticks.

2. Mix the carrot and cucumber with the sugar and allow to marinate for 10–15 minutes.

3. Place a damp cloth onto the yuba and allow the damp to soften it then cut it into thin strips.

4. Pour the sunflower oil into a hot wok over a medium heat. Add the yuba and garlic purée. Cook and toss lightly for 2–3 minutes then add the vegetables and sea kale. Stir and toss to prevent sticking. Cook for 3–4 minutes.

5. Add the soya beans, fish sauce, sesame oil, coriander and soy sauce. Cook and stir for 2 minutes then serve with a squeeze of lime juice.

Measurements	Ingredients
20g	Sea kale
100g	Soya beans (cooked)
$\frac{1}{2}$	Cucumber
60g	Onion
70g	Carrots
1	Red pepper
10g	Caster sugar
10g	Yuba (soya sheets)
20g	Sunflower oil
20g	Garlic purée
10g	Fish sauce
10g	Sesame oil
10g	Coriander (chopped)
20ml	Rich soy sauce
1	Lime (juice only)

Chef's Notes

• This salad can be served with most fish dishes, but goes really well with fish or shrimp cake.

Cơm Nếp Xôi

Sticky Rice

Method

1. Wash the rice 3 times under cold water. Place into a suitable pan and add salt to taste. Stir the salt in well.

2. Bring the water to the boil then add the rice. Bring back to the boil, keep at the boil for 3 minutes and then tip off any excess water (keep the water in the pan at the same level as the rice), then lower the heat and cook for 30 minutes with a tight-fitting lid. Serve immediately.

Measurements	Ingredients
300g	Glutinous (sticky) rice
1.25lt	Water
	Salt

Chef's Notes

- For coconut scented rice (Dùa nê´), add 200ml coconut milk and 20g white sugar at the beginning of the boiling process and continue as above.

- For fried sticky rice (Cợm nếp chiên), take 50g cooked sticky rice then roll into a ball and flatten with the palm of your hand into the shape of a cake and fry in hot oil until golden brown.

Chan Gà Hâp Ăn Vói Xóât Nẫm

Chicken Feet and Mushrooms

Method

1. Blanch and refresh the chicken feet, then remove the outer skin by using a pulling motion with a clean cloth. Brush the chicken feet in dark soy and allow to dry (better left overnight). Deep fry the feet until crispy golden brown.

2. Soak the mushrooms in warm water for 15 minutes then remove stalk and slice the flesh. Keep the water for stock.

3. Peel and slice the shallots. Mince the garlic and ginger and then sweat them off with the shallots in sunflower oil, on a medium to high heat.

4. Add the fish sauce, rice wine, remaining soy sauces, mushrooms, shallots, hoi sin and oyster sauce. Bring to the boil and add the mushroom water and the water. Add the chicken feet and then simmer for 15 minutes. Stir to prevent sticking.

5. Mix the cornflour with a little water and if required thicken the sauce with a little of the cornflour at a time until you have achieved the required consistency.

6. Serve with a garnish of chopped coriander.

Measurements	Ingredients
12	Chicken feet (cleaned and de-clawed)
40ml	Dark soy sauce
8	Dried Chinese mushrooms
50g	Shallots
20g cloves	Garlic (peeled)
3cm	Ginger (peeled)
30ml	Sunflower oil
10ml	Fish sauce
20ml	Rice wine
20ml	Sweet soy sauce
10ml	Rich soy sauce
5ml	Hoi sin sauce
5ml	Oyster sauce
100ml	Water
10g	Cornflour
10g	Coriander (chopped)
	Oil for deep-frying
	Salt and black pepper

Chef's Notes

- This dish was served to me in a side street café in Saigon and I was told politely that you have to use your fingers to hold the feet and suck the meat off.

- Chicken feet are very popular not only in Vietnam but anywhere there is a thriving Chinese community.

Nem Nu'ó'ng

Skewered Pork Balls

Method

1. Deseed the chillies and purée them. Ground the roasted peanuts. Purée the shallots.

2. Cut the pork fat and bacon into 5mm dice.

3. Mix all the ingredients except the oil together thoroughly and stand in the fridge for 1 hour covered with clingfilm.

4. Rub a little oil on your hand and take approximately 50g of the mixture and roll it tightly into a ball.

5. Lightly oil the skewer and place three balls onto it. Lightly brush with the remaining oil.

6. Place them onto a preheated charcoal grill and cook for 10–15 minutes over a medium to low heat, turning regularly until golden brown and cooked through.

7. Place garnish neatly onto the plate and serve.

Chef's Notes

• You can also serve a fish sauce dip or peanut dip with this dish.

Measurements	Ingredients
2	Red chillies
40g	Roasted peanuts
30g	Shallots (peeled)
50g	Pork back fat (diced)
150g	Streaky bacon (diced)
500g	Minced pork
40g	Brown sugar
20g	Garlic purée
20ml	Fish sauce
30ml	Vegetable oil
8–12	Bamboo or sugar cane skewers
	Salt and ground black pepper
Garnish	Ingredients
60g	Cucumbers (peeled, decored and sliced)

continued over →

- If you can obtain the sugar cane to make into skewers, it adds another dimension to the flavour. This recipe comes from Ho Chi Minh City.

...continued

4 sprigs	Mint
4 leaves	Lettuce
4 wedges	Lime

Mục Nú'ó'ng
Grilled Squid

Method

1. Clean the squid out under running water, rub with salt and rinse under the cold water again. Cut in half and then criss-cross the surface of the skin to make a chessboard pattern, then cut into 5cm dice.

2. Mix all the ingredients except the squid together in a bowl.

3. Place the squid into the marinade and leave covered in the fridge for 90 minutes.

4. Take out and pat dry and then place into the preheated deep-fryer (230°C, 425°F). When golden brown remove onto kitchen paper.

5. Place the garnish neatly onto the serving plate and then add the hot drained squid. Serve immediately.

Measurements	Ingredients
500g	Squid
20g	Garlic purée
40ml	Nut oil
10g	Lemongrass powder
10ml	Sweet dark soy sauce
10ml	Rich soy sauce
10ml	Lemon juice
10g	Palm sugar
5g	Chinese allspice
2.5g	Ground black pepper
2.5g	Mild curry powder (korma)

continued over →

Chef's Notes

- You may use this marinade for deep-fried flounder or deep-fried prawns. You can also serve a fish sauce or garlic type dip.
- You will see this type of dish in most southern and central parts of Vietnam.

...continued

Garnish	Ingredients
4 leaves	Lettuce
4	Spring onions
4 wedges	Lime
8 sprigs	Mint
4 sprigs	Coriander

Thịt Bò Măng Tre

Beef and Bamboo Shoots

Method

1. Dry roast the sesame seeds in a wok or suitable pan until golden brown.

2. Dip both sides of the beef in the sesame seeds and then put to one side. Trim the spring onions and cut in half.

3. Pour the oil into the wok and over a medium heat fry off the garlic, shallots, spring onions and the bamboo shoots for 2–3 minutes.

4. Add the beef and stir and cook for 2–3 minutes then add all the other ingredients (except the water and coriander) to the wok and cook for 2 more minutes.

5. Remove the ingredients with a slotted spoon and add the water and stir into the sauce until heated through, then pour over the beef. Serve immediately with coriander.

Measurements	Ingredients
50g	Sesame seeds
600g	Fillet or sirloin of beef (sliced 3cm × 6cm and 0.5cm thick)
8	Spring onions
40ml	Peanut oil
10g	Garlic purée
20g	Shallots (peeled)
220g	Bamboo shoots (sliced)
20ml	Fish sauce
20ml	Oyster sauce
20–30ml	Water
4 sprigs	Coriander
	Ground black pepper

Chef's Notes

- This is a simple but tasty meal that you can serve with a bowl of plain rice or noodles. I was served this dish in Nha Trang in the local bus station.

Bún Thịt Nướng

Rice Noodles and Grilled Skewered Pork

Method

1. Purée the shallots. Remove any outer leaves from the lemongrass and then cut in half lengthways and remove the root, then very finely dice the leaves.

2. Thoroughly mix all the ingredients together and marinate the pork covered in the fridge for at least 1 hour.

3. Lightly oil the skewer and place the diced meat onto your skewer. Then lightly brush with the remaining oil.

4. Place them onto a preheated charcoal grill and cook for 20–25 minutes over a medium to low heat, turning regularly until golden brown and cooked through.

5. Place the hot noodles in the centre of the plate and place the skewers on top sprinkled with deep-fried shallots. Add the rest of the garnish neatly to the plate and serve.

Chef's Notes

- This dish is often served with sautéed noodles. You can also serve a hot chilli sauce rather than the fish sauce dip if you wish.

Measurements	Ingredients
50g	Shallots
1 stalk	Lemongrass
30g	Garlic purée
20ml	Fish sauce
10ml	Whisky
20g	Brown sugar
	Fresh ground black pepper
600g	Pork tenderloin or loin (diced 2cm thick)
20ml	Vegetable oil
12	Wooden skewers
Garnish	Ingredients
300g	Rice noodles (cooked)
20g	Shallots (deep-fried)
100g	Mixed pickled vegetables
60ml	Fish sauce dip
60g	Cucumbers (peeled, deseeded and sliced)
4 sprigs	Mint
4	Lettuce leaves

Bánh Chuối

Mung Bean Cake

Method

1. Drain the mung beans then remove the skin (hull) and cook them in water for $2\frac{1}{2}$–3 hours. Drain and allow to air dry, then purée.

2. Bring the coconut milk and vanilla pod to a simmer then add the brown sugar and stir in

Measurements	Ingredients
275g	Mung beans (soaked overnight)
130ml	Coconut milk (thick or thin)

continued over →

until it has been absorbed.

3. Pour the coconut mixture, mung bean purée and cornflour into a blender and blend to make a smooth paste.

4. Pour this mixture into a greased ovenproof dish. Then place in a preheated oven at 180°C (350°F, gas mark 4) for approximately 1 hour, until golden brown.

5. When cooked dust with a little icing sugar.

...continued

$\frac{1}{2}$	Vanilla pod
210g	Brown sugar
130g	Cornflour
10g	Icing sugar

Chef's Notes

- Remember never to add salt either when soaking or cooking pulses. Only right at the end of cooking should you ever add salt. This is because they will remain hard no matter how long you try cooking them!

- You will need a dish 18cm × 6cm.

Bánh Chuô'i

Banana Cake

Method

1. Mix the coconut milk, cream and sugar together until the sugar has completely dissolved. Peel 3 bananas and slice lengthways, then peel and purée the other 3.

2. Very lightly toast the bread, then cut the corners off and dip the bread into the cream mixture.

3. Put a layer of the bread into a greased ovenproof dish. Spread some of the mashed banana on top of the toasted bread, then lay some sliced banana on top of the mash.

Measurements	Ingredients
50ml	Coconut milk (thick or thin)
170ml	Whipping cream
40g	White caster sugar
6 medium	Bananas (ripe)
10 medium slices	White bread

4. Repeat this process until you finish with a layer of bread, then slowly pour any leftover cream mixture over the top.

5. Place in a preheated oven at 180°C (350°F, gas mark 4) for approximately 1 hour until golden brown. Serve when slightly cooled.

Chef's Notes

- You will need a dish 18cm × 6cm.

- You can also add a layer of very thin pineapple, sliced and grilled with a little added sugar.

Chè Dậu Xanh

Sweet Mung Bean Soup

Method

1. Drain the mung beans then remove the hull and cook them in water for $2\frac{1}{2}$–3 hours. Drain and allow to air dry, then purée.

2. Place a damp cloth onto the yuba and allow the moisture to soften it, then cut into thin strips.

3. Soak the lotus seeds in water for at least 3 hours. Once soaked rub off the outer shell. Cook for 1 hour in 1lt water. Once cooked drain well and refresh under cold running water, then pick out the middle shoot and discard the rest.

4. Cut the prunes into quarters.

5. Cook the mung beans, prunes, vanilla pod and yuba strips in the coconut milk and 650ml water on a low heat for 40 minutes. Skim the debris from the surface.

6. Add the lotus seeds and sugar and cook out for a further 20 minutes. Then serve.

Measurements	Ingredients
300g	Mung beans (soaked overnight)
1,650ml	Water
10g	Yuba (soya sheets)
100g	Lotus seeds
8	Prunes (pitted)
$\frac{1}{2}$	Vanilla pod
500ml	Coconut milk (thick or thin)
30g	Caster sugar

Chef's Notes

- Serve either hot or cold.

Thịt Heo Kho Nướ́c

Clay Pot Pork

Method

1. Trim the spring onions and cut in half.

2. Mix the soy sauce with the fish sauce and the sugar until it has dissolved.

3. Pour the oil into clay pots (1 or 2 per person) then place the pork in and seal the pork.

4. After 2–3 minutes add all the liquid and vegetables to the pot, stir and place on a low heat with the lid on. Cook for 10 minutes

5. Serve in the clay pots, with the garnish separate.

Measurements	Ingredients
100g	Spring onions
40ml	Light soy sauce
20ml	Fish sauce
50g	Palm sugar
40ml	Vegetable oil
600g	Pork (sliced 3cm × 6cm)
100g	Mustard greens

continued over →

Chef's Notes

- This recipe is different to the Malaysian clay pot version. The biggest difference is that here the rice is served separately, whereas in the Malaysian recipe, the rice is cooked in the pot first, and the meat and vegetables are cooked on top of the rice.

- If you cannot obtain the mustard greens substitute with bok choi or choi sum.

- If you do not have a clay pot you could use a non-stick pan with a tight-fitting lid.

...continued

80ml	Chicken stock
4	Clay pots
Garnish	Ingredients
80g	Cucumber (peeled, deseeded and sliced)
2	Tomatoes (sliced)
500g	Jasmine rice (cooked)

Cambodia 5

Clockwise from above left: Cambodian curry, Pork and duck with roasted peanuts and noodle salad, Fried noodles with dried shrimp, Fried fish in a star fruit sauce.

CAMBODIA

Cambodia is one of Asia's poorest countries and is emerging from decades of war, and violence. Situated between Vietnam in the east, Thailand in the west and Laos in the north, it has a 435-kilometre coastline on the Gulf of Thailand in the south.

From 1975 to 1979 the Khmer revolutionaries led by Saloth Sar, later known as Pol Pot, took total control of Cambodia and plunged the country into a period of genocide. No one knows exactly how many people were murdered during this part of Cambodia's history, but official estimates are 2 million.

Cambodia's history dates back to the first century when it formed part of the Funan Kingdom and made its wealth from being positioned on the main trade routes from India to China until the sixth century.

Around the ninth century the rise of the great Khmer Kingdom encompassed much of Thailand, Vietnam, Laos and Cambodia. This mighty empire lasted six centuries leaving an incredible legacy of magnificent architectural monuments and sculpture, such as the Temples at Angkor.

The Angkorian period began with the rule of King Jayavarman II in 802, when he was crowned by the Brahmin priests and then declared himself 'god-king' (Khmer deva-raja).

Cambodia has two river systems and consists of two low-lying fertile plains surrounding the Mekong River valley and the great lake of Tonle Sap. Vast irrigation systems in the form of small canals were introduced to cultivate the land. They were also used to protect the empire from their enemies, by raising crocodiles in them. This irrigation brought a huge increase in rice production that then allowed an increase in population. At the empire's height around the twelfth century a population of 30 million was sustained and the capital Angkor supported over a million inhabitants.

Influences from the West came in the sixteenth century from the Portuguese and Spanish traders, followed by the Dutch and the French. In 1863 the French took control of Cambodia for 90 years. Independence was declared in 1953 and for 15 years King Norodom Sihanouk ruled and alienated all political parties with oppressive policies. In 1970 he was overthrown by a coup and fled to China.

General Lon Nol took control and became a more unpopular leader. His regime was more cruel and corrupt than those of the previous kings. The Americans propped up his unpopular rule. They also began to carpet bomb parts of Cambodia, killing thousands of people in their attacks on the Vietnamese communists and their supporters. This caused thousands to flee to the capital, Phnom Penh. Soon after the coup the Americans and the South Vietnamese invaded on the pretext of rooting out North

Vietnamese training camps, but this failed. Savage fighting took place and engulfed the country in a struggle between the Lon Nol regime and the Khmer Rouge.

Two weeks before the fall of Saigon, on 17 April 1975, the Khmer Rouge finally took control of the capital Phnom Penh and Pol Pot became leader and began the brutal restructuring of Cambodian society to a Maoist, peasant-dominated, agrarian cooperative society.

Most of Cambodia's educated people were taken to the country and either worked to death or tortured and executed. Reasons for this could be that they spoke a different language or had differing political views or even wore glasses.

All this ended when Vietnam invaded in 1978 and overthrew the Khmer Rouge. Pol Pot and his supporters fled to the northern border of Thailand and continued guerrilla warfare from there.

1993 saw the first free elections administered by the United Nations with the drawing up of a new constitution. The main threat of the Khmer Rouge ended with the death of its leader in April 1998.

Cambodia covers an area of 181,035 square kilometres and has a population in excess of 12 million. The capital Phnom Penh is in the centre of the country. Ninety per cent of the population are ethnic Khmers and the other 10 per cent is made up of ethnic Chinese and Vietnamese (Cham Muslims) and hill tribes.

The official language is Khmer, although French and English are also spoken, but not widely, and the currency is the Riel.

Cambodia's location means it is in the world's tropical zone and is always hot and warm. It has two seasons. The hot or dry season is between November and April and the wet season is May to December. The temperature is between 25°C and 31°C with an annual rainfall of 1,500–3,000m.

Over the centuries Cambodia has been affected by many influences, even as early as the ninth century when struggles with China, Vietnam, Thailand (Siam) and Laos all left impacts on the culture. The trade with India and Java made an impact not only in architecture and cuisine but also on the clothing, for example, the skirts worn by Khmers are a replication of the sari.

The Hindu and Buddhist religions and Pali Khmer script are all a legacy from those times.

The official state religion is Hinayana Buddhism. It was also the religion before 1975, but during the four-year regime of the Khmer Rouge almost all the monks were eliminated along with thousands of ancient wats and temples.

The finest Khmer examples from the Angkorian era are the temples at Angkor Wat and the structures at Angkor Thom. Some of the finest

sculptures can be found in the National Museum at Phnom Pehn. Traditional dance is at the root of Cambodian society intertwined with its very culture. According to legend, the goddess of Cambodia was a dancer. Its origins can be traced back to the Khmer Temples and city of Angkor a thousand years ago, when dancers were employed to act as a medium between the god king and the divine spirit. The dancers displayed traditional Khmer ideals such as feminine movement, grace and form in colourful costumes.

The temples are adorned with images of the dances. There are a number of different dance styles. The best known is the court or classical dance based on characters and stories from the Reamaker (similar to the Hindu Ramayana), then there is folk dancing, mask dancing and shadow puppetry.

One astonishing fact is that it takes at least ten long years of arduous training before you can become an accomplished dancer. Most young Cambodian girls dream of becoming a celestial dancer.

Cambodia's cuisine is different to that of its neighbours, but there are similarities to Thai and Vietnamese cuisine. The early influences of India and Java have seen the introduction of blending spices for curries, allowing the spices to infuse and release their flavour and aromas before any other flavours or spices are added. This style of cooking and blending of spices in Cambodia is called 'Kroeung'. The custom of eating everything with a spoon (except noodles where chopsticks are used) is inherited from India. The Chinese influence can also been witnessed today in the use of soy sauce, noodles and stir-frying in the cuisine. French influence is seen in the abundance of baguettes and pâtés that can be purchased at every market in Cambodia as well as street vendor stalls.

The country is just starting to develop its infrastructure and come to terms with its own period of peace, security and freedom.

During my time in Cambodia I made many new friends and three in particular: Arnfinn Oines, Shelia Connelly and Paul Hay. Arnfinn runs a guest house called Earthwalkers with other students and friends (see Useful Addresses, page 359) and took a lot of time out to help me research the cuisine. Shelia Connelly runs a new hotel school for the local population in Siem Reap, to study and train in a trade. Her fiancé Paul Hay (a Khmer resident) runs a biking tour company (see Useful Addresses).

I visited Cambodia in 2002 and found the people to be very friendly, kind and hard working. They were always ready to share the little they had with a guest and loved to talk about food. The level of poverty the people have to endure is mind blowing. On one occasion, I witnessed a man ploughing a field with his oxen close to the Thai border and asked my friend Paul Hay why the man was in the field, when it was clearly sign posted 'Danger Mines'. He replied, saying if he does not work the land he and his family would starve.

The disintegration of Cambodian society resulted in its cuisine being almost completely lost during the dark days of the Khmer Rouge.

The mass murders, refugee camps, displacement and migration of the Cambodian people around the world, and the passing of time, have left a huge hole in the cuisine of Cambodia. The loss of great cooks, recipes and the knowledge of recipes and dishes handed down from generation to generation and the infinite knowledge of the spices and pastes will be hard to replace.

There is a dividing line between the cuisine and food eaten in Cambodia, depending on whether the people are rich or poor, urban or rural. People in the cities can choose from well-stocked markets and stalls with endless choices, and restaurants on the whole able to offer luxury items and food. This is not the case in smaller towns around the provinces where residents, due to the lack of transportation and infrastructure, can only purchase and cook what is grown and sold in their local markets. They cannot pop down to the local supermarket for a chicken or salmon fillet. There is a great difference in the amount of protein in the dishes that I was served. On the whole peasant food contained approximately 100g per person and at times less.

Fish and rice are the two main ingredients in the cuisine. The fish comes from two inland areas, the Mekong and Tonle Sap Lake. Fish and other seafoods come from the ocean around the Cambodian coastline. With rice being the main staple diet in the country, whether in the shantytowns or the cities, around 60 per cent of the daily protein comes from fish, with the remainder from meat.

Although there are similarities to Cambodia's neighbours in the cuisine such as the use of coconut milk (especially in desserts), cane and palm sugar, plus numerous ingredients like lemongrass, galangal, coriander, garlic, etc., it does have subtle differences. For example, if there is a lack of fish and meat content, there is less use of chillies and the amount in each dish is drastically reduced compared to Thai cuisine. Water is used rather than stock and bouillons. Dishes are sweeter than those in Vietnam, and a little less sweet than in Thailand. There is a tendency to use more Monosodium Glutamate (MSG) than in Thailand – this enhances savoury flavours. There is also a use of sour tastes, for example in the use of fruit, similar to those found in Vietnam and Thailand. The Cambodians use their own style of fish sauce liberally in their dishes along with fish paste (prahok). The cuisine as a whole uses far fewer spices than their neighbours and you are nearly always asked in restaurants (especially in rural areas) if you like it spicy or not. This could be because spices and ingredients are very expensive and hard to obtain.

The Cambodians have also adopted a number of dishes from the Vietnamese, for example a soup they call Soup chnang day, spring rolls (Koung) and wrappers called Tay yor. The difficult thing to understand is that Cambodians often make no differentiation between fruit and vegetables, which results in fruit appearing in some savoury dishes.

In this chapter I have simply and briefly covered the cuisines of north, central and southern Cambodia.

NORTHERN CAMBODIA

Along the northern border with Thailand are the Dangkrek Mountains. Travelling down to the ancient city of Angkor and the provincial capital Siem Reap, you can see the old colonial town and the gateway to Angkor Wat. Angkor and its world famous temples, built between the sixth and eleventh centuries, are one of man's most magnificent architectural structures from where the kings ruled the mighty Khmer kingdom. The kingdom at its height stretched over a vast area from the southern tip of Vietnam to Yunnan in China to the Bay of Bengal. The temples at the moment are largely unspoilt by commercial tourism, but the effect when you see these incredible structures puts it in the super league of the Pyramids, Machu Pichu and the Taj Mahal.

The temples at Angkor are truly an incredible sight to behold, from the friezes of the celestial dancers along the great walls to the ornate decorations and sculptures adorning the five beehive-shaped towers that rise and dominate the skyline. You can see man's efforts to honour the gods at the temple Ta Prohm, and the giant fig tree reclaiming the temple back into the jungle.

Once the destination of travellers from the sixth century, Angkor acted as the capital of the Khmer Empire from the ninth century until 1431. It is now a favourite of archaeologists, with its mysteries and unsolved questions. Abandoned to the jungle in 1432 as the capital moved to Phnom Penh, it was rediscovered by King Ang Chan in 1550, while he was out hunting. So stunned was he by the beauty and magnificence of the buildings that he moved his entire court there, bringing life back to Angkor. Many missionaries from Spain and Portugal visited Angkor during this period, such as Diego do Couto.

The kingdom was attacked, and conquered by the Thais in 1594. Then Angkor once again disappeared.

Father Charles-Emile Bouillevaux (1823–1913) was the first tourist in Angkor. He published his book, *Travel in Indochina in 1848–56, The Annam and Cambodia*. It was Henri Mouhot who was credited in 1860 with the discovery of Angkor Wat, with his book, *Travels in Siam, Cambodia, Laos and Annam*.

Angkor is littered with temples, and wats, the more popular ones require the purchase of tickets and entrants are rigorously checked.

Many of the sights will have locals, especially children, selling anything from cold drinks and postcards to trinkets every few metres.

Siem Reap is five to six kilometres from Angkor and is a base from which to visit Angkor. The town was a collection of small villages that have settled around individual pagodas and has been receiving visitors for hundreds of years.

The streets are full of potholes like most of the towns in Cambodia and the economy is poor, but the people are gentle and gracious. The town has two markets, the new market (Psa-len), and the old market (Psa-ja), which is actually the newer market!

The place has a unique odour to it, and is claustrophobic with all the stalls and vendors jammed tight together with little room to move around the enclosed corrugated hall.

The produce is excellent with the mainly freshwater fish still moving on the tables. The sizes ranged from a few centimetres to over a metre in length.

Women and children run most of the stalls and do much of the cooking and work. Men tend either to work in construction or on motor vehicles, as guides or just sit around. It is not uncommon to see a 5–6-year-old child descaling, gutting and chopping the head off a catfish with a chopper bigger than the child's own head. The skill at such a young age is incredible.

The chickens were fresh and still had their innards in and necks attached, but at least the feathers were removed. An impromptu restaurant that looked like total chaos and a frenzy of activity occupied part of the market.

The new market is just off the Phnom Penh highway. Produce is sold either side of the road and outdoors. It was quite an education to wander along the stalls. They sold all manner of things from dried frogs, to fresh (live) chickens. At one point I witnessed a young girl and her mother crouched down on the floor with two plastic bags and a wok and burner. They would place their hands one at a time into one bag, take hold of an object and then pull something off it very quickly and place it into a separate bag that moved.

I asked my friend Arnfinn what was going on, and he told me that the women had caught crickets earlier that morning and were in the process of removing their wings, to prevent them from flying away when the girls tip the contents of the bag into the hot oil and wok. I suppose that is what you could term a Cambodian ready meal. If you walk around the edge of the rag market you can see the French influences, with hot and cold baguettes stuffed with fillings of pâté and meats. There were only a few little stalls and makeshift restaurants where you could take a break and eat, but they did look cleaner than the food stalls in the old market.

Between the hours of 12 o'clock until 2pm everything – construction, markets, shops, cafes – stops for a siesta.

For the Cambodian people, breakfast is the most important meal of the day, as their working day starts at sunrise, which is at 5 or 6 am. The meal can be a bowl of porridge with salty egg or dried fish. It can also be a bowl of chicken or pork noodles. Lunch or dinner could be soup, rice, vegetable dishes and either a fish or meat dish – a total of 5 or 6 dishes. The rural food eaten at supper or dinner time could be tongue, pig's ears and snout of pig, which would normally be deep-fried. In the villages of the north the hill tribes will eat wild birds and deer as well as frogs.

I was lucky enough to be invited to Paul and Shelia's house for a meal. All the food was placed at the same time on a mat on a table, in bowls. Some Cambodians still eat seated on the floor with the food in the centre placed on a mat. Everyone indulges themselves at the same time. Eating to the Khmers is culturally very important, and not just fuel for the body. Paul was very insistent that he had plenty of rice for us while we were eating and made sure our bowls were very full. He told me at the end of the meal that if you run out of rice before the other food on the table you may be rich but you are very mean.

As I walked along the road to Earthwalkers, the dusk drawing in towards the end of the day, I noticed that there were many little plastic makeshift paddling pools along the side of the road. These had aluminium poles on both sides and a neon light suspended over the top, connected to a car battery. Later that week I asked Arnfinn why his staff were so excited that morning and he explained that they had a swarm of crickets and his staff had caught bagfuls. These crickets can be up to 8 centimetres in length.

I asked him how they had managed to do this. He explained that the little pools and neon lights would attract the crickets, causing them to jump or fly towards the lights and fall into the water, then they are collected by his staff. They would also catch them with large nets as well. Crickets are a valuable source of protein as well as a hand snack for the locals.

As there are no refrigerators most of the meat is sold live or, if dead, it must have been killed within just a few hours of being sold.

This also creates transport problems for the locals; how do you transport a live 100-kilogram pig to market, when all you have is the family 50cc motorbike? The answer is to feed the pig magic mushrooms to help sedate it and strap it to the back of the bike, before the effects wear off.

Touring the restaurants and food stalls in Siem Reap with Paul was a great experience because I was able to talk to the chefs and cooks about the cuisine and dishes that they served. I was utterly amazed and delighted to get a chance to go into the kitchens of the Peak Poub Timei restaurant. It was like travelling back in time. It was brick built with wood fires, and double boiling pots in the centre of the kitchen containing stocks simmering away. The kitchen was divided into areas, as a modern kitchen would be, but everything was fuelled by wood. No extraction systems or instant gas-powered flames. Cooking on the embers in this Khmer kitchen, with basic kitchen implements made from wood and coconut shells, is a sight one rarely witnesses these days. The grilled chicken with garlic and lime had an excellent flavour as did the beef and noodles.

The Serei Sour Sdei restaurant on the main road as you enter Siem Reap from Angkor is more modern looking, but very simple. The family cook on two portable gas burners with the preparation table at the front of the restaurant. Plastic garden chairs and tables are the order of the day.

The house special is pork with oyster mushrooms with bean thread noodles, and the pork and green bean soup spiced with black pepper was also very good. You can inform the cook how much of each ingredient you want in the dish if you wish, or just sit and watch them hard at work preparing your meal.

Khmer Krom Num Pachok Chon

Snail and Noodle Soup

Method

1. Soak the noodles in water for 10 minutes, then blanch them in 3 litres boiling water and refresh them in cold water. Use as required.

2. Bring the hock to a boil in the water and the chicken stock and cook at a simmer for 1 hour then remove and allow to cool. Keep the liquid. Skim all the debris and fat from the surface and then add the garlic purée, galangal and pepper. Bring back to the boil and simmer

3. Wash and clean out the snails. Bring the snails to the boil for 5–6 minutes in some water and drain and rinse. Keep to one side.

4. Cut the lemongrass stalks in half, remove the roots and pound, then add the diced galangal, 2 chillies and black pepper to form a smooth paste. Separately mix thoroughly the Prahok, fish sauce sugar and rice.

5. Add the Prahok and lemongrass mixture and stir in well to the liquid. Bring back to a simmer and add the snails Cook for 40 minutes to allow the flavours to infuse.

6. Divide the noodles into four soup bowls and then divide the garnish between the bowls (except the lime). Break up the hock meat into the bowls then pour over the hot soup and serve immediately.

7. Garnish with lime wedges and the four remaining chillies.

Measurements	Ingredients
1.5kg	Rice noodles (vermicelli)
1.5lt plus extra for soaking and boiling	Water
400g	Pork hock
500ml	Strong chicken stock
30g	Garlic purée
3cm	Galangal (peeled and chopped)
5g	Black pepper
200g	Snails (meat only)
2 stalks	Lemongrass
6	Green chillies (deseeded)
30g	Prahok (fish paste)
20ml	Fish sauce
20g	Sugar
30g	Ground rice (roasted)
Garnish	Ingredients
70g	Shallots (peeled and chopped)
220g	Chinese spinach (chopped)
10g	Mint leaves (chopped)
1	Lime (cut into 8 wedges)

Chef's Notes

- This is a hearty Khmer soup that is tasty and filling.
- You must ensure that you clean the snails well to remove any grit or sand.

Kro Jeak Chrouk Paklau Conj Plaeh Dohng

Braised Pigs' Ears and Coconut

Method

1. Ensure that the pigs' ears have been cleaned of all hair (either singe over a flame or shave) and thoroughly washed.

2. Peel and thinly slice the garlic cloves.

3. Bring the pigs' ears to the boil in the stock and cook for 20–25 minutes at a simmer. Remove and drain them. Allow to cool, then slice them.

4. Pour the oil into a hot wok and add the ears and fry them until they begin to colour.

5. Add the garlic and stir well. Add the palm sugar, allspice and soy sauces cook for 2–3 minutes.

Measurements	Ingredients
4	Pigs' ears
3 cloves	Garlic
3lt	Chicken or pork stock
40ml	Corn or sunflower oil
20g	Palm sugar
2.5g	Allspice
20ml	Thick soy sauce
10ml	Rich soy sauce
400ml	Coconut milk
5ml	Fish sauce
	Salt and black pepper

6. Add the coconut milk and cook for 5 minutes then add the remaining ingredients and reduce to a thick caramelised liquid. Remember to stir continually to prevent sticking.

Chef's Notes

- This traditional dish is often served as a snack rather than a main meal. It is a little chewy and you could replace the ears with frog's legs or well-cooked belly pork if you find the idea of eating pigs' ears unpalatable.

- Serve with plain boiled or steamed rice.

Moen Neung Tirk Doung

Chicken with Coconut Juice

Method

1. Make two incisions with a sharp knife just deep enough to break the surface of the flesh in each of the legs to aid marination.

2. Peel and mince the shallots. Purée the galangal, then mix all the marinade ingredients with the chicken stock and cover the legs, and allow to marinate for 6 hours, turning regularly.

3. Pour the oil into a hot wok and add the legs and fry them until they begin to colour. Tip off any excess oil.

4. Pour the coconut milk onto the legs and cook over a low heat until the milk has reduced to a syrup and the chicken has thoroughly cooked. Remember to turn the chicken to give an even cooking.

5. Place the chicken onto lettuce leaves and serve with slices of cucumber and tomatoes. Serve with hot plain boiled or steamed rice.

Chef's Notes

- For grilled dishes most Khmers prefer to use the darker meat of the legs as the breast dries out quicker.

Measurements	Ingredients
4	Chicken legs (fresh)
150ml	Chicken stock
30ml	Coconut oil
400ml	Coconut milk
Marinade	Ingredients
50g	Shallots
2 slices	Galangal
20ml	Thick soy sauce
20ml	Rich soy sauce
20g	Palm sugar
20g	Garlic purée
2.5g	Salt
2.5g	Freshly ground black pepper
Garnish	Ingredients
1	Lettuce (washed)
4	Tomatoes (washed and sliced)
$\frac{1}{4}$	Cucumber (washed and sliced)
400g	Jasmine rice (cooked)

Bai Damnoep Thouren

Sticky Rice with Durian

Method

1. Bring the coconut milk and water to a simmer with the durian flesh and the sugar and salt for 10–15 minutes.

2. Wash the rice then soak for 30 minutes in fresh water. For 1 part rice add $1\frac{1}{3}$ parts water. Season and place in a thick-bottomed pot with a tight-fitting lid and cook over a low flame for 20–25 minutes. Do not lift the lid before the cooking time is up as precious steam will escape and the rice will not cook evenly.

Measurements	Ingredients
400ml	Coconut milk
100ml	Water
400g	Durian flesh (diced)
200g	Palm sugar
2.5g	Salt
400g	Glutinous rice

3. When the rice has cooked pour the coconut milk and durian over it and mix in well.

4. Serve in suitable bowls.

Chef's Notes

• This is a simple dessert and is very popular, especially in the north of the country.

• You may add a little more sugar if you wish, but the palm sugar is quite sweet. You can use brown sugar if you are unable to obtain palm sugar.

• You can also use tinned durian if fresh is unobtainable.

CENTRAL CAMBODIA

Central Cambodia is where the majority of the people live and farm. The central region is dominated by one of the world's largest freshwater lakes, the Tonle Sap Lake. The lake is the world's richest source of freshwater fish. It has been the lifeblood of the Cambodian people for over one thousand years and covers an area of approximately 3,120 square kilometres. From November to April the river flows down to the Mekong in the south. During the rainy season from June to October, the lake triples its size to approximately 10,000 square kilometres, and then the Tonle Sap River reverses its flow and travels northwards to the lake, bringing silt and fertilising the planes. The lake also stores floodwaters from the Mekong River, which helps prevent flooding valuable farmland through the country.

The geographical anomaly of the river reversing its flow is also responsible for the fertile land. The lake and its tributaries and canals have been the major transport system for centuries, and because the land is so fertile it has been a major producer of plants, rice and vegetables. The lake is one of the world's richest fishing areas, and is home to many kinds of fish. During the flooding period many people come from the provinces and help local fishermen who live in house boats to catch the fish. The fish are sold or made into smoked fish, dried fish or made into Prahok (fish paste). The output per square kilometre is 15 tonnes of fish. At the end of the rainy season the large numbers of fish travel back down the Mekong and get caught in nets along the way. The most popular way to cook fish in Cambodia is to grill it.

The Cambodian fish paste called Prahok is made by salting the fish and allowing it to dry for a few days. The fish is then washed and lightly pounded and the bones, skin and guts are removed. It is then re-pounded, salted and sealed in jars and allowed to gather flavour and strength for three to four months.

Obviously fish dishes heavily influence the area; for example, Sngor treys is a sour fish soup scented with lime, chillies, lemongrass and soldier fish. There is also Som lor num bagn chock, which is green soup with noodles, enriched with coconut, garlic, long beans, nuts and white fish, then there is a Khmer soup called Som lor kako that has catfish, bacon, baby sour aubergines and pumpkin.

As you travel through this central region towards Phnom Penh you will see houses, some on stilts surrounded by a patchwork of paddy fields as far as the eye can see. The only unsettling thing was the number of signs warning 'Danger Mines', but after a while you tend to not notice them, as there are so many.

Sngor Treys

Sour Fish Soup Scented with Limes

Measurements	Ingredients
1kg	Soldier or river fish
3	Limes (juice only)
4	Green chillies (deseeded and diced)
2 stalks	Lemongrass
4	Spring onions
10g	Asian basil (or Holy basil)
10g	Chinese watercress or spinach
75g	Jasmine rice
4 sprigs	Mint
1.25lt	Light fish stock or water
	Salt and fresh ground pepper

Method

1. Descale the fish, then gut and remove the fins, wash well. Cut the fish into 4 even portions. Add the lime juice and half of the diced chillies, salt and pepper, rub over the fish and leave for 10–15 minutes.

2. Remove the stalks from the lemongrass then cut in half and remove the stalk and cut the first two inches into fine dice.

3. Cut the root off the spring onions and chop. Wash and shred the basil and watercress leaves. Wash and drain the rice. Chop the mint.

4. Place the rice into a suitable pan and add the lemongrass and either the stock or water and bring to a gentle simmer.

5. Once the rice is simmering add the fish (and lime and chilli marinade) then season and cook for 10–12 minutes.

6. Place the remaining half of the diced chillies, the mint, spring onions, watercress and basil into four separate bowls and then divide the fish and rice into them with a little of the cooking liquid.

Chef's Notes

- A simple fish dish that could also be served with a little extra rice.

- You could use a small carp, catfish or as a last resort trout if you cannot get the soldier fish.

Som Lor Num Bagn Chock

Green Soup with Noodles

Measurements	Ingredients
1.5kg	Rice noodles
600g	Fish fillets (catfish or any fresh water white fish)
1.5lt	Coconut milk
80g	Prahok
30g	Palm sugar
5–10g	Salt
Garnish	Ingredients
100g	Kenya beans
300g	Cucumber
100g	Bean sprouts
10g	Mint leaves
Paste	Ingredients
5g	Turmeric (peeled)
70g	Red chillies (deseeded)
2 stalks	Lemongrass
2cm	Galangal (peeled)
10g	Garlic purée
20g	Roasted peanuts
2	Kaffir lime leaves (shredded)

Method

1. To make the paste slice and chop the turmeric, chillies, lemongrass and galangal. Place them in a pestle and mortar with the garlic, peanuts and the shredded lime leaves and pound into a paste.

2. Soak the noodles in water for 10 minutes, then blanch in boiling water and refresh in cold water. Use when required.

3. Steam and flake the fish fillets and allow to cool. Add the fish to the paste, then continue to pound coconut.

4. Bring 1 litre milk to the boil and add the Prahok and stir until it has completely broken up. Then add the palm sugar and salt. Stir until it has all dissolved then strain through a very fine sieve. Throw away the debris and bring the milk back to the boil.

5. Add the fish and turmeric paste to the sieved coconut milk and continue to simmer. Add the remaining coconut milk and cook for a further 15 minutes at a simmer, removing any debris from the surface.

6. Wash and cut the beans into fine strips and cut the cucumber into matchsticks. Wash the bean sprouts and drain.

7. To serve, place a little of each ingredient from the garnish into suitable bowls with some noodles, then ladle the soup on top of the garnish and noodles. Serve hot.

Chef's Notes

- Prahok (preserved fish purée) is often called 'Cambodian cheese'.

- Traditionally this dish would be placed in the centre of the mat and guests would place their own ingredients and noodles into their soup bowls as they desired. You can also serve extra garnish with the soup in little bowls or on a plate.

Som Lor Kako

Green Soup

Method

1. Slice and chop the turmeric, lemongrass and galangal. Place them into a pestle and mortar with the garlic, and pound into a paste.

2. Peel and cut the papaya, baby aubergine and pumpkin into strips, and cut the long beans into 4–5cm lengths.

3. Clean and cut the catfish fillets into four even portions and cut the bacon into lardons.

4. Take the paste and then add the palm sugar and salt (dissolved in fish sauce) and pound for a few minutes, then add the Prahok and pound a little further.

5. Pour the oil into a hot pot and roast off the pea aubergines, then add the paste and stir and cook until it becomes fragrant. Add the bacon and cook for 2–3 minutes until the fat begins to disperse. Add the rice and stir in.

6. Stir in the vegetable strips and then add the fish. Cook for 2–3 minutes then slowly incorporate the fish stock or water.

7. Add all other ingredients and cook for 2–3 minutes. Check seasoning and then serve hot.

Chef's Notes

- This is a hearty and popular staple Khmer meal, often eaten at family meal times.

Measurements	Ingredients
1	Green papaya
1	Baby aubergine
100g	Pumpkin (segment)
100g	Long beans
400g	Catfish fillets
250g	Bacon
10g	Palm sugar
2.5g	Salt
25ml	Fish sauce
5g	Prahok
20–30ml	Oil
16	Pea aubergines
50g	Rice (ground and roasted)
600ml	Light fish stock or water
10	Chilli leaves
Paste	Ingredients
5g	Turmeric (peeled)
1 stalk	Lemongrass
2cm	Galangal (peeled)
10g	Garlic puree

Chai Thang Hon

Fried Noodles with Dried Shrimp

Method

1. Reconstitute the squid and shrimps in water for 20 minutes. Wash and shred the mushrooms. Peel and purée the garlic.

2. Soak the noodles in water for 10 minutes, then blanch in boiling water and refresh in cold water. Use when required.

3. Pour 40ml oil into a hot wok and cook off the garlic, then add the fish sauce and sugar and stir until all the sugar is dissolved.

4. Add the pork, stir and seal the meat to ensure that it does not form into lumps, then add the squid, shrimp and mushrooms.

Measurements	Ingredients
50g	Dried squid
100g	Dried shrimps
100g	Pigs' ear mushrooms
2 cloves	Garlic
200g	Rice noodles (vermicelli)
60ml	Vegetable oil
60ml	Fish sauce
10g	Palm sugar
250g	Minced pork

5. Add the noodles and the remaining oil to the wok and fry until the noodles and pork are thoroughly cooked.

6. Serve immediately.

Chef's Notes

- This dish is of Chinese origin and is served in Cambodia at the New Year celebrations. It is made and presented to the ancestors and then eaten.

Saik Dtai Daehk Dey Nom Sah Laht

Pork, Duck with Roasted Peanuts and Noodle Salad

Method

1. Soak the noodles in water for 10 minutes, then blanch in boiling water and refresh in cold water. Use when required. Crush the roasted peanuts.

2. Mix the sugar and fish sauce together over a low heat until the sugar has dissolved.

3. Mix the alfalfa with the coriander.

4. Very thinly slice the pork and the duck and dice the tofu and cucumber.

Measurements	Ingredients
230g	Rice noodles
50g	Roasted peanuts
30g	White granulated sugar
100ml	Fish sauce
50g	Alfalfa
20g	Coriander (chopped)

continued over →

5. Place the noodles in the bowl together with the meat on top.

6. Add the alfalfa, cucumbers and tofu. Pour the fish sauce over the top and sprinkle with peanuts and serve in suitable bowls.

Chef's Notes

- This is a dish that I was served at a roadside food stall on the main highway out of Siem Reap towards the Tonle Sap Lake early one morning for breakfast.

...continued

50g	Pork loin (cooked)
50g	Duck breast (cooked)
50g	Pressed bean curd (tofu)
50g	Cucumber

SOUTHERN CAMBODIA

The southern area of Cambodia is dominated by the Mekong River Delta. The Mekong travels from the Tibetan mountains through Burma (Myanmar), Thailand and Laos and ends in Vietnam. It is 4,200 kilometres long, with 500 kilometres flowing throw Cambodia. Annually the Mekong brings valuable residues of silt and mud into the Tonle Sap Lake making the plains fertile. The river is also a means of transport and of electric power.

According to archaeologists this area around the Mekong Delta is thought to have been settled in over 6,000 years ago, but the tropical climate and conditions have erased the physical evidence of this. Archaeologists believe that there were two migrations: one from the Malay Peninsula and the Indonesian region; the other believed to be from the area that is now called Tibet and China. The first records of a kingdom in Cambodia are of the Hindu Kingdom of Funan in the third century. Its wealth and power grew with highly sophisticated irrigation systems that it built and it also managed to harness the mighty floodwaters of the Mekong. Its power spread along with its Indian culture of dance, literature and religions like Hinduism and Buddhism. This also brought about the system of the semi-divine ruler.

A Chinese ambassador in the third century described his visit to this area: 'There are walled villages, places and dwellings. The men go about naked and barefoot ... Taxes are paid in gold, silver and perfume. There are books and libraries and they can use the alphabet.' Then came the Chenla Kingdom, the Kambuja and the Khmer Empire. The capital city of Cambodia is Phnom Penh, which was the last place to fall to the Khmer Rouge. It has been the capital since the fifteenth century. It has a population of 1 million and is slowly increasing. It was built on the confluence of the Mekong, Tonle Sap and Bassac rivers. It was once considered the most beautiful of French-built cities in all of Indochina.

The city's name is connected to the legend of Wat Phnom. The Wat is on top of a tree-covered knoll and can be seen from all over the city, so is an excellent landmark. The hill was the original site for a pagoda, which was erected after a flood. A woman called Penh (thus Phnom Penh, i.e. the hill of Penh) found four statues of Buddha after the Mekong River receded and in 1373 the pagoda was built.

Ounalom Wat is the centre of the Buddhist religion in Cambodia. Before the city fell to the Khmer Rouge, the Wat was home to 500 monks. Today it has just over 50.

The central market is in art-deco style and is full of shops selling gold and silver jewellery, antiques and coins, etc. Other less luxurious items like clothes and perfumes are sold at the Russian market (O Russei Market). Like elsewhere in Asia the markets attract many customers with the diversity of food products on stalls in and around the market area. Their tin tables and plastic chairs are put out on display. The aroma of grilled spiced duck or chicken (Ang moan pralak kreoung) marinated in garlic, sugar, lemongrass and turmeric fills the air. Sounds of chopping and the sizzling of frying, people talking, and sipping their freshly made Sngar soup (beef bone soup) with the hustle and bustle of daily life is played out all in this one area. Every day people from outside the city, usually dressed in sarongs, bring the fruits of their labour to sell from their bicycles, on the streets or from the stalls.

You will see dried fish, squid, frog's legs and eels on one stall, dried meat and sausages on the next. Jars of pickled vegetables and fruits together with soy and fish sauces fill the shelves and the spaces on the next stall.

As you move through the market stalls, you see plastic bowls with water hoses pumping water into them. They are filled with live fish, prawns, crabs, lobsters and eels, splashing around under the nets that cover the bowls. There may be live chickens in cages and cuts of meat in baskets on the next stall.

Rickshaws, cyclos and motorbikes all are whizzing along, often with baskets full of fruit or textiles and live produce to sell and trade. As one market closes another opens. In late October or early November as the mighty Mekong River changes its direction and flow, the festival Bon Om Touk or Sampeas Prea Khe in Khmer takes place. It also goes by the simpler name of the Water Festival. Canoe races are held on the river.

You are never too far from somewhere to eat in Phnom Penh. Whether you are in the street, park or market, there is always someone willing to help you indulge, from a glass-fronted cart selling a baguette with your choice of filling or a food vendor standing behind his makeshift table and wok happily creating dishes such as Chhar khngey, stir-fried fish with garlic, cloves and ginger. As you walk around the parkland or in the street you will see families happily eating and drinking together.

You will find many people will travel as early as 6am to the markets to get the best and freshest meat, fish, shellfish, vegetables, fruit and spices.

Shelia Connelly told me that if you go a number of times to one vendor and make friends you will be rewarded a hundred times, as they will keep the best for you and they will tell you what is good and what is not so good. They will also ask you what you intend to cook and advise you on how to get the best out of the ingredients. In my case, once that they knew I was a chef, they suggested numerous recipes and ideas on what to cook. What more can you ask – just like our supermarket staff!

Fifteen kilometres southwest of Phnom Penh is Choeung Ek and the 'killing fields' where between 1975 and 1978, 17,000 men, women and children were executed in the Khmer Rouge extermination camps. At the memorial Stupa erected in 1988 there are over 8,000 skulls lying behind clear glass.

Kampot is just 5 kilometres from the sea. It has a population of just 14,000 and is situated on the Tuk Chhou River. It is a very pretty town and has kept much of its original charm. North towards the hills is the To Chu Waterfalls. The seaside fishing village of Kep with its palm trees and wonderful villas was the place to visit for the rich Cambodians and French society. After the Khmer Rouge took control, they completely wiped the village off the map and even turned the petrol station's underground tank into a mass grave. It is understood that there are plans to rebuild Kep and restore it to its former glory.

Cambodia's only maritime port is Sihanoukville, or better known as Kompong Som. It has a population of 15,000 and has some of the best beaches, diving and fishing around the town. The locals boast that the best seafood is sold in the town's beach restaurant.

Shopping around Asian markets can be stimulating, challenging and mystifying and sometimes you need a strong stomach, but if you love food it can be an extraordinary experience and highly rewarding. It challenges your senses, with stinky fruit (fermented durian), tempeh, fried crickets, fish scaled alive, chickens and ducks sold alive. Walking around the fish markets without air conditioning is an altogether different experience around late breakfast time.

Trey Chamhuy

Steamed Fish with Sweet Sauce

Method

1. Wash and gut the fish, remove the scales.

2. Slice the lemongrass into thin slices and then place with the strips of galangal into the fish's belly with 4 sprigs of coriander. Take four very thin slices from the galangal, place to one side, and finely dice the rest.

3. Mince the cloves of fresh garlic. Chop the peanuts really well and keep to one side.

4. To make the sauce place the sugar, lime juice, vinegar and fish sauce in the pan with the water and warm up slowly until all the sugar has dissolved.

5. Then add the garlic and cook on a low heat for 2 minutes. Add the peanuts, stir well and cook for 1–2 more minutes on a high heat, then remove.

6. Wash all the garnish. Peel the onions and cucumber, then slice.

7. Brush the fish with the sauce.

Measurements	Ingredients
1.5kg	White round fish (see Chef's Notes)
3cm	Galangal (peeled)
2 stalks	Lemongrass
4 sprigs	Coriander
Sauce	Ingredients
3 cloves	Garlic
100g	Roasted peanuts
40g	Palm sugar
20ml	Lime juice
10ml	Vinegar
50ml	Fish sauce
100ml	Water
Garnish	Ingredients
200g	Mixed lettuce leaves
300g	Cucumber

continued over →

8. Place the fish on a greased sheet of tin foil and put into a steamer. Cook for 25–40 minutes depending on the size of the fish.

9. Place the fish on a suitable serving platter and pour the sauce over. Serve with garnish and hot cooked rice.

...continued

100g	Spring onions
100g	Bean sprout
4 sprigs	Coriander
400g	Rice (cooked)

Chef's Notes

- As a general rule of thumb when grilling or steaming fish remember that for every 2.5cm of thickness it takes 10 minutes to cook.

- The traditional way to steam the fish is to leave the scales on, but this would not be really acceptable in the West.

- Any round white fish is acceptable such as catfish, snake fish, carp or even bream.

Trey Chhar Khngey

Fish with Fried Ginger

Measurements	Ingredients
400g	Catfish or trout fillets
250g	Ginger (peeled)
50ml	Vegetable oil
50ml	Sunflower oil
10g	Garlic purée
20g	Palm sugar
2.5g	Salt
4 sprigs	Sweet basil
400g	Rice (cooked)

Method

1. Ensure the fillets are clean and have no bones in. Cut into 6cm lengths.

2. Cut the ginger into fine strips.

3. Pour the vegetable oil into a wok and cook the ginger over a medium heat for 5–6 minutes then remove with a slotted spoon onto kitchen paper. Discard the oil.

4. Pour the sunflower oil into a separate pan and add the garlic. Cook and stir for 2–3 minutes then add the fish and fry. Mix the sugar and salt together until it is broken up.

5. As the fish begins to change colour add the ginger, sugar and salt and stir-fry until the fish is cooked. Be careful not to break up the fish.

6. Place the fish onto a serving dish and garnish with the sweet basil and hot cooked rice.

Chef's Notes

• You could use any firm fleshed fish for this recipe, such as snapper, mackerel, etc.

• This dish can be served at lunch or dinnertime. The recipe can also be used with chicken, pork or duck.

• This recipe is as simple as it gets, quick and easy.

Ang Saht Dtia Pralak Kreoung

Spicy Grilled Duck

Method

1. Remove the legs and separate the thigh from the drumstick through the joint. Chop the breast of duck from the carcass, but leave on the bone and cut in half.

2. Cut the lower third of the lemongrass and cut it in half, then remove the hard root and roughly dice. Place the lemongrass, spring onions, turmeric, garlic, and sugar into a pestle and mortar or a food processor and pound until smooth.

3. Add the soy sauces to the paste and then add the duck portions to the marinade. Leave covered in a fridge for 10–15 minutes.

Measurements	Ingredients
1.5kg	Duck
4 stalks	Lemongrass
4	Spring onions
5g	Turmeric powder
3 cloves	Garlic
10g	Brown sugar
10ml	Dark soy sauce
20ml	Rich soy sauce
400g	Rice (cooked)
	Salt

4. Gently remove the duck from the marinade, then place it onto the greased bars of the griddle and cook for approximately 10 minutes. Bring the remaining marinade to the boil in a saucepan and use it as a basting liquor for the duck.

5. Remember to turn the duck regularly to aid even cooking.

6. Served with hot cooked rice and vegetables.

Chef's Notes

• You can serve it with fried string beans, sliced corn, cucumbers, tomatoes and even bread.

• Chicken (Moan) is interchangeable with the duck if you prefer.

Khao Poun

Pork Ball Soup

Measurements	Ingredients
400g	Bean thread noodles
50g	Shallots (peeled)
30g	Spring onions
40g	Water chestnuts
2 cloves	Garlic (peeled)
100g	Diced ham (smoked)
300g	Minced pork
20ml	Rich soy sauce
10g	Cornflour
10ml	Fish sauce
1.25lt	Chicken or pork stock
	Ground black pepper

Method

1. Soak the noodles in water for 10 minutes then remove and cut into 15cm lengths. Then blanch in hot water for 1–2 minutes and refresh.

2. Slice the shallots and mince the spring onions. Very finely chop the water chestnuts. Slice the garlic and deep-fry until golden brown.

3. Place the ham, water chestnuts, pork, soy sauce, cornflour, fish sauce and spring onions in a suitable mixing bowl. Season with ground black pepper. Thoroughly mix all the ingredients together.

4. Roll the mixture into 50g balls and place on a tray until all the mixture has been used up.

5. Bring the stock to the boil and add the balls and shallots. Cook for 10–15 minutes at a simmer and skim any debris from the surface.

6. Place the noodles into the serving bowls and spoon the balls evenly on top. Then pour over the hot stock. Garnish the soup with the deep-fried garlic.

Chef's Notes

- This is a wonderfully easy soup to make and can be prepared well in advance. Try not to use too much fatty pork mince otherwise you will get grease floating on the surface.

- You should not need salt due to the stock, fish sauce and soy sauce.

- This dish was given to me when we stopped at the O Russei Market.

Sngar Soup

Beef Bone Soup

Method

1. Soak the noodles in water for 10 minutes then remove and keep to one side. Cut the shallots into quarters.

2. Trim off all the fatty bits from the bones, and cut them into 5–6cm lengths. Roast the galangal in the oven until it becomes fragrant, then break open and remove the pulp.

3. Peel the papaya and cut in half and remove all the seeds. Then cut into eight portions and clean.

4. Bring the water to the boil and add the beef bones and bring back to a simmer and cook for 1 hour.

5. Add the papaya, galangal, shallots, fish sauce and sugar to the water and continue to cook for a further 90 minutes. Skim off any debris from the surface. Season with pepper.

Measurements	Ingredients
100g	Vermicelli noodles
4	Shallots (peeled)
1kg	Beef rib bones
3cm	Galangal
1	Papaya
1.25lt	Water
40ml	Fish sauce
20g	Palm sugar
	Ground black pepper
Garnish	Ingredients
100g	Cucumber
100g	Spring onions
200g	Mixed lettuce leaves
1	Lime (cut into quarters)

6. For the garnish wash the ingredients and then peel and cut the cucumber and spring onions into slices and arrange neatly on the plates.

7. Check the seasoning and skim any debris from the surface.

8. Divide the noodles evenly into the soup bowls and then divide the bones, shallots and papaya into each and then pour over the soup. Serve immediately.

Chef's Notes

- This is a very popular soup throughout Cambodia, but I managed to get this version from a vendor at the Russian market (O Russei Market).

- There are versions with rice instead of noodles.

OTHER CAMBODIAN RECIPES

Sahj Jruk Jia Moouy Neung Khtuem So

Pork with Garlic and Lime

Method

1. Remove any fat from the pork then cut it into thin slices and grill until cooked.

2. Soak the rice, then drain. Bring 850ml of water and a dash of oil to the boil and then add the rice with a little salt. Cook, drain, and keep hot in serving dishes with slices of pork over the top of the rice.

3. Mix the sugar and the water together.

4. Place the oil into a hot wok and over a medium heat add the garlic leaves, mouli and cucumber. Stir and cook the vegetables for 3–4 minutes, then add the soy sauce.

5. Add the stock, water and sugar and a squeeze of lime juice and serve with the rice and pork immediately.

Measurements	Ingredients
500g	Pork loin
140g	Rice
850ml	Water
60ml	Sunflower oil
20g	Sugar
100g	Garlic leaves (chopped)
100g	Mouli (sliced and peeled)
100g	Cucumber (thick sliced)
60ml	Soy sauce (thin)
200ml	Chicken stock
1	Lime

Chef's Notes

- I have adapted this recipe from a dish that I was served at the Peak Poub Tmei Restaurant that served Khmer food in Siem Reap.

- If you cannot obtain the garlic leaves use Chinese celery leaves or onion leaves.

Sahj Koh Jia Moouy Neung Mi Soou

Beef with Bean Thread Noodles

Method

1. Cut the beef into thin strips (3cm x 7cm). Soak the noodles in water for 10 minutes then remove and blanch in boiling water for 1–2 minutes then refresh and keep to one side.

Measurements	Ingredients
600g	Sirloin beef
200g	Bean thread noodles
50ml	Oil

continued over →

2. To make the meatballs, place into a mixing bowl the ham, water chestnuts, pork, soy sauce, cornflour, fish sauce and spring onions. Season with ground black pepper. Thoroughly mix all the ingredients together and divide equally into 16 balls.

3. Slice the garlic and fry for 2–3 minutes until golden brown, add the shallots and the mouli and cook for a further minute. Check seasoning and remove any excess oil or debris from the surface.

4. Add the stock, shrimp paste, fish sauce and meatballs. Bring to the boil and simmer.

5. Place the noodles into four suitable bowls followed by the meatballs (4 in each). Spoon over the other ingredients and top with the grilled beef.

6. Serve immediately garnished with spring onions.

Chef's Notes

- This is a nice light meal and is best served piping hot.

- I have adapted this recipe from a dish that I was served early one morning at the Peak Poub Tmei Restaurant that serves Khmer food in Siem Reap.

...continued

6 cloves	Garlic
50g	Shallots (peeled)
100g	Mouli
1.5lt	Light chicken stock
20g	Shrimp paste (Prahok)
60ml	Fish sauce
16	Pork meatballs
4	Spring onions
	Ground black pepper
Meatballs	Ingredients
100g	Diced ham (smoked)
40g	Water chestnuts
300g	Minced pork
20ml	Rich soy sauce
10g	Cornflour
10ml	Fish sauce
30g	Spring onions (chopped)

Sach Chrouk Chea Moie Sandik Barange

Pork and Green Bean Soup

Method

1. Remove the top and bottom of the gourd, then cut in half lengthways and remove the centre from each half. Cut the gourd into small batons.

2. In a suitable pan add the oil and place over a medium heat. Add the pork and cook for 4–5 minutes.

3. Bring the liquid to the boil and add it to the pork, then add the gourd and cook for 3–4 minutes.

Measurements	Ingredients
2	Green gourd
20–30ml	Oil
500g	Minced pork
500ml	Light chicken stock *or* water
	Ground black pepper
	Salt

4. Check the seasoning and cook for a further 3–4 minutes. Skim any debris from the surface.

5. Serve hot.

Chef's Notes

- You can use most green gourds, but try to choose the ripe ones and not the very hard and very bitter types.

- This is a simple peasant dish and sometimes contains 50–100g rice, but this is how I was served it at the Seri Sour Sdei Restaurant, although it did contain MSG as opposed to salt.

Chai Sandeik Barange Chea Moie Matai, Teak Si Eauv

Fried Green Beans with Chillies and Soy

Method

1. Peel and slice the garlic and wash the green beans and cut them into 6cm lengths.

2. Pour the oil into a wok over a high heat and fry off the garlic. Tip off the excess oil.

3. Add the green beans and chillies and fry without any colour.

4. Add the water to the beans and cook for 2–3 minutes then add all the other ingredients and stir.

5. Cook for 2 further minutes and then serve.

Measurements	Ingredients
4 cloves	Garlic
400g	Chinese green beans (including leaves)
30ml	Oil
6–8	Bird's eye chillies
60ml	Water
20g	Caster sugar
50ml	Thick soy sauce
50ml	Thin soy sauce
	Fresh ground black pepper and salt

Chef's Notes

- If you do not like the heat of this dish then add the chillies halfway through stage 4 rather than at stage 3.

- This recipe did include MSG, which I have replaced with salt, and is a reproduction of a similar dish that I was served at the Seri Sour Sdei Restaurant.

- This dish is a good accompaniment to most fish and meat dishes.

Chha Sandek Kour

Fried String Beans

Method

1. Place the string beans in water for 30 minutes (to aid softening and cooking), then drain and cut into 6cm lengths.

2. Mix the fish sauce into the sugar and stir until it has dissolved.

3. Place the pork into a mixing bowl and add the garlic, salt and fish sauce mixture. Mix together really well.

Measurements	Ingredients
300g	Chinese string beans
10ml	Fish sauce
10g	Palm sugar
300g	Minced pork
10g	Garlic purée
60ml	Sunflower oil
	Salt and black pepper

4. Pour half the oil into a hot wok and fry off the garlic mixture until it becomes fragrant then add the pork and stir well to break up the mince so that it is thoroughly cooked.

5. In a separate pan add the remaining oil on a high heat. Add the well-drained string beans and fry for 2–3 minutes until cooked, season.

6. Remove onto kitchen paper.

7. Place the mince onto a suitable plate and put the beans on top. Serve immediately.

Chef's Notes

• This dish can be served for lunch or dinner, and string beans are a suitable vegetable for the frying process. You could replace the Chinese string beans with long beans or as a last resort fine Kenya beans.

• You can also serve this dish with plain boiled rice.

Chai Sach Chrouk hea Moie Piseith

Pork and Oyster Mushrooms

Measurements	Ingredients
150g	Marrows
8 cloves	Garlic
200g small	Oyster mushrooms
200g	Bean thread noodles
30ml	Sunflower oil
400g	Minced pork
60ml	Water
	Freshly ground black pepper

Method

1. Wash and remove the top and bottom of the marrow and cut in half. Remove the centre and cut into large slices. Peel and slice the garlic and clean the mushrooms.

2. Soak the noodles in water for 10 minutes, drain and blanch in hot water for 2–3 minutes, then refresh in cold water and drain.

3. Pour the oil into a suitable wok over a medium heat and fry off the garlic and then add the pork and cook for 2–3 minutes without colour.

4. Add the mushrooms and sliced marrows and stir. Cook for 2–3 minutes.

5. Add the noodles and water, stir and season with salt and pepper.

6. Serve immediately.

Chef's Notes

- This dish is an excellent lunchtime meal that I had on my way through southern Cambodia.

- You can replace the pork with minced chicken if you wish.

Trey Chien Plei Spu

Fried Fish in a Star Fruit Sauce

Method

1. Remove the scales, gills, eyes and gut the fish, then clean.

2. Remove the stalk and seeds from the peppers and the tomatoes then cut into 15mm dice. Peel and cut the onions into small dice. Peel and finely chop the garlic.

3. Wash the star fruit and then cut the tips off the fruit. Slice widthways and remove any seeds.

4. Pour 100ml fish stock into a bowl and add the fish paste, fish sauce, sugar, cornflour, soy sauce, oyster sauce, hoi sin sauce and black pepper. Mix together really well.

5. Pour the oil into a hot wok over a high heat. Fry the fish until golden brown and the skin is crispy on both sides. Remove and drain onto kitchen paper and keep hot.

6. Tip off the excess oil in the pan and fry the garlic until it becomes fragrant.

7. Add the peppers, onions, tomatoes and the star fruit and stir. Add the remaining stock and bring to the boil, then add the fish sauce mixture and gently stir until it thickens. Correct the seasoning and add the coriander. Stir.

8. Place the fish onto suitable serving dishes and ladle the sauce over each fish. Serve immediately with plain boiled or steamed rice.

Measurements	Ingredients
4 × 500g	Any small white round fish
3	Red peppers
3	Tomatoes
2	Onions
3 cloves	Garlic
3	Star fruit
230ml	Fish stock
40g	Fish paste (Pharok)
30ml	Fish sauce
30g	Palm sugar
20g	Cornflour
30ml	Dark soy sauce
30ml	Oyster sauce
10ml	Hoi sin sauce
220ml	Palm oil
50g	Coriander (chopped including stalks)
400g	Rice (cooked)
	Salt and fresh ground black pepper

Chef's Notes

- This is an excellent dish, which has the hallmarks of Chinese influence. This is from northern Cambodia and you can use any white fish. If you cannot find white fish use trout.

- The Cambodians, Thais and Chinese use juice of the star fruit to treat dehydration, hangovers, liver and gastro-intestinal tract problems, and also chicken-pox and eczema.

Sangkya Lpeou

Steamed Sweet Pumpkin

Method

1. Wash the whole pumpkin and dry.

2. Remove the top and keep to one side.

3. Remove the centre seeds and any debris.

4. Place the eggs into a suitable bowl and add the sugar, salt and coconut milk and whisk well until the sugar is fully dissolved.

5. Pour the mixture into the pumpkin and replace the lid.

Measurements	Ingredients
1 small (400–800g)	Pumpkin
400ml	Eggs (whole)
250g	Palm sugar
420ml	Coconut milk (thick or thin)
Pinch	Salt

6. Place the pumpkin into a steamer and cook for 15–20 minutes or cover with tin foil and place in a preheated oven and cook for 15–20 minutes on 180°C (gas mark 4).

7. Remove from the oven when the pumpkin is soft and allow to cool slightly, then cut into slices.

Chef's Notes

- You can serve this either hot or cold, but it is best warm.
- The smaller pumpkins like Jack-be-little or a small Patty pan are ideal.

Ang Moan Prolak

Salty Chicken

Method

1. Cut the chicken into 8 pieces and leave on the bone.

2. Place all other ingredients into a pestle and mortar or a food processor and blend to a fine paste.

3. Coat the chicken with this paste and leave for 30 minutes.

Measurements	Ingredients
1.5–2kg	Whole chicken
50g	Garlic purée (fresh)
50g	Sea salt
30g	Palm sugar
20ml	Fish sauce

4. Place the chicken onto a preheated griddle or under the grill and turn regularly to enhance even cooking and colour.

5. Serve immediately with salad or plain cooked rice.

Chef's Notes

- This dish is very simple and you can replace the chicken with pork but remove the fish sauce, otherwise it will be over-salty.

Trey Dot

Salt Grilled Fish

Method

1. Clean, descale and remove the fins from the fish and cut into 4 portions left on the bone.

2. Slice the garlic and chillies. Peel the mangoes and cut into fine strips. Dissolve the sugar in the fish sauce and mix the mango, garlic, chillies and fish sauce together.

3. Place the salt into a thick-bottomed pan and place the fish on top.

4. Cook over a medium heat until done, turning only once to avoid breaking the fish up.

5. Place the fish on a suitable serving dish, spoon over the garlic and mango dressing and serve.

Measurements	Ingredients
2.5–3kg	Catfish or snake fish
2 cloves	Garlic
2	Red chillies
2	Mangoes
20g	Sugar
60ml	Fish sauce
2.25kg	Rock salt
Pinch	Freshly ground black pepper

Chef's Notes

- Again this is another way to grill fish and occasionally chicken in the home or in restaurants in Cambodia.

- Do not cover or place a lid on top of the pot at any time you are heating or cooking with salt in this way as any moisture will not be able to escape.

Som Lor Curry

Cambodian Curry

Method

1. Cut the chicken into 8 pieces and leave on the bone.

2. Peel the potatoes and cut into small dice. Roast the shrimp paste in a little tinfoil in the oven until fragrant. Cut the lemongrass in half and remove the roots then cut the stalks into dice.

Measurements	Ingredients
1.5–2kg	Whole chicken
400g	Sweet potatoes
10g	Shrimp paste
2 stalks	Lemongrass

continued over →

3. Remove the vein from the lime leaves and shred. Cut the ginger and the galangal into small dice.

4. Place the garlic, sea salt, galangal, ginger, turmeric, lime leaves, 600g finely diced red onions, lemongrass, shrimp paste and curry powder into a pestle and mortar or a food processor and blend to a fine paste.

5. Slice the remaining red onions and fry off in oil until golden brown, then add the paste and cook over a medium heat, stirring all the time until it becomes fragrant.

6. Add the chicken and cook over a gentle heat and seal. Continue to stir to prevent any sticking and burning. Stir in the sugar and fish sauce once the chicken has been sealed.

7. Stir in the coconut milk and stock and reduce over a low heat for 2–2½ hrs until it is thick.

8. Then add the potatoes and cook for a further 15 minutes until the potatoes are cooked, check seasoning.

9. Serve with boiled rice and bread.

...continued

6	Kaffir lime leaves
1.5cm	Ginger (peeled)
3cm	Galangal (peeled)
50g	Fresh garlic puré
30g	Sea salt
2.5g	Turmeric powder
700g	Red onions
20ml	Coconut oil
20g	Mild curry powder
10g	Palm sugar
30ml	Fish sauce
800ml	Coconut milk
500ml	Chicken stock or water
400g	Rice (cooked)

Chef's Notes

• This type of dish is often served at special occasions such as Khmer New Year.

• You can serve this dish with noodles should you wish, and replace the chicken with small pork ribs that have been cut in half.

Lok Lak

Fried Beef with Dipping sauce

Method

1. To make the dipping sauce, place the garlic cloves, pepper and sugar in a pestle and mortar and pound, then add the lime juice and a dash of water.

2. Cut the beef into 2cm dice, then roll in the cornflour.

Measurements	Ingredients
2 cloves	Garlic
10g	Freshly ground black pepper
50g	Palm sugar
1	Lime (juice only)

continued over →

3. Seal the beef in a wok with palm oil over a high heat, add the garlic purée and stir until the beef is cooked.

4. In a separate pan, fry two eggs and drain off any excess oil. Deep-fry (165°C,330°F) the sliced potato until golden brown then drain onto kitchen paper.

5. Wash the tomatoes and then cut them into quarters. Wash the lettuce and allow to dry, then place onto serving plates with the tomatoes.

6. Place the beef on the middle of the plate and put the eggs on top.

7. Deep-fry the onions until golden brown. Serve on the same plate.

8. Serve with the dipping sauce.

Chef's Notes

- This dish is very French in origin and is popular among the Cambodian people. It is cooked at home as well as in restaurants.

...continued

1kg	Sirloin, fillet or rump steak
10g	Cornflour
50ml	Vegetable oil
20g	Garlic purée
5g	Salt
30ml	Palm oil
Garnish	Ingredients
2	Eggs
400ml	Vegetable oil
500g	Potato (peeled and thinly sliced)
350g	Tomatoes
200g	Lettuce
150g	Onions (peeled)

Chek Ktis

Sweet Banana and Sago

Method

1. Peel and slice the bananas. Pour the coconut milk into a suitable pan with the water and bring to the boil.

2. Add the sugar and salt, then stir in the sago and bring back to the boil. Add the banana and remove from the heat.

3. Stir, check seasoning and serve.

Measurements	Ingredients
4 small	Sweet bananas
400ml	Coconut milk (thick or thin)
450ml	Water
220g	Palm sugar
Pinch	Salt
80g	Sago flour

Chef's Notes

- You could use caster sugar instead of palm sugar if you do not like the colour or really sweet flavour.

- Small sweet ripe bananas produce the best results for this dessert.

Bampong Trey

Deep-Fried Fish with Peanuts and Herbs

Method

1. Wash, descale, gut and remove the gills from the fish.

2. Trim the spring onions and cut into julienne (fine strips). Peel and remove the centre from the cucumber, then slice.

3. Place the dipping sauce ingredients into a bowl and stir until the sugar has dissolved. Keep to one side for service.

4. Fry the fish carefully in oil 180°C, 350°F . This should take 12–15 minutes. Lift out and drain onto kitchen paper, but keep hot.

5. Place the lettuce, cucumber and herbs onto a plate, then place the fish in the centre and garnish with chillies and a spoonful of dipping sauce over the fish, then sprinkle the spring onions and ground peanuts over the top.

6. Serve with the dipping sauce.

Chef's Notes

- The dipping sauce should taste sour and salty.

Measurements	Ingredients
1kg	White fish fillets (catfish, perch, eel or carp)
4	Spring onions
300g	Cucumber
2lt	Oil (for frying)
200g	Lettuce
100g	Picked herbs (parsley, coriander, chives and dill)
4	Red chillies (see Chef's Notes)
100g	Roasted peanuts (ground)
Dipping sauce	Ingredients
60ml	Lime juice
5g	Salt
2.5g	Brown sugar
10g	Garlic purée

- This is a very common way to serve fish at home or in small restaurants. Any firm-fleshed fish can be cooked and presented this way.

- Cut the red chillies into the shape of flowers by making two cuts from the tip of the chilli to three-quarters of the way towards the stalk. Let the chillies soak in ice-cold water for 30 minutes and the ends should open up like a flower.

Gnom Lahong Kchei Chea Moie Bangkea

Green Papaya Salad with Shrimps

Method

1. Mix the water with the tamarind paste, and strain off and keep the liquid and discard the remaining pulp.

2. Mix the tamarind juice, fish sauce, garlic purée, mint, shrimp paste and sugar together and keep to one side for the dressing.

3. Peel the tomatoes and papaya and cut into fine strips. Remove the stalks from the beans and green chillies and cut into fine strips.

4. Place all the vegetables, nuts, shrimps, crab meat and chillies in the dressing and mix until all the ingredients are coated.

5. Arrange the lettuce on the plates then place the mixture onto the lettuce leaves.

6. Garnish with sprigs of coriander, basil and chillies.

Chef's Notes

- This is a simple salad from Phnom Penh.

- You can change the shrimps for fresh ones to add a little more flavour and texture to this dish.

- Cut the red chillies into the shape of flowers by making two cuts from the tip of the chilli to three-quarters of the way towards the stalk. Let the chillies soak in ice-cold water for 30 minutes and the ends should open up like a flower.

Measurements	Ingredients
60ml	Water
30g	Tamarind paste
50g	Fish sauce
50g	Garlic purée
5g	Mint (chopped)
20g	Shrimp paste
10g	Palm sugar
100g	Tomatoes
300g	Green papaya
100g	String beans
25g	Green chillies
20g	Peanuts (chopped and crushed)
60g	Dried shrimps
20g	White crab meat (cooked)
Garnish	Ingredients
1	Lettuce (washed and picked)
10g	Coriander
5g	Basil
4	Red chillies (cut into flowers)

Gnom Svay Chea Moie Trei Chai ea

Green Mango Salad and Smoked Fish

Method

1. Peel and slice the onion, and mangoes. Cut the lemongrass in half and remove the root and cut the lower third into fine strips. Finely chop the galangal.

2. Remove any skin from the smoked fish, cut into strips and place into a suitable container for marinating. Mix all the ingredients together and marinate for 20 minutes.

3. Arrange the lettuce onto a suitable plate and then arrange the fish mix on top. Garnish with chilli flowers, coriander, mouli, shallots and carrot shreds and serve.

Chef's Notes

- Using the green mango adds to the sour taste that characterises this dish.

- You can use most smoked fish but traditionally Cambodians tend to use mackerel.

- Cut the chillies into the shape of flowers by making two cuts from the tip of the chilli to

Measurements	Ingredients
100g	Onion
2	Green mangoes
2 stalks	Lemongrass
2–3cm	Galangal (peeled)
100g	Smoked fish (eel, mackerel, trout, etc)
20g	Roasted peanuts (crushed)
10g	Mint (chopped)
10ml	Fish sauce
Garnish	Ingredients
1	Lettuce (washed and prepared)
4	Red chillies (see Chef's Notes)
4	Green chillies (see Chef's Notes)
10g	Coriander

continued over →

three-quarters of the way towards the stalk. Let the chillies soak in ice-cold water for 30 minutes and the ends should open up like a flower.

...continued

20g	Mouli (finely shredded)
20g	Carrot (finely shredded)
20g	Shallots

Trei Chai ea Bonpong Chea Moie Svay

Deep-fried Smoked Fish with Raw Mango

Method

1. Peel the prawns and remove the central vein.

2. Remove the stalk and seeds from chilli and cut into fine shreds. Cut the onion into fine slices.

3. Remove any skin from the smoked fish, cut into strips and deep-fry.

4. Mix the onion, mango, fish sauce, prawns, mint, and chilli together.

5. Arrange the lettuce onto a suitable plate and then place the prawn mix on top with the fish on top of that.

6. Garnish with chilli flowers, coriander and carrot shreds and serve.

Chef's Notes

- This is another simple salad from the Phnom Penh area.

- You can change the shrimps for dried ones to add a little more flavour and texture to this dish.

Measurements	Ingredients
60g	Prawns
1	Red chilli
100g	Onion (peeled)
200g	Smoked fish (mackerel, eel, etc.)
2	Green raw mango
30ml	Fish sauce
5g	Mint (chopped)
	Oil for deep-frying
Garnish	Ingredients
1	Lettuce (washed and prepared)
10g	Coriander
4	Red chillies (cut into flowers)
20g	Carrot (finely shredded)

Plei Sach Koh

Sliced Beef Marinated with Chilli and Mint

Method

1. Remove the stalk and seeds from 3 chillies, then cut into fine shreds. Place half of the mint, the garlic pureé and chillies into a pestle and mortar and pound until a smooth paste has been achieved, then add the lime juice and a dash of water.

2. Remove any sinew or fat from the fillet and then cut into very thin slices.

3. Cut the lemongrass in half and remove the root, and cut the lower third into fine strips. Add the lemongrass to the chilli marinade.

4. Place the sliced beef into the marinade, cover with clingfilm and place in the fridge for 20–25 minutes.

5. Cut the onion and spring onions into fine slices. Deseed the peppers and cut into fine strips the same size as the onions.

6. Mix the vegetables with the remaining mint and the fish sauce.

7. Place the lettuce in the centre of the plate, then take the meat out of the marinade and arrange on top of the lettuce. Place the vegetables in the centre of the beef. Pour some of the marinade over the beef.

8. Serve garnished with coriander, chilli flowers and carrot and mouli.

Measurements	Ingredients
3	Red chillies
10g	Mint leaves (chopped)
10g	Garlic purée
20ml	Lime juice
500g	Beef fillet
2 stalks	Lemongrass
150g	Onions (peeled)
6	Spring onions
1	Red pepper
1	Green pepper
20ml	Fish sauce
20ml	Oil
Garnish	Ingredients
1	Lettuce (washed and shredded)
10g	Coriander
4	Red chillies (cut into flowers)
20g	Carrot (finely shredded)
20g	Mouli (finely shredded)

Chef's Notes

- This is a traditional Khmer salad dish and is served raw from the marinade, similar to the popular European dish carpaccio.

- You can serve it lightly grilled rather than raw if you wish.

Chai La Pow Chea Moie Sach Chrouk

Stir-fried Squash and Pork

Method

1. Cut the squash, shallots and spring onions into strips 4–5cm long. Mix the sugar and fish sauce together.

2. Pour the oil into a wok over a high heat and add the garlic purée and shallots. Stir to prevent burning, and once fragrant add the pork and seal it.

3. Add the fish sauce and then stir in the squash and stir-fry gently for 3–4 minutes until the pork has thoroughly cooked.

4. Finish with the spring onions and season with black pepper.

5. Garnish with coriander, chilli flowers and serve with hot cooked rice immediately.

Chef's Notes

• This dish has a touch of sweet and sour flavour about it. The sourness from the fish sauce is countered by the sugar and sweetness of the squash.

Measurements	Ingredients
200g	Squash (peeled)
50g	Shallots
4	Spring onions
30ml	Fish sauce
10g	Palm sugar
50ml	Sunflower oil
20g	Garlic purée
300g	Diced pork (3cm long x 1cm wide)
	Fresh ground pepper
Garnish	Ingredients
10g	Coriander
4	Red chillies (cut into flowers)
400g	Rice (cooked)

Gnom Khroeung Sak Mot Sm Rbieb Khmer

Khmer Seafood Salad

Method

1. Peel the prawns and remove the central vein.

2. Prepare the squid by removing the body from the tubes then remove the transparent quill and wash thoroughly. Also remove the beak and any fatty tissue from the main body. Wash well and cut the tubes into rings and cut the tentacles up roughly.

3. Cut the onion and spring onions into fine slices. Deseed the peppers and chillies and cut into fine strips the same size as the onions.

4. Mix the garlic purée, fish sauce and the lime together and keep for a sauce.

5. Cook off the prawns and squid in a suitable wok over a high heat in the coconut oil. When the prawns have changed to a pink/red colour they are cooked.

Measurements	Ingredients
300g large	Tiger prawns
300g	Squid
50g	Onions (peeled)
6	Spring onions
1	Red pepper
1	Green pepper
3	Red chillies
10g	Garlic purée
20ml	Fish sauce
10ml	Lime juice
30ml	Coconut oil
1	Head of lettuce

6. Arrange the lettuce in the centre of the plate then mix the vegetables with the sauce and place in the centre of the lettuce, then add the prawns and squid on top.

7. Serve immediately.

Chef's Notes

- This recipe is from Phnom Penh. It is a spicy salad that can incorporate fried white fish if you do not like squid or prawns.

- You could also serve a dipping sauce and sliced cucumbers.

Sak Meon Chnang Dai Chea Moie Bai

Chicken Clay Pot with Rice

Measurements	Ingredients
40ml	Fish sauce
1	Lime (juice only)
30g	Palm sugar
4	Red chillies
1 stalk	Lemongrass
300ml	Chicken stock (strong)
4	Lime leaves (shredded)
100g	Jasmine rice
400g	Raw chicken (sliced)
5g	Basil (chopped)
2.5g	Ground black pepper

Method

1. Mix the fish sauce and lime juice with the sugar until they are well dissolved. Deseed and finely shred the chillies.

2. Cut the lemongrass in half, remove the root and cut the lower third into fine strips.

3. Bring the stock to the boil together with the lemongrass, lime leaves and chillies.

4. Add the rice to the stock and then cook at a simmer for 10 minutes with a lid on.

5. Stir in the fish sauce and the chicken, replace the lid and simmer for a further 10 minutes.

6. Remove the lid and stir in the basil and correct seasoning if required.

7. Serve hot in the clay pot.

Chef's Notes

- This way of cooking in a clay pot is classic Asian-style cookery. If you do not have a clay pot which helps to add that extra flavour and is cooked over hot coals, then use a casserole dish, but it must be cooked on the top of the stove.

- This dish is popular all over Cambodia, but this particular recipe is from the Angkor region.

Hawker Food

Ground beef-style omelette

HAWKER FOOD

I decided to include this as a separate chapter as it shows the fascinating diversity of food. Whether you are in Thailand, Singapore or Vietnam, one of the most fantastic experiences you can have is eating on the streets or canals with the locals at a hawker stall or in a food hall. These eateries show the ethnic, cultural and religious differences. They also show the cultural diversity of the people in these countries and their tolerances and contributions to this everyday gourmet extravaganza.

Hawker food is 'food from the streets', and is normally cooked and served from a portable cart or stall. The trolleys or carts can be as simple as a wooden box cart on pram wheels with a camping stove or a stainless steel, glass fronted, double boiling trolley with a turbo wok built in! They can be powered by wood, charcoal or gas, with a neon light hooked up to a car battery, and a colourful umbrella or canopy overhead.

The bustling pavements can be difficult to navigate, walking between the stalls. They are also a feast for the senses, with the tempting aromas and sounds emanating from the makeshift stalls and wheeled trolleys. The stir fries and bubbling soups on portable burners are a sight to behold. When late afternoon draws near you will see streets that were deserted during the morning and afternoon periods begin to fill up slowly, when one vendor arrives followed by another, until it is difficult to walk down the pavements.

Everything seems to be for sale, from fruit, soups, satays, noodles, rice, desserts and sweets, to garlands of flowers.

This pastime of eating on the streets from mobile carts is classless. You can be sitting next to a multi-million-dollar company director eating the same sort of dish around the same tin table and no one bats an eyelid. This acceptance and support has allowed the hawker business to grow.

There can be 20 to 30 stalls on a street or in a food court, which gives great variety.

Hawker food is synonymous with fast food. You can eat on the plastic tables and chairs or have it to take away. It is much cheaper than Western-style commercial burger, pizza and fried chicken outlets, and much healthier too.

The incredible thing is the variety of dishes that are made to order and modified to suit tastes, cooked and served before your very eyes. It can be mesmerising to see the chefs and cooks in action hour after hour, making wontons and rice noodles filled with seafood and dusted with spices, served up in piping hot soups.

The great thing is one day you may decide, 'I feel like something spicy, but light' and choose to have a spare rib soup. The next day you may think, 'I like that soup but I would like it less spicy', and go to a different stall for a different version of the dish.

In Asia there is a great tolerance for deviation and interpretation, which not only reflects the creative talents of the people cooking the food but also the regional and individual tastes.

The vast majority of the people behind the cooking never learned to cook by using a recipe or book, nor in fact trained in a school of cookery, but learned through experience by osmosis, watching others within the family from an early age, and through experimentation. They do not blindly follow a recipe or obsess by following the written text of some long-gone authority. Take Nasi lemak (coconut scented rice) which on one stall has a handful of dried chillies and tamarind in the dish, and on another has sliced chillies and no tamarind on its plate. Who is to say which is right or wrong? The permutations are endless.

Some of the great chefs have adapted or added a secret ingredient or given a dish a twist to complete a new look, taste or aroma that is different from other stalls or restaurants. This is true of many of the world's greatest cuisines, chefs and cooks throughout history, and is true today. One thing these cooks take into account is what is freshest and best in the marketplace. What can I substitute in its place and can I make a variation on my dish? This is because different ingredients grown in different locations can taste, look and smell slightly different, due to soil, weather and variety.

The food courts have a kind of carnival atmosphere and the noise from hundreds of people talking and eating is a little bewildering at first. You are first greeted by a beverage server who will take you to a table and order drinks for you. You can walk and wander around the court and order your food from each stall, giving your table number if you have one, and then the food is cooked and delivered to your table where you pay the stallholder.

It is incredible how these food servers bring the correct food to the right table when on occasions when there are no table numbers.

Don't think for one minute that if you order a soup then a salad and a curry with rice, your food will arrive at your table in course order; it is best that you just tuck in and enjoy the food as it arrives. The atmosphere also allows for relaxed eating, so if you are given chopsticks, just ask for a knife and fork if you feel you need them.

As I explained earlier, I have sometimes had to adjust, adapt and on occasion guess what a cook has added to his or her dish or recipe. This has been because of difficulties in translation, or not knowing or having the exact ingredient. I have not categorised these dishes by country.

Traditional dishes like Satay, Rojak, Hokkien mee and Fish head soup have made the move into the restaurant market, but are still very popular hawker dishes.

Many local councils and countries are slowly trying to move or relocate hawkers from the streets to the more aesthetic and hygienic surroundings

of food courts and food complexes, as is the case in Singapore. This is likely to take generations to accomplish because getting a bite to eat from the hawker stalls is deep within Asia's culture.

Many top-class hotels in Asia often have a week or weekend food festival and dress up heated trolleys or bring out their own colourful hawker stalls as a promotional monthly or bi-monthly event, cooking local dishes.

Bergedel Goreng

Meat Patties

Method

1. Peel, dice and boil the potatoes. Drain the water off and let air dry.

2. Peel and then finely dice the shallots, spring onions and celery.

3. Mash the potato, and mix well with the minced beef, ghee, garlic purée, shallots, spring onions, celery, spices and egg yolk.

4. Take 50g mixture and roll into a ball, then flatten out with the palm of your hand. Repeat until all the mixture has been used.

5. Whisk up the egg whites and dip the patties in the whites and deep-fry until golden brown in a preheated fryer (160°C, 350°F).

Measurements	Ingredients
850g	Potatoes (peeled)
400g	Shallots
4	Spring onions
40g	Celery
140g	Minced beef
20g	Ghee
10g	Garlic purée
5g	Ground black pepper, nutmeg and salt
1	Egg yolk
2	Egg whites

6. Drain onto kitchen paper and serve with salad or plain boiled rice.

Chef's Notes

- These patties are made with beef in Malaysia and often with pork in Thailand.
- This dish can be served with rice or salad.

Ikan Panggang

Grilled Mackerel

Method

1. Take all the paste ingredients except the vegetable oil, and pound until a smooth paste has been achieved.

2. Gut the fish and remove the gills and eyes. Wash and make three incisions on each side of the fish.

3. Mix half the salt with lime juice and rub into the fish. Marinate for 10–15 minutes.

4. Pour the vegetable oil into the pan over a high heat. Fry off the paste until fragrant. Mix the sugar and the remaining salt with the coconut milk then add to the paste. Allow to cool, then add the fish and marinate for 90 minutes.

5. Then remove the fish and bring the coconut milk to the boil. Reduce to a simmer and cook until it is thick.

6. Place the fish onto a grill and continually baste with the coconut milk until cooked.

7. Remove the seeds and cut the chillies into flowers. Cut the orange in half and then cut each half into slices. Cut the spring onions in half and cut each end to make little palm trees.

8. Place the fish onto a suitable plate and garnish with the oranges, onions, spring onions, and chillies. Spoon over the coconut milk. Serve with hot steamed rice.

Measurements	Ingredients
4 × 250–300g	Mackerel
5g	Salt
1	Lime (juice only)
20g	Palm sugar
300g	Thick coconut milk
Paste	Ingredients
5	Shallots
30g	Garlic (peeled)
4	Red chillies
2cm	Ginger (peeled)
10g	Turmeric powder
20ml	Vegetable oil
Garnish	Ingredients
2	Red chillies
1	Orange (sliced)
4	Spring onions
1	Onion (peeled and sliced)
300g	Rice (cooked)

Chef's Notes

- You could use any oily fish if you cannot obtain mackerel.

- This dish is Malaysian and Singaporean in origin.

Tauhu Sumbat

Bean Curd filled with Cucumber and Bean Sprouts

Method

1. Cut the bean curd into 50g squares. Peel, remove the stalk and shred the spring onions, and cucumber.

2. Place the garlic and the chillies into a pestle and mortar or blender and pound to a smooth paste.

3. Blend together all the other sauce ingredients to make a sauce. Place the sauce in small ramekins or bowls.

4. Make an incision in one side of the bean curd and then scoop out the inside to make a pocket.

5. Then fill with the cucumber, spring onion and bean sprouts.

6. Serve either warm or cold. Place the sauce in the centre of the plate then arrange the bean curd around the edges.

Measurements	Ingredients
400g	Bean curd
½	Cucumber
4	Spring onions
300g	Bean sprouts (washed)
	Salt and ground white pepper
Sauce	Ingredients
3 cloves	Garlic
8	Red chillies (deseeded)
30ml	Dark soy sauce
20ml	Rich soy sauce
20ml	Rich wine vinegar
340g	Ground peanuts
350ml	Water
	Salt and ground white pepper

Chef's Notes

- I first had this at a night market in Ipoh in Malaysia. It is normally served cold, but I think it is better warmed through in the oven or steamer.

Century Egg and Minced Pork Congee

Method

1. Shell the eggs and cut into eights. Cut the ginger into very fine strips, blanch in a little boiling water and refresh. Peel and shred the shallots and spring onions.

2. Bring the stock to the boil, add the rice and simmer for 70–80 minutes.

3. Run your knife through the pork to ensure that it is thoroughly minced and not in big lumps.

Measurements	Ingredients
2	Century eggs (preserved eggs, Chinese in origin)
2cm	Ginger (peeled)
4	Spring onions
2	Shallots

continued over →

Add this to the rice and stir to make sure there are no lumps. Simmer for a further 10 minutes.

4. Season the congee, and when the pork is cooked spoon the congee into the serving bowls and garnish the top with nuts, ginger, shallots and spring onions and flavour with sesame oil.

Chef's Notes

- This is a popular dish in Malaysia. This particular dish and recipe comes from Penang.

- It is also possible to use minced chicken as opposed to pork, as in Malaysia pork is mainly confined to the Chinese areas and restaurants, as it is a Muslim state.

...continued	
1.5lt	Light vegetable stock or water
150g	Rice (long grain)
150g	Minced pork
60g	Roasted peanuts (chopped)
10ml	Sesame oil
	Salt and ground white pepper

Kanom Hua Pak Gard

Fried Radish Cakes

Method

1. Chop the prawns in half, skin the sausage and chop up into small dice.

2. Mix the rice flour, cornflour and water and stir well. Then add the mouli and sausage and stir in well. Season with salt.

3. Pour the radish mixture into a suitable well-greased tray (2–3cm deep).

4. Place into a steamer and cook for 30–40 minutes, remove and allow to cool. Turn out and cut into 2.5cm dice.

5. Pour the oil into a wok and stir in all the prawns over a high heat for 1–2 minutes then add the garlic and stir. Add the beaten eggs, stir in and cook.

6. Add the radish cakes and fry until golden brown. Add the fish sauce. Turn out onto kitchen paper.

7. Place onto a suitable plate and garnish with spring onions, coriander, chilli flowers and chilli sauce.

Measurements	Ingredients
4 large	Prawns (deveined and shelled)
1	Chinese sausage
400g	Rice flour
10g	Cornflour
220ml	Water
500g	Mouli (Chinese white radish) (grated)
100ml	Vegetable oil
20g	Dried prawns
20g	Garlic purée
2 medium	Eggs (beaten)
20ml	Fish sauce (Thai)
Garnish	Ingredients
50ml	Sweet chilli sauce
4	Spring onions (trimmed and chopped)
10g	Coriander (chopped)
4	Chillies (cut into flowers)

Chef's Notes

- This is one of the most popular hawker dishes in Thailand and also in Singapore.

- This dish and recipe changes from stall to stall and place to place. Some have Chinese sausage and prawns, others do not.

- This dish can be prepared in advance and finished off in a few minutes, which makes it ideal for dinner parties.

Leng Chee Kang

Sweet Nut and Barley Broth

Method

1. Bring the syrup ingredients to the boil in the water for 30 minutes and then let stand.

2. Cut the plums, peanuts and sweet potatoes into 1cm dice.

3. Soak the barley, sago, lotus seeds (with centre removed) and gingko nuts in water.

4. Cut the Agar Agar strips into 2.5–3cm lengths and soak.

5. Bring each group of ingredients to the boil seperately, and then drain and keep seperate.

6. Take a spoonful of every ingredient and place into a suitable bowl, then ladle in the hot syrup, add a little grated nutmeg and serve.

Chef's Notes

- Logans are similar to lychees and are often called dragon's eye.

- If you would like it cold then you can serve with a portion of crushed ice.

Measurements	Ingredients
20g	Dried plums
100g	Peanuts (halves)
150g	Sweet potatoes
60g	Barley grains
50g	Sago grains
50g	Lotus seeds
50g	Gingko nuts
15	Agar Agar strips
20g	Lychees
10g	Dried nutmeg
Syrup	Ingredients
300g	Sugar crystals
300g	Caster sugar
300g	Dried logans
3lt	Water

Roti Canai

Method

1. Sieve the flour and salt together and then add the sugar.

2. Mix in the water and then knead really well. The dough is ready when it no longer sticks to the hand and is elastic.

3. Divide into eight portions, return to the bowl, brush with melted ghee and then cover with a damp cloth and allow to prove and rest for 30–40 minutes.

4. Take the portions and flatten with the palm of your hand. Take the edge of the dough and swirl around in a circular motion to help the dough to thin out or use a rolling pin to thin out.

5. Take each portion of dough and fold in the corners and flatten out again. Repeat this 3 times.

6. Once flattened brush lightly with ghee and place on a preheated griddle until cooked.

Measurements	Ingredients
310g	Plain flour
2.5g	Salt
2.5g	Sugar
120ml	Warm water
125g	Ghee

Chef's Notes

- This is popular all over Asia and is served with curry, Dhal pickled onion and Murtabak (Malay), Martabak (Thai).

Murtabak

Ground Beef-Style Omelette

Method

1. Take all the paste ingredients and mix together to make a paste. Deseed and finely slice the chillies, and finely dice the onions.

2. Purée the galangal and ginger, then mix with the garlic purée.

3. Place half the ghee into a frying pan and fry the garlic and ginger purée over a high heat until it becomes fragrant. Add the spice paste and stir. Cook for 3–4 minutes.

4. Place the remainder of the ghee into the frying pan, add the minced meat and cook for 3–4 minutes. Then add the stock or water and continue to cook. Stir to ensure there are no lumps and reduce.

5. Add the onions and chillies and cook over a medium heat then add the beaten eggs and stir in. Add the minced beef, fold over the edges and divide into 4 portions.

6. Once the Roti Canai has been flattened out and placed onto a greased griddle, place one of the portions of the egg and minced beef into the centre and fold over the edges. Seal all the sides and continue to cook and turn over continually.

7. Once golden brown all over, place onto a suitable serving dish and garnish with lettuce, chillies and spring onions.

Chef's Notes

- This dish has its origins in India and is very popular among the Indian communities in Malaysia, Thailand and Singapore.

- You can also serve diced cucumbers, sliced shallots, sliced red chillies, shallots mixed with a sweet rice wine vinegar or fish sauce.

Measurements	Ingredients
4	Green chillies
100g	Onions (peeled)
1cm	Galangal (peeled)
1cm	Ginger (peeled)
10g	Garlic purée
20g	Ghee
250g	Minced beef
100ml	Light stock or water
4 medium	Eggs (beaten)
4 portions	Roti Canai (see page 341)
	Salt
Paste	Ingredients
5g	Madras curry powder
5g	Chilli powder
5g	Turmeric
5g	Garam masala
2.5g	Ground black pepper
50ml	Water
Garnish	Ingredients
4	Lettuce leaves
4	Red chillies (cut into flowers)
4	Spring onions (chopped)

Masalvade

Chickpea Fritters

Method

1. Soak the chickpeas overnight, then mince them. Finely dice the onion and dried chillies.

2. Chop up the shrimps. Whisk the eggs and season with salt.

3. Place all the ingredients except the plain flour into a bowl and mix well. Cover with clingfilm and place in a fridge for 1 hour.

4. Dust your hand with flour and take 50g (approximately) of the mixture and roll it into a ball. Then flatten out onto a lightly floured surface and place on a tray until required. Repeat this process until all the mixture has gone.

5. Preheat a deep fat fryer and fry the fritters until golden brown.

6. Drain onto kitchen paper and then serve on a suitable plate.

Measurements	Ingredients
300g	Chickpeas (dried)
70g	Onion (peeled)
4	Dried chillies
170g	Shrimps (peeled, deveined and shelled)
2	Eggs
10g	Madras curry powder
2.5g	Garam masala
5g	Fresh curry leaves (chopped)
Pinch	Methi
10g	Cornflour
30g	Plain flour
	Salt
	Vegetable oil for deep-frying

Chef's Notes

• This is a simple and very popular snack item from Singapore and Malaysia that can be served either hot or cold and at any time of the day or night.

• This can also be a vegetarian option if you remove the shrimps, and ensure that the eggs are free range.

Kuih Lapis

Rose Rice Cakes

Method

1. Sieve the flour and cornflour together and then add 500g coconut, the sugar, rose essence and a pinch of salt and stir.

2. Split the mixture in two and dye half with the red food colouring.

Measurements	Ingredients
220g	Rice flour
30g	Cornflour
600g	Desiccated coconut
200g	Caster sugar

continued over →

3. Grease a 5cm-deep tray and pour some red mixture into the tray to just cover the bottom ($\frac{1}{2}$ cm thick), and then place into a preheated steamer. Cook for 8 minutes until the sponge is firm to the touch.

4. Then add a thin layer of plain mixture, place into the steamer and cook for 5 minutes. Repeat this process of alternating the colours, finishing with the red colour on top, and a dusting of the remaining desiccated coconut.

5. Allow to cool, then cut into 4cm dice and serve.

...continued

10ml	Rose essence
	Salt
	Red food colouring

Chef's Notes

• This is a simple dessert that is popular in Singapore and Kuala Lumpur.

Toasted Shrimp

Method

1. Remove the centre vein from the tails of the shrimps. Place the shrimps into a blender with the onions and garlic, season and blend to make a smooth paste.

2. Beat the egg white into the paste.

3. Spread the shrimp paste over the slices of bread, cut the crusts off and cut into 3cm x 6cm portions.

Measurements	Ingredients
230g	Shrimps (shelled)
30g	Onion puréed
15g	Garlic purée
1	Egg white
10 thin slices	White bread

continued over →

4. Roll each portion in the sesame seeds.

5. Chill them in the fridge for 30 minutes and then place into a preheated fryer (160°C, 350°F), and cook until golden brown.

6. Drain onto kitchen paper and then place on a suitable plate with sliced cucumbers, carrot and lettuce and finish with a sprig of parsley.

Chef's Notes

- There are numerous versions in Cambodia, Vietnam and in Thailand, but this one is simple to make.

- This is best served hot, but can be served cold, either as a snack or a light starter to a meal.

...continued

100g	Sesame seeds
	Salt
	Ground white pepper
	Oil for deep-frying
Garnish	**Ingredients**
½	Cucumber (sliced)
1	Carrot (peeled and sliced)
1 sprig	Flat parsley
4 leaves	Lettuce (washed)

Hokkien Mee

Fried Yellow Noodles, Bean Sprouts, Chillies and Pork

Method

1. Remove the centre vein from the tails of the prawns. Blanch and refresh the yellow noodles and soak the vermicelli in water for 10 minutes then drain.

2. Wash, trim and cut the choy sam into 4–5cm lengths.

Measurements	Ingredients
200g	Prawns (shelled)
250g	Yellow noodles (Mee)
100g	Rice vermicelli
100g	Choy sam (mustard greens)
80g	Red chillies
100g	Shallots (peeled and sliced whole)
2 cloves	Garlic (sliced)
20ml	Palm oil
300g	Tenderloin of pork (sliced)
20g	Palm sugar
1lt	Chicken or pork stock
250ml	Prawn or fish stock
	Salt
200g	Bean sprouts (washed)

3. Deseed the chillies and pound to a smooth paste. Deep fry the shallots and garlic until golden brown and keep on kitchen paper until required.

4. Pour the oil into a wok and add the chilli paste and fry over a medium heat until fragrant. Remove half and keep to one side.

5. Add the prawns and pork to the chilli paste in the pan and continue to fry for 2–3 minutes, then add the sugar and choy sam. Cook and stir for a further minute then add the stocks. Bring to the boil and season.

6. Place the vermicelli into the serving bowls, then the noodles on top with the fried chilli paste and bean sprouts on top of the noodles.

7. Ladle the prawns, pork, choy sam and stock onto the noodles and garnish with the fried shallots and garlic. Serve piping hot.

Chef's Notes

- Hokkien Mee has two quite different versions. The one above is the Malaysian 'Penang soup' style version. The other is a Singaporean and southern Malay dry version, that uses approximately 60ml stock, but has 20ml rich soy and 30ml dark soy together with 500g yellow noodles, 100g onions, 180g sliced pork, 100g prawns, 60g pork liver, 100g choy sam and 4 sliced (medium) red chillies. This is all fried off in a hot wok with 30ml palm oil.

- The trick is to have a hot wok when you start this dry version.

Kuih Teow

Ipoh Teow Soup

Measurements	Ingredients
150g	Prawns (shelled)
200g	Chicken breast (cooked)
2	Red chillies
1.5lt	Light chicken stock
6	Spring onions (cut into diamonds)
500g	Rice noodles
4 sprigs	Coriander
	Salt
	Ground white pepper
	Sesame oil

Method

1. Remove the centre vein from the tails of the prawns and cut them in half. Skin and cut the chicken breast into fine strips. Deseed the chillies and cut into thin slices.

2. Bring 250ml stock to the boil and add the seasoning, prawns and chicken. Cook for 3–4 minutes, then add the spring onions.

3. Bring the rest of the stock to the boil and add the noodles and chillies. Cook for 2–3 minutes, then drain (keeping the stock) and divide into 4 even portions. Top with the chicken, prawns and spring onions.

4. Top up with stock and finish with a sprig of coriander.

5. Serve piping hot.

Chef's Notes

- When I am in Ipoh in Malaysia I always look forward to three meals when I go out to the local markets to wander around. This is one of those favourites.

- Just like the Hokkien Mee dish this is a complete meal on its own, either for lunch or dinner.

Char Koay Teow

Flat Rice Noodles with Prawns and Bean Sprouts

Method

1. Remove the centre vein from the tails of the prawns. Cut the prawns in half. Peel and chop the garlic. Destalk and remove the seeds of the chillies and then finely dice them and chop them into a purée. Whisk the eggs.

2. Blanch the noodles and refresh under cold water then drain and keep to one side.

3. Pour the oil into a suitable wok and fry off the garlic for 1 minute over a medium heat then add the prawns, bean sprouts, noodles and chilli purée.

Measurements	Ingredients
250g	Prawns (shelled)
4 cloves	Garlic
2	Red chillies
4 medium	Eggs
500g	Flat rice noodles
50ml	Palm or corn oil
250g	Bean sprouts (washed)
20ml	Sweet soy sauce

4. Push the ingredients to the back of the wok and allow the excess oil to run to the front, then add the whisked eggs and stir until they are cooked. Then incorporate all the ingredients with the eggs and add the soy sauce.

5. Divide the ingredients onto four suitable plates and serve immediately.

Chef's Notes

- This dish traditionally has 200g diced lard as its cooking medium, but for modern Western tastes I have adapted it with palm or corn oil.

- Again it is a very quick and easy dish to make and serve.

- I had this dish in both Malaysia and in southern Thailand.

Suun Goreng

Fried Glass Noodles

Method

1. Remove the skin and shred the chicken. Slice the bamboo shoots and the carrots. Peel and slice the spring onions into 3cm lengths.

2. Soak the vermicelli in water for 10 minutes then drain.

3. Pour the oil into a suitable wok and fry off the spring onions for a minute over a medium heat then add the chicken, bamboo shoots and carrots. Stir well.

4. Add the stock and bring to the boil. Add the vermicelli, soy sauce and seasoning. Stir and serve hot.

Measurements	Ingredients
300g	Chicken breast (cooked)
100g	Bamboo shoots
50g	Carrot (peeled)
4	Spring onions
300g	Rice vermicelli
40ml	Vegetable oil
20ml	Rich soy sauce
600ml	Chicken stock
	Ground white pepper
	Salt

Chef's Notes

- There should be little or no stock left over from this dish.

Nasi Ayam Dan Rebung

Rice with Chicken and Bamboo Shoots

Measurements	Ingredients
150g	Bamboo shoots
100g	Carrot (peeled)
500g	Jasmine rice
400g	Chicken meat (chopped)
1lt	Chicken stock
10g	Coriander (chopped)
Marinade	**Ingredients**
3cm	Ginger (peeled)
50g	Shallots (peeled)
4 small	Shallots (peeled)
4	Spring onions
5g	Palm sugar
5ml	Sesame oil
50ml	Rich soy sauce
	Salt

Method

1. Cut the bamboo shoots and carrots into small dice. Soak the rice for 30 minutes in water, then wash and drain.

2. To make the marinade, pound or blend the ginger, shallots, small shallots and spring onions. Mix well with salt, sugar and sesame oil.

3. Mix the chicken with the marinade and leave for 30 minutes.

4. Bring the stock to the boil with a dash of oil, and add the rice, bamboo shoots and carrots and boil for 6–7 minutes. Then add the chicken, including the marinade and continue to cook for 12–15 minutes.

5. Take off the heat for around 5–10 minutes and place a lid on top, then serve piping hot with a sprinkling of coriander.

Chef's Notes

- A simple rice dish from Singapore and southern Malaysia.

- You can use pork or beef in this recipe.

Jiu Hoo Char

Yam with Dried Cuttlefish and Belly of Pork

Method

1. Remove the skin from the pork belly, bring to the boil from cold water then remove and shred. Wash the lettuce leaves.

2. Soak the cuttlefish in cold water, remove and then shred. Soak the mushrooms then trim off the stalk and shred. Peel and mince the onions.

3. Wash, trim and shred carrot and cabbage. Skin and shred the yam.

4. Pour the oil into a suitable wok over a high heat and add the garlic and onions and cook for 2–3 minutes. Add the miso and stir and cook for 2–3 minutes over a medium heat.

5. Add the cuttlefish and the pork, stir and cook, then add all the other ingredients except the stock and cook out for 2–3 minutes. Stir to ensure that the ingredients do not stick.

6. Add the stock and cook until all the liquid has evaporated. Season and stir.

7. Garnish suitable plates with cucumber and tomatoes, fill the lettuce leaves with the pork and cuttlefish mixture and serve while hot.

Measurements	Ingredients
250g	Pork belly
150g	Cuttlefish (dried)
8	Dried mushrooms
120g	Onions
150g	Carrot
300g	Cabbage
300g	Yam
50ml	Vegetable oil
10g	Garlic purée
20g	Miso
5g	Palm sugar
250ml	Chicken stock
	Salt
Garnish	Ingredients
8	Chinese lettuce leaves
$\frac{1}{4}$	Cucumber (peeled)
4	Tomatoes (washed and sliced)

Chef's Notes

- Miso is made by fermenting soya beans and cereal grains with salt and water for up to two years in wooden kegs.

- This can be used as a snack or main meal.

Khao Tom Moo

Rice Soup with Pork

Method

1. Finely chop the garlic. Season the minced pork and roll into 30g balls then chill in the fridge.

2. Pour the oil into a suitable wok or pan over a medium heat and brown off the garlic and then keep to one side.

3. In a separate pan bring the stock to the boil with the fish sauce and soy sauce.

4. Place the balls one by one into the stock and reduce to a simmer.

5. Cook the balls for 2 minutes and then add the rice. Bring back to the boil, then cook for 3 minutes at a simmer. Add the spring onions and cook for a further 3 minutes. Add the coriander and stir.

6. Once the rice has cooked and been reheated thoroughly, divide into 4 suitable portions and add a spoonful of the garlic and oil to each portion.

7. Serve piping hot.

Measurements	Ingredients
4 cloves	Garlic
150g	Minced pork
50ml	Corn oil
1lt	Chicken stock
40ml	Fish sauce
40ml	Soy sauce
400g	Rice (cooked)
4	Spring onions
20g	Coriander
	Ground white pepper

Chef's Notes

- This is the most popular breakfast dish in Thailand, and is normally made from the evening's left-over rice. It is somewhat bland when you put it against other Thai dishes.

Moo Pad Pak

Fried Pork with Vegetables

Measurements	Ingredients
50ml	Rich soy sauce
300g	Rough pork mince
	Black pepper
60ml	Vegetable oil
20g	Garlic purée
100g	Mange tout
75g	Cauliflower florets
75g	Broccoli florets
50g	Courgettes (sliced)
100g	Spring onions (cut into 2–3cm lengths)
10g	Brown sugar
30ml	Light soy sauce
50ml	Fish sauce
200ml	Pork or chicken stock

Method

1. Mix 20ml rich soy sauce with the minced pork and some freshly ground black pepper.

2. Pour the oil into a suitable wok and fry the garlic off over a high heat until golden brown.

3. Add the pork and stir-fry until cooked.

4. Add all the vegetables and the fish sauce and stir-fry for 2–3 minutes. Then add the sugar, soy sauces and freshly ground pepper. Stir well.

5. Add the stock and continue to cook for 3–4 minutes. Correct the seasoning.

6. Do not overcook the vegetables.

Chef's Notes

- This Thai dish is served for lunch or dinner and is available in many areas of Thailand.

- Serve with either rice or noodles.

Gai Pad Prik Haeng

Fried Chicken with Nuts and Chilli

Measurements	Ingredients
100g	Snow peas
50g	Roasted peanuts
4 small	Shallots
4 medium	Red chillies (deseeded)
50ml	Corn oil
10g	Garlic purée
400g	Sliced chicken
30ml	Light soy sauce
30ml	Sweet soy sauce
40ml	Fish sauce
5g	Palm sugar
100ml	Chicken stock
2.5g	Coriander (chopped)

Method

1. Cut the snow peas into 3cm lengths. Chop the peanuts and the shallots. Slice the chillies.

2. Pour the oil into a suitable wok over a high heat and fry off the garlic and shallots until golden brown, then add the chillies and cook for 1–2 minutes and stir.

3. Add the chicken and stir to prevent sticking. Add the snow peas, peanuts, soy, fish sauce and sugar. Stir well.

4. Add the stock, stir in well for 1–2 minutes and serve.

5. Garnish with coriander.

Chef's Notes

• A typical Thai stir-fry dish that is hot!

• There are normally 6–7 chillies in this recipe, but I have toned it down a little.

• You would normally have plain rice with this dish, but you could serve noodles if you wish.

Glossary

Asian fish balls
These are available precooked and chilled or frozen from most Asian supermarkets.

Aubergines There are several kinds of aubergine and they are called eggplants, long eggplants and small pea eggplants in Asia. There are also different colours – green, white and purple. The small ones are the size of a small grape. They taste very bitter and sour and are added to curries, dipping sauces and soups. The medium-sized ones are normally white (and green) and the size of a tomato and are often stuffed or pickled. The taste is bitter. The long purple aubergine is often peeled and sliced or diced and used in curries and stir fries.

Bamboo shoots
These are the new shoots from the bamboo tree. The flavour is comparable to that of the artichoke. If you purchase it fresh, wash and then peel the outer leaves. Boil in just enough water to cover the shoots for 10–15 minutes and then drain. The shoots will remain crispy but the bitter taste will have been reduced. Bamboo shoots are widely available in tins and jars, but fresh will be obtainable in Asian supermarkets.

Banana There are numerous varieties of banana. The smaller Asian banana is sweeter than the larger varieties we have in the West. The red skinned variety used in Vietnam has a wonderful taste, but is only available from July to August. The paler green ones are available all year round and the larger versions of these are used for cooking.

Blossoms are the purple-coloured tips that form a bunch measuring 15–30cm in length. The flavour and texture are comparable to that of the artichoke; they also need to be soaked in acidulated water to prevent browning when peeled. To prepare them you first must remove the hard outer leaves and you will see an undeveloped banana inside. The tender inner leaves are cut and then sliced and placed in the acidulated water. Blossoms are available from most Asian supermarkets.

Leaves The dark green leaves are used for a variety of functions, whether as a wrapper, container, bowl or decorative sheets under plates or trays of food. The leaves are available from most Asian supermarkets and can be frozen. If the recipe states the use of banana leaves and they are unavailable, use tinfoil.

Basil In Asian cookery, there are three types of basil. These are:

Holy or purple basil. It has a purple stem and leaves with a slightly bitter taste and a hot flavour. It is used in stir fries and is added to dishes at the last minute. Thais believe it helps to get rid of toothache. Substitute with Western basil as a last resort.

Lemon basil has a light green stem and leaves, and a slightly peppery lemon flavour. It is used in fish dishes, soups and curries.

Sweet basil has a purple stem with dark green leaves and a slight aniseed flavour. It is used in curries, pastes and stir fries.

Wrap all basil stems in a damp cloth and placed either in a jar with a little water in the fridge, or in the fridge with a damp cloth over the top of the leaves.

Bean sprouts There are two varieties, one is from the soya bean

and the other, which is often used in Vietnamese cuisine, is grown from the mung bean. Both can be purchased at different stages of growth either in tins or jars, but fresh will be widely available in supermarkets. They are good blanched fresh in salads, stir fries, soups, etc.

Bean thread noodles

Often called bean thread vermicelli, cellophane noodles and glass noodles, these are all made from mung bean paste. They vary in width and length. Thin, transparent and shiny becoming transparent when cooked or soaked. Normally used in soups, stir fries and salads. To cook, soak in warm water for 10 minutes and drain. Cook for only 1–2 minutes.

Bird's eye chillies

These are a common ingredient, especially in Thailand. The bird's eye chilli is very hot and sharp in flavour with a chilli fragrance. They are 1–2cm in length and start out green and then progress to a dark red, the colour increasing in intensity. They are

widely available fresh or dried in tins and jars, but fresh will be obtainable in Asian supermarkets.

Jalapeno chillies are mainly used for their colour making pastes. They are less spicy than the bird's eye chillies.

Common chillies are the least spicy and hot and are normally reserved for salads and stir fries. They are often used for drying over five days or used when making chilli powder. For reconstitution of dried chillies, soak for 10 minutes in warm water.

Remember to remove the seeds where possible and store in a paper bag in the fridge.

Black fungus (pigs' ear mushrooms)

Also known as wood ear, cloud ear, tree ear and rats' ear mushrooms, these are sold either dried, tinned or fresh. For reconstitution of dried pigs' ears, soak for 10 minutes in warm water, making sure any dirt is removed. The mushroom will at least double in volume. Then drain and prepare as required. The

mushroom has a good earthy flavour. Other mushrooms include, straw, Chinese and button. If dried, reconstitute as above.

Catfish

A freshwater fish that also lives in brackish water such as estuaries. Specimens have been caught up to 150kg, but are normally purchased around 2.5kg to 5kg in the Asian markets.

Cassava

There are two types of this vegetable, sweet and bitter. The bitter version has a poisonous outer peel of prussic acid, which is removed by boiling at high temperature either peeled or unpeeled. Both should be washed, peeled, boiled and grated. It can be added to any meal containing potato.

Chayote squash

Pear-shaped squash approximately the size of an avocado with a light green colour and hard flesh until it is cooked. It can be used directly as a vegetable, sliced and deep fried in batter, for example. Also used in soups, stir fries and pickles. A green papaya can be used as a substitute.

Chinese celery

It is much slimmer and a darker green than the Western celery, with a much stronger taste. They are available from most Asian supermarkets. If unavailable, use the hearts of the Western celery or the leaves with stalks. It also looks similar to coriander and the Asian people believe it helps to get rid of urinary tract infections and gives one a healthy appetite.

Chinese cabbage

This is an elongated vegetable with a white stem and green leaves and has a sweet, tender and slight mustard flavour. If unavailable use another curly leaf cabbage.

Chinese lettuce

This vegetable is called Chinese celery or Napa cabbage. It is tightly packed and approximately 30cm long. It looks like a cross between a lettuce and a cabbage, with white at the bottom of the leaf turning yellow with green edging around the upper leaf.

Chinese sausage

These are red with white speckles of fat approximately

12–14cm in length with a parchment paper covering. They need to be cooked before being eaten.

Chinese spinach (or water convolvus)

This has spear-shaped leaves and long stems. It also goes under the name of 'morning glory'. It has a very mild spicy flavour.

Often used as wrappers for small bundles of food, eaten fresh or cooked. If unobtainable use spinach leaves. Available from most Asian supermarkets. The Thais also think it is healthy for skin and eyes.

Chinese watercress

Grown in fresh water this has larger triangular leaves than the Western counterparts.

Coconut

Grown from the coconut palm tree, refers to the nut from the much larger seed. When the seed is green the coconut juice inside is sweet. It is difficult to obtain the green seed with the nut in the UK. The coconut milk is taken from the fleshy inner part of the nut. When extracted it is creamy white and thick.

It is available in tinned form (thick or thin), powdered form and creamed form. Only use the creamed coconut to enrich a dish at the end of the cooking process. Remember to shake tinned coconut milk first before using.

Coriander

Often referred to as cilantro and also Chinese parsley. The roots, seeds and leaves are all used in Asian cookery. The roots and seeds are used for curries and the dark green leaves are used for soups, salads and garnishing, added at the last minute to avoid the loss of colour and to keep its musty fragrance.

The stems and leaves can be substituted in recipes if the roots are not available.

Custard apple

The apple is light green in colour and has an uneven shape. The fruit is white with black seeds. The apple has a mild flavour and the texture is smooth. It is available from May through to July.

Durian

This is often called stinky fruit and comes in a variety of

sizes. It has a spiky outer skin and a very distinct odour. The meat is white to yellow in colour and is very sweet, with the texture of marshmallow. The fruit is very popular and the taste is nothing like the smell.

Did you know that the combination and consumption of the durian fruit and alcohol has actually killed people?

Fish

In Asian cookery just as much freshwater fish and shellfish are used as saltwater fish. Freshwater fish such as catfish, snakefish and carp are the best varieties to use. Saltwater fish such as tilapia, snapper, bass, mackerel and pomfret are the varieties to use.

Fish sauce

This comes in a number of different colours, flavours and with names such as Nam pla in Thailand or Nuoc mam in Cambodia and Vietnam. The sauce has a distinct fishy smell and is made from freshwater fish, sea fish or shrimps depending on the country.

The fish is salted and allowed to ferment in the sun for a long period and then drained off.

Five spice

This is a well-known Asian spice made from blending star anise, cinnamon, cloves, fennel seeds and either ginger or pepper. It is used for stewing, grilling and marinating meats. This powder is widely available from most supermarkets.

Galangal

This looks a little like ginger, but that is where the similarity ends. The flavour and aroma is like a perfumed scent and is superb in curries, stews and marinades, with meat, fish or shellfish dishes. Also called ginza and Siamese ginger. It has a pale yellow to white skin, with light pinkish stalks. You must remove the outer skin with a sharp knife, as you would do with ginger. You can buy dried slices of galangal, but you need to soak them well.

It is not to be confused with lesser galangal or rhizome in Cambodia and krachai in Thai. This is cream coloured

with a slightly less bitter flavour than ginger. Prepare and use in the same way as ginger. It is used with fish and curries.

The Chinese and Thais believe that it is good for the skin, helps get rid of diarrhoea and improves the appetite.

Garlic There are several kinds of garlic used in Asian cookery. One in particular has very small cloves that are slightly pink in colour; it is called Thai garlic. When using this type, cooks do not remove the skin. The Thais also believe that garlic helps the skin and helps prevent coughs and cancer and reduces cholesterol.

Ginger A wonderful aromatic ingredient. It is used in almost all areas of Asian cookery from stir fries to desserts and drinks. It is believed by Asians to have properties that aid the digestive system and improve the appetite. It should always be peeled before use.

Glutinous rice This goes under the name of sticky rice. It has

high starch content and really needs to be soaked for 2–3 hours prior to use. It can be obtained from Asian supermarkets. It is small and round with a creamy white colour.

The rice needs to be drained and then placed in a steamer with a tight-fitting lid and cooked for 12–15 minutes until cooked, then allowed to stand for five minutes before serving.

Guava This green pear-shaped fruit has a very tart taste, but is widely available and should be peeled and cut into dice then stewed in a light syrup for the best results.

Jackfruit This is much larger than the durian fruit with less of a sharp spiny outer shell. It has less of an odour than the durian fruit. It also has a milder taste.

Jasmine rice This is often referred to as fragrant rice, and is the preferred rice in Thailand, Vietnam and Cambodia. It is a long grain rice that has a delicate fragrance, unlike basmati for example.

Kaffir lime The actual limes have warty outer skins, and

a rather sour juice. The juice and blanched rind are used for soups and curries. The lime leaves look a little like bay leaves, but the fragrance of the leaf is unmistakably lime scented. Used in most areas of Asian cookery, from soups to cool drinks. They also freeze well with little or no loss of flavour and colour. You must remove the stringy vein from the centre of the leaf if you are going to chop or pound them.

Lemongrass This is one of the signature ingredients for Thai and Cambodian cuisine. Its distinctive lemon balm fragrance combined with galangal and kaffir lime leaves give one the sensual aromas of the orient. It looks like any large grass stalk.

Only the lower third of the stalk is used. If you are cooking rice and you wish to add a little more flavour you can place the two-thirds that has been cut away into the rice, and it will impart a gentle lemon scent. Lemongrass can also be purchased in powder form and in dried, sliced or

diced form. It needs to be soaked in a little warm water before being used.

It will keep for two to three weeks in the fridge and also freezes well. It is thought that it helps to relieve backache and headaches.

Long beans These are also called snake beans, Chinese beans and are between 15 and 30cm long. They are green and can be purchased in bunches. The beans are sweeter than their Western string bean counterparts and are excellent in stir fries as they keep their crunchiness after cooking.

Lotus This is grown in ponds and swamps throughout Asia and is a symbol in the Buddhist religion. It is also the base food from which lotus seeds, lotus roots and lotus rootlets are obtained.

Lotus seeds have a coriander-type taste and can help to flavour a dish. *Lotus root* is the sweet, crunchy part of the lotus plant that has to be peeled before using. *Lotus rootlets*, considered similar to

asparagus, are the stems of the lotus plant, often sold in jars.

Mango This is one of the most favoured fruits in Asia. It is eaten ripe in desserts and green (unripe) in savoury salads as a sour vegetable. Mango contains enzymes that will aid the tenderising of meat.

Mushrooms
Mushrooms commonly used in Asian cookery are straw mushrooms, Chinese mushrooms, shitake mushrooms and oyster mushrooms. They all have their own distinctive flavour. You can purchase them dried, tinned or fresh. If dried, remember that they must be soaked for at least for 20 minutes before use.

Noodles There are many different types of noodles made from mung beans or rice. The best way to have noodles is to purchase them fresh if possible. Yellow noodles are made with the addition of eggs, and are also called egg noodles. If you use dried vermicelli noodles, it is best to soak them for at least five minutes. You can also deep fry them from dry until crispy.

They are used in soups, salads and as accompaniments to curries, stir fries and spring rolls, etc.

Palm sugar There are two types of palm sugar. It ranges in colour from light brown to dark brown. One version is thick, hard and crumbly and has a caramel flavour. The other is syrupy and is tapped from the trunk of the tree, and is then boiled down. Palm sugar is not the same as coconut palm sugar.

Pickled vegetables
These can be found in glass jars or tins in most Asian supermarkets. They can be used as snacks or as an accompaniment to your meal.

Prahok This is crushed, salted and fermented fish. Once the fish are caught, they are gutted, scaled and cleaned by hand and then trampled underfoot.

The fish migrate from the Mekong Delta up the Tonle Sap River into the Tonle Sap Lake in Cambodia.

Foreigners often refer to it as fish cheese. It is a strong acquired taste.

Shrimp paste This is made from fermented dried fish or shrimp depending on the country of origin. It is brown and has a strong odour. It is also often called shrimp sauce, which is the same thing but let down with a little water. Use it in moderation and if you are unable to obtain it use a tin of anchovies with 30ml water and blend it to a smooth paste. This will be a useful substitute. It can keep for up to a year, and does not need to be refrigerated.

Tamarind paste This comes from the sour pulp of the tamarind tree. The tree produces a sweet version that is often eaten as fruit, but the sour one is peeled and dried and pressed into block form. To use you break off a portion and place it into water and rub between your fingers, then drain off the liquid and throw the pulp away. Use the tamarind water (juice) as required. The Thais believe it reduces hypertension. It can be purchased in bottled form at some Asian stores. You can also use lime or lemon juice as a substitute.

Tofu (bean curd)
Originally from China, tofu is made from pressed soybean residue and placed into blocks and then water. There are numerous versions, smoked, spiced, marinated and silken. Will keep for 3–4 days if refrigerated once opened. Obtainable from health food shops and good supermarkets.

Turmeric A member of the ginger family, turmeric (means 'yellow' in Khmer) is a deep yellow in colour. It is often used to colour curries and sometimes as a poor man's saffron. In the West it is rare to obtain whole turmeric, you are much more likely to obtain the powdered version.

Useful addresses

Shelia Connolly
Ecole d'Hôtellerie et de Tourisme Paul Dubrule
P.O. Box 934412, La Glacière
Route No. 6, Siem Reap
Kingdom of Cambodia

Earthwalkers
Sala Kanseng Village, Sangkat No 2
P.O. Box 93073
Siem Reap
Kingdom of Cambodia
www.earthwalkers.no

Mr Paul Hay, (Buntheoun),
Trail bike tours throughout Cambodia
Cullinagh, House No 124, Street 0, Trang Village
Slokram Commune
Siem Reap
Kingdom of Cambodia
hiddencambodia@yahoo.com

Michael Chew
Kolej Hill Citi College
Pengkalan Emas Mall
Jalan Pasir Puteh
31650 Ipoh, Perak
Malaysia
Tel: 05- 3227878
Fax: 05- 3211827
Kolej_hillciti@hotmail.com
www.kolejhillciti.edu.my

David Chua
Asian Tourism Institution
1st Floor, 85 Gaya Street, 88000 Sabah
Kota Kinabalu, Sabah (Borneo)
East Malaysia
P.O. Box 11600, 88817 Kota Kinabalu,
Sabah (Borneo)
East Malaysia
Tel: (088) 241222   Fax: (088) 216916
Ati_education@hotmail.com

Lee Lean Suan
Flamingo Institute of Further Education
No 2, 2nd Floor
Bangunan Institut Flamingo
Tasik Ampang
Jalan Hulu Kelang
68000 Ampang, Selangor Darul Ehsan
KL Malaysia
fife@fife.edu.my

Busara Boonmakham
Sompet Thai Cookery School & Travel
Chiang Inn Plaza
GLF 100/1 Chiangklan Rd
Chiangmai 50100
Thailand
Tel: 66 53 280901-2
Sompet2000@hotmail.com
Http://welcome.to/sompet

Paul Young
E&P Catering Butchers Ltd
Unit 3 Bishopgate Park
Widdrington Road
Coventry
CV1 4NA
Tel: 024 76 559909
Fax: 024 76 559828

Mannan Impex PTE Ltd
Provision & Sundry Goods
No 118, Serangoon Road
Singapore 218023
Tel: 2998424
Fax: 2911404

Birmingham College of Food Tourism and Creative Studies
Business and Community (International Cookery Courses)
Summer Row
Birmingham
B3 1JB
Tel: 0121 604 1000
Fax: 0121 236 7996
www.bcftcs.ac.uk

John Artis Limited
Cox Lane
Chessington
Surrey
KT9 1SF
Tel: 020 8391 5544
Fax: 020 8391 4595
email: tvine@john-artis.ltd.uk
www.johnartis.co.uk

Index